Dynamic Publishing with ColdFusion® MX

By Benjamin Elmore

Contributions by:
Allen Benson,
Dan Blackman,
Jon Briccetti,
Robin Hilliard,
Anthony McClure,
Kevin Webb,
and Rob Rusher

www.newriders.com

201 West 103rd Street, Indianapolis, Indiana 46290
An Imprint of Pearson Education
Boston • Indianapolis • London • Munich • New York • San Francisco

Dynamic Publishing with ColdFusion® MX

International Standard Book Number: 0-7357-1312-X

Library of Congress Catalog Card Number: 2002105978

Printed in the United States of America

First Printing: October 2002

06 05 04 03 02 7 6 5 4 3 2 1

Interpretation of the printing code: The rightmost double-digit number is the year of the book's printing; the rightmost single-digit number is the number of the book's printing. For example, the printing code 02-1 shows that the first printing of the book occurred in 2002.

Trademarks

All terms mentioned in this book that are known to be trademarks or service marks have been appropriately capitalized. New Riders Publishing cannot attest to the accuracy of this information. Use of a term in this book should not be regarded as affecting the validity of any trademark or service mark.

Warning and Disclaimer

Every effort has been made to make this book as complete and as accurate as possible, but no warranty of fitness is implied. The information provided is on an "as is" basis. The authors and the publisher shall have neither liability nor responsibility to any person or entity with respect to any loss or damages arising from the information contained in this book.

Publisher
David Dwyer

Associate Publisher
Stephanie Wall

Production Manager
Gina Kanouse

Managing Editor
Kristy Knoop

Senior Acquisitions Editor
Linda Anne Bump

Senior Development Editor
Lisa Thibault

Project Editor
Suzanne Pettypiece

Copy Editor
Karen A. Gill

Product Marketing Manager
Tammy Detrich

Publicity Manager
Susan Nixon

Manufacturing Coordinator
Jim Conway

Cover Designer
Aren Howell

Interior Graphics
Seth Wynne

Compositor
Ron Wise

Proofreader
Debbie Williams

Indexer
Angie Bess

Dynamic Publishing with ColdFusion® MX

Contents at a Glance

Table of Contents

About the Authors

Benjamin Elmore holds the position of Chief Technology Officer at RemoteSite Technologies, Inc. His expertise regarding web development technologies and the associated market was instrumental in defining the functionality of RemoteSite's flagship content management system, OASIS, which is currently in use within New York State government.

In addition to his leadership role within RemoteSite, Benjamin has fulfilled technology roles with the Allaire Corporation, Macromedia, and Travelers Insurance Company that have had a significant impact on the web development community.

The Allaire Corporation contracted Benjamin to be its worldwide Spectra Evangelist, the one person who is believed to be the most effective and proficient in the use of that major web development product. While maintaining his CTO role at RemoteSite, Ben educated the Allaire client and partner base regarding the appropriate implementation of the product. With his guidance, Allaire defined subsequent releases of the Spectra product in keeping with the needs of the worldwide development community.

RemoteSite was engaged by Macromedia to provide guidance regarding the use of their MX technologies within the Dylan 65 Project, with Benjamin specified as the requisite lead within the associated contract document. This project is critical to Macromedia because it represents the next generation of `Macromedia.com`. Benjamin served as the lead engineer, responsible for architecting the project's workflow and publishing subsystems utilizing Macromedia's pre-release MX technology. In this role, he worked directly with the CTO of Macromedia, providing feedback regarding the need for enhanced features and functionality within emerging technology—ultimately assisting Macromedia with the evolution of that technology in preparation for its pending market debut.

Benjamin also was a key player in building the Bond Internet Application for Travelers Insurance Company. He provided leadership and mentoring for a group of Travelers' developers as they constructed their first major content management application. The success of this new application was pivotal in the decision to move forward with the overall construction of the Bond Intranet Application as well as an internal intranet. These activities were more than just technical implementations. During these engagements, Benjamin also assisted the Traveler's Property Causality Management team with its understanding of content management concepts, and its applicability to its specific business environment.

A member of the board of advisors for the Albany ColdFusion User Group and a certified instructor, Benjamin is an active promoter of technological excellence.

He has been a speaker at many user groups across the nation as well at various international vendor developer conferences, including Rational Software, Macromedia, and Sybase.

Benjamin served as the primary mentor and Technological Director of the Allaire Spectra Ace Program during 2000. He was a key presenter at Macromedia's Worldwide Developers Conference for both 2000 and 2001. Ben co-authored the book *Macromedia Advanced ColdFusion 5.0* with Macromedia ColdFusion Evangelist Ben Forta. He holds industry certifications as an advanced developer and senior instructor for Macromedia's ColdFusion technology, including the most advanced technologies. He was co-author of two articles on web development methodologies appearing within the *ColdFusion Developers' Journal*, the international periodical for emerging web technologies. The Allaire Spectra Methodology three-day training course, offered worldwide, is based in large part on those articles.

Seth Hodgson is currently a web engineer working for Macromedia. He is a certified Macromedia ColdFusion and Macromedia Flash developer. Before heading to northern California, Seth did the impossible along with an amazing team at Impossible, Inc. in Santa Barbara, California building solutions for commerce, communications, intranets, and extranets for a wide variety of industries using the full range of Macromedia technologies.

Michael Mazzorana currently manages Internet development and solution strategies for Travelers Life & Annuity, which is a member of Citigroup. From 1997 through 2001, he held a similar position with Travelers Property Casualty that included working with various internal business areas to create Internet solutions related to selling and servicing insurance products. Starting in 1997, Michael led an effort to hire a new team, chose new products, and started a development effort of the Travelers corporate intranet. Much of Michael's career has been focused on trying to understand the business and technical challenges around web site technology management and growth. His current projects are focused on e-business solutions with evaluation of various products and trends that meet business objectives.

Jeff Tapper is a Certified Macromedia Instructor as well as a Certified Advanced ColdFusion Developer. He has been developing web-based applications since 1994, and has used ColdFusion for many significant projects since 1995 (version 1.5). He was a speaker at the 2000 Allaire Developer Conference, as well as a regular speaker at several Macromedia user groups and events. Jeff co-authored two books for Macromedia Press, and is pleased to be included as a contributing author of this book.

About the Contributing Authors

Allen Benson has been involved in object-oriented software development for more than 10 years as a developer, consultant, mentor, and instructor. He has written for publications including *Java Report* and *VisualAge* magazines. Allen has presented at the Allaire Developers Conference and SPG's Internet/Intranet Application Development Conference. He also was a member of the SIGS Java Seminar Series presentation team. Allen now does Java/J2EE consulting and training.

Dan Blackman is a Senior Technologist for RemoteSite Technologies. He is experienced at developing and deploying complex web applications using technologies such as ColdFusion 5.0/MX, Flash MX, JavaScript, HTML, and DBMS (Oracle, SQL Server). He is a Certified Macromedia Professional holding certification in web site development, a ColdFusion developer, and is a Certified Advanced ColdFusion Developer. He has worked with clients around the country, such as at the University of Buffalo, Macromedia, and NASA in web application development and business development roles.

Jon Briccetti is a senior technologist at RemoteSite Technologies, with expertise in Macromedia ColdFusion, Dreamweaver MX, and Flash MX. He is a Certified Macromedia Instructor and Certified Macromedia Professional. Jon's IT experience began at age 12 with a TRS-80 and hasn't stopped since; he's developed software applications in various environments for many years. Jon has extensive analysis skills, polished from various career excursions in non-IT positions and business ownership. As the Founder and Co-President of the Albany NY Macromedia User Group, Jon is well known in the capital district as an expert in Macromedia technologies and has delivered presentations at user groups and at the ColdFusion seminars for Macromedia.

Robin Hilliard is a senior technical sales engineer at Macromedia Australia/New Zealand, having originally joined Allaire as the technical support engineer for the Asia/Pacific region. After obtaining a BSc in computer science and pure mathematics at Sydney University, Robin worked for four years at Andersen Consulting in a variety of enterprise computing engagements before moving to Internet design firm Zivo, where he took a technical lead role on projects for Subaru and BHP Steel. Robin is an experienced ColdFusion and Spectra developer, and he is passionate about simplifying the processes used in software design. Robin is also a bass in the chamber choir Cantillation, and he enjoys flying, sailing, and tinkering with his content management tag library, Speck (`www.speckcms.com`). Robin can be reached at `robin@zeta.org.au`.

Anthony McClure is a senior technologist with RemoteSite Technologies. He has more than seven years of experience in various information technologies, including architecting, developing, and maintaining Macromedia-, Microsoft-, and Java-based Internet applications in various aspects of e-business. Recent major projects have produced a specialty for Macromedia Spectra-based applications. Projects that Anthony has had a significant impact on in recent times include being a co-lead for the FAO Schwarz Spectra e-commerce application, a co-lead for the Screaming Media product integration for the Spectra 1.5 release, and offering implementation and architecture support for North Point Domain and its new product. Anthony is a Macromedia Certified Instructor for the ColdFusion technologies.

About the Technical Editors

Kathy Hester spends most of her time as a trainer for web designers and developers. When she's not involved with training sessions, Kathy works as an independent contractor doing project management, web programming, and user interface design. In her spare time, she manages the New Orleans ColdFusion User Group and works with Hal Helms teaching Fusebox methodology. Kathy can be reached at `kathyhes@realsheep.com`.

Tracy Smith, who is based in Washington, D.C., is an independent web developer, specializing in Internet solutions for small businesses and non-profits. He has been working with computers since he was 10 and has been programming in ColdFusion for more than four years. Tracy's first ColdFusion application was a small "baby pool" application for the person who first introduced him to ColdFusion as a means to connect the database with the web. He assisted his co-worker with troubleshooting ColdFusion code, upgrading the web server to newer versions, and ultimately taking over the project when this person left the company. He learned enough ColdFusion in a short time to secure a position with an Internet startup company called PrizeCentral.com as a remote developer. At PrizeCentral.com, Tracy lead the ColdFusion and database development from a 250,000 member database to more than 6 million members. Prizecentral.com was re-invented as Flipside.com as the company was acquired by Vivideni-Universal Publishing. Tracy left Flipside.com in 2001 to become a freelance web developer.

Paul Wille is currently a senior programmer at ISITE Design (a Macromedia Premier Solutions Partner) and Certified Advanced ColdFusion 5.0 Developer. He has spent his past three years at ISITE mastering ColdFusion, leading most of ISITE's major accounts and developing an ASP solution for the automotive industry composed of CRM, customer profiling, and XML data integration. Paul's current research centers on Web Services, .NET architecture, and how ColdFusion MX and Flash MX interact within that space. Outside of development, he has developed and delivered multiple customized training engagements for clients on ColdFusion development, best practices, project planning, and specifications. Prior to working at ISITE Design, Paul trained for four years on desktop applications and database architecture.

Amy Wong is currently the Technical Editor for the ColdFusion MX Application Designer and Developer Center (`www.macromedia.com/desdev/mx/coldfusion`) at Macromedia. Developing with ColdFusion since version 1.5, she decided to work in the ColdFusion technical support forums at Allaire in 1999 because of its helpful developer community. She feels she's come full circle because she now works to produce instructional articles and tutorials with authors whom she admired as a ColdFusion newbie. Amy has worked with ColdFusion and Macromedia Spectra, and she is enjoying learning Flash MX, Dreamweaver MX, and Fireworks MX. When she's not asking for, nagging about, or editing new articles, she's usually paddling her whitewater boat (a Pyranha Sub 7, One Ball) on the river.

Dedication

Great efforts call for great sacrifice. Over the years, my great sacrifice has been time with my wife, Mary, and my two kids, Haydn and Olivia. I would like to dedicate this book to my daughter, Olivia Elmore, on her fifth birthday. Happy birthday, Olivia. May all your dreams and wishes come true.

—Benjamin Elmore

Acknowledgments

When a close friend of mine encouraged me to write a book about building dynamic applications, I failed to realize that the complexity in writing a book is on par with the subject matter of the book. Throughout this process, there were many different groups of talented individuals who worked extremely hard to make this book a success.

It was my privilege to command such a fine group of writers and reviewers in pursuit of such a lofty goal. It is only right for me to sing the praises of my comrades in arms whose feats of greatness have made this book so successful. Without the fine writing of Dan Blackman, Jon Briccetti, Jeff Tapper, Seth Hodgson, Allen Benson, Dan Blackman, Anthony McClure, Michael Mazzorana, and Robin Hilliard, this book wouldn't be the same. The success of this book is as much theirs as it is mine. I encourage you to write to these authors with questions, comments, and feedback. Each one has shared a part of his experience with us to help plant the seeds of ideas that will bring about applications of the future.

No book can be complete without the willingness of colleagues to share ideas, review materials, and provide feedback and support. Although they didn't author any of the book's chapters, the behind-the-scenes support and input of Ashley King, Rob Rusher, and Kevin Webb was invaluable to the team.

Editors are the unsung heroes of every book. They battle the forces of nature to bring to all of you the finished product. Their untiring spirit, their unending patience, their unending source of knowledge, and their candor is to be applauded. I would specifically like to thank Linda Bump, Senior Acquisition Editor, Lisa Thibault, Senior Development Editor, and Suzanne Pettypiece, Project Editor. I would also like to say a special thanks to New Riders in supporting a solutions book for ColdFusion MX.

This book's completion and organization can also be attributed to the assistance given by Janice Dolan and the Zazil Media Group. Janice played the role of tasks master so sweetly as she held the whip in one hand. An acknowledgment is also due to Seth Wynne for support on several of the graphics for this book.

Over the past two years, I was given a backstage pass to watch the development of the Macromedia MX product suite. During this time, I learned to laugh and cry over the changes in the product at sometimes a weekly interval. However, I would never change this experience for anything in the world. To this, I owe my gratitude and thanks to Jeremy Allaire and Libby Freligh, who kept me involved throughout this evolution of the next great Internet platform. Great products are written by engineers who process one great quality: vision. The engineers at Macromedia showed that quality with great abundance, and I would like to thank them all for the job they did.

Last, I would like to acknowledge all of you for your desire to move forward in your own knowledge. It is our collective hope that this book provides you with new perspectives, new ideas, and information to guide your career and expertise to new heights.

A Message from New Riders

As the reader of this book, you are our most important critic and commentator. We value your opinion and want to know what we're doing right, what we could do better, in what areas you'd like to see us publish, and any other words of wisdom you're willing to pass our way.

As associate publisher at New Riders, I welcome your comments. You may fax, email, or write me directly to let me know what you did or didn't like about this book—as well as what we can do to make our books better. When you write, please be sure to include this book's title, ISBN, and author, as well as your name and phone or fax number. I will carefully review your comments and share them with the authors and editors who worked on the book.

Please note that I cannot help you with technical problems related to the topic of this book, and that due to the high volume of email I receive, I might not be able to reply to every message. Thanks.

Fax: 317-581-4663

Email: `stephanie.wall@newriders.com`

Mail: Stephanie Wall
Associate Publisher
New Riders Publishing
201 West 103rd Street
Indianapolis, IN 46290 USA

Visit Our Web Site: *www.newriders.com*

On our web site, you'll find information about our other books, the authors we partner with, book updates and file downloads, promotions, discussion boards for online interaction with other users and with technology experts, and a calendar of trade shows and other professional events with which we'll be involved. We hope to see you around.

Email Us from Our Web Site

Go to `www.newriders.com` and click on the Contact Us link if you

- Have comments or questions about this book.
- Want to report errors that you have found in this book.
- Have a book proposal or are interested in writing for New Riders.
- Would like us to send you one of our author kits.
- Are an expert in a computer topic or technology and are interested in being a reviewer or technical editor.
- Want to find a distributor for our titles in your area.
- Are an educator/instructor who wants to preview New Riders books for classroom use. In the body/comments area, include your name, school, department, address, phone number, office days/hours, text currently in use, and enrollment in your department, along with your request for either desk/examination copies or additional information.

Introduction

Businesses are constantly faced with the need to effectively leverage technology in every aspect of their processes. These needs are driven from a legal requirement to run a light and cost-effective operation model. When you want to adopt a technology, very rarely are you dealing specifically with the bits and bites of a technology implementation. Instead, adoption is based on the understanding of the series of solutions that provide measurable impact to organizations and then the actual application development that surrounds it. Dynamic publishing is one of those types of solutions, and this book is focused to help you understand the business implications and the subsequent application development.

The following issues factor into the ease of application development:

- The composition of the team who is doing the development
- The language in which the application is written
- The functionality that is contained within the application

The authors who wrote this book have built their careers around being able to effectively minimize the impact that each of these influences has on projects. This book reflects their experience and is organized in a way that helps present these three main themes in a concise and intertwined manner.

The chapters attempt to clarify the team issues as well as provide information around building a dynamic publishing application. Dynamic publishing is not an exact science with a set number of pieces, attributes, and variables. Instead, it is a term to describe a set of functionality or a solution to a problem. Effectively writing about dynamic publishing requires base functionality to be covered with a focus on the options that can be taken to solve the problem. Through this sort of writing, you will find more building blocks to be assembled together rather than an exact recipe for construction.

The Audience

Multiple players are involved in bringing an application to completion. This book targets three roles—technical manager, architect, and mid- to senior-level developer—in which these players are involved. In the section "How to Use This Book," we will discuss how this book is laid out for these roles more specifically. Therefore, the audience is an exact mapping over the roles in which we're targeting.

Thus, the mission statement for this book is as follows:

> To present a book that interweaves the three roles that make application successful. Focusing around dynamic publishing, we want to impress upon the technical manager the aspects of dynamic publishing to successfully understand the associated return on investment (ROI) and complexity; provide the architects with the alternatives available to develop with; and provide the technical depth for the developer to be able to draw the essence of this type of application.

To provide a baseline for keeping the target true to these roles, we created a set of personas to depict to whom we were writing. The following sections describe each role being targeted and the persona that was created.

Technical Manager

The technical manager is responsible not only for managing a development and infrastructure staff, but also for interfacing with senior management in IS (CIO, IS security, networking, and so on). The technical manager must understand how business works and work closely with business areas. This manager finds technology solutions to meet business problems and articulates solutions to the business community on how the technology can help them solve problems, save money, and so on. Although the technical manager interfaces and ultimately makes the technical solutions, he is generally not technical enough to actually use the tools that he chooses.

> I am George, the technical manager. As a technology manager who is leading a web development team or e-business team, I must always be in the position of clearly understanding how the business works. In most cases, I will be expected to understand the business nearly as well as the business area I am interacting with. The challenge I face is to find a technology solution that fits the core IS infrastructure and meet business demands. When a solution has been found, the next step is to articulate the power of a solution via discussions and illustrations. The real challenge is to articulate them in a way that both technology and business groups can equally understand to be of value to the overall organization. I will say this more often than not, "If I don't understand the solution, then the technology groups and business groups won't buy into it. Make me effective."

Architect

The architect is responsible for planning the way that the system rolls out within the team. He decides how to meet the requirements that are set in business objectives and requirement documents. The architect fits all the services and functionality of the application together, which he delegates to the team. Because one of the calls or goals of an architect is combine the business requirements with the design of the application, the architect is generally someone who understands the business domain fairly well. As you will see in the way this book is laid out, the architect acts as a middle ground between a developer's implementation and technical manager's business needs.

I am Jerry, the architect. I come to this book already knowing the principles of architecture, but I never complain about a few pages that tell me how great I am or miss an opportunity to reassess my capabilities. I need to know how the problem of dynamic publishing relates to what I already know about application development and existing web application architectures. In the end, I am looking for something that will make me think but not tell me *how* to think. As an architect, I like options and abstract thinking. I will solve the problem if you give me enough information to get my creative juices flowing. I have great interest in the content or "how to" chapters of this book because I do not like to craft a technical vision without having been there myself. I will use this book as a dynamic publishing field manual.

Developer

The developer is the person who does the actual work. He is told what to do at a level and then builds it. This book is targeted to this role more than the others. Due to the extremely technical nature of this role, you will find that developers have a much heavier focus on getting the things done than on enforcing requirements to match the business need. Their only real contact with the business world is through the design of the architect.

I am Newman, the developer. I need a book that will explain the things I need to know clearly and concisely and then provide more detailed information that I can reference. I never read technical books cover to cover unless I am totally unfamiliar with a technology, and even then I still skip around. I want to go to a chapter, read a few pages to get the concept, and reference the rest as I need to. I love chapters that tell me what I need to know in the first part and then show me how the concept applies in different situations in each section of the chapter. That way, I can say "Okay, I can read this first part and then this part over here that shows me how to do it in a similar way to what I need." But the book still needs to be readable all the way through.

I also want to know tips and pitfalls along the way. That's why I go to the developer forums. I search the forums and see how other people have screwed up so that I can avoid the same fate. If the book can say "Watch out for this" or "It's easier this way," then I will keep it on my desk. If the book doesn't do this, then why do I need it when I have forums and documentation?

The Content of the Book

Over the years, applications have gone through phases or fads in which labels described their functionality. Great examples are content management, commerce, community, and portal applications. Although there are definitely some differences between these types of applications, there are far more similarities. For example, both a content management application and a commerce site can use a process automation service (workflow) to track approval of content that is shown to a user. By focusing on the functionality that makes up these varieties of application types, this book can present these common functional units in a way that we can assemble into these labeled application types.

Each language brings its own complexity that causes us to struggle to become masters of the syntax so that we can build our applications using the full set of features of that language. Therefore, the combination of solution building and language features drive the bulk of the book's content. The particular languages we will cover in this book include ColdFusion MX, Flash Remoting, and Flash MX.

Wrapped around this technically rich content are the chapters concerned with understanding a management and architectural view of the topic being covered. This gives us a blend of what we want to accomplish, what the approaches can be, and how to construct them when we're using this book to learn. Following are the highlights that this book covers:

- **Design options**—Instead of providing absolutes to a solution, this book provides an abstract description of the problem with possible options to solve it. However, most examples focus exclusively on one item.
- **MX platform overview**—With the introduction of the Macromedia MX product suite, we now draw upon functionality that several products provide. One chapter is dedicated to explaining the rich client application that this platform supports and that Macromedia wrote.
- **MX features**—Specific features are covered outside of their usage in solving a problem to show off the new features without constraints.
- **Dissection of a dynamic publishing application**—A dissection provides us with more than a look at solving a specific type of application problem; it provides a framework so that we can understand all derivatives of the application.

The Application of the Book

To support the content of the book, we created a sample application and example files. In addition, we used architectural models and the requirements that the application is based on that were created to support its construction.

The location of the combined Zip and installation instructions are available from the New Riders web site at `www.newriders.com`.

How to Use This Book

Because there are a few different veins following through this book, this section shows you how the book is organized so that, depending on which role you are playing on your development engagements, you will benefit. This book is organized so that you can focus on any particular part of an application's needs.

Therefore, there are three ways in which you can approach this book:

- By role
- By feature
- By functionality group

If you decide to take the role approach, we suggest that you read all the chapters that were targeted for your role as shown in chapter types in the following section. If you are looking for a particular feature, you will find that the chapter names highlight either the technology or the solution-specific focus. Finally, if you want to read about a specific functional grouping, such as your content repository, we suggest you read the chapters that are presented in the virtual section, as noted in the next section.

The Format of the Book

To support the multiple types of content that we wanted to have appear in the book, we created a classification for each chapter that specifies how it was written. These three chapters types are listed next with the associated chapters.

Foundation Chapters

These chapters describe the core concepts needed to understand what we are building as well as the basic building blocks for organizing a dynamic publishing application. These chapters are targeted to both technical managers and architects. The chapters that fall into this category are 1 through 4, 13, and 19.

Dunk Chapters

These chapters are tightly written to concisely point out and explain one feature in ColdFusion MX in great detail. The focus on the feature is dealt with outside of the context of the application so that you can understand the full usage. The supporting examples are either part of the application or in their own example directory. These chapters were targeted to both architects and developers. The chapters that fall into this category are 5 through 7, 14, 15, and 20.

Content Chapters

These chapters outline and discuss how to implement a specific piece of functionality as it relates to dynamic publishing. These are detailed for the particular problem that we are covering and provide a set of options that we can pull from. In these chapters are specific usages of the features that are explained in the dunk chapters. These chapters were targeted primarily for developers. The chapters that fall into this category are 8 through 12, 16 through 18, and 21 through 23.

The Parts of the Book

The book follows a natural progression to help you see the application build from the ground up. It is important to call out that the layering segmentation that the chapters follow is the same one that the presented architecture is based on. This layered architecture, covered in detail in Chapter 3, "Architecting a Dynamic Publishing Application," is based on an MVC-style architecture and provides an excellent way to digest technical and business requirements.

This layering of the chapters to organize around the architecture provides consistency between chapter introduction and feature dependency. This is accomplished through five logical groupings of the chapters in this book. Each section has a consistent way in which it organizes the chapter types. The foundation chapters are presented first to set the overview for the sections. These are followed by dunk chapters that are needed to explain a specific ColdFusion MX feature that the proceeding content chapters reference.

Part I: The Why

This section discusses the essence and purpose of Dynamic Publishing. It also covers the information about the technology that we are working with as well as the architecture with which we are going to use to build. Chapters 1 through 3 are included in this section.

Part II: The Content Layer

This section deals with the ground layer in a dynamic application and dives into the mysteries of the content repository in an organization. Chapters 4 through 12 are included in this section.

Part III: The Repository Management Layer

This section covers the mysteries of managing the content repository for the application as well as an organization. This includes building effective business interfaces as well as implementing process automation effectively into an organization. Chapters 13 through 18 are included in this section.

Part IV: The Publishing Layer

This section exposes content that is residing in the repository to multiple clients and streamlines the management of the presentation. Chapters 19 through 22 are included in this section.

Part V: The Aftermath

This is the go-live section. The part contains just one chapter, 23, "Development of Dynamic Publishing Applications." This chapter highlights items that are needed to successfully bring an application to launch.

Summary

This book provides so many different options for pursuing planning and construction of a dynamic publishing system. This supports a casual skimming to keep certain key topics of a system we are working for all the way to a complete in-depth read to help us see the whole picture of how a dynamic publishing system is assembled.

In whatever role you are viewing this book, you're encouraged to challenge yourself against the ideas and information provided to assist in the best construction of your next venture.

I

The Why

1

Overview of Dynamic Publishing

by Michael Mazzorana

WHEN YOU THINK OF THE WORD *publishing*, one of the thoughts that might come to your mind might be the book you are reading right now. This book is composed of thousands of words, images, and styles on hundreds of pages structured in a consistent format for you, the reader. Now think about the process that took place before this book hit the bookstore shelves. Contributors were defined with roles of how or what would be contributed. The writing process began with rules, guidelines, and procedures. After the content for the book was complete, the editing and approval process began. Then the book was approved, printed, and bound together to be presented in the structured format you're experiencing right now.

If we put the word *dynamic* into the mix, the word *publishing* takes on a slightly different meaning. We begin to immediately think of a faster, more efficient way of managing the content assets that make up this book and how the participants contributed to the process of creating the book. Content assets, such as titles, book covers, author bios, and illustrations are combined by the process in place. Naturally, technology solutions are one way to make this happen.

This book will focus on dynamic publishing as a technical solution that fits a business process. Content assets will be discussed as any type of company asset that might include video, audio, graphics, legacy system data, newly created content, and anything else that would support a business process and company web site. We will explain how participants can contribute content changes to a central location with an automated workflow through an easy interface that will immediately populate a production web site. The management of static HTML templates is a cumbersome and costly process for your organization. This chapter will introduce a fictitious company to bring the problem and solutions to life.

We can define *dynamic publishing* as a way to manage and present content assets in a consistent, efficient, timely, and cost-effective manner.

As a reference to this book and a way to absorb how you can understand dynamic publishing as an application solution, think of dynamic publishing as individual application layers. Each layer solves specific business problems and uses a specific technical solution. By understanding each logical layer individually, you will be able to digest an understanding of this powerful solution for your business users and technology peers.

In this introductory chapter, you will learn how each technical layer will solve specific business problems. Throughout this book, we will use a fictitious company with real-world productivity and process issues. Whether you're a business manager, technical manager, or developer, you should be able to use some of the explanations and examples in this book for your success with dynamic publishing.

The Four Layers

Dynamic publishing can be segmented into four key layers: the Content layer, the Management layer, the Publishing layer, and the Client layer (see Figure 1.1).

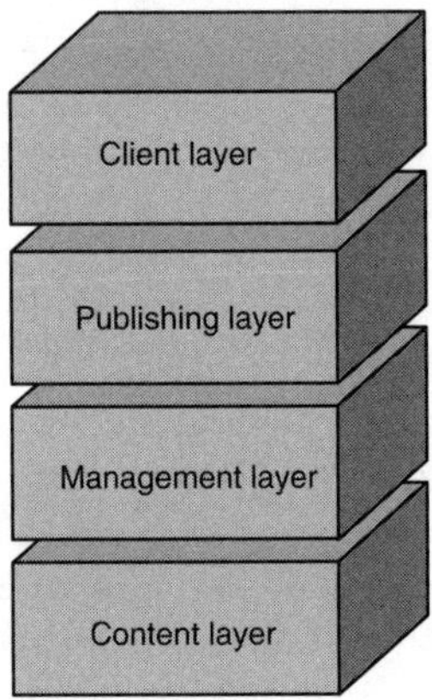

Figure 1.1 The four main layers of dynamic publishing.

Note

In web development over the years, business owners have associated the end result of their projects with how the web site functioned and what the design and functionality looked and felt like. Before the concept of dynamic publishing or Web Content Management, web sites were designed with a top-down approach, and the result was often a poorly thought-out content structure. A web site would grow horizontally without depth, which in turn would grow out of control with poor navigation and a bad user experience. These "bad habits" still linger today.

The illustration of layers in the order shown is not to fight that thought process that is embedded in business owners' and web designers' minds, but instead to support it with a "re-education" on how web development should be approached. Imagine if we were building a house. The siding, trim, paint, and roof shingles would not come before the foundation was poured, but when you sat with your contractor, all you would care about would be the plan and the final result. For the project to be successful, the builder must ask the right questions, and the buyer needs to understand the results based on mutual decisions between himself and the buyer. Therefore, both parties need to go through the whole process from the ground up to achieve good results.

The IT Challenges of Managing Internet Content Today

When Tim Berners-Lee invented HTML in the late 1980s and early 1990s, he couldn't have imagined the success we are seeing today: a simplistic way to create information that can be linked together easily. HTML has created an explosion of easily accessible information at people's fingertips, but in recent years, HTML has shown that simple has its problems. A major portion of the information on the web today is managed in a labor-intensive fashion:

- Billions of static pages and documents exist with content enclosed in HTML tags on static templates. Manageability and reusability have become a major issue for organizations that leverage the Internet to expand their businesses.
- The way most sights are built today makes the business content that lives on them impossible to reuse, manage, and retrieve for presentation to web users.
- HTML is not the only means by which you will be confronted when you're building client front-end experiences.

The way that content is stored and managed will become critical to meet these demands.

The Current Publishing Process in a Static System

In most well-run business organizations today, it is not uncommon that strong processes are in place for check and balance of system stability and business continuity. In a static HTML managed site today, a company that makes it a priority to ensure it keeps its information updated will dedicate teams of "template developers" who take requests from business units and manually update pages on-the-fly with tools like Dreamweaver, FrontPage, and even Notepad. Operations of the web servers avoid traditional "change control" processes to keep up with frequency of content change requests. In most company operations, it is necessary to wrap application code in a consistent way so it migrates smoothly from one environment to another. Packaging a change multiple times a day for HTML pages that need to go to production have not fit control models for companies that depend on complex enterprise tools that migrate the wrapped code, such as IBM's Tivoli, Hewlett-Packard's OpenView, and Computer Associates' TNG-Unicenter. Many situations in development units still require a webmaster role to fulfill the managing and moving of HTML files from one environment to the next until it is in production. Another factor when changes are made in this non-structured environment includes old versions being accidentally published, new versions being overwritten, and template developers stepping on top of each other. IT managers who are uncomfortable with this approach do not have many choices and risk the instability of their environments if a breakdown occurs in the process.

Frequent changes to company web sites can be attributed to the increased economic demands that are driving our businesses. IT departments are being challenged to meet the importance of keeping up with competitors. Each company jockeys for position by streamlining business models to contribute the most recent products, services, and overall presence in the newest communication channel. In a static HTML model, time-to-market demands are impossible unless increased resource supports the increased demand from business units. Portal strategies become impossible to implement unless content is fresh, structured, and stored separately from other text, layout, and graphics. Cobranding and other various business channels need to tailor user experiences for a specific need or audience and are taking hold as a critical part of any company who does business on the web. If the technical foundation is not in place to support these initiatives, development units find themselves creating additional sites by copying them and then applying a different look and feel. This approach is not scalable and can be costly to a department in the long term.

As these strategies grow, so does the IT maintenance of the many web sites that begin to exist. Unfortunately, cut budgets and thinning staff resources do not allow for additional developers to support the copy and paste development approach. The unknown danger for most business areas that are budgeting for their IT departments is an unclear understanding of the growing maintenance problem and the increasing fragility of their web presence. Web development needs to take a more mature development approach. Content demands that are supporting these business requirements are changing the way we need to develop web applications. We need to think of a web site more like an application. The transition from static sites to dynamic sites will require a different thought process for both technical and business staff alike.

Managing a Business Web Site: DuvalShock, Inc.

If you are a technical manager, one of your biggest challenges is articulating and judging return on investment (ROI) for a dynamic publishing solution. If we take a more detailed look of how most companies manage content today, you will become aware of the time and effort it takes to make simple changes on a targeted template. This section discusses how a typical business web site can be managed. From this example, we can break down the issues and build a basic ROI understanding.

As a prototype throughout this book, we will focus on a company named DuvalShock, Inc. DuvalShock, Inc. is a fictitious electrical component manufacturer that requires frequent updates on its home page for independent manufacturing representatives who use this information to operate and sell DuvalShock, Inc. products. Breaking down the company's web site, we can see in Figure 1.2 that DuvalShock's home page consists of business-critical information that is related to the electrical industry and the independent middle sales representatives who sell DuvalShock, Inc. products.

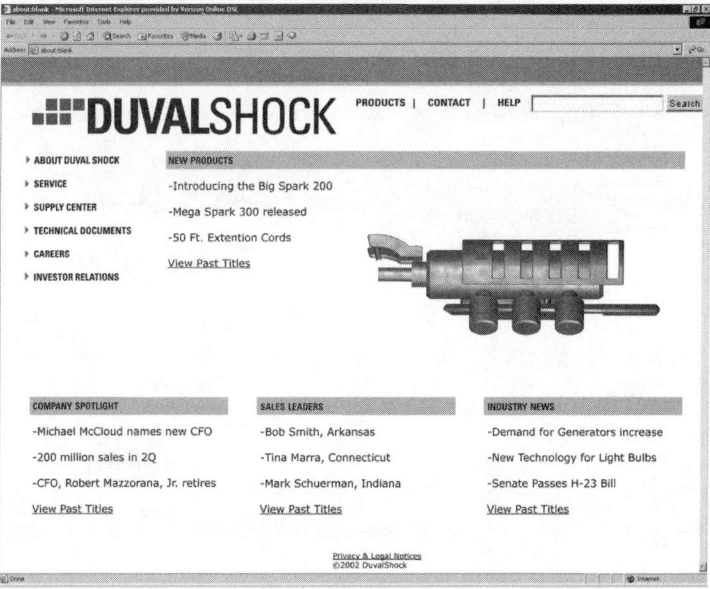

Figure 1.2 DuvalShock home page.

The marketing department enters a request into a home-grown "change request" application that asks for the details needed to begin development of a new model diesel-powered generator that is soon to be available. Even before the content reaches this stage, the intended marketing material that is already written goes through a series of edits and approvals in the Generator Marketing Unit. An employee in the unit writes the first draft of the marketing material on a word processor and saves it to a shared server. Then many individuals edit and re-edit the draft until business and compliance areas give final signoff. The frustration level of going through these approvals via unread emails, voice mails, and meetings leaves no room for delay of sharing the information with the sales reps when it finally is entered into the development team's change request application. Often, a project manager is needed to keep track of the documentation that is created and the approvals that are needed with various spreadsheets and project formats.

The development process begins with a developer being assigned to handle the change request. He takes the request and most likely has a series of templates to work from that affect different components of the web site.

In this case shown in Figure 1.3, three HTML templates are developed. The development team is responsible for meeting the requirements described for each template.

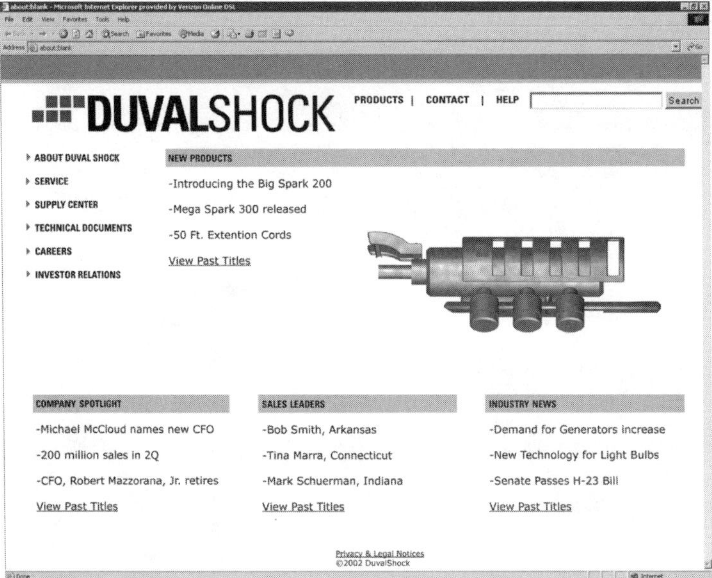

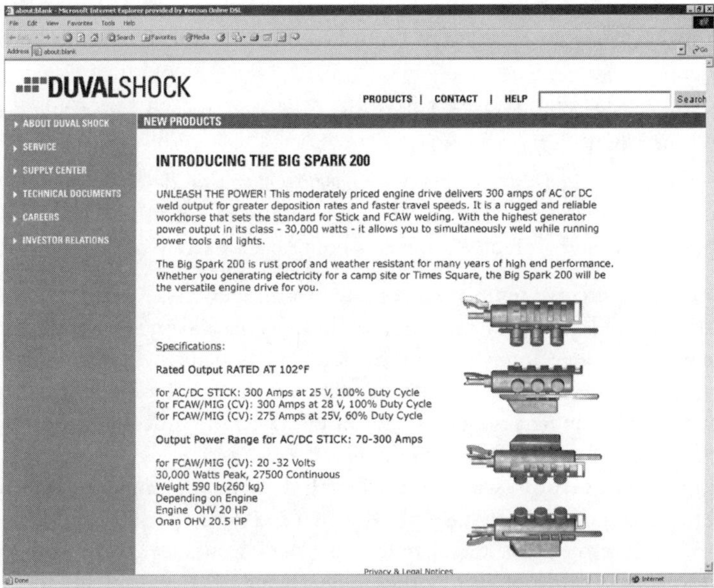

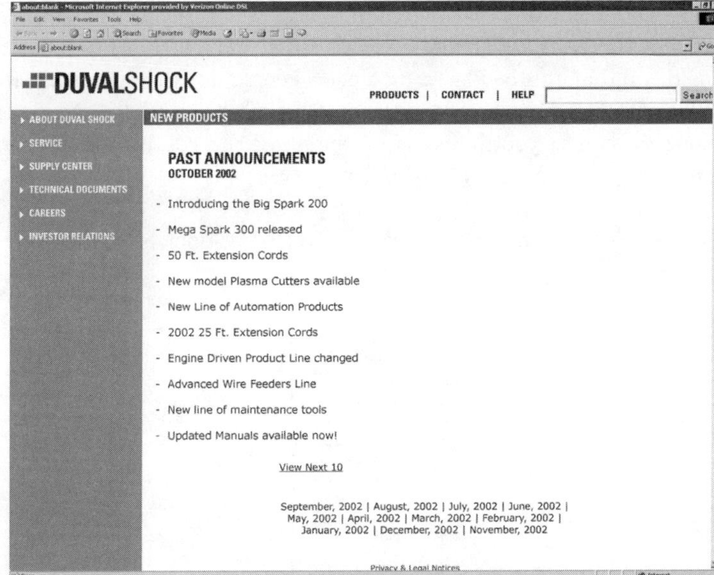

Figure 1.3 DuvalShock web site.

- A *home page template* has a title description that links to the *body template*. Three title descriptions are required to show, and then the fourth oldest is bumped off this page.
- The *body template* holds the details of the marketing material. The title description hyperlink points here.
- An *archive template* lists bumped *home page template* title descriptions (10 at a time) in chronological order for the current month. This template also has links to previous months' archive templates going back exactly one year.

At month end, the archive template is restarted to the new month and previous months are separated on a dedicated *month template*. This is a once-a-month activity requirement that the development team needs to track manually. Depending on how critical and timely the content needs to be archived, the development team can spend many hours of development time and a lot of effort on the process, which might entail extra hours on weekends and evenings.

Discussions and questions with the marketing department employee who originally requested this change inevitably take place. When the developer has completed the work, the webmaster migrates the change to a quality assurance (QA) environment. The business employee is notified by the project manager to thoroughly test and sign off on the change. If he sees something that is not correct and cannot get signoff for this change, development and QA migration repeat.

Figure 1.4 shows the complete life cycle discussed and a formula to judge the cost of a new marketing item to be placed on a page. People don't always realize the number of roles involved in the process and the amount of time it takes to move out a simple change. Of course, you should adjust the hours and cost on the illustration according to your department's culture and skill level.

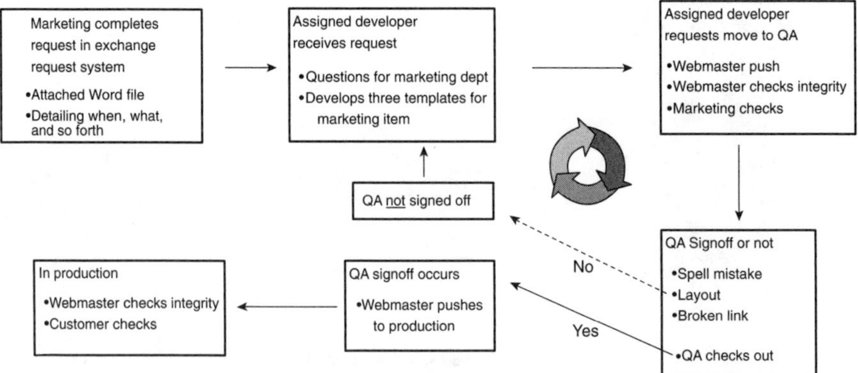

Figure 1.4 Steps for migrating content to production with a manual process.

Buy or Build?

If you are convinced that everything pointed out until now is a valid reason for seriously looking at a dynamic publishing solution, the next critical decision to make is whether to buy or build. The build versus buy issue can be a daunting one in the world of managing information on the web. The theory on how to approach this decision has changed directions exponentially to the Internet technology in the past five years. The controversy has created a confusing product market labeled Web Content Management (WCM). Companies and consultants in this space have interpreted Web Content Management in different ways. Enterprises have spent millions of dollars trying to solve problems that they were not quite clear about. Based on the nature of web applications built today, it is clear that not one tool or platform will meet all your requirements, and you can almost be assured that you will be integrating in several areas.

You must also consider how to leverage your staff and the skills they possess. This decision is critical to building and maintaining any solution path you decide to go down. Business requirements take priority on the solution you choose, but this is one area in which a technical manager needs to influence final decisions with business partners.

This book focuses on Macromedia's Java and ColdFusion technologies by showing their strengths through building a dynamic publishing application backend. Macromedia Flash and other traditional scripting languages will be applied to the Client layer. Tying these languages and platforms together will create a powerful solution that can co-exist with your development team's skills.

The rest of this chapter attempts to break down the requirements so that you can understand the application layers and decide the best approach for your organization. Again, it is important to understand the logical separation of each layer and the requirements within. It will help you to pick a product(s) and develop a solution described in this book. Whether you are a technical application architect, a business manager, or a developer, understanding these layers will help you define whether buying or building a dynamic publishing is right for you.

The Content Layer

The Content layer (see Figure 1.5) consists of an aggregation of many corporate assets that are found in almost any size company.

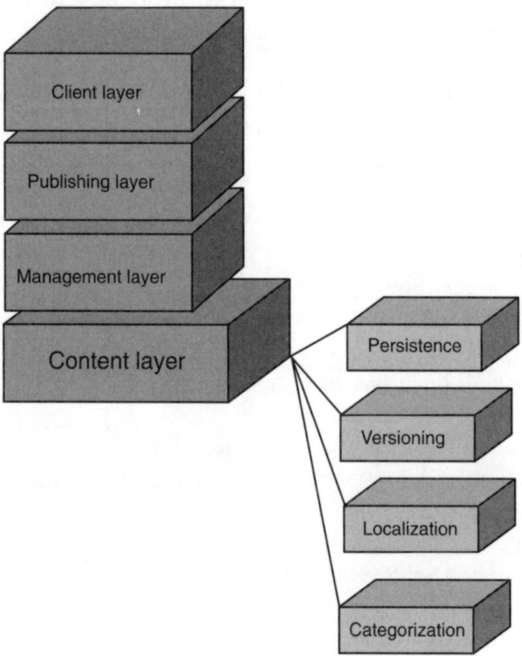

Figure 1.5 The Content layer.

Looking at the list of vital existing legacy systems and digital assets in a company, (see Figure 1.6), the biggest challenge that companies and IT organizations face today is how to leverage these existing assets. The way that these systems exist today does not transpose well with strategic web initiatives that businesses are trying to implement. One thing is certain: IT organizations will be forced to leverage existing invested infrastructures to meet business requirements for their web strategies.

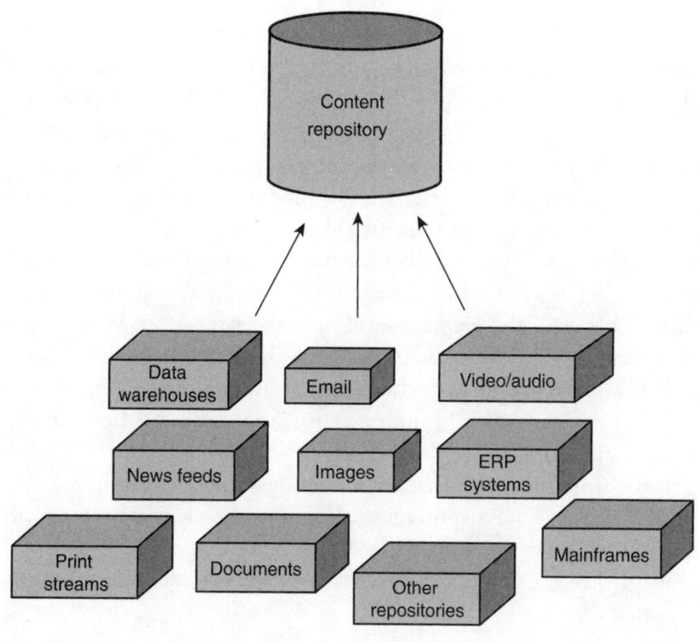

Figure 1.6 Types of digital assets in an organization today that can be fed into a content repository.

A key concept of the Content layer is that after solutions are designed to leverage existing digital assets or new solutions are built to support an initiative, a content repository acts as the nucleus to the life cycle of content in a dynamic publishing strategy. A *content repository* is simply a location where content can be stored as a structured, yet loosely coupled format to be used in almost any way. In many cases today, the approach would be to store content as XML in an enterprise database solution. XML will tag content assets in a granular way to be effectively searched and presented to the end user.

You need to consider introducing a database that is scalable and can handle these common content repository options. You also should consider the following features in your dynamic publishing solution.

Versioning

We can begin to understand the requirements of the Content layer by first discussing versioning. Versioning can be thought of a way to track and save changes made to content living in the repository. Versioning of content is an important business requirement when building a dynamic publishing application. Internal audit and legal departments will look for ways to improve the validity of content that is presented on a web site, and, versioning, is key to meeting this requirement. If a graphic designer updates your logo or a business unit changes the text on your web sites pages, versioning assists in archiving, tracking, and reporting these events. Versioning also plays a role in rolling back a change at the element level or at the page level. More important, version tracking is necessary for accountability.

Content that is not stored in your database repository is most likely versioned with the static HTML template with a "source control" tool, such as Microsoft's Visual Source Safe or Merant's PVCS.

Content that is stored in your database with a dynamic publishing solution has versioning built in based on your requirements. Your business, legal, and internal audit departments need to determine how far back and how long to keep backups of your database. A process needs to be put in place to synchronize static template source with content repository versions.

Internationalization and Localization

Also required for developing the Content layer are internationalization and localization. For many businesses, selling, servicing, or partnering with their products in foreign countries is critical. Even if you are not currently getting requirements to develop solutions to meet foreign markets, it might pay off if you begin your Content layer foundation efforts with foreign markets in mind.

Following are some of the challenges to think about for existing content:

- **Translation of content**—This is most likely a third-party tool or process that needs to be integrated. Third-party translation tools rarely translate content accurately, so having an outside workflow can support the tool effectively.
- **Fitting local business processes**—This involves being prepared to spawn off separate workflows. This topic is discussed in more detail in the section titled "The Management Layer."
- **Content modification for revision or cultural customization of content**—This could be the English language in another English speaking country (for example, color/colour).
- **Preparing for character set displays and resolution of character-set issues in double-byte languages**—Example of this can be related to Japanese characters or the Farci language.
- **Targeting content to be localized**—An example of localization can be how insurance regulations slightly differ from state to state, so subtle content modifications need to reflect this.

Leveraging Existing Digital Assets

As we mentioned earlier, being able to tap into existing digital assets (shown in Figure 1.6) is critical to your success in leveraging the abilities of the web. Your requirements will most likely define how you will need to reach business partners, customers, and employees with your content assets that live deep in the abyss of your company. Many employees manage important company assets without a formal process or system and become inaccessible to others in the organization because this information is stored on a local hard drive. Storing information in a central repository insures others in the company, and therefore, your customers, can access those assets.

After you have tapped into these critical assets, the Content layer assists the following areas:

- **Categorization of existing and newly created content**—This is needed against your repository to define the content that is available. It assists you in search and personalization capabilities when the Client layer is executed.
- **Persistence of content**—This is important because it stores the content in a hierarchical manner. Content is more accessible and scalable through how it is stored and cached. Separation of application logic from the specifics of how and where persistent data is stored allows for abstraction, scalability, and database independence for your content repository.

The Management Layer

After you have your content layer defined and designed, you need a way to add, change, and manipulate the data living in the content repository. Think of the Management layer (see Figure 1.7) as a workflow or a set of tasks required for content items before they are published to production. The essence of a workflow should be in synergy to the business process it is trying to support.

Following are some of the common tasks in a Management layer:

- **Entry of metadata**—The process should support tagging of content to ensure it has an identity.
- **Authoring of content**—Whether it is massaging existing digital assets or creating new content, the flow should include a way to author it in a consistent process.
- **A selection of keywords or categories**—Predefined keywords and categories are the key to leveraging structure in any web site. This affects how your dynamic publishing solution behaves with other layers.
- **Notification features**—These include sending emails or paging individuals when key tasks are complete and action is needed to complete the flow.

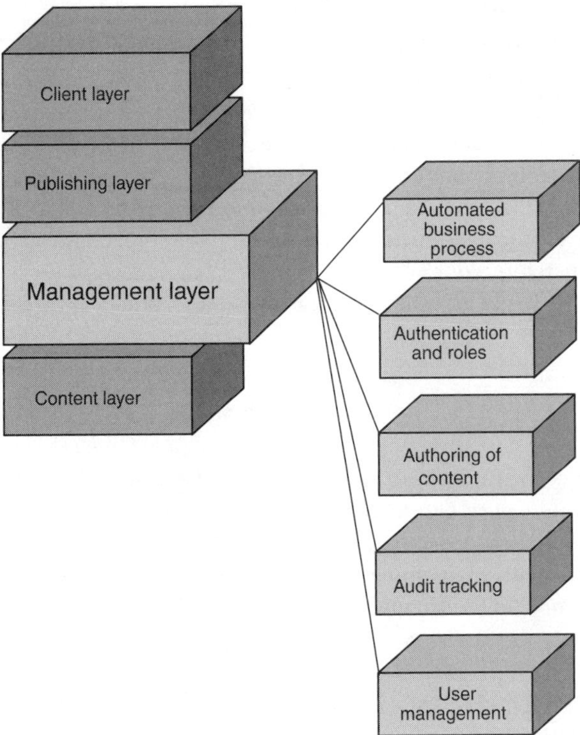

Figure 1.7 The Management layer.

The big advantage with the Management layer is developing a way to automate business processes. In Chapter 12, "Categorization of Content," we will look at DuvalShock's business process from a use-case scenario and break down how automation can make the process more efficient through automation of tasks. We will explore how to re-educate your business partners to see the advantages automation will offer at the same time support your strategy for dynamic publishing. Also important, we will look at leveraging pieces of your existing infrastructure, such as like LDAP and other directory services, to ensure single sign on that co-exists with other daily corporate applications used in your organization.

The Publishing Layer

At this point, we have considered the requirements of the Content layer, which gives us a solid foundation for how the content will span its existence over time. The Management layer gives you a mechanism control process and enforces how the business and content repository work together. The next critical layer to dynamic publishing is the Publishing layer (see Figure 1.8).

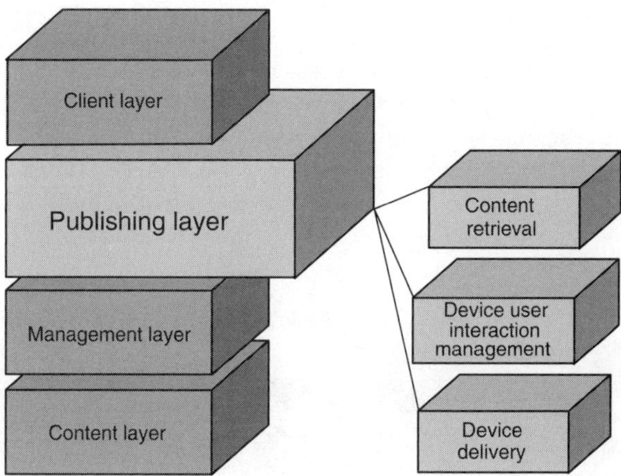

Figure 1.8 The Publishing layer.

The Publishing layer is simply the publishing of your content assets that have been through the first two layers. It becomes the final step after the Management layer is completed. Publishing releases the content in the repository to the Client layer.

Publishing can be broken down into the following business rules:

- **How content is published**—Will it be served up as HTML, a PDF, or to a Flash interface? Where on the site is it targeted for?
- **When content goes live**—Are there rules that apply to a specific date when content should be presented or when existing content should be removed?
- **What to display in a category or page**—Will the list of titles be dedicated to one template and the body to another designated template?
- **The order in which content is listed**—Should items be listed newest to oldest or in alphabetical order? A publishing rule can also combine the creation and metadata to publish the most recent content for a specific category.

When metadata and categorization are properly set up in the Content and Management layers, the Publishing layer can perform powerful functions that could drive your site's navigation dynamically or expose your content to third-party tools that assist in building portals or search capabilities.

Businesses will have better control of their content by being able to set up marketing campaigns with rules that minimize mistakes. One example of a mistake would be when products are reduced in price one week but the message still exists on the web site two weeks later. This creates disgruntled customers and hurts a company's reputation. Publishing can also be powerful in targeting content to specific audiences. The life of content items on a web site can have expirations embedded to ensure old content is not featured and is eliminated or stored in an archive.

The Client Layer

The final application layer and the layer we have been building up to is the Client layer (see Figure 1.9). After proper architecture and building of the first three layers, the user experience becomes the most important aspect of your web site. This is the final presentation of your organization's content assets, but the content still has the ability to dynamically change and be reused as defined by the business requirements.

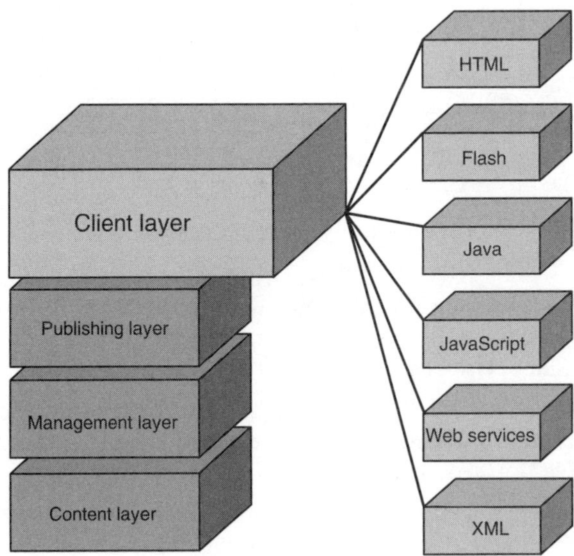

Figure 1.9 The Client layer.

The process, management, and rules around the content continue to exist in the repository. A user experience is enriched by the foundation below it, but it is not limited to just HTML web pages. The Content, Management, and Publishing layers are a solid approach for traditional web templating and scripting languages, such as HTML, JavaScript, and DHTML. Also supporting the Client layer in dynamic publishing are the dynamic options to build your site by embedding the necessary elements in templates to call databases, middleware, and other data sources. The major application servers in the market today support standard and proprietary options to support the dynamic areas in your pages.

These include (but are not limited to) the following:

- ColdFusion Markup Language (CFML)
- Java ServerPages (JSP)
- Active Server Pages (ASP)

Most likely, your current web application servers and developer staff development tools will support the construction of the web Client layer.

Although we have been concentrating most of our discussions around today's traditional web technology options, we should also consider other ways that content will be used. Our dynamic publishing application layers described are not web dependent. Other Client layer experiences are possible with existing technologies and unknown innovations that will inevitably arrive in the future. Flash technology has made an interesting development migration from simple dynamic navigation and other various screen animations to a more end-user rich application experience. Macromedia's latest innovations with Flash technology now natively support the development of content and data-driven applications with a Flash Player. Think of rich Windows OS-like interfaces through a web browser. Future chapters of this book will detail more of those features and how the Client layer can take advantage of them.

With our application layers in place, we can make our content reusable in various ways. One way to consider making your dynamic publishing application an asset to the rest of your organization and partners is to leverage web services or web syndication. The content stored in the repository is separated from any ties to layout logic, so the possibility of sharing your content with other web sites becomes much less complex. Companies are starting to realize that they need content from business partners, distributors, subscription feeds, and even other internal areas of their organization. Companies also are recognizing that their own content is in demand by the same external areas. Macromedia's latest MX technologies take advantage of this and make the process of receiving or exposing your content data to others a simple one.

The MX technology in question is the built-in web service generation that is tied to ColdFusion Components. Web services is a standard way in which an object can be exposed and communicated to across a network. Web services as a technology consists of two major parts: the description of the service through a WSDL file and an invocation of the web service request through a SOAP message. Web services is quickly becoming the industry standard for distributed communication due to the ease in which it is called and the message format it uses, which is XML. This book covers Web services in much greater detail in Chapter 20, "Web Services."

Hardware devices have driven the need for dynamic publishing. Content is starting to be prevalent in devices with unique operating systems, such as PDAs, cell phones, audio-web clients such as VOXEO, and even public monitors that exist in elevators. The first three application layers will position these latest Client layers as well as the future innovations around the corner.

Conclusion

In this chapter, you read a high-level overview of the different facets of dynamic publishing. Before explaining the solution, we first evaluated a problem in the web development units today. Developers spend too much valuable time acting as a scribe for the business units that need to get out important business information on their web pages. Also discussed was how business organizations cannot afford to continue to manage their sites statically if they want to effectively execute customer, partner, and employee Internet strategies in the future. IT managers need to begin focusing the talents of their development units with building and managing enterprise solutions that will have positive long-term effects.

Approach this solution in four different layers:

- The Content layer is where your content repository lives. Content from disparate existing or different repositories and legacy systems can be collected as needed and stored, versioned, and formatted in a way that your business customers, partners, and employees can reach through a simple web interface.
- The Management layer is where content has a life cycle and evolves. This layer mirrors your business process in an automated fashion. Defined roles fit a workflow to ensure auditing, compliance, and business continuity for your company. This layer empowers your business to control your web site's information.
- The Publishing layer is a configuration of the rules on how content should be managed. Content expires, needs to display a certain order, has to behave on a page or pages as defined in the application requirements, and content needs a deployment mechanism for being available to your targeted audience.
- The Client layer is where the content displays. For the web, templates assist in accomplishing this. Dynamic pages interact with the other layers to drive how the user experiences your site. Outside of traditional web development, this layer has other alternatives like Flash technology to enrich a user's experience. The Client layer is unlimited to how you want to leverage the first three layers.

When you're trying to explain dynamic publishing to your peers or management, breaking it down into logical separate identities makes it easier for your audience to digest. Each layer has a specific role and solution to help your organization meet business objectives. Keep in perspective that you're trying to solve a business problem for your company by building a strategic application that supports business processes, but at the same time enables the business to be successful with the audience. Use this chapter as a foundation and refer to the following chapters to come.

2

Understanding the MX Platform

by Benjamin Elmore

THIS BOOK IS BUILT UPON THE REVOLUTIONARY product suite that Macromedia recently introduced. This chapter is included in this book to give you a viewpoint of the product set as a whole without the filtering that a specific implementation brings. By providing a view of what Macromedia's intent is for the product set, we can compare our usage of the product to see if our application growth is inline with the projected growth of the product suite.

Macromedia has been gracious enough to allow us to repurpose an article from the Macromedia Developer Center called "Developing Rich Internet Applications with Macromedia MX." You can find the article at `http://www.macromedia.com/desdev/mx/studio/whitepapers/rich_internet_apps.pdf`.

Introduction

Summary

The Internet's potential as a platform for commerce, communications, and business automation is being constrained by the limitations of today's user experience. To address this challenge, a new class of applications—Rich Internet Applications—is emerging, promising to change Internet application development. This white paper outlines the need for a new generation of applications, provides a technical overview of Rich Internet Applications, and describes how the new Macromedia MX product family lets you develop these applications.

Evolution of the Internet

During the last six years, the web has seen explosive growth. With more than 4 billion static pages and 400 million users, it has affected the conduct of business, education, and government worldwide.

Despite the growth and success of the web, however, the Internet's potential as a platform for commerce, communications, and business automation remains untapped, constrained by the limitations of today's user experience.

While the web provides an excellent user experience for browsing content, the experience for applications makes even simple activities like online shopping too difficult, and more complex interactions like those in traditional client/server and desktop applications almost impossible.

The key to tapping the Internet's potential is twofold: to deliver more effective user experiences through the browser; and to extend the capabilities of the web to deliver richer, more interactive, and more responsive user interfaces that can be deployed not just to personal computers, but across many devices.

In response to the opportunity for a more effective Internet, a new generation of Internet applications is emerging: Rich Internet Applications.

Defining Rich Internet Applications

Rich Internet Applications take advantage of interactive, or rich, client technology to offer more intuitive, responsive, and effective user experiences on the web. They combine the interactive user experiences of desktop applications with the deployment flexibility and cost profile of traditional web applications to create a single, integrated user experience.

Rich client technology makes it possible to build Rich Internet Applications by providing a runtime environment that can host compiled client-side applications that are delivered as files via HTTP. The client-side applications connect to existing application server back-ends using an asynchronous client/server architecture that's secure, scalable, and well suited to the new service-oriented model being driven by the adoption of web services.

The growing adoption of rich client technology is an evolutionary step that will not replace HTML; rather, it will extend browsers and devices for more effective and responsive user interfaces. Most Rich Internet Applications run within the browser, and many run within a web page along with HTML content. HTML will continue to play a critical role in delivering content, user interfaces, and navigation.

Because rich client technology can run in both browsers and devices, it promises the ability to create applications that are deployed consistently across a broad array of Internet-connected platforms. Moreover, because rich client technology can support motion graphics, video, audio, two-way communications, and complex forms, it provides a significantly more robust environment for creating application user interfaces.

Examples of Rich Internet Applications

The best way to understand how Rich Internet Applications can advance Internet application development is to look at a few examples:

- **Broadmoor hotel**—The Broadmoor uses a Rich Internet Application to deliver a better user experience for online reservations. While the original reservation system used five HTML pages, the new system provides a single, intuitive screen. By moving the reservation form from HTML to a rich client technology, the Broadmoor reduced the average time to complete a reservation from more than three minutes to less than a minute, and increased the number of online reservations (`www.broadmoor.com`).
- **ETrade**—ETrade used a Rich Internet Application to create a control that was embedded into an HTML page to look up stock quotes. The quote widget eliminated the need to do a full page refresh every time a user searched for a new quote. This reduced the time for the lookup, improved the user experience, and lowered costs by reducing the amount of pages delivered and the bandwidth used on the site (`www.etrade.com`).

Although relatively simple, these two examples show how Rich Internet Applications can enable a whole new class of Internet solutions with intuitive, responsive, and effective user interfaces that incorporate content and application functionality into a single, integrated user experience.

Requirements for Rich Internet Applications

Delivering Rich Internet Applications requires three elements: rich client technology, server technology, and development tools.

- **Rich client technology**—Rich client technology provides the client-side capabilities that make Rich Internet Applications possible by taking advantage of local processing power on personal computers and devices. The two key factors in choosing a rich client technology are the adoption of the technology and its capabilities.
- **Server technology**—Server technology provides the mechanism to connect rich clients to application logic and data. The server technology for Rich Internet Applications should extend existing infrastructure to offer a rapid scripting environment, enterprise integration, client connectivity, and support for key standards. In addition to enabling traditional database applications, Rich Internet Applications promise to integrate two-way communications and real-time data into applications, so they also need a new generation of communication server capabilities.

- **Development tools**—Having the client and server technology is meaningless without a set of easy and powerful development tools that let you get started quickly and deliver advanced solutions. Because of their client/server architecture, Rich Internet Applications require a range of development tools that work together.

The new Macromedia MX product family is specifically designed to address these requirements, making it possible to build the next generation of Internet solutions quickly and easily.

Building Rich Internet Applications

Overview

Macromedia MX is the first complete family of products and technologies designed to work together to deliver Rich Internet Applications. The Macromedia MX product family includes major new releases of existing Macromedia products, as well as new technologies and products. It includes solutions for each of the three key elements required to create Rich Internet Applications: rich client technology, server technology, and development tools.

- **Rich client technology**—Macromedia MX takes advantage of the new capabilities of Macromedia Flash Player 6. Macromedia Flash Player 6 builds on the success of Macromedia Flash with powerful new capabilities specifically designed for enabling Rich Internet Applications.
- **Server technology**—Macromedia MX includes a major new release of the ColdFusion server-scripting environment, ColdFusion MX. ColdFusion MX offers a completely new architecture that runs on Java servers and Windows .NET. In addition, the Macromedia MX product family will include an entirely new server technology for two-way communications and real-time data exchange.
- **Development tools**—Macromedia MX offers a complete suite of development tools for building rich applications in the new Macromedia Studio MX release. Macromedia Studio MX includes Macromedia Flash MX, Dreamweaver MX, Fireworks MX, and FreeHand 10.

The Macromedia MX products are designed to work together seamlessly, while also flexibly supporting a wide range of other technologies and industry standards.

Rich Client Technology

The first key element to delivering Rich Internet Applications is rich client technology. This technology provides the runtime environment for deploying rich user interfaces.

Macromedia Flash Player

Although a variety of rich client technologies are available, the most widely adopted is Macromedia Flash Player. Through broad and free distribution, wide industry acceptance, and the availability of a published file format standard (SWF), it has become the de facto standard rich client technology on the Internet.

With more than 2 billion downloads since 1997, Macromedia Flash Player is the most ubiquitous rich client and the most widely distributed software on the Internet. Macromedia Flash Player is currently available to over 98 percent of web users, reaching more users than any other rich client technology. It runs in every major browser and on Windows, Macintosh, Linux, Solaris, and other operating systems.

Macromedia Flash Player also has broad distribution on Internet-connected devices. Through agreements with leading personal computer and device vendors including AOL Time Warner, Apple, Casio, Ericsson, Microsoft, Nokia, OpenTV, Samsung, and Sony, Macromedia Flash Player is on everything from Pocket PCs to mobile communicators to game stations.

The player supports a runtime environment for applications that are delivered in the SWF file format. These files are created in an authoring environment such as Macromedia Flash MX. The player itself is less than 500k, and through compression and the ability to load components on demand, even complex SWF files remain small and easy to deploy on the Internet.

Rich Internet Application Capabilities

The new Macromedia Flash Player 6 is the cornerstone of the rich client technology in the Macromedia MX product family, building on the success of previous player releases and adding significant new functionality for Rich Internet Applications. It offers a wide range of key capabilities that are not available in any other rich client:

- **Client-side scripting**—Macromedia Flash Player provides a robust client-side scripting environment that uses ActionScript, a scripting language based on the industry-standard ECMAScript. Version 6 of the player includes a powerful new object and event model, as well as new APIs for client/server application development.
- **High-performance server connectivity**—Macromedia Flash Player supports a new technology called Macromedia Flash Remoting that enables high-performance connectivity with ColdFusion MX and other server technologies. It uses a binary message format, called Action Message Format (AMF), which lets you invoke server-side objects with a single line of code. The result is transparent client/server connectivity for applications.
- **Real-time server communication**—Macromedia Flash Player supports real-time communication including two-way audio and video, and real-time data exchange. These capabilities let you build applications that natively incorporate communication functionalities traditionally found only in instant messaging and video chat clients, as well as open new types of collaborative applications by sharing application data in real time.

- **Offline data persistence**—With the new Shared Object technology, Macromedia Flash Player can persist data locally. As a result, you can build mobile Rich Internet Applications that run in both online and offline modes, seamlessly synching data when connected.
- **Accessibility**—Macromedia Flash Player supports assistive technologies, such as screen readers, which let you build applications that are accessible to all users.
- **Localization support**—Macromedia Flash Player is localized in a wide range of languages including English, French, German, Italian, Portuguese, Spanish, Swedish, Japanese, Korean, and Simplified and Traditional Chinese. This makes it an effective solution for global applications.
- **Vector graphic display**—Because graphics, user interfaces, and rich content created with Macromedia Flash are displayed by the Macromedia Flash Player and are based on vector graphics, they download quickly and display cleanly.

While all of these features are critical to building effective Rich Internet Applications, the most important characteristic of Macromedia Flash Player is its wide distribution.

More than 2 million downloads of Macromedia Flash Player occur each day; at this rate, it will be deployed to approximately 80 percent of web users in about a year. However, because the player downloads and installs quickly and seamlessly, developers can begin using the new Macromedia Flash Player 6 capabilities immediately with the knowledge that users will be able to easily access it.

Rich Internet Application Delivery

Using Macromedia Flash Player to deliver Rich Internet Applications is straightforward. The client-side of an application is sent to the Macromedia Flash Player as a SWF file, much like HTML content is delivered to a browser. The client application can then communicate with the server as needed using AMF over HTTP and Macromedia Flash Remoting without requiring the browser page to reload. On the server, application logic is provided in ColdFusion MX pages or components. See Figure 2.1

The same model works with applications built using Microsoft .NET or Java application servers. ColdFusion MX runs on Windows .NET servers and Java application servers. In addition, Macromedia Flash Remoting is available separately for applications built natively with ASP.NET, C#, or Java.

(For more information about Macromedia Flash Player, see the new Macromedia white paper, *Macromedia Flash MX — A Next-Generation Rich Client*).

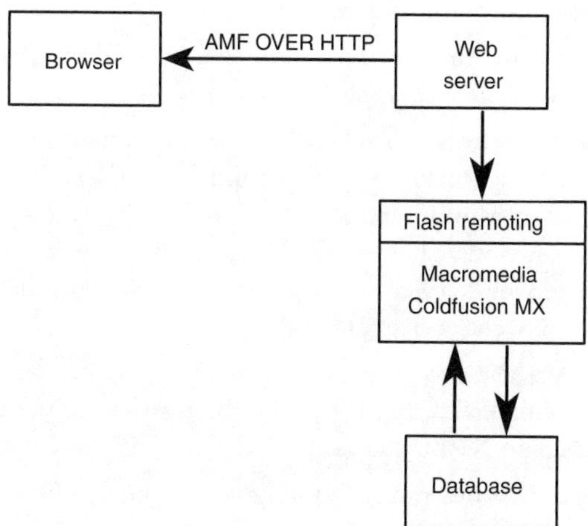

Figure 2.1 A Rich Internet Application delivered with ColdFusion.

Server Technology

The second key element to delivering Rich Internet Applications is server technology. This technology lets you connect to the rich client technology and rapidly develop on Java and Windows .NET servers.

Macromedia ColdFusion MX

On the server, the Macromedia MX product family introduces ColdFusion MX, the next generation of ColdFusion server-side scripting technology.

ColdFusion MX provides a server-side scripting environment for application logic created with ColdFusion Markup Language (CFML) and now, server-side ActionScript. CFML uses an intuitive tag-based syntax that's easy to use yet offers powerful capabilities. Server-side ActionScript provides a scripting environment that uses the same scripting language found in Macromedia Flash Player.

In addition to the scripting environment, ColdFusion MX offers a number of advanced application services including full-text searching and indexing, dynamic charting, security, state management, and language extensibility with Java, C++, COM, EJB, and CORBA.

ColdFusion, one of the first commercial application server technologies on the market, defined the page-based model for web application development. More than 10,000 companies have adopted it as the foundation for rapid Internet application development.

Rich Internet Application Capabilities

ColdFusion MX delivers an entirely new runtime architecture and a number of powerful new features for Rich Internet Applications:

- **ColdFusion Components**—A powerful new component model—ColdFusion Components, or CFCs—makes it easy to build reusable components in CFML. CFCs can be accessed as web services, Macromedia Flash Remoting services, custom tags, and functions. They're self-describing, so it's easy to share them on teams and generate Web Service Description Layer (WSDL) files automatically for consumption by web services clients.
- **XML**—ColdFusion MX has deep support for XML. XML is treated as a native data type, easily manipulated, and handled with a variety of standard processing functionality including XPath and XSLT.
- **Web services**—Publishing and consuming web services with ColdFusion is straightforward and easy. ColdFusion Components can be automatically deployed as web services, providing one of the easiest mechanisms on the market for creating a web service. For consumption, ColdFusion MX makes it possible to invoke a web service with a single line of code, and then automatically generate custom tags to interface with the methods provided by the service.
- **Server-side ActionScript**—The ColdFusion server-scripting environment now supports server-side ActionScript, which, like the client-side ActionScript used in Macromedia Flash Player, is based on the industry-standard ECMAScript. This lets Macromedia Flash developers create server-side scripts with a language they are already familiar with.
- **Native Macromedia Flash remoting services**—For connecting with client applications running in Macromedia Flash Player, ColdFusion MX offers native support for Macromedia Flash Remoting. CFCs can be used to automatically deploy services for Macromedia Flash applications, and server-side ActionScript can be used to script services.
- **Java technology architecture**—ColdFusion MX has been entirely rebuilt on a Java technology architecture. As a result, it can now run stand-alone or be deployed natively on leading Java application servers including IBM WebSphere and Sun iPlanet. In addition, the environment has strong interoperability with Java and support for deploying JavaServer Pages (JSP) and Java Servlets.
- **Microsoft .NET support**—ColdFusion MX is built to run on Microsoft Windows .NET servers. It delivers strong integration with the .NET Framework through support for Microsoft .NET web services as well as COM.

These are just some of the new features in ColdFusion MX, all of which build on the legendary ease of use and productivity of the ColdFusion scripting environment. This ease of use is further enhanced through strong integration with the Macromedia Flash MX and Dreamweaver MX development environments.

Communication Server Technology

In addition to ColdFusion MX, Macromedia is planning to release a new communication server technology that will let you deliver two-way communications and real-time data with Macromedia Flash Player.

This new technology will support multi-way, real-time audio and video, as well as one-to-many, broadcast-style streaming audio and video. It will allow real-time data transfer for applications that monitor live information, and other advanced capabilities for communication and collaboration-oriented applications.

The new technology will interoperate with other server technologies, such as ColdFusion MX, through Macromedia Flash Remoting, using the same services-oriented architecture that Macromedia Flash Player employs.

Development Tools

The third key element to delivering rich applications is the set of development tools that lets you create the various pieces of an application—from graphics to web pages to rich user interfaces to server-side application logic.

Macromedia Studio MX

The Macromedia MX product family offers a complete suite of development tools for creating Rich Internet Applications: Macromedia Studio MX.

Macromedia Studio MX includes Macromedia Flash MX, Dreamweaver MX, Fireworks MX, and FreeHand 10. Each new Macromedia MX tool is a major release in its own right, with powerful new functionality. Together, they comprise the first complete set of integrated tools for Rich Internet Application development.

Macromedia Studio MX also includes ColdFusion MX Server Developer Edition, a fully functional, single-user version of ColdFusion MX that developers can use to easily develop and test Rich Internet Applications at their workstations.

With more than 2.4 million designers and developers already using the products in Macromedia Studio MX, the software suite builds on the momentum that Dreamweaver and Macromedia Flash have in the market today.

Macromedia User Interface

Designed to work together, the Macromedia MX development tools share a new standard Macromedia user interface. As a result, they deliver significantly better productivity for both design- and code-oriented tasks:

- **Workspace organization**—The powerful new Macromedia user interface supports collapsible and dockable floating panels, which you can customize for a variety of different work modes.
- **Property inspection**—The Property Inspector offers common conventions and a consistent organization across the programs. This reduces the number of panels you need to work with and lets you build complex applications faster.

- **Design and coding**—Dreamweaver MX and Macromedia Flash MX both offer powerful visual design and code editing tools in a single environment, which significantly increases productivity by eliminating the need to switch environments. Dreamweaver MX includes visual HTML design tools and new hand-coding tools for HTML, XHTML, XML, and scripting languages, including JavaScript, ActionScript, CFML, ASP, ASP.NET, JSP, and PHP. Macromedia Flash MX includes visual design tools for rich user interfaces and robust ActionScript editing and debugging tools.
- **Server integration**—Consistent integration with ColdFusion MX and other server technologies lets you easily access server-side data and rapidly develop applications.
- **Productivity enhancements**—Common design tools, keyboard shortcuts, and menu structures let you effortlessly switch between tools.

Rich Internet Application Capabilities

Each of the tools in Macromedia Studio MX has a broad range of new features and capabilities that support development across the spectrum of Internet solutions. Among these are a number of specific capabilities for developing Rich Internet Applications:

- Dreamweaver MX provides the development environment for constructing the dynamic pages that contain Rich Internet Applications and server-side application logic.
- For developing server-side application logic, Dreamweaver MX has strong support for working with CFCs, web services, and server-side ActionScript.
- For developing the client-side application logic and user interfaces, Macromedia Flash MX provides a robust development environment that works with Dreamweaver MX.
- Macromedia Flash MX adds a powerful editing environment for coding client-side ActionScript, visual tools for working with Macromedia Flash Components, and support for integrated ActionScript debugging. Macromedia Flash MX also supports distributed debugging for applications built with Macromedia Flash Remoting on the server.
- Macromedia Flash MX supports a flexible model for building components. Macromedia Flash Components can encapsulate functionality for reuse, and can be customized visually and functionally at design time and runtime. The Macromedia Flash MX authoring environment ships with a set of pre-built components for common form controls. Third-party components also are available.
- Fireworks MX is an ideal environment for developing graphics for interface elements and content in Rich Internet Applications. It exports to Macromedia Flash MX and offers powerful new tools such as bitmap-editing support.

These products support a seamless workflow for building web sites and applications. Rich user interface elements built in Macromedia Flash MX can be dropped into pages created with Dreamweaver MX. Dreamweaver MX can be used to code server-side logic with tools that integrate with ColdFusion. Graphic assets built in Fireworks MX and FreeHand 10 can be easily imported into Macromedia Flash MX or Dreamweaver MX, and modified via launch and edit. Applications and dynamic pages can display live dynamic data from ColdFusion MX.

Overall, Macromedia Studio MX is the only integrated suite of products that gives developers all the tools they need to build Rich Internet Applications.

Websites and Web Applications

While the entire Macromedia MX family is uniquely suited to build Rich Internet Applications, the individual Macromedia MX products also let you create effective user experiences across the spectrum of Internet solutions:

- **Web sites**—Dreamweaver MX and Fireworks MX work together to enable visual page design; handle advanced coding requirements for HTML, XHTML, and XML; and create professional web graphics.
- **Web applications**—Dreamweaver MX can be used with ColdFusion MX to create everything from simple database applications to advanced e-commerce solutions. In addition, Dreamweaver MX has strong support for developing applications with ASP, ASP.NET, JSP, and PHP.
- **Rich content**—Macromedia Flash MX provides the premier authoring environment for creating rich content and operates with Fireworks MX and FreeHand to create professional bitmap and vector graphics.

Macromedia MX in the Enterprise

Macromedia MX was designed to adhere to established IT best practices and make it possible to deliver Rich Internet Applications that leverage existing infrastructure, support the development of maintainable solutions, use XML and web services, and implement strong security standards.

Leveraging Existing Infrastructure

The Macromedia MX runtime technologies on the client and server extend existing infrastructure and support key interoperability standards within the enterprise. See Figure 2.2

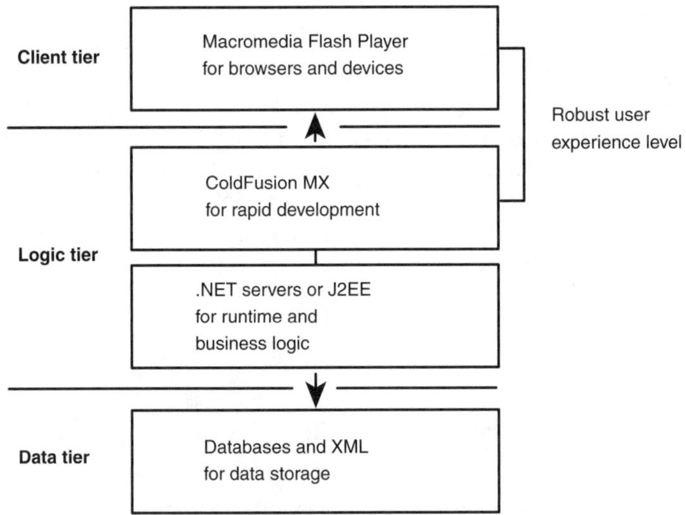

Figure 2.2 Macromedia MX extends existing infrastructure.

Macromedia Flash Player runs as an extension of the browser, desktop, or device operating environment, and already has very broad adoption. Distribution of the player is straightforward. When installed, it offers significant benefits for subsequent deployment of Rich Internet Applications.

On the server, ColdFusion MX can run on all major operating systems including Windows, Solaris, and Linux. It can also run on Windows .NET Server or be deployed within a standard Java application server such as IBM WebSphere and Sun iPlanet. As a result, ColdFusion MX can be used to increase productivity and lower costs in an enterprise environment.

The ColdFusion MX server environment interoperates with the key IT infrastructure—from mail servers to databases to distributed object middleware—through support for industry standards including LDAP, SMTP, POP, HTTP, JDBC, ODBC, COM, EJB, CORBA, XML, and web services.

Macromedia tools and players also work with other server-scripting environments including ASP, ASP.NET, JSP, and PHP.

Working with the Microsoft .NET Platform

The Microsoft .NET platform includes a broad range of products and technologies aimed at delivering distributed applications. Macromedia MX is designed to integrate with .NET to enable the creation of Rich Internet Applications.

Macromedia MX features a variety of integration points with .NET technologies:

- Macromedia Flash Player is available as an ActiveX control for Microsoft Internet Explorer; it is included with Microsoft Windows XP and is available for Microsoft Pocket PC. The player offers a rich user interface for applications using .NET through either ColdFusion MX on the server, or directly to ASP.NET and C# with Macromedia Flash Remoting for .NET. Using these connections, Macromedia Flash Player can remotely call CLR code as if it were a local ActionScript object.
- ColdFusion MX runs on Microsoft Windows .NET servers; integrates with Microsoft servers such as SQL Server, IIS, and Exchange; and supports integration with the .NET Framework through .NET web services, and with .NET objects through COM APIs.
- Dreamweaver MX offers strong support for building applications with ASP.NET including authoring tools, behaviors, and support for standard ASP.NET controls. In addition, Dreamweaver MX supports authoring and using Microsoft .NET web services, making it an ideal rapid development environment for ASP.NET applications.

Overall, Macromedia MX provides a powerful way to get more out of IT investments in .NET technologies by expanding the range of developers who can use .NET, accelerating .NET web development and enabling the use of .NET for building Rich Internet Applications.

Working with the Sun Java Platform

The Sun Microsystems Java technology platform has become an industry standard for enterprise applications. Macromedia MX delivers exceptional support for the Java technology platform.

Macromedia MX features a variety of integration points with the Java technology platform and Java application servers based on the Java 2, Enterprise Edition (J2EE) specification:

- Macromedia Flash Player provides a rich user interface for applications built on J2EE through either ColdFusion MX on the server or directly to Java with Macromedia Flash Remoting for J2EE. Using these connections, the Macromedia Flash Player can remotely call any Java class or package, JavaBean, Enterprise JavaBean (EJB), or Java Management Extension (JMX) as if it were a local ActionScript object. The player can also integrate with session management and security frameworks.
- The ColdFusion MX runtime is built on Java, and CFML and ActionScript files dynamically compile directly to Java code.
- ColdFusion MX can be easily installed on popular J2EE application servers including Macromedia JRun, IBM WebSphere, and Sun iPlanet.

- ColdFusion MX includes a built-in JSP and servlet container based on JRun. Developers can import and use JSP tag libraries in CFML as native ColdFusion tags.
- ColdFusion scripts can directly invoke and use any Java class or API from within pages or components. ColdFusion MX can publish web services for Java technology-based web services engines, and consume web services published by Java engines.
- Dreamweaver MX has strong support for building applications with JSP using JSP authoring tools. Dreamweaver MX supports authoring and using web services that work with Java servers, making it an ideal rapid development environment for JSP applications.

Overall, Macromedia MX provides a powerful way to get more out IT investments in Java technologies by expanding the range of developers who can use Java servers, accelerating Java web application development, and enabling the use of Java servers for building Rich Internet Applications.

Because Macromedia MX supports both the Microsoft .NET and Sun Microsystems Java platforms, IT organizations don't have to choose between them, and can even use both platforms together.

Supporting Modularity and Reuse

One of the key requirements for both rapid development and application maintenance is support for modularity and reuse. The Macromedia Flash Components and CFCs make it simple to rapidly develop maintainable applications with Macromedia MX.

The Macromedia Flash component model lets developers easily pick from pre-built user interface components or build their own components. This encourages a consistent design across applications and supports reuse.

On the server, CFCs provide a straightforward mechanism to create reusable code that's accessible through custom tags or function calls. CFCs can be automatically deployed as web services or Macromedia Flash Remoting services.

Macromedia MX supports building applications that use an n-tier application architecture with clear separation between client-side user interface, server-side presentation-tier logic, business logic in distributed objects, and data stored in relational databases. Macromedia MX applications can work with distributed objects deployed using COM and EJB.

Macromedia MX also supports building applications that take advantage of the service-oriented architectures enabled by web services. Rich Internet Applications are ideally suited to deployment in a services-oriented context because their support for asynchronous user interface updates makes it possible to provide an effective user experience during the consumption of web services.

Using XML and Web Services

XML and web services are becoming increasingly important to the delivery of enterprise solutions. Macromedia MX makes working with them easy and productive.

Rich Internet Applications are ideally suited to delivering effective user experiences for applications that are built by assembling web services and using XML for data exchange.

Macromedia MX offers a variety of ways to work with XML and web services:

- Macromedia Flash Player 6 has enhanced support for XML that makes parsing XML on the client significantly faster than in Macromedia Flash Player 5. As a result, it's now easy to use XML to exchange data between Macromedia Flash clients and application servers over HTTP or sockets.
- ColdFusion MX has new XML scripting features that help developers easily load XML into ColdFusion objects and translate ColdFusion objects into XML, all without needing to directly work with the complexities of parsing and traversing XML documents and nodes.
- ColdFusion MX supports advanced XML capabilities, such as XML searching using XPath notation and XML transformation using XSLT, that let developers easily transform XML documents into HTML or other XML formats.
- Using CFCs, developers can easily author and deploy web services with a built-in web services engine that supports Standard Object Access Protocol (SOAP) and WSDL.
- Web services client support in ColdFusion MX makes it possible to import and use any remote web services as a custom tag or object, or through a declarative invocation mechanism.
- Macromedia Flash Remoting, included with ColdFusion MX, lets you access web services directly from Macromedia Flash clients. Web services are visible to developers as if they were local ActionScript objects on the client.
- Dreamweaver MX fully supports XML authoring and editing with color coding, XML validation, and the ability to import XML Schema and Document Type Definition (DTD) to define new tag libraries for the editor.
- Dreamweaver MX offers web services tools for browsing remote web services and dynamically generates client proxies for those web services using ColdFusion, ASP.NET, or JSP. From the web services browser, developers can drag and drop web service methods into Code view for rapid development, and then view the live data from the web services directly in the page.

Overall, deep support for XML and web services makes Macromedia MX an ideal solution for working with these technologies in the enterprise.

Delivering Secure Solutions

Because they're built on existing Internet and enterprise standards and infrastructure, Rich Internet Applications can take advantage of an existing security infrastructure:

- Applications deployed to Macromedia Flash Player that use Macromedia Flash Remoting to talk with application servers can use Secure Sockets Layer (SSL) for client/server data exchange.
- Macromedia Flash Player provides a secure runtime sandbox on the client. Applications running in the player in a browser do not have access to client machines and can only make server requests to the domain they originated from.
- ColdFusion MX fully supports integration with existing security infrastructure for user authentication through standard mechanisms including LDAP and databases.
- ColdFusion MX provides a robust role-based application security framework and enables server sandboxing for securing resources hosted on a shared server.

Macromedia works closely with industry groups to continue the advancement of security in new technology areas. As with all security, it's crucial that developers and server administrations configure, design, and maintain Rich Internet Applications with security in mind.

3

Architecting a Dynamic Publishing Application

by Benjamin Elmore

I CAN STILL REMEMBER THE FIRST TIME I was referred to as a systems architect. I thought to myself, "What's a systems architect?" Apparently, someone much wiser than me at the time recognized that my contributions to the project warranted this classification that I was unfamiliar with. So, like any good techie, I set out to research this subject and understand what information architecture is and what a system architect does. I have talked to many people who have discovered architecture in quite the same way that I did: by doing it and not realizing what it was. Unfortunately, this is not the best way to approach the subject of information architecture.

The goal of this chapter is to discuss the subject of information architecture and the role of the architect as it's related to developing a dynamic publishing system for the web. We will focus on the reasons behind the dynamic publishing challenges and an architecture that can be created to support them. We'll look at the issues facing the architect and the concerns that need to be met by setting the technical vision for system construction to lay the proper foundation for success.

Why Use Architecture in a Dynamic Publishing System?

Some view learning architecture and following the necessary guidelines it imposes in an application as a daunting task. There's a constant learning curve before an individual can be called proficient in architecture. With that said, understanding why you would even bother learning architecture is a valid question.

There are several reasons for an organization or a developer to take the time to immerse in this thing called architecture.

The first reason behind using architecture is that it saves development time for the project by helping plan the entire application before development starts. This is because *architecture* in its simplest term is the mapping out and visualization of what the application is intending to do. With architecture in place, an application has the capability to discover flaws before a single line of code is written. Software studies have shown that requirement flaws captured this early can have a return on investment (ROI) in cost savings of upward to 10 times of what it would have been if caught during the designing steps of the application. One particular report illustrated in Karl E. Wieger's book *Software Requirements* (Microsoft Press, 1999) estimated the cost to change a requirement at 200 percent more than the initial cost of building that requirement into the application. Looking at these numbers, we can deduct that just a single discovery can lessen the actual time needed to implement and cost justify the time spent creating and implementing an architecture.

With architecture comes design standards, guidelines, and consistent approaches to development (referred to as *patterns*) that allow the application to be more easily understood by new members to the team, better maintained, and also support changes without the threat of rippling the code base.

This benefit also has its criticism against it. The main points of contention are that the design of the application's architecture actually adds time to a project's development cycle, or that ramping up on architecture is too costly for an organization. As we can see from the base ROI statement, this is quite the opposite. However, there is some validity to the time investment to set this in place. Both an organization and a developer who are first approaching leveraging architecture should realize that during the first implementation, they won't see the same magnitude of time savings as noted earlier. The reason for this is that a learning curve absorbs a majority of the time saved, as noted above. You will start to see the benefits pay off in subsequent implementations.

The second reason behind using architecture comes out of the ability to create a set of documents that describe the application. This is where architecture starts to intersect with methodology or the process in which the application is built. Different methodologies call for different diagrams, requirement formats, and other bits of information to ensure not only sound information architecture but also a clean transition between a user's need and the final product. We will pass on the methodology discussion and instead focus on the documentation that surrounds architecture. It is here that the main point of contention is raised: Many developers and managers feel that the level of detail necessary to properly document an application is much too time consuming. This misconception is due to a lack of understanding of how to effectively leverage the documentation notation.

In the software industry, there has emerged a standard notation for describing the functionality and data associated with the application. This notation is called *Unified Modeling Language* (UML) and is managed by the Object Management Group, which is a committee of companies that governs this and other languages. The web site for this standard is `www.uml.org`.

Circling back to the point that brought us to UML, it should be noted that although there is a variety to the notation used to document your architecture, it is not a requirement that all of it be used in every design. Relating this to programming, this is like saying you aren't required to use all the functionality of the language on each application. The only requirement is that you document the design enough to guarantee a clear description of the application's functionality—nothing more, nothing less.

For an organization, the benefits to *why* are clear. They include a faster development time and a living documented design repository of your application. To a developer, though, what is the attraction to become an information architect? One of the most appealing facets is that architecture is abstracted from languages. (This is also another benefit to an organization.) Instead of having to look at what is apparent in the constructs of a development language, architecture allows you the freedom of solving the problem using the abstract basic building blocks and principles found in a design notation. Thus, as languages change, the way you approach a problem doesn't. We'll expand this point a bit in the next section.

Some Architectural Progression

Information systems, like any other industry in history, have evolved from the days of invention and hand craftsmanship into the realms of automation and dynamic structure. At the same time, this evolutionary process has been reciprocal with each major development trend. We have gone from mainframes with text-based interfaces to client-server with rich graphical interfaces and back again with the advent of the Internet and the web with text-based browser interfaces. We now see this coming full circle, first with the introduction of dynamic HTML and now with the graphical benefits of Flash.

Looking to the future, we are heading down this path again with wireless and device-driven systems.

It seems that with each new paradigm, we want to throw out ideas from the past, burn our notebooks, so to speak, and feel that we need to unlearn and relearn to embrace a new technology. It is actually quite the contrary, and the concepts and strategies that we discuss here have been in existence for a long while. If we keep as open a mind to what we already know as we are with what is to come, we'll realize that learning a new technology is merely a question of a new application of our existing architectural knowledge.

What Is Information Architecture?

In its most basic form, *information architecture* is essentially the collective decisions that are made concerning the design and construction of the various artifacts (components, business entities, packages, subsystems, and so on), such as how they will collaborate and interface with each other to develop an information system.

In the construction industry, a building cannot be constructed without having a blueprint. A blueprint ensures the success and safety of the construction project. Laws exist both in nature and in society that govern the construction of buildings. Architecture is applied to different levels of projects that call for various levels of detail and completeness. The blueprint for a doghouse would be in stark contrast to a blueprint of a 20,000-seat arena.

In the realm of information systems, architecture is just as important to the process of system construction as it is with building construction. You wouldn't let someone build your house without a plan and a blueprint that ensures your home will be the configuration you desire, provide the services you need for survival, and be safe for your family to live in. In the same respect, as a business, we shouldn't let anyone build an information system without a plan and a blueprint that ensures that the system will be configured correctly, provide the services that our business requires, be scalable to meet the business demands, and be safe for our business to operate.

Following this thought through to completion, failure of design can be determined by looking at the two extremes: uncontrolled and nonexistent. Because all systems have an architecture, not starting out with a planned one results in an ad-hoc pieced together system that lacks a consistent flow. Any changes that are needed to this sort of system are difficult to make because the capability to pinpoint exactly where the change needs to made is impossible. On the other extreme is an over-scoped architecture. In this extreme, the needs of the business requirements are not met because the architecture is the focus. In this sort of system, the blueprint is crafted to support unrealistic demand and functionality for the application. Consequently, the timeline to build this is much longer.

New Riders published a book titled *Information Architecture* that can provide further information on this subject.

The Principles of Architecture

By understanding and applying architecture, we ensure the success of our information system. Architecture, besides being theoretical, is composed of distinct building blocks and governed by some basic principles. These components of architecture permeate all discussion and all ranges of topics from describing a simple interaction between a product and a shopping process to an overall application design. Given the fact that our designs throughout the book and this chapter are described with UML, we will show the corresponding notations that these principles are reflected with. Being mindful that many of you are experienced with this these concepts, we will keep them to a brief summary.

Components, Classes, and Objects

One of the core building blocks in a system is the modular unit that represents a set of functionality and data. From the object-oriented world of design and programming, the term to describe this concept is *class*. We know that a class definition consists of properties (attributes or variables) that define the data that will sustain its existence, and behaviors (methods, functions) that are the class's functional and dynamic revelation of itself to its various consumers. For example, a `Product` class might contain a series of properties, such as `Name`, `Description`, and `Price`, and a set of behaviors, such as Purchase or Discontinue. This core structure is implemented as objects in the system that are the exact manifestation of the data and functionality. For example, a `Product` class would describe the data that a product comprises, but an object would actually store the data, one object for each product.

In UML, the notation for a class is shown in Figure 3.1. It has three compartments. The top shows the class name, the middle shows the properties, and the bottom shows the methods. These classes are shown on what is called a *class diagram*, which are generally shown with other classes along with their relationship with them. Class diagrams don't represent specific objects or specific functional flows.

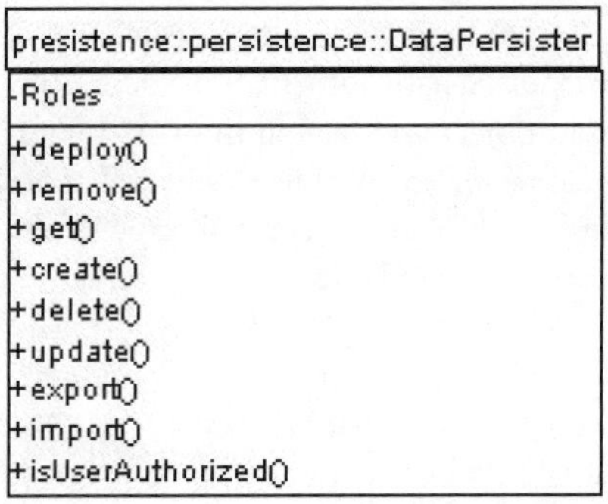

```
presistence::persistence::DataPersister
-Roles
+deploy()
+remove()
+get()
+create()
+delete()
+update()
+export()
+import()
+isUserAuthorized()
```

Figure 3.1 UML symbol for a class.

Classes have a couple of implementations that are important to us. One is statically, which signifies that the class is without internal data and instead is just a set of logic (methods) grouped together. The other way is with an object instance, and as illustrated in an earlier example, object instances need to be populated with data *before* being used. When you are designing your system, you have to model both data and functionality. Data is more commonly shown as instances, whereas functionality, such as publishing or persistence, can be implemented through static classes.

Another modular unit concept is that of the component. We can look at components in many ways, but for the purposes of this discussion, we'll consider a *component* any replaceable part of an information system that adheres to and realizes a set of interfaces. Components can consist of one to an entire package of classes and objects. They can play the role of the smallest part of the application or the role of an entire service, such as publishing, for the application. Figure 3.2 shows the UML notation for a component. As mentioned, a component can contain classes internally, but the symbol is void of additional markings to show this.

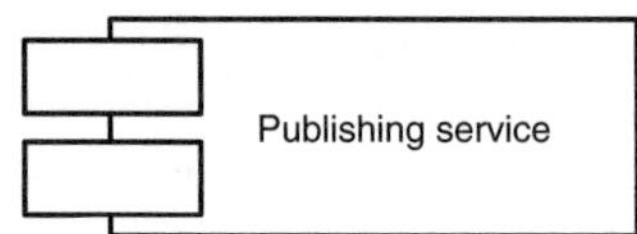

Figure 3.2 UML symbol for a component.

In ColdFusion MX, the introduction of ColdFusion Components (CFCs) is a new paradigm in the world of ColdFusion development. It is with this language construct that we can implement physically the mapped out object, class, or component. Chapter 5, "ColdFusion Components," contains a full discussion of components, and Chapter 8, "ColdFusion Components with Persistence," focuses on persistent components (instances).

It is impossible to talk about classes and components without discussing the object-oriented concept called *encapsulation*, or information hiding. This basic premise of protecting the data related to an object and having the class reveal itself in the form of behaviors is the most critical factor to an object's survival as an asset to the information system. If the changing of an object's data is allowed without its knowledge, the object will be transitioned to an altered state. This might cause the object to stray from its intended purpose and result in an unstable system.

For example, let's say that we have an Inventory component that has a property called `NumInStock`. The business rule is that when the `NumInStock` property goes lower than the minimum inventory number set by the product it is related, it automatically issues a reordering of the product. This logic is encapsulated in a method called `placeOrder`. If I follow encapsulation every time I want to place an order for the product, I fire the `placeOrder` method and keep the inventory at the right levels at all times. If I violate encapsulation and just change the `NumInStock` property directly, I end up with an unstable system and incorrect inventory levels. Violating encapsulation means violating the business logic of your application.

Relationships

It is safe to assume that our entire application isn't going to be built on the back of a single component or class and instead is going to involve a multitude of components working with each other to get the job done. Associations are used to describe how the objects relate to each other and the mechanism on which communication is made possible. An *association* simply means that one object knows of or creates the existence of another object and understands how to communicate or collaborate with it via its interfaces.

When one object relies on another object to fulfill its intended purpose, a dependency exists. The management of these dependencies is the most important task that we have in designing the information system architecture. Why do we care so much about this? Reuse. Reuse is the key benefit that we are seeking, but I'm going to give you a new benefit to think about: unuse. Although Webster probably wouldn't agree that unuse is actually a word, the concept rings true in information technology. By correctly structuring our class definitions and managing the dependencies between them, we can replace or extend existing classes with new ones without worrying about the effects the change will have on the other parts of the system. A simple example of why unuse is valuable in a system is when you think of functionality over time. Let's say that you had a sales tool that you interfaced to pull your current sales opportunities from. By architecting your dependencies correctly, you could easily unuse the interface to the tool in favor of an interface to a new sales tool in the future.

Several types of relationships between classes are important to notate. Table 3.1 shows the three main notations that you will use. In turn, each one of these relationships is shown in Figure 3.3.

Table 3.1 **Basic Relationship Symbols**

Type	Symbol	Definition
Generalization	A line with an open triangle on one end	This is when one class extends another component, thus obtaining the extended component's methods and properties. The class on the symbol side of the relationship is the parent.
Association	A line	This is when one or both of the classes needs to know of the other to do its job. The classes are unaware of how the other classes are created instantiated.
Aggregation	A line with a diamond on the end	This is when one of the classes is considered part of the other class. The class on the symbol side of the relationship is the class that contains the other one.

To see how this pulls together, let's look at Figure 3.3 and see what the visual notations look like inside a class diagram. The class diagram here depicts the relationship between the classes in the repository package of the DuvalShock application and how they are associated. These classes specifically deal with persisting data for the system.

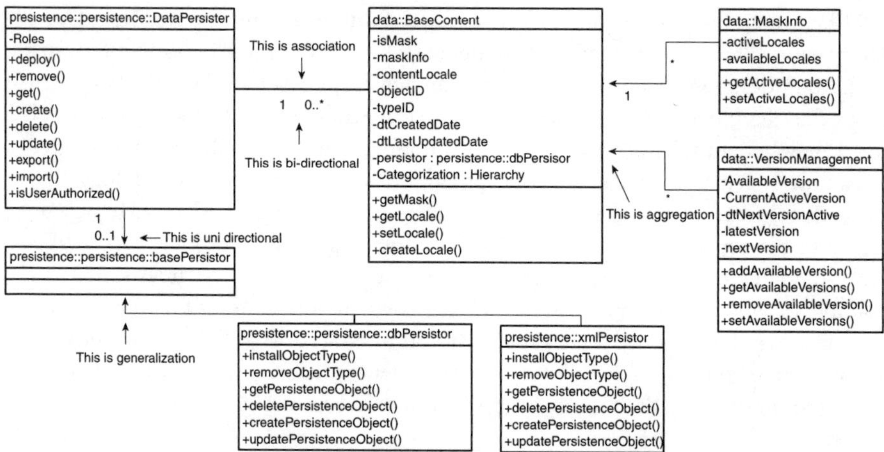

Figure 3.3 UML class diagram with callouts to the relationships.

I should call out two other items when discussing relationships: navigability and cardinality. *Navigability* is used to show awareness between classes. It allows us to show that an Inventory component and a Product component are mutually aware of each other, and that a Product component is not aware of the Shopping Cart component that points to it.

The default navigability is bi-direction and doesn't change the aggregation or association notation on the model. *Bi-directional navigability* means that both classes are aware of each other.

Uni-directional navigability is used to show that one class is aware of the other, but the receiver is unaware of the other class. This is illustrated by adding an arrow at the end of the relationship from the caller to the receiver. In figure 3.3 we see this called out on the relationship between `dataPersister` and `basePersistor`. This is a key notation to make when looking for reuse in an application because when a change is required, you must validate that each component associated to the one(s) you are changing will still function. As a general rule, the less the awareness a component has to itself the easier it is to change without effecting the rest of the system.

In our example shown in Figure 3.3, we have an association between `dataPresister` and `baseContent`. Because they both know of each other, a change in one can affect the functionality of the other and could require change if you wanted to deal with a different persistent object then `dataPresister`. However, looking at our example between `dataPresister` and any of the children of `basePresistor`, we notice that it is uni-directional; therefore, a change in `dataPresister` won't affect any of the `Persistors`.

Note

What you are seeing in the example is the `dataPersister` used as a broker to handle all the persisting of data. This is considered a Singleton class because this is the single component created for this purpose. These sorts of Singleton (*Singleton* is a pattern in software development; see the "Patterns" section later in this chapter) or application-level services, commonly have relationships to several components, but they actually have few components that are aware of them.

Note

Cardinality describes whether one class knows of more than one of the other classes at any point in time. This is used to show that an inventory component only knows of one specific product and that the Shopping Cart component knows of several products. *Cardinality* is shown for a component by noting the other side of the *association* between the component and another.

Packaged Functionality

When we look past the fundamentals of object-oriented technology, we find that we need a little more than just classes, associations, and components. Reality is that just as we can't have all our functionality of the application embedded into one component, we also can't have all the class thrown into one pot. It's necessary to separate the components further. When a collection of classes seems to form a greater purpose as a group than as individual classes, a subsystem is born. In UML, this is considered to be a *package*. Figure 3.4 shows the UML representation of a package.

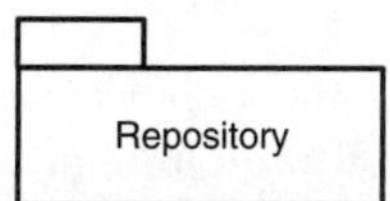

Figure 3.4 UML symbol for a package.

Sometimes subsystems are planned and designed, and other times they happen by accident. Obviously, we want to plan and design them. If we look at the design of our subsystems in the same light that we look at designing our classes and components, we can use the same principles and concepts. Encapsulation of subsystem data and management of the dependencies between subsystems are essential. These jobs become more difficult as an application grows. It will be common to have packages including other packages as a way to relate and at the same time specialize functionality. Figure 3.5 shows the top-level package diagram of the DuvalShock application with an exploded Repository package. The dashed arrows show dependencies between packages. Unlike relationships between classes, the default dependency is uni-directional, in which one package shows its reliance on another.

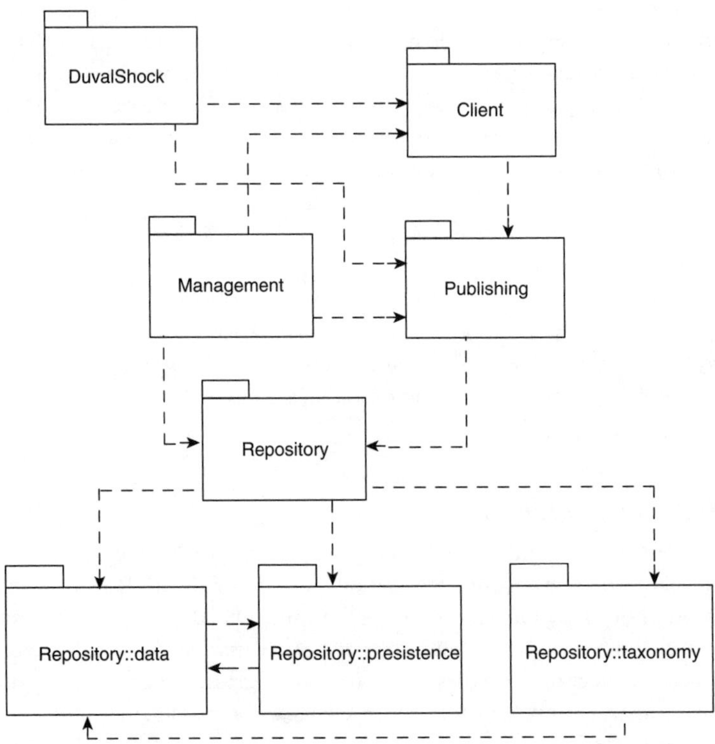

Figure 3.5 Top-level package diagram with exploded subpackage.

In ColdFusion MX, it is possible to physically package your application through the use of CFCs. The implementation of this feature in ColdFusion is similar to that of the J2EE packaging functionality. In addition to describing behaviors that can be used by the entire system, when using packaging, you can describe behavior that is only accessible to other classes in the package.

Patterns

As we march through the principles of architecture, we can start to see how the overall shape of our application is going to be laid out. It starts with classes working with classes and moves quickly into packages containing classes working with other packages. Each core principle builds on the earlier one to deal with its inherit weakness. For example, we need associations because we don't want to put all of our logic in one class. We also use packages to keep from having our entire application grouped under one location.

As we start seeing the shape of our application form, another interesting thing starts to happen. You start to realize that you have several of your class/packages relationships set up at the same. If you look at it further, you notice that it's because you're trying to solve a similar problem.

Welcome to patterns. A *pattern* is a well-defined repeatable solution to a commonly occurring problem. The design pattern has become a cultural icon in the world of information systems development. Patterns provide us with a way to describe and categorize the knowledge we have gained in solving the same problems repeatedly. Patterns outline the fundamental problem that is being addressed. These problems are manifested in many of the issues that face us; therefore, they are transposable over all the different business needs that arise. Design patterns are a great thought tool that everyone should understand and explore. They help us to be more productive by working smarter and not harder. They allow us to be more comfortable because the solutions have been proven over time.

A catalog of patterns is not a substitute for systems architecture and design; rather, it's an essential tool for implementing stable and proven solutions. One of the most widely known books about patterns is *Design Patterns: Elements of Reusable Object-Oriented Software* published by Addison-Wesley. This book is helpful for both experienced and novice users alike.

The problems that a pattern can be used to solve vary widely. A pattern can be used to solve something as simple as organizing linked objects to another object or as complicated as masking the interface of several security subsystems into one common interface or defining the way in which the application is laid out.

To consciously build using patterns requires that you first have a good understanding of the needs of the systems and then identify an approach to use. That would make the basic steps for developing with patterns as follows:

1. Understand your business needs.
2. Determine your approach to the situation.
3. Find a pattern that matches your approach and business problem.

Let's walk through this using the object model shown in Figure 3.3 as the end result. One of our needs is to have the ability to store content in a variety of formats. In addition, we desire that the manner in which we interface the algorithm to store the data remains the same regardless of the format. In looking at these requirements, we can determine that we need to have a class that handles the storage of each unique type of data. Also, we want to do this with a consistent interface.

We now have the business problem and the approach we want to take. From here, we want to see if a pattern maps to this, which it does. The pattern that best solves this is the Strategy pattern. The intent of this pattern is to "define a family of algorithms, encapsulate each one, and make them interchangeable." With the pattern comes a class diagram that describes the classes and association needed to solve this problem. This is shown in Figure 3.6.

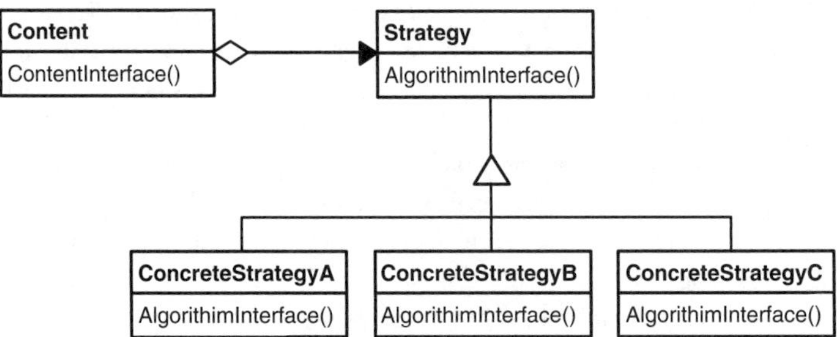

Figure 3.6 Class diagram of the Strategy pattern.

In our specific example (Figure 3.3), we have mapped this pattern to the `DataPerister` and the children of the `BasePersistor` class. Each specific class of the `BasePresistor` contains the same algorisms but specific implementation.

It rarely happens in real implementations that you actually plan all pattern usages. More commonly, you build out the necessary functionality and look back to see that you have followed a similar pattern. Going back and completing or modifying the implementation toward a set pattern is referred to as *refactoring*. This statement is especially true when you are first starting out.

Architectural Designs

The overall design of the application influences and sometimes governs the way we use patterns, components, classes, and associations. In some cases, it is easier to think of this as the overall application pattern because it sets the boundaries and rules that we work under.

Two types of architectural designs are in use. One, a partitioned approach specifically geared toward managing user interfaces, is probably the most well known and is referred to as the *Model/View/Controller or MVC Architecture*. The other one is more of a loosely coupled wholly contained functionality, referred to as a *Service Oriented Architecture (SOA)*.

Each of these approaches brings its own rules and has set objectives it is trying to accomplish. Strangely enough though, these approaches don't have to be considered independent of each other. It is possible to have an MVC approach that has several of its core services exposed through an overlapping SOA. Later, we cover a layered architecture for building a dynamic publishing system in which this application is written against and in which the chapters are organized against. It is important to note that this isn't technically a coexistence of these designs because one primary design needs to be followed. It is impossible, as you will see from the architecture covered later in the chapter, to follow both. Figure 3.7 is an illustration that depicts how this is arranged.

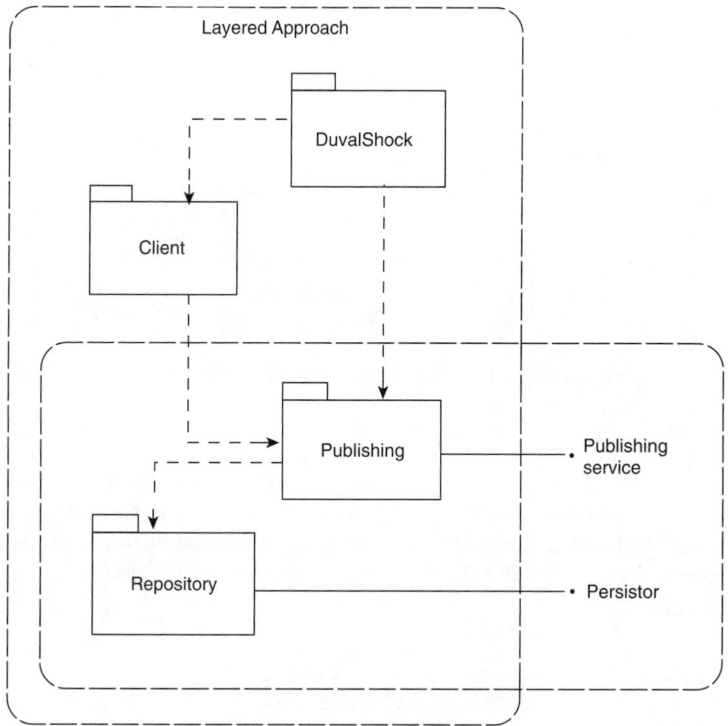

Figure 3.7 Intersection of architectural designs.

Model/View/Controller Architecture

This is one of the most popular architectures out there in the market place today and has been around for more than 30 years. The Model/View/Controller (MVC) is a set of classes organized to build user interfaces. Figure 3.8 shows how the three major sections of the application work together.

MVC consists of three kinds or categories of objects. The Model consists of objects that represent the data and state of the application. The View is its screen presentation and interface control. Finally, the Controller defines the way the user interface reacts to user input. Before MVC, user interface designs tended to lump these objects together. MVC decouples them to increase flexibility and reuse.

MVC decouples views and models by establishing a subscribe/notify protocol between them. A view must ensure that its appearance reflects the state of the model. Whenever the model's data changes, the model notifies views that depend on it. In response, each view gets an opportunity to update itself. This approach lets you attach multiple views to a model to provide different presentations. You also can create new views for a model without rewriting it. This feature alone is extremely valuable given the rate in which an application's interface tends to change.

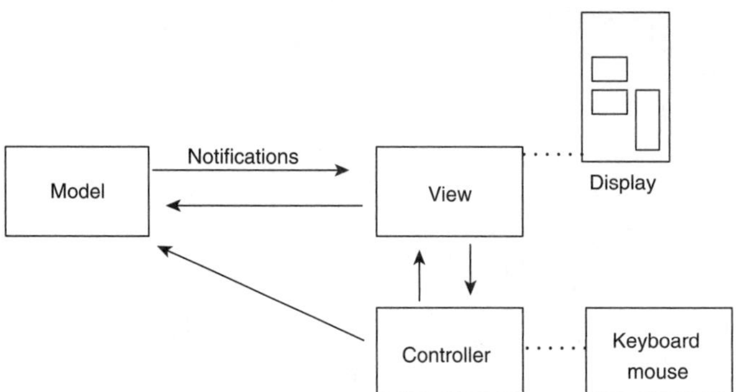

Figure 3.8 The Model/View/Controller architecture.

The architectural approach that we'll use in the book (a layered architecture) is based on this core basis of separation. A layered architecture at its basic implementation requires the separation of data from process and user interface (which is the core principle of a MVC design), and in a basic web application, these lines can be drawn between server lines. This is distributed computing at its most basic (shown at a top level in Figure 3.9).

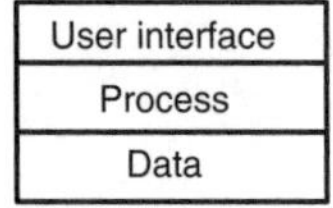

Figure 3.9 The basic structure of a layered architecture.

Service-Oriented Architecture

Service-Oriented Architecture (SOA) is the latest strategy for architecting distributed web applications. This architecture is a clear, logical progression from the distributed computing models that precede it. The following is a walkthrough of each of the steps that have brought us where SOA is today:

- **Client-server model**—The rapid growth of network computing—and more recently, the Internet—has led to a variety of strategies for architecting distributed applications. The client-server model was a predominant approach for building distributed applications.

In this model, the core of an application runs on a central server that interacts with a client application on the end user's computer. The client-side application often has extensive program logic built in, making it a thick client. Updates to a distributed application often require that end users update their client software. Major database vendors provide an example of the client-server model, in which the database runs on a central server and end users can install client programs on their local computers to interact with and manage the database across the network.

- **N-tier model**—The explosive growth of the Internet and rapid adoption of web browsers led to a new approach, the n-tier model, which is the predominant strategy for building distributed web applications today.

  In this model, application logic is distributed across several tiers of backend servers (a database server and an application server in a 3-tier approach), and the end user interacts with the application through a web browser. The rapid adoption and development of n-tier application architecture has given rise to the Internet we know today, but it is difficult to share functionality between and across these applications.
- **Composite computing model**—In response to the shortcomings of the n-tier model, the composite computing model has risen in importance. At its foundation, this approach is concerned with building distributed applications by assembling small, individual software components into a larger, functional whole. In addition, these components must be available for remote discovery and invocation across the network.

  Technologies that have attempted to accomplish this include Microsoft's DCOM and Sun's Enterprise Java Beans. These technologies provide a way to build reusable software components that other components and clients can discover and use across the network. However, the promise of these technologies has never been fully realized due to their proprietary nature.

This brings us to the SOA, a vendor-neutral, XML-based incarnation of the composite computing model. In the SOA, the components that are assembled into full-featured applications are Web Services. Web Services use Web Services Description Language (WSDL) to describe their functionality. You can register each service in a Universal Description, Discovery, and Integration (UDDI) registry. UDDI registries serve as a phone book of sorts for Web Services. Data is passed to and from Web Services as XML packets that conform to the Simple Object Access Protocol (SOAP). Each of these standards has broad industry support, and each is covered in depth in Chapter 22, "Assembling a Dynamic Application."

The SOA is built around three roles:

- The requestor is any client that finds, binds to, and uses Web Services.
- The provider publishes its Web Services to the registry and exposes them for client consumption.
- The registry stores published descriptions of Web Services so that requestors can find services as needed.

In a ColdFusion MX application, the requestor role contains any of the devices that can access your application's functionality, such as a browser, a Flash MX movie, or a web-enabled PDA. The provider role is the ColdFusion MX application, composed of Web Services implemented as CFCs. The registry could be one of the UDDI registries covered in Chapter 22, and the Web Services that the application provides can be published to these registries if you want to make them globally available. Figure 3.10 provides a graphical overview for the SOA.

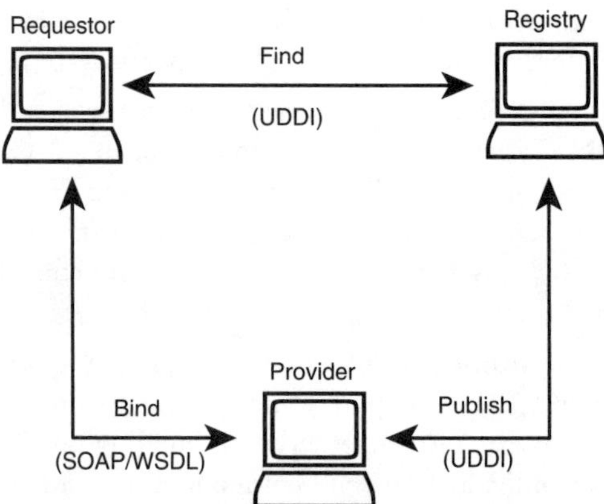

Figure 3.10 Service-Oriented Architecture.

In Chapter 22, we will see that exposing a CFC as a Web Service is as simple as creating a function in the CFC with the `access="remote"` attribute. ColdFusion MX automatically generates the WSDL file for a remotely accessible CFC so that its functionality can be exposed and consumed as a Web Service. CFCs provide a clean way to modularize our code into components, but we can instantly expose these same components as Web Services, making a ColdFusion MX application the perfect provider for dynamic applications that implement the SOA.

Building a dynamic application using the SOA ensures that the functionality of the application is exposed in a format that any client can consume. That client can be CFM pages in the Presentation layer of your application, Flash MX SWFs that access functionality via Flash Remoting, or other devices or applications that fill the role of requestor and access the functionality of your application as a pure Web Service. This architecture simplifies multiple device support within the application and promotes component reuse within the Enterprise. In addition, it allows for the functionality of the application to be shared across internal sites, partner sites, and applications. Application functionality can even be made globally available if its services are published to a UDDI registry. The ability to expose CFCs as Web Services is truly revolutionary, and the process could not be simpler than it is in ColdFusion MX.

The Layered Dynamic Publishing Architecture

This chapter has built up to the presentation of this one architecture to use as a guideline for building your application. The primary difference in using an application-specific architecture is that more specific services and functionality segmentation are available, as if you were creating a guideline for generic application development. Most application-specific architectures derive themselves from a more generic one, thus specializing it to their needs. This architecture is no different. The parent architecture is a layered architecture.

In relation to the other chapters in this book, you will notice how this architecture is used as a logical breakdown of the business domain for the technical manager, as should proper architecture. The benefit to this overlapping is that it will help properly communicate the complexity or impact of a request because the same model in which they break down their requirements is used to build it up. This also allows an illustration and comprehension of dependencies between layers that will then translate into their understanding of the same logical dependencies between requirements. How much you should leverage this capability to overlap the architectural design with the breaking down of the business domain model is completely subjective. I would use this at a base minimum to help bridge the gap between technical managers and architects.

So that you can understand how to work with this architecture, it is important to walk through the overview of how it was constructed, the objectives for which it was targeted, and the development guidelines and steps for construction.

Overview

Now we will employ the layered architecture by separating the concerns of our problem space, which is dynamic publishing, into several layers of functionality. These layers are Repository, Management, Publishing, and Client. With each layer, we need to keep the job of managing dependencies at the forefront. We also need to separate data from process and user interface. Figure 3.11 shows the layered architecture of our dynamic publishing system.

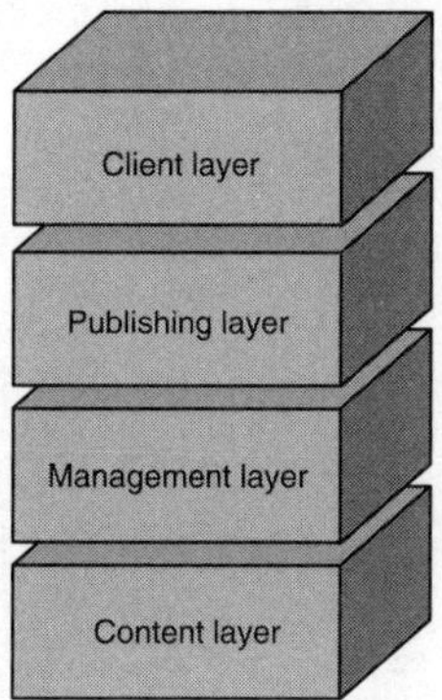

Figure 3.11 The layered dynamic publishing architecture.

We layered for two reasons. First, layering allows us to create a delegation-based architecture for implementation so that different groups of people can work on parts of the system that they're experienced with. Second, we can create a system that has its layers functionally independent of each other so that each layer can respond to change and potentially be replaced with new technology. This is the hard part, and it's why defining the architecture is so important. For example, in the Repository layer, you must classify content. However, not every application needs this, so you won't look to build it out right away. By separating the application and maintaining this delegation and detachment between the layers, you can then build out a global classification system without impacting the other layers.

The true uniqueness in this application-specific architecture is the way that each layer is responsible for specific grouping of functionality and services. It's not required that the implementation of these services be generic, but this separation does allow you to refactor your code into a framework over time. We casually mentioned earlier that it is possible to make portions of design accessible to an SOA-based application. This is done by modularizing the individual functionality in a given layer and then encapsulating it into a service that is publicly available. The very nature of an MVC-based design shows the separation of a view from a control, thus allowing different clients to use the control and model.

Now let's look at some of the specific architectural concerns of dynamic publishing at a layer level. Figures 3.12, 3.13, 3.14, and 3.15 show the layers with the specific functionality called out.

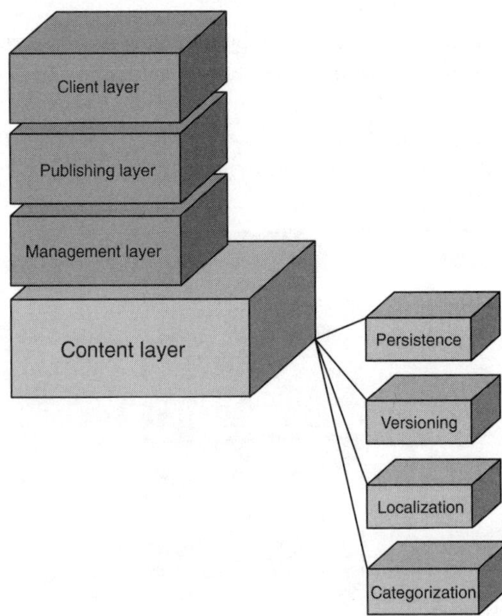

Figure 3.12 The layered dynamic publishing architecture with the Content layer exploded.

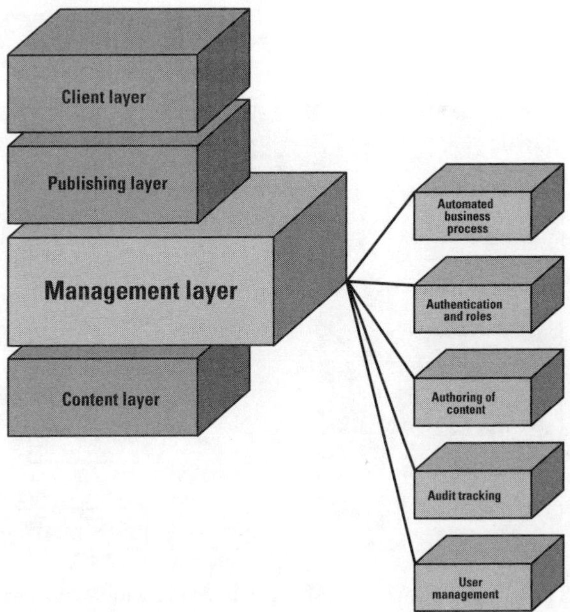

Figure 3.13 The layered dynamic publishing architecture with the Management layer exploded.

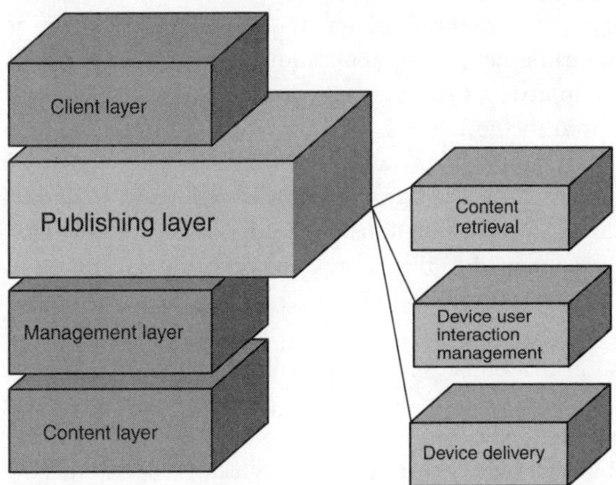

Figure 3.14 The layered dynamic publishing architecture with the Publishing layer exploded.

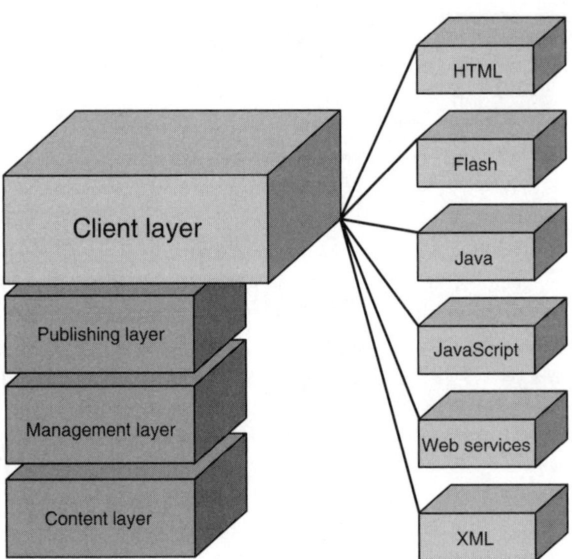

Figure 3.15 The layered dynamic publishing architecture with the Client layer exploded.

Your application can fit into a layered approach in several ways. The first way is to completely disperse your applications into these layers, such as by putting your content entity components into the repository component, your specific publishing rules into the Publishing layer, your application view into the Client layer, and so on. The other way in which you can arrange your application to work within this layered approach is in a framework approach. This approach would be a logical separation of potential reusable services into the core layers, thus creating a framework and then your specific application logic into a new layer on top of or embedded into the Client layer.

The Content layer of the application is fully described in Chapter 4, "Basics of a Content Repository." From a functionality standpoint, this means that the following services would be contained to this layer: Categorization, Data Persistence, Data Relationships, Data Localization, and Data Versioning. This is a pure data and data retrieval layer.

In an application that embeds its functionality into the different layers, this would mean that the specific taxonomy or metadata classification services and the actual defined content would exist into this layer. The only constraint on the content components defined in this layer is that because they can be distributed, nothing visual can be defined in its methods. If this is the way you want to build your front-end view, you need to move the components to the Client layer.

The Management layer of the application is fully described in Chapter 13, "Basics of Managing Content." From a functionality standpoint, that would mean the layer would include the process automation engine (workflow), security/resource management, and user management. This is a pure process tier.

In an application that will embed its functionality into the different layers, this would mean that the specific tasks that would perform the work of your processes would be located in this layer. The client for a management tier is a bit different from that of the application. Therefore, the same rules that you apply for constructing your visual client facing front end do not necessarily apply. A primary reason is that you change your management front end far less frequently than a visual client. However, even with this separation of public versus private client generation, it is modeled that the Client layer should contain both interfaces even if it doesn't touch the Management layer directly in the diagram. This is because a layer can see and use all layers below it.

With that being said, a task of an automated process would be moved into the client or application-specific tier if it were presenting a visual interface.

The Publishing layer of the application is fully described in Chapter 19, "Basics of Publishing." From a functionality standpoint, the layer would include the publishing rules engine, content retrieval logging, and content audit reporting. Also, the publishing might allow for a persistent rule search request and decide to handle the persistence itself or delegate it to the repository tier. By self-containing the persistence, the publishing tier acts purely as a service to the application architecture rather than a control process in MVC style application. This is a pure content retrieval process tier.

In an application that embeds its functionality into the different layers, this would mean that the specific rules for retrieval and massaging of the data would be contained in this layer. Because there is nothing visual about rules, this would not apply to the need to optionally store information in the Client layer.

The Client layer of the application also is described in Chapter 19. This layer is the most dynamic of the layers we are working with in that it contains the specific implementation of the application's public view and management view. Also, it contains the most change in your application's lifecycle. Little is reusable at this layer because it is meant to map to your specific business needs.

From a functionality standpoint, that would mean the layer would include a range of functionality depending on specific implementations, as noted earlier.

If an application is embedding its functionality into these four layers, it would be safe to say that it could include process tasks, management interfaces, client interfaces, defined content components with visual methods, and other application-specific services.

The other alternative to embedding into these layers directly is to create an application-specific layer into which the logic, data, and visual interfaces of the application are built. In that case, this layer would contain rules, tasks, content, and other application-specific services.

Motives

The design is constructed with a set of objectives or motives. You can look at these motives and use them to see if this application design is the best option for a particular instance. These are the main motives:

- **Detachment of core logic from presentation**—This dictates that the services are constructed without an attachment or knowledge of the front-end requestor.
- **Consolidations of functionality**—Instead of having content and functionality scattered throughout the different packages or locations, this consolidates like-minded services into core layers so that all needs for that service are routed directly to that layer for work to be done.
- **Multiple client support**—This dictates that our design has the ability to be queried through a variety of interfaces.
- **Ability to support a framework design**—This was a need to have the layers really pull out the functionality so much that it wasn't just the visual view that was separated. In this case, the content, rules, workflow, taxonomy, and other application-specific needs could be pulled into their own package and just leverage the services as a framework of reusable functionality.

Starting the Development

The first question we have to face is when to start building the architecture of the application. Successful construction of the application's architecture is based on a good understanding of the application's requirements. Some refinement to the requirement will come of the architectural design, but it is a critical mistake to use the designing of the system as a way to define what the application needs. It is not until you reach this point that the starting of the design should commence.

The whole process in which this is coordinated in relation to design and implementation is referred to as a *development methodology*. However, this is one area that we won't touch. The key point is that the health of the application design is based entirely on the accuracy of the requirements used to build it. The form in which the requirements are constructed varies greatly between methodologies. It ranges from stakeholder requests to functional requirement documents to use case scenarios.

> **Warning**
>
> As part of a set methodology, an application's requirements go through a series of stages whereby they become more specific and start mapping into usages of the system. This is all best practices in software development and cannot be skipped. By cutting to the chase and talking about the actual development of the application, I am in no way endorsing skipping this step. At this point, I have assumed that I have gone through the proper development cycle with requirements, user cases, and high-level business domain models.

When you're learning to create an application design, you first need to understand the basics of classes and relationships and then move up to packages and so on. When it comes down to actually designing the application, the process is reversed and follows something like this:

1. Set the application design pattern.
2. Define the high-level breakout of functionality into packages. This will be drive from your specific business model and the application design you are going after.
3. Identify key functionality inside of each package.
4. Identify key patterns that map to the problems that you want to fix.
5. Build out supporting classes and objects to accomplish needed functionality.

Looking at this sort of drilling down of our application to drive our application, we get a sense that we are riding a wave of macro to micro back to macro to micro and so on. This process is repeated until you have adequately described the entire functionality of your system.

We can see an example of this process in a construction of a commerce application. The application breaks into major macro packages: inventory management and product purchasing. At this point, we choose just one of the macro sections and drill into it, in effect flushing out all the details. This is the micro view that we are creating. With this completed, we go back to the other macro section and repeat the process.

Let's start this process and look at some detail to further clarify it.

The first step is to set the application design pattern that we will use to model our architecture against. As you will probably guess, this is going to be the layered dynamic publishing architecture that we have spent so much time with. Right away, we know that our business needs, requirements, and functionality are going to be grouped and organized into the three primary layers in which this design dictates. We also are assured that the functionality in these three core layers is going to be extracted from anything visual. Finally, we have guidelines we use to direct the functionality into the set parts of the application. What we *don't* have set for us is which functionality is going to be used. The business requirements specify the actual functionality.

Note

Remember that the application architecture is not a framework in which you will automatically have the functionality available to you. It simply states the guidelines where certain types of content will reside.

We determine which functionality to use by dissecting the business requirements that the application is built on. The heart of the design is the focus on business needs and translation into what it represents in our design. During this focusing of our application's requirement, we start to see the further segmentation of the application's packaging. To start, we design a top-level package diagram that shows the key points of separation, and in our case, this is mostly due to the application design pattern we are using. Figure 3.16 shows this top package diagram with the key interfaces in which the other packages work with it.

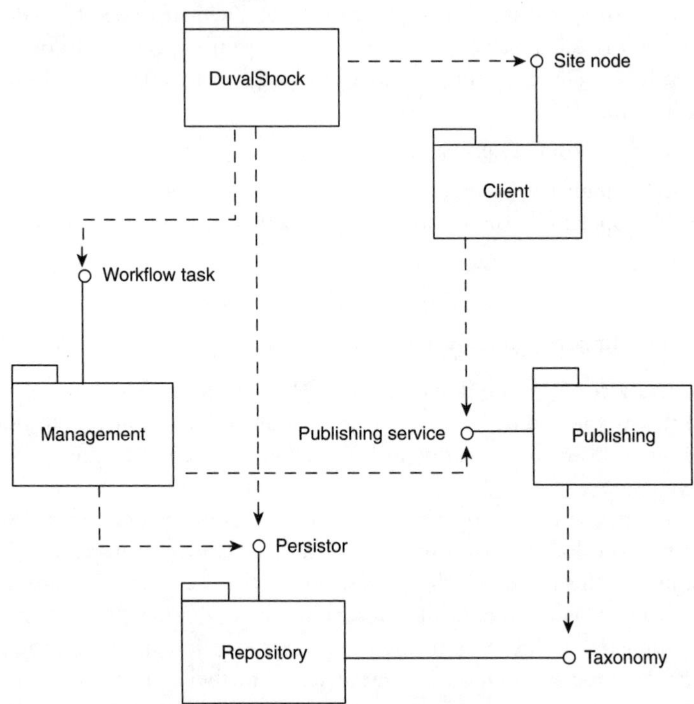

Figure 3.16 The top-level package diagram of the DuvalShock application.

This is our baseline. From here, we will continue to explore the specific nature of our business domain and further segment the packages into subpackages. This segmentation provides a much more maintainable code application design because it enforces the encapsulation of functionality and provides a structural organization to the application. As you discover the needs of the system, you will add further subpackages (noted by the *parentPackageName:subPackageName* notation). Figure 3.17 shows a more robust and segmented package diagram. In this case, we expanded the Repository package to deal with the persistence requirements, the DuvalShock package to store the specific application requirements, and the Management package to handle security and process automation.

At this point, we get a sense of how we are able to organize our business requirements into packages and the like. The way we are going to structure our code, through pattern usage, isn't the only reusable factor to our code. Several of the services that an application needs are repeatable in other similar applications. This is a good time to pause and decide whether to create additional technical requirements to make the service more reusable and part of a framework. The benefit of doing this is the law of the masses: The masses use, and each time they do, they save time.

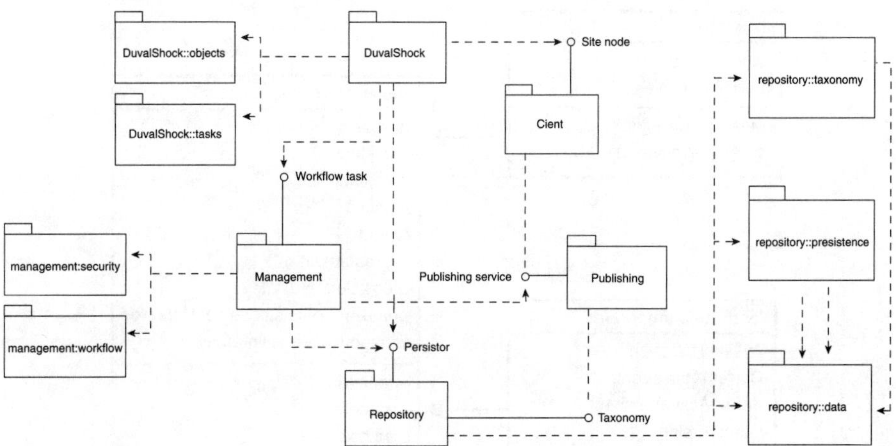

Figure 3.17 An exploded package diagram of the DuvalShock application.

There are basic principles that govern the creation of a service as part of a framework. First, realize that the particular application requirements are less important than the need to keep the service reusable. To that point, the package cannot contain other non-framework classes or components. This allows the framework to be ported almost anywhere it is needed without having to bring along other support classes from a unique application. As you can see, the encapsulation principles discussed earlier in this chapter are highly important.

After we determine the specific functionality, we need to lay out the classes and associations. To avoid reinventing the wheel, we can turn to pattern usage to match our functional needs with a pattern that can solve it. This alone causes an accelerated development cycle as well as a more stable product, as long as the pattern match is correct.

Let's look at an example by diving our 'Repository' package. Inside we can see a subpackage called Data. The general functional requirements for this are to provide a composite structure of entity components (components that represent data) that support some global data properties as well as version and localization support. A good pattern to use, from our brief analysis, is the composite pattern that states that it helps objects truly be a collection of other data elements. This is perfect because a version and a locale are really different objects contained inside the content object. By laying out the pattern, we are able to build out the supporting class diagram that contains the classes and relationships. Figure 3.18 shows the class diagram for the Repository:Data package.

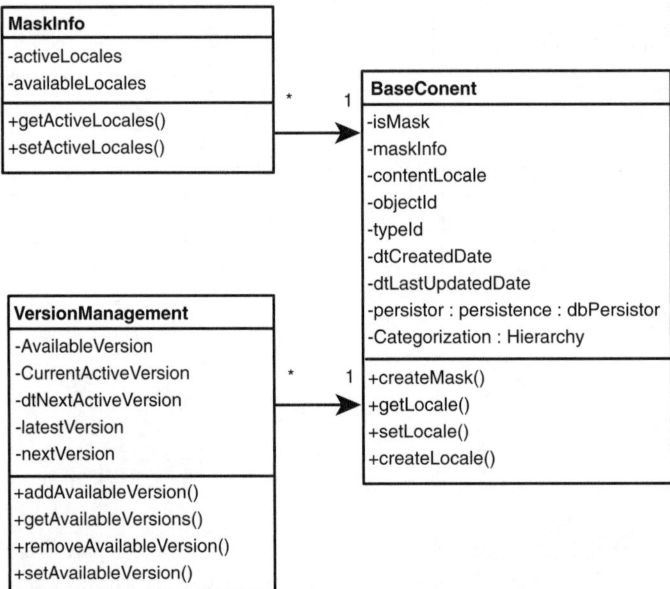

Figure 3.18 Class diagram for the Repository:Data package.

This repetition of requirements to the model is what it takes to come up with the overall design of your application. The application design pattern helps set the boundaries and overall service interaction. This book is set up to cover each layer one at a time and even further dissect the layer into particular services. In these chapters, you will find the alternatives and options available to you when you're solving specific problems.

As your application unfolds, never be happy with the way it currently stands. Keep an eye on the relationships and dependencies between packages and classes. If you notice too many circular relationships in which every class knows every other one, then consolidate the similar classes. This constant critiquing of your design creates a simple, elegant, and powerful application.

Building Blocks for Architecture in CFMX

Some say that it isn't until implementation that you should start considering the strengths and limitations of the language with which you are building. However, it is important to know the support blocks that the platform does support to help with an implementation decision. With the introduction of CFCs into the CFML language, few blocks are unavailable to you.

Static Components

A CFC can be just a collection of related methods. A static component requires that all the data it needs to perform its task be passed to it through its arguments. You can use this sort of block for independent application functionality that creates content and searches taxonomy hierarchies. You also could implement patterns such as singleton and strategy this way. You can have just certain methods that are static. Again, the static nature of a method or component is determined by whether it receives all of its processing data from its arguments.

Storage of Data (Entity)

A component can have a set of properties that it can access using an internal scope called `this`. When the component maps over a set piece of data, such as an article, and the properties match the fields found on the data, it is considered an entity component.

Persistent Service Settings

Components that have properties don't have to be mapped over data or be persistent. A component can be created, initialized, and then used over the course of the application without having to store any of its properties in a database. This sort of component is typically set up to be globally available where the application load routine initializes and places the component in a shared scope.

Custom Tags

It's not correct to think that with CFCs entering the CFML language, custom tags are no longer needed. Custom tags play a vital role in crafting a front-end application interface. Their strong point is their ability to have child data and generated content to manipulate.

> **Note**
>
> The general rule about when to use a component over a custom tag is that if it deals with process or data, use CFC. Otherwise, use a custom tag to handle the encapsulation of the visual manipulation.

Performance in an Application

It is unfortunate that next to architecture, the only other item that is forgotten as often is embedding performance into your application from the beginning. In a distributed application, such as the Internet, milliseconds are compounded by thousands of hits that in turn result in minutes of delays during response times. Generally, the course of action when the application is deployed and running slowly is to open the application and attempt to make drastic changes, thus sacrificing the entire process just walked through, in hopes of speeding up performance.

Instead of having to deal with this 11th hour fire drill, proper planning of application caching from the beginning can result in a much more reliable and higher performing site.

The easiest way to build caching into your application is by delegating to the individual services that make up your application. By creating an application standard of having each service include its own custom caches and expose public management methods to those caches, we can find the optimized way of accomplishing a finely tuned site.

Conclusion

The world of designing and architecting an application carry with it a different way of thinking. By following an application-specific architectural pattern, we gather the benefit of organization and proper segmentation of our application. The pattern discussed in this chapter laid out an approach to the design and a solid way in which you can organize and describe the business domain.

II

The Content Layer

4

Basics of a Content Repository

By Michael Mazzorana

IN THIS CHAPTER, WE WILL EXAMINE THE Content layer in greater detail. A core component of this layer is a centralized content repository. We will detail the importance of having a dedicated repository for holding digital assets that might exist in your organization. After you have fed these various types of business assets into your repository, we will talk about what key elements are needed to transform your content into effective business processes and customer experiences.

In a content repository, content becomes categorized, structured, and prepared for reusability and aggregation for a multitude of business and technical solutions. The business strategy of your company can benefit by identifying existing information that is relevant for exposure to your customers and business partners. Your repository also is an asset to your internal business process because it is easily accessible for workflow systems and various internal applications. The content that you stream into your repository is transformed into Extensible Markup Language (XML). XML breaks the barriers of the various proprietary asset repositories that couldn't co-exist in the past.

The business process interacting with your repository lives and breathes; the business rules on how content is presented are dynamic and purposeful. Your web site becomes a true application and leverages the concept of portals and customer relationship management in the truest way possible. This is the basis of understanding the remaining layers of your dynamic publishing solution.

What Is a Centralized Content Repository?

A *centralized content repository* is similar to any other data repository. Like a traditional data repository, it is business-critical data that lives in some kind of relational database. It's an application programming interface (API) sitting on top feeding, managing, and retrieving data based on various business-related rules.

A centralized content repository differs from other data repositories in its enterprise. Try to imagine it as common ground where content or data from different areas of your company can be fed into or new content can be contributed to an open standard format that can be redistributed, reused, or repurposed to any other system or format. The technical community has clearly defined and accepted this as an open standard data format with which other systems and applications can communicate. XML has become the prominent open standard that every major software solution is migrating toward. With the use of XML, categorization and granular identification of your content positions your organization for various publishing abilities. Your content repository will use XML.

Your organization's return on investment (ROI) for a content repository is focused in two areas:

- By leveraging your content repository, how can your business become less dependent on repurposing content in a manual and labor-intensive fashion for the web and other channels? Aggregation of content in a common interface is critical. Disparate systems that don't talk well with each other need a neutral XML repository for cost-effective solutions.

> **Note**
>
> *Repurposing content* refers to the redistribution or the massaging of content for various displays or system formats, such as Word documents, PDFs, and web sites.

- How can content that is exposed to your customers and partners be positioned for better management and versioning for a more efficient time to market approach? Meeting strict internal company processes for contribution and exposure of your content through automated workflows, can keep information consistent and compliant.

The rest of this chapter is focused on explaining to developers and business users alike the benefits and challenges that surround the building of a content repository.

Challenges of a Content Repository

The most challenging phase of your project to build a content repository is clearly identifying what data is really necessary to pull into it. Another challenge in the same requirement process is determining what requirements your web site might need that your current digital assets do not do a good job of filling. Treat each of these requirements as two different needs that must be satisfied in your requirements gathering phase.

For example:

- Your company might have product description material that is already being managed by a homegrown legacy solution created several years ago. It is a critical system to your organization and is mainly used by your internal business employees to input and use as reference to assist in keeping abreast of current and new product information. The marketing department relies on this legacy system for information needed to create brochures and advertising material. Their process today is to print out the legacy system's material and rework it in their own system or word processor until it is "market ready" for print or a change request to a web development team. This legacy digital asset could become a strong requirement for your content repository.
- The CEO of your company writes a letter each quarter to your distributor sales force. Your company policy has been to stay in close touch with your partners who make you successful even at the senior management level. Senior management has recognized the web as a channel that can quickly and frequently communicate their company strategy and goals. Currently, there is no system or other automated way for a company executive to write the message and have it go through the necessary approval workflow before it is distributed to the sales force. The few communications that are sent out are done in a word processor and manually passed around for approvals. A requirement has been identified that a content repository can assist in the tracking, versioning, and publishing of company executive letters to their distributors in a timelier manner.

The first example is clearly a system that has many company employees already using it. Rewriting it or reworking the existing code that operates this product application might not be the most cost-effective option for leveraging data reuse on the company web site. A more efficient option might be to extract the pertinent content data and place it in XML format in the content repository. After the content lives in the repository, it can begin a new life of its own with a marketing department involved in the process. In Chapter 16, "Securing the Application and User Management," we discuss how different contributors in the Management layer have a role in reworking the content to become market ready for the company web site.

The second example has a different requirement approach. It has no legacy system and no clear process for creating content even in the beginning stages. Data is not fed from an existing system location; therefore, it is necessary to create a complete solution in the content repository to meet the needs of the information to be published on the company web site.

No matter which option you run into, the base requirements for why a content repository needs to exist will be the same. The compliance and legal department want a better way to receive the information they need to review and the internal audit department wants a track record of what is being created. Further, content needs to be reused, re-purposed, and shared to different companies and partners. Your existing data repositories do not meet these requirements because they were not originally designed to do so. Taking your company assets one step closer to being exposed on your web site requires a common repository for your disparate systems data.

Considering Digital Assets in a Content Repository

What digital assets must you consider? Many different types of digital assets exist in a company, and all have a function and a process that have already gone through a requirements gathering phase and development effort. Figure 4.1 shows how a digital asset funnels into a repository.

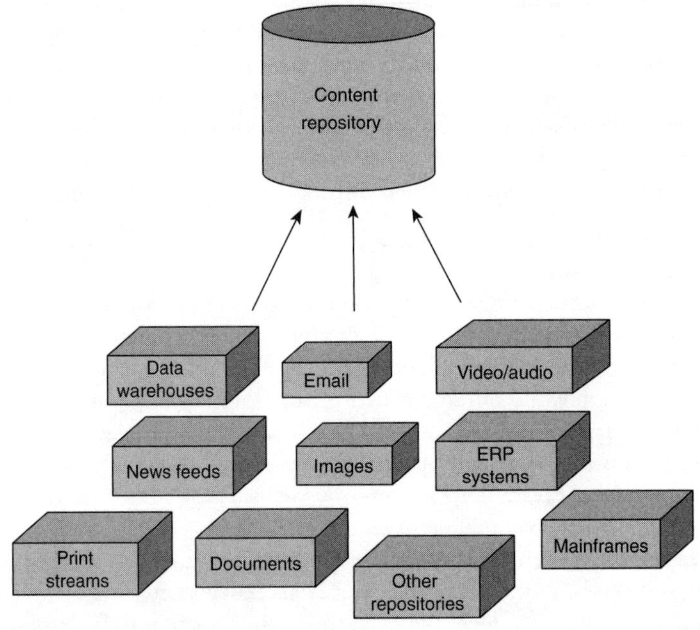

Figure 4.1 Digital assets funneling into a repository.

Let's explore a few digital assets that might be candidates for your content repository:

- **Mainframe systems**—Large corporations have invested heavily in the mainframe system environment because of its ability to handle large amounts of data and complex business logic. Because of its stability and strength, the mainframe shows no sign of going away, and companies continue to grow and maintain these large systems critical to their business. Where mainframe technology has lagged behind has been the ease of how to expose and tailor the data to the web. Product descriptions, marketing material, and other data might live in these systems and the benefits could be great by allowing data feeds into an XML-based content repository to position the information for easier exposure.
- **Newsfeeds**—Many organizations use external vendors that specialize in the aggregation of news data to assist with informing employees and partners in making critical business decisions. Companies such as Reuters and Dow Jones now sell their news content to companies to assist in business decisions. In fact, the integration of this information to existing web applications is now becoming a necessity. Being able to feed or syndicate the content in a repository can bring advantages to your business. News content can be tagged and exposed to different areas when it's made available in a workflow for appropriate distribution to targeted audiences.
- **ERP Systems**—Enterprise Resource Planning (ERP) Systems might be a major component to your organization's infrastructure. ERPs combine many types of core departmental applications into a single platform solution. Most companies have invested in some sort of Enterprise System, such as SAP or PeopleSoft, that assist in human resource management, supplies ordering, or management capabilities. If chosen carefully, content that is managed in those systems can be leveraged in content repositories. You might want to make some internal marketing supplies available for partners on the Internet. Also in ERP Systems, exposing corporate directories to different audiences has great advantages in a content repository.

It's good practice for any technical manager to show the business management how to leverage or reuse existing investments in your organizations. As a technical manager, you're expected to look at how to leverage your existing digital assets. As mentioned earlier, these systems might have millions of dollars already invested in them. Most have been well thought-out and already fit perfectly to a business need and process. One disadvantage of data contained in existing systems is that it can be hard to scrub/massage and expose it for other applications because of the proprietary nature in which it was stored. In all cases of the requirements phase, you should avoid reinventing the wheel if possible. You will get more return on your development investment if content is leveraged in its original form. Reusing or repurposing existing content stores such as mainframes is far more cost effective than replacing them. Letting mainframes do what they were designed to do and have done well for so many years, and simply repurposing their data for additional uses, is the best choice in most cases.

Often, you will have to create new solutions in the content repository. Existing content in a digital asset might be so obscure that developing connecting solutions for data repositories to content repositories might be a wasted effort. The Internet has brought fresh thinking about changing business models; therefore, the outcome of requirements might find little synergy with existing systems data.

The bottom line is to avoid over-engineering when you're leveraging various assets. Clearly define in business requirements what is necessary to bring into a content repository. Not all data sources make sense. Minimal scrubbing or no scrubbing at all should be the basis for an effort to bring data into a content repository. *Scrubbing* can be thought of as rewording or restructuring content during the Management Layer phase (explained in Chapter 16).

Content Management Versus Document Management

An important topic to examine when identifying your business requirements is the content within documents and the content outside of documents. The topics of content management and document management have been a topic of confusion for IT and business professionals because the two have co-existed in the market. To understand the differences and similarities and be able to decide what solution fits the problem your organization is trying to solve, we will first look at the solution that entered the market first.

Document management was first on the scene soon after word processors became dominant in the workplace. Soon after, Portable Document Format (PDF) and other proprietary document creation tools made an appearance. The focus of document management is the document—not so much the finer details of the content that lives within the document. Some document management systems can perform granular activity of meta-tagging, merging, and separation of document information, but in most cases, the content still has a dependency on the proprietary origin in which it was created. Searching within the document, repurposing the content, and personalizing fragments of information become less effective for the end user. Document management was designed to meet the needs of the client/server market for internal management of whole documents and did not address today's most recent needs of dynamic web content.

Table 4.1 compares content management and document management.

Table 4.1 **Content Management Versus Document Management**

Content Management	Document Management
Content assets are granular.	Content assets are less granular.
Updates can be localized to individual pieces of content.	Updates need global changes to the whole document.

Content Management	Document Management
Several content assets are available to satisfy need.	One content asset is available per identified need.
There is no proprietary dependency to platform or technology, XML based.	Content is encapsulated in a proprietary container like word processing software.
It conforms well with changing business uses.	Business use is mostly for internal needs.
Reuse is easy.	Reuse is difficult.

Content management became a niche to fill the business requirements of more frequent updates on web sites and less updating to one-dimensional HTML templates that were clumsy to manage. Taking a lesson from document management, content management solutions now come packaged with a workflow system, can have check-in check-out functionality, and have several other similarities that can make comparing them a confusing task unless you look carefully at these distinctly different solutions.

Both vendor-packaged solutions claim they can assist in your web site management requirements, but when you look closely at document management, it is clear that it was not designed for integration with web template development. Document management does not separate content from a Presentation layer and is not designed for dynamic delivery of content. Content management is designed to take advantage of granular assets and has the ability to be sliced and diced in multiple ways, formats, and targeted audiences. With a content repository, separation of content from the presentation layer is accomplished easily, unlike document management.

The latest trend of the two circles is that many traditional document management vendors are entering the content management market. Their mature knowledge in the workflow and versioning space has made it a natural fit to begin integrating the two solutions into a single product. These integrated solutions will continue to confuse the market until proprietary document formats conform closer to XML standards and other web consortium standards (`http://www.w3c.org/XML/`). As we mentioned earlier, most major software solutions companies will be leveraging XML in some way if they are not already.

Depending on your requirements, content management and document management can live well together. In many content management solutions, documents can be uploaded and tagged a metadata category so that they can be searched easily and dynamically driven to user roles and areas of a web site. In many business solutions, document management systems live seamlessly behind content management front-ends. They hold a repository of forms or documents that might be required to perform business with an organization. Most well-designed document management systems include a way to manage the forms and documents on one side and then expose the forms to Internet users to search and categorize.

Internationalization and Localization

As mentioned in Chapter 1, "Overview of Dynamic Publishing," for many businesses that sell, service, or partner their products in foreign countries, having content presented in different languages or customized to a culture is critical. If you are not currently getting requirements to develop solutions to meet foreign markets, it might pay off if you begin your Content layer foundation efforts with foreign markets in mind. As the economic world shrinks, it might soon become a requirement that a centralized content repository can assist you with.

Some of the challenges to think about before building a repository are mentioned in the following sections. The intent of this book isn't to give you an understanding of all the challenges and hidden gems of building an international application. Instead, it provides you with an implementation understanding to ground your further exploration into this topic.

> **Note**
>
> Not all translated languages use the letters of the alphabet that we are used to. You need to be able to tap into your repository in a way that it can display differently. Alternatively, translation solutions must be able to turn into the necessary displays needed for a language; this is accomplished by choosing a character set that is broad enough to support the languages of your site. For example, the default encoding ISO-8859-1 (Latin) supports characters from languages with Latin roots (Spanish, French, and English). To be able to truly support an international presence, it is important to choose a character set (also referred to as a character encoding) that supports languages from Chinese to Farsi to English. The common character encoding for this need is UTF-8 (UNICODE). There is a requirement on the application server to support the character encoding to perform data manipulation with the information in the repository. With the release of ColdFusion MX, ColdFusion can now handle UNICODE encoding.

Translation of Content

Manual translation is extremely expensive. A more cost-effective solution is using a third-party tool or processes that can bulk translate your content. You can pull these internally through integration. No translation solution to date does a perfect job of taking content and translating it exactly, so dynamic translation of your sites without reviewing or checking might be damaging to your organization. Instead of a direct translation, you will more than likely have automated translation as the first step to create a localized copy of your data. You then store this data in a repository that can co-exist with your primary content and that the Management layer process can use to automate the translation with language specialists who can sign off on it.

Fitting Local Business Processes

Being prepared to spawn off separate workflows on the same repository information that is translated is advantageous to your international needs. Your office in Hong Kong can interact effectively remotely with content originating in New York with a centralized content repository. This ability to have a dynamically modifiable business process is discussed in more detail in Chapter 13, "Basics of Managing Content."

> **Caution**
>
> Content isn't the only thing that causes the business process to change. International and sovereign laws have a great impact as you take your business overseas. Be aware that delivering content to an international client base is different from bringing your business international.

Content Storage

As noted earlier, it is important to be able to store localized content with your primary data so that you can present the correct information to your international clientele. For example, the word *color* in the United States might need a change to *colour* in Great Britain. You can handle this in a variety of ways from storing the data in a single repository to having a repository for each localized version. A primary objective of storing the content in these repositories is to be able to programmatically deal with content with desired versions or without. Cultural differences might make the same content live in different sentence structures and formats.

Versioning of Content

At the beginning of this chapter, we looked at the differences between a data repository and a content repository. Content versioning is an area that is unique to the centralized content repository. Versioning is simply a way to keep track of changes made to the content. It can list *what* was changed, *who* changed it, and *when* it was changed. The design of the application determines the manner in which the actual versioning is done (where the versions are located, what format the versioned content is stored in, and so on). It can range from custom written versioning using files and database storage to interfacing well-known third-party Source Control Systems such as Microsoft's Visual SourceSafe, CVS, or Rational's ClearCase. This implementation is explored in further detail in Chapter 11, "Persistence with Versioning."

> **Note**
>
> It's easy to get the versioning of content mixed up with the versioning of our application. Content versioning is used during the live execution of the application to provide us with a history of the data in relation to the web site. Versioning of our application is the process of versioning files, server settings, and other artifacts used to develop the application.

Enterprises that lean heavily toward an internal audit process usually ask how your solution or product can track changes that were made and how you can re-create an older version if litigation issues occur. Perhaps a sales representative claims that a web site stated that commission would be 50% on a sale of a product when it was supposed to be advertised at 5%. You need to be able to go back and re-create a change or track activity to settle internal and external issues that might occur.

The web has become a critical means in how to run your business. If you're a financial company, the regulatory government agencies expect you to have a versioning infrastructure in place. No longer do you trust the webmaster to update your site and control the information within.

Internal audit and legal departments look for ways to improve the validity of content presented on a web site, and versioning is the key to meeting this requirement. If a graphic designer updates your logo or a business unit changes the text on your web site's pages, versioning assists you in archiving, tracking, and reporting these events. Versioning also plays a role in rolling back a change at the element level or at the page level. More important, version tracking is necessary for accountability.

The Actions of Versioning

Looking through the examples stated earlier as well as your own situation, you can see that the variety of business needs fundamentally revolve around a set of actions embedded in the content versioning:

- **Creation of version**—This is the basis of the versioning system. The action creates a version and stores it in the repository. A version can be created and made the current one or it can be created for further use and manipulation.
- **Rollback to older version**—This reverts the current content to a different saved version.
- **Comparison of older version**—This shows the delta between the current content and a saved version. This is only used in specific cases and is not generally present in all version control situations.
- **Merging of versions**—This functionality allows you to selectively merge the delta between one version and another into one or the other. This is not a base need for all content versioning situations.

File Versus Content Versioning

Our description of content versioning to this point has been somewhat nebulous in the fact that it hasn't accounted for the specific types of content that we can deal with. To clarify, a system can be composed of two main types of content: file based and data storage based. Each of these formats requires slightly different manners for handling.

Content that is represented as a file is generally worked with using a handle to the file. For the most part, the data that it contains is kept separate from the internal workings of the system. Typically, versioning of this type of content is not custom written because of the complexity of reading the different file types. If all the actions are needed, it is generally accomplished through the programmatic interfacing with a document management server.

Content that is stored in some sort of data storage mechanism, such as a database, has much less complexity associated with it when needing to version. Unlike file-based content in which the file is kept external to the application, this type of content is pulled from the data storage, worked with, and returned. Versioning is much simpler to accomplish and typically doesn't require interfacing specialized products or components.

Categorization of Content

Categorization can be a complex topic, and at the same time, it can be the most critical topic to understand when you architect how your business content will live in your repository. Keep in mind the following points:

- Dynamic publishing is as effective as the accuracy of how your content relates to the categories and how your company or organization functions.
- The manner in which your Client layer presents content, the effectiveness of your search on your site, and your success with dynamic navigation are all critical to accurate content categorization.
- Metadata is an XML tag that corresponds to related content. Think of it as keywords on a tab when you're trying to find a book in the library.

Figure 4.2 illustrates another analogy for understanding categories and metadata. Imagine going to the supermarket and looking at the aisle signs for something you're going to buy.

You walk into a store knowing you need milk and butter. The supermarket is a large place with thousands of items categorized for you in logical groups. You search for an aisle that has a sign describing dairy products, and you logically understand how the business works, so you head over to that aisle. After you're in the dairy section, you're able to minimize your search to subcategories that are contained in one physical location, and you're able to find the product you're looking for.

Obviously, this is a fairly over-simplified description of categorization. Regardless, the way that the supermarket prepared for the categorization, designed it to save you time, and personalized the service was carefully thought-out. The store was able to take you through a maze of information in a quick and effective manner. To take it a step further, how the supermarket got you to the dairy section could have been deliberate. You might have been routed through the cereal section just in case the milk you were buying was for oatmeal, and you realized you were almost out of it.

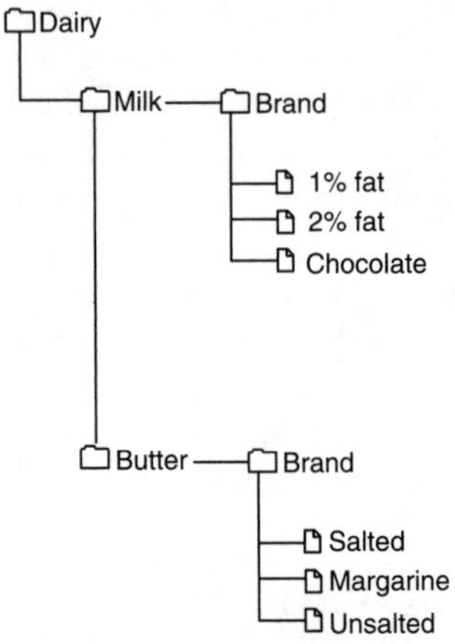

Dairy
Milk
Brand
1% fat
2% fat
Chocolate
Butter
Brand
Salted
Margarine
Unsalted

Figure 4.2 Categorization of supermarket items.

Let's think about categorization in a business and content repository situation. Going back to our example of the electrical product company named DuvalShock, imagine that the company has many products it develops and sells (see Figure 4.3).

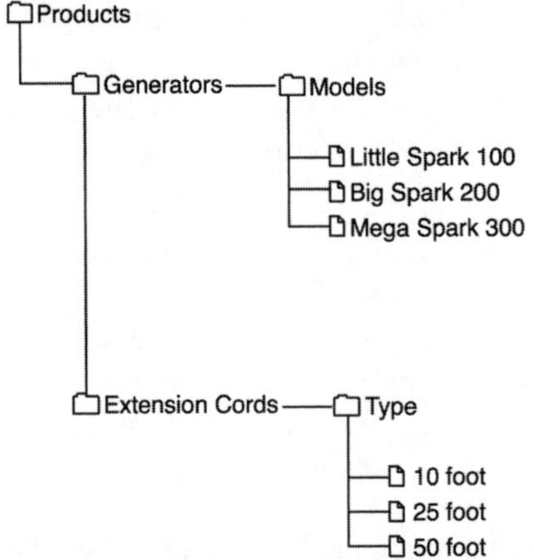

Figure 4.3 Categorization of company items.

When you are defining the requirements for your centralized content repository for your dynamic publishing solution, you need to carefully plan out the categorization of the information to be stored. In the illustration for DuvalShock's products, Products has been determined the top-level metadata. After Products is found, subcategories or additional pieces of metadata are tagged on the appropriate areas of content and continue a logical drill down of the information that someone is trying to find.

With this basic example of categorization and metadata, let's look at some of the benefits that this web site could leverage for a better user experience.

Search

If we are at DuvalShock's Internet home page, we could search the site. Before even giving an option to enter a keyword, we might want to give users a category to search within a category. For example, we might suggest an option button or a drop-down box to search within Products so that an end user's search results are more concise to that category and not to everything in the web site (see Figure 4.4).

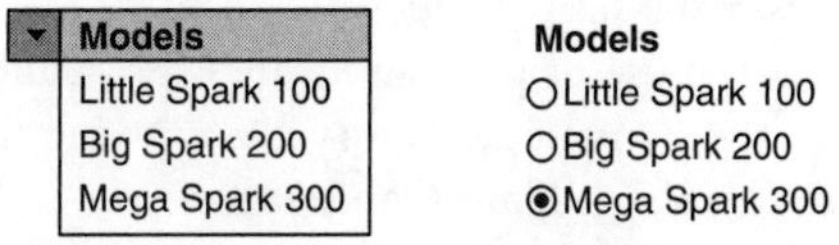

Models
Little Spark 100
Big Spark 200
Mega Spark 300

Models
Little Spark 100
Big Spark 200
Mega Spark 300

Figure 4.4 Example of using categorization to narrow searching of content items.

Dynamic Navigation

In a site design, navigation "breadcrumb trail" can be part of a horizontal navigation as an end user traverses a section of a web site. Instead of manually creating and updating this experience, metadata from a content repository can assist with this. Starting at DuvalShock's home page, a choice for Products is listed as a link. A user who is looking for product details might begin to drill down to the Products link to find a list of categories related to Products. Using our example, the two (or more) that are listed are Generators and Extension Cords. The end user chooses Generators to have the content repository dynamically drill down to the next level, which is Models of Generators that are Stored. Finally, the user can choose a model of generator to show the description, price, warranty, or whatever was decided in the full description requirements.

The dynamic navigation "breadcrumb trail" could look something like Figure 4.5.

Breadcumb trail

Homepage | Products | Generators | Little Spark 100

Figure 4.5 Example of using categorization to drive dynamic navigation.

Each category can be a hyperlink back to the dedicated page level for that piece of metadata.

Personalization

Another excellent use of metadata and categories is targeting or tailoring an end user with content that is specific to him. With your authentication infrastructure, identify your site visitor upon logging in. Based on the role or group he belongs to, build a web page dynamically using your repository. For example, a sales representative who only sells extension cords will see only product choices for that particular line of product. Alternatively to driving personalization from a user's role in the system, you can build a page that lets the end user build his own profile to control the display by adding or removing categories of metadata. Doing this allows the user to decide what content repository assets make him productive.

Later chapters discuss the use of publishing rules (pre-built content retrieval logic) to extract content from the content repository. By applying these category-aware publishing rules to HTML templates, Flash Components, and web services, we can satisfy particular request based on end users. These sort of publishing rules are used most often by portal solutions, in which displays need metadata to dynamically build web sites for a particular user. Thus, we have a publishing rule that is set to play a role in a personalized site.

What Is Metadata?

The topic of categorization brings to the front the concept of tagging content with extra information that describes more about the content than its core structural elements. This is known as the content's *metadata*.

When you're defining a piece of content, you focus on the core structural elements, such as title, summary, city, and so on to drive its definition. This is the essence of what the content is about. However, the content also has a secondary set of arbitrary data, called metadata, which gives it a relation or additional information to the application in which it works. For example, an article consists of a title, body, and summary. In an energy company, that article would have a relationship to the product offerings, the company, or any other part of the organization. This relationship has to do with the sort of content it contains based on what the business is about.

In some cases, the metadata that is defined is a category or keyword of the classification hierarchy, but that is not a requirement. The benefit to using a classification hierarchy to map out the available metadata that can be assigned to a piece of content would be in the ability to use the classification engine's functionality. An additional benefit is the fact that it would be a structured way of associating and managing the metadata. This would not be the case if you were to assign straight text to the object as metadata.

Conclusion

In this chapter, we defined the components of the Content layer in detail. We covered the Content layer both from a business and a technical understanding. Technical leaders need to clearly understand the differences between a data repository and a content repository and articulate that to business groups. Using some of the explanations and descriptions in this chapter can help guide you through the mystery of what a content repository is and why an additional repository is necessary to your company's success.

The topic of content management versus document management is an important area that all audiences need to understand. Share the explanation in this chapter to get all areas of your organization on the same page. It can be a costly mistake to misunderstand one or the other. Realize that both content management and document management have strengths and fit into a business model for different requirements. In addition, recognize that the two solutions can co-exist and improve the overall user experience on your web site if the strengths are leveraged with the two in mind.

Consider internationalization and localization even if you don't have an international presence today. If you're a moderately sized company and you continue to grow, chances are that you will need to take future steps to be prepared for the challenges explained in this chapter. The accessibility of the Internet has begun to require certain audit controls and restrictions that have changed the roles of internal audit and compliance to have greater focus on how applications are built for the Internet. The nature of dynamic publishing will certainly catch the attention of your internal regulators as you architect your content infrastructure.

Categorization was one of the larger topics in this chapter and because of this, it can be considered one of the most important topics to understand for a successful dynamic publishing effort. Do not underestimate the effort it will take to get various business departments to break down your business categories by agreeing on terms, recognizing overlaps in business process, and understanding the end user impact. One of the better approaches to breaking down the content that will ultimately live in your content repository is to convince your requirements group not to think about what it will do on your Client layer. Keep the requirements group focused on how their business works and what logical structure makes sense to the content that will be managed and presented.

The next several chapters focus on the technical details that developers need to achieve to build what was discussed in this chapter. ColdFusion MX introduces a variety of features that you can used to effectively create the services and functionality of this business area, particularly the introduction of ColdFusion Components. Chapter 13 offers a detailed explanation of how your business departments will manage the content that lives in your repository.

5

ColdFusion Components

by Anthony McClure

APPLICATION DESIGN IN COLDFUSION MX IS QUITE a bit different than in previous versions. One of the key reasons for this difference is the introduction of ColdFusion Components (CFCs).

CFCs provide developers with an exciting new way to structure code into modular, reusable units. CFCs are more than just a new way of organizing code, however; in actuality, they're an entirely new paradigm for ColdFusion application development. With a series of application services built around them, CFCs allow applications to execute their embedded code as a single reusable unit, provide access security, and expose themselves as Web and Flash Gateway Services.

This paradigm forms the backbone architecture for application development in ColdFusion MX. Because CFCs are new to ColdFusion MX and our dynamic publishing application is built on this platform, a discussion of CFC code syntax, application, and use is warranted at this time.

By way of a close examination of how CFCs are structured and work, this chapter focuses on the value of using this new paradigm in ColdFusion MX applications and how it is implemented.

What Are ColdFusion Components?

Good application design typically separates the architecture into three sections:

- User interface
- Business logic
- Data access

This architecture is sometimes referred to as *Model View Controller* (MVC) *architecture*. Other forms of this architecture include Microsoft's DNA, 3-tier, or n-tier architecture and distributed application development.

> **Note**
>
> For more information on MVC architecture and building distributed applications, try these resources:
>
> - Microsoft DNA—`http://msdn.microsoft.com/library/default.asp?url=/library/en-us/vsent7/html/vxconAnOverviewOfDistributedApplications.asp`
> - N-Tier architecture—`http://www.webopedia.com/quick_ref/app.arch.html`

The ability for architects and developers to implement MVC architecture is based largely on the programming language that is used in application development.

Previous to ColdFusion MX, ColdFusion developers and architects had access to templates, custom tags, and user-defined functions (UDFs) in which to implement MVC architectures. Versions of ColdFusion prior to ColdFusion MX did not provide a consistent design approach to do this. Therefore, it has become the responsibility of the developers to implement the architecture with no help from the language.

With the advent of ColdFusion MX and CFCs, developers now have a reliable and language-supported mechanism to develop MVC architectures from. In addition, CFCs allow similar functionality to exist together in a single template, allowing for easier long-term code maintenance and extensibility.

The following sections cover the various functions and services that CFCs expose. By using these features, developers can create the business logic and data access layers of the MVC architecture in a consistent and language-standardized method, and project managers are presented with standardized reusable code for further project development.

Web Service Integration

Components not only organize functionality together, but they also describe the component completely. With the capability to describe which methods/functions on the component are remotely accessible, it is possible to generate the necessary WSDL file (an XML document that describes the exposed web service to all clients) to make the component available as a web service. The *WSDL generation* is a default method for all components. The necessary Java stub components are generated automatically upon the first invocation of the component.

Function Organization

Components are a series of functions that are grouped together into a single unit. By being able to group functions together (using `<CFFUNCTION>` tags) inside of `<CFCOMPONENT>` tags, related services can be put together into a single cohesive unit.

Property Declaration

In addition to grouping functions together, a component also can describe properties that are meant to be available across multiple function calls.

In traditional object-oriented programming, a property represents a value that describes the object in some way. For example, if we were using an automobile as an object, one of its properties would be color because all automobiles are painted in some way. The automobile might have many other properties as well, such as engine size, number of passengers, body style, and so on.

> **What Is a Web Service?**
>
> Web services are relatively new to the world of Internet development. Web services allow for the publication or use of application logic from one server to another through the Internet. By creating web services, a developer opens the functionality in question to requests from remote clients. In converse, by using (or *consuming*, as it is called) a web service, a client remotely accesses the functionality that a server exposes.
>
> For more information on web services and how ColdFusion MX handles them, see Chapter 20, "Web Services."

Although ColdFusion MX only uses these declared properties when a component is published as a web service, the properties are exposed through a process called *component introspection* and become a basis for creating component-based custom persistence.

Component Inheritance

Inheritance, a common feature of object oriented programming languages, is now available for the first time to ColdFusion developers with the introduction of CFCs and Component Inheritance in ColdFusion MX. Simply put, component inheritance allows a component to extend another component. The new component's definition will consist of locally declared functions, arguments, and properties as well as those declared in the component it extends.

A good example of this is our automobile object. If we create an automobile CFC, we provide all of the basic properties and methods that we know all automobiles need. However, in addition to the basic properties and methods, specific types of automobiles (cars, trucks, and so on) need additional definition. Trucks might have a towing capacity and a bed size that a car would not.

We could just place all of the truck properties in the automobile CFC, but that would not be the most efficient use of the code. Luckily, component inheritance comes to the rescue. We create a new CFC called Truck that extends the Automobile CFC. In doing this, the Truck CFC automatically gains all of the properties and methods of the automobile, but it can add additional properties and methods as needed.

Ultimately, this allows many components to reuse a generalized set of base functionality, such as custom persistence information, without rewriting the same code repeatedly.

Component Class Compiling

New to ColdFusion MX, all code is now compiled in Java class files. This, along with standard libraries from a J2EE server (ColdFusion MX uses an OEM version of the JRun server by default), is a dramatic change from previous ColdFusion versions and becomes the basis for ColdFusion on the Java platform.

Component Packaging

Component packaging allows developers to place similar CFCs together in logical directory hierarchies. Other components in the same directory are considered packaged together with this component and are aware of the components in the same package. References to the other components in the same package are made without the need to prefix the component with its full package name. Also, it is possible to restrict the access of methods on the component only to other components inside the same package or subpackages.

> **Note**
>
> For more information on component packaging and its use, see Chapters 8, "ColdFusion Components with Persistence" and 9, "Centralized Data Persistence."

Component Introspection

A component is described with a set of properties, functions, and arguments. At runtime, it is possible to dynamically determine what the makeup of the component is. The properties and methods of the component as well as the component it inherits from are available. The tags that are used in component creation can have additional attributes that ColdFusion does not use but will be passed through during component introspection.

This process of introspection becomes the basis for the custom persistence engine examined in this book. For more information on component introspection, see Chapters 8 and 9.

Multiple Invocation Mechanisms

Components can be invoked through Web Services, a URL, the `<CFINVOKE>` tag, the Flash Gateway Service, a Form Post, and using `object.method()` and `createObject()` in CFSCRIPT notation. The ability to call a component from within a CFSCRIPT block makes it superior to a custom tag.

Built-In Validation

When executing a function, the built-in validation feature ensures that the arguments passed in and passed out are both provided and valid. Validation can occur for both simple and complex data types.

Function Security

When you're describing a function of a component, you can assign an attribute that sets the roles that have permission to access a function. When the function is invoked, ColdFusion MX verifies that the authenticated user is indeed in one of the roles assigned to the function. This is accomplished using the new ColdFusion MX security model, which has changed drastically from previous versions.

> **Note**
>
> To find out more information on the new security model in ColdFusion MX, see these resources:
>
> - **ColdFusion MX documentation**—Chapter 16, "Securing the Application and User Management" and Chapter 14, "Leveraging Security in ColdFusion MX."
> - **Articles in the Macromedia ColdFusion MX Application Developer Center**—`http://www.macromedia.com/desdev/mx/coldfusion/`

Built-In Component Explorer

This feature allows developers to view the components that are located on the ColdFusion server. The Component Explorer shows the components that are bundled together into packages, depicts inheritances, and demonstrates functions and properties. In addition, if the component leverages the optional `hint` attribute on the component tags (`<CFCOMPONENT>`, `<CFPROPERTY>`, `<CFFUNCTION>`, and `<CFARGUMENT>`), the Explorer will show this additional user generated documentation. To access the Explorer, go to `http://server/cfide/componentutils/componentdoc.cfm`.

Component Structure

To create CFCs, a series of ColdFusion tags (`<CFCOMPONENT>`, `<CFFUNCTION>`, `<CFARGUMENT>`, and `<CFRETURN>`) are used together and saved in a template with a .cfc extension. In fact, CFCs are essentially the same as any other ColdFusion template and can contain all existing CFML tags (including `<CFTRY>`/`<CFCATCH>` for custom error handling), UDFs, `<CFSCRIPT>` blocks, calls to custom tags, and calls to other CFC functions.

How does this look from a code standpoint? The best way to examine CFC construction is to build a useful CFC. A common problem that faces developers is user authentication, or accepting the input of a username/password combination and verifying the credentials against a database. In the past, this functionality most likely would have been placed within a login template or perhaps a custom tag. With ColdFusion MX, a CFC becomes the perfect place to handle security interactions.

<CFCOMPONENT> Tag

To begin the security CFC, you need a start and end `<CFCOMPONENT>` tag set. This tag set surrounds the entire template and identifies the code as a CFC. Listing 5.1 shows the `<CFCOMPONENT>` syntax.

Listing 5.1 ***<CFCOMPONENT>* Syntax**

```
<cfcomponent output="no" extends="testComponent">
        .
        .
        .
</cfcomponent>
```

The `<CFCOMPONENT>` tag contains two optional attributes, which are summarized in Table 5.1.

Table 5.1 ***<CFCOMPONENT>* Attributes**

Attribute	Required	Data Type	Description
`Output`	No	Boolean	This attribute controls output behavior for the component. If it's set to `false`, then HTML is not generated.
`Extends`	No	String	Used in component inheritance, this attribute tells the CFC the name of another component that this CFC inherits from.

In the security code, the <CFCOMPONENT> does not use the `extends` attribute because this CFC does not inherit from another component. The `output` attribute is set to a Boolean `false` value because our CFCs are used in the middle tier of the MVC architecture and do not provide user interface elements. Although it is possible to enable user interface output from a CFC, it's best to use CFCs mainly for business logic and data access points for applications. Standard CFML templates, custom tags, and include files should still be the basis for user interface code.

<CFFUNCTION> Tag

By itself, the <CFCOMPONENT> tag does not accomplish much at this point. To expose functionality for use in ColdFusion MX applications, you must declare functions within the start and end <CFCOMPONENT> tags by using the <CFFUNCTION> tag set (see Listing 5.2).

Listing 5.2 *<CFFUNCTION>*

```
<cfcomponent>
   <cffunction
      name="functionName"
      returnType="boolean"
      roles="role1,role2"
      access="public"
      output="false"
   >
         .
         Function Logic Here
         .
   </cffunction>
</cfcomponent>
```

The <CFFUNCTION> tag attributes describe the basic properties of the function call (see Table 5.2).

Table 5.2 *<CFFUNCTION>* **Attributes**

Attribute	Required	Data Type	Description
`Name`	Yes	String	Name of the component function. This name is used when executing the function.
`ReturnType`	No	String	Data type for the return value from the function call.

continues

Table 5.2 **Continued**

Attribute	Required	Data Type	Description
`Roles`	No	String List	List of ColdFusion MX roles that have access to this function. When the function is invoked, the authenticated user is checked for roles-based permissions to access the function. Uses ColdFusion MX security features.
`Access`	No	String	As various client types access the component function (URI, internal application templates, Flash Gateway, Web Service, and so on), a check against this attribute takes place. If the access level does not match the client source, an error is generated.
`Output`	No	Boolean	Similar to the `<CFCOMPONENT>` output attribute. Used to suppress component output.

All code within the start and end tags is executed when the function is invoked. In the security component example, you should add a function of `"authenticate"` to the security component. This function will contain the necessary ColdFusion MX code to check the database against the user-supplied credentials.

Listing 5.3 shows the start of this component. It is saved into a file called security.cfc.

Listing 5.3 **The Security CFC (security.cfc)**

```
<cfcomponent output="false">
   <cffunction
      name="authenticate"
      returnType="boolean"
      access="public"
   >
         .
         Security Check Here
         .
   </cffunction>
</cfcomponent>
```

The `"authenticate"` function is set up to have a Boolean return type (indicating the successful or unsuccessful authentication of user credentials) and has `Public` access. This access level tells the component that it can be executed from any internal ColdFusion templates on the server. If we wanted the function to be available through the Flash Gateway or Web Services, the access would have to change to `Remote` instead. Table 5.3 shows the acceptable values for this attribute.

Table 5.3 **Access Parameter Values**

Access Value	Description
`Private`	Only the same component that defines this function can access it. Only a function within the same CFC file can call this function.
`Package`	This function is available to the component that declares it and all others within the same package. Packages form the basis of component organization and represent the directory hierarchy that your components reside in. Another component within the same directory as the declaring component can access a function with Package access.
`Public`	This is the default access value. The function is available to all ColdFusion templates on the server and is still protected from external invocation (Flash Gateway, URL, Form Post, Web Service).
`Remote`	All client types (including remote clients) can access the function.

<CFARGUMENT> Tag

To authenticate a user, you must pass some information into the component. `<CFARGUMENT>` declarative tags and the `arguments` variable scope handle CFC data passing inside a `<CFFUNCTION>`.

The `<CFARGUMENT>` tag contains a simple structure of attributes that is used to describe the nature of the data passed into the function. Arguments can be set as required or not. If a required argument is not passed into the function, an exception occurs. Table 5.4 shows the attributes of `<CFARGUMENT>`.

Table 5.4 ***<CFARGUMENT>* Attributes**

Attribute	Required	Data Type	Description
`Name`	Yes	String	This is the name of the argument.
`Type`	No	String	This is the data type of the passed data. The defaults of any ColdFusion data type are acceptable. In addition to traditional ColdFusion data types, another component can be passed in by referencing its name.
`Required`	No	Boolean	Determines whether the argument in question should be required or not. If set to a `true` value, then the argument must be passed into the CFC for the function to run.

continues

Table 5.4 **Continued**

Attribute	Required	Data Type	Description
`Default`	No	String	This is the default value to use if the argument is not passed to the function. This attribute is mutually exclusive with the `Required` attribute.

For the `"authenticate"` function example, two arguments are needed to authenticate: the username and password of the user. A single `<CFARGUMENT>` tag defines each of these. Listing 5.4 shows the `"authenticate"` function, including the two `<CFARGUMENT>` tags.

Listing 5.4 **Adding Arguments to the Security CFC (security.cfc)**

```
<cfcomponent output="false">
   <cffunction
      name="authenticate"
      returnType="boolean"
      access="public"
   >
      <cfargument
         name="cfcUsername"
         required="true"
         type="string"
      >

      <cfargument
         name="cfcPassword"
         required="true"
         type="string"
      >
   </cffunction>
</cfcomponent>
```

In Listing 5.4, `"cfcUsername"` and `"cfcPassword"` are both set as type `"string"` and `Required`. Therefore, a string data type value must be present for each argument when you're invoking this function call. These two values can then be used within the function logic to determine successful authentication against a database.

To gain access to arguments passed into a CFC, a special variable scope was created. This variable scope is named `arguments`, and it operates in a similar manner to the custom tag `attributes` scope.

To gain access to the data within the `arguments` scope, dot notation is used. For example, the `"cfcPassword"` argument can be evaluated by the code `arguments.cfcPassword`. Putting these concepts together, the `"authenticate"` security CFC functions logic can be added.

Note

The `arguments` variable scope, like many others in ColdFusion MX, is in fact treated as a CFML structure. Because of this, you can output the entire scope in a formatted table by using the <CFDUMP> ColdFusion tag. This is extremely helpful for code development and debugging purposes. Just be sure to set the `output` attribute for the component and function to `true` when doing so.

Listing 5.5 **Creating the Security CFC (security.cfc) Function Logic**

```
<cfcomponent output="false">
   <cffunction
      name="authenticate"
      returnType="boolean"
      access="public"
   >
      <cfargument
         name="cfcUsername"
         required="true"
         type="string"
      >
       <cfargument
         name="cfcPassword"
         required="true"
         type="string"
      >
     <cfquery name="checkCredentials" datasource="security">
         SELECT username
         FROM security
         WHERE username = '#arguments.cfcUsername#'
         AND password = '#arguments.cfcPassword#'
      </cfquery>
   </cffunction>
</cfcomponent>
```

A <CFQUERY> checks the security database table for a matching username and password. The function is fully operational at this point, but one problem remains: No return value is sent to the invoking client after the check completes.

<CFRETURN> Tag

CFCs handle return values in functions using the <CFRETURN> tag. This tag has a simple syntax, which is shown in Listing 5.6.

Listing 5.6 ***<CFRETURN>***

```
<cfcomponent>
   <cffunction
      name="functionName"
      returnType="boolean"
      roles="role1,role2"
      access="public"
      output="false"
   >
         .
         Function Logic Here
         .
      <cfreturn expression>
   </cffunction>
</cfcomponent>
```

The `<CFRETURN>` tag contains no attributes. Only the return value, in expression format (an evaluation of an expression can occur), is needed.

For the `"authenticate"` function call, a Boolean result should be returned to the invoker to indicate the successful or unsuccessful result of the check. To accomplish this, the code checks the `recordCount` property of the checkCredentials query. If the result is greater than zero, then a match has been made and a Boolean `true` result is returned.

Final Output of security.cfc

Listing 5.7 shows the final security CFC in its entirety:

Listing 5.7 **Returning a Value from the Security CFC (security.cfc)**

```
<cfcomponent output="false">
   <cffunction
      name="authenticate"
      returnType="boolean"
      access="public"
   >
      <cfargument
         name="cfcUsername"
         required="true"
         type="string"
      >
       <cfargument
         name="cfcPassword"
         required="true"
         type="string"
      >
      <cfquery name="checkCredentials" datasource="security">
         SELECT username
```

```
         FROM security
         WHERE username = '#arguments.cfcUsername#'
         AND password = '#arguments.cfcPassword#'
      </cfquery>
       <cfif checkCredentials.recordCount>
         <cfreturn true>
      <cfelse>
         <cfreturn false>
      </cfif>
   </cffunction>
</cfcomponent>
```

The security CFC has one complete function call. Other functionality (an "authorization" function for instance) can be added with additional <cffunction> blocks.

Working with Components

You can invoke the functions within a CFC in many ways, such as via ColdFusion templates, custom tags, other CFCs, a Flash movie, a form submit, a URL, and as a web service.

You can invoke the functions within ColdFusion templates in several ways as well, including usage of the <CFOBJECT>, <CFINVOKE>, and <CFSCRIPT> (along with the ColdFusion function CREATEOBJECT()) tags.

<CFINVOKE> and *<CFOBJECT>*

Invocation of a function using <CFINVOKE> is straightforward. The <CFINVOKE> tag contains attributes that are used to identify the CFC to execute against and the function to call and to set up a return variable if needed. Table 5.5 shows the <CFINVOKE> attributes.

Table 5.5 ***<CFINVOKE>* Attributes**

Attribute	Required	Data Type	Description
Component	Yes	String	This is the name of the CFC and its package location. For the security component, this would be security (corresponds to the name of the CFC file).
Method	Yes	String	This is the name of the function to invoke.
ReturnVariable	No	String	This is the name of the variable to place return results.

continues

Table 5.5 **Continued**

Attribute	Required	Data Type	Description
`ArgumentCollection`	No	Structure	This is the structure of argument names and values to pass into the function call.
`WebService`	No	String	This is the URL location of the WSDL file for the web service in question.
`Input parameters`	No	Per Argument	Similar to the ArgumentCollection, but instead of a structure of names and values, a parameter is passed in the format of `argument name = "argument value"` for each argument of the function.

The invocation happens in three steps.

1. A CFC object is created.
2. One or more functions are executed against the object.
3. The object is destroyed.

If a `<CFINVOKE>` call is made without a `<CFOBJECT>` call, all three steps happen in sequence. That is, the object is instantiated, executed against, and then destroyed. Because of this, if multiple actions against the same CFC are to take place within the template, a better solution is to instantiate the object using a `<CFOBJECT>` call. In this case, the `<CFOBJECT>` tag will create the object for use throughout the template and will destroy itself upon template completion, avoiding the object instantiation for each function call.

Listing 5.8 shows an example of calling the security CFC.

Listing 5.8 **Invoking the Security CFC**

```
<cfobject name="mySecurityComponent" component="security">
<cfinvoke
   component="#mySecurityComponent#"
   method="authenticate"
   returnVariable="bSecResult"
   cfcUserName="amcclure"
   cfcPassword="password"
>
```

```
<cfinvoke
   component="#mySecurityComponent#"
   method="authorize"
   returnVariable="bAuthResult"
   cfcUserName="amcclure"
   lAcceptedGroups="administrators"
>
```

Notice that the code uses a `<CFOBJECT>` call to create an object called `mySecurityComponent`. By doing this, the object is not instantiated twice by the two function calls. When the code finishes, the object is destroyed automatically.

Using *<cfscript>* and the *createObject( )* Function

In a similar method to using `<CFOBJECT>` and `<CFINVOKE>`, `<CFSCRIPT>` blocks can be used to instantiate and execute CFC functions. This is a great feature of CFCs because custom tags (along with all other ColdFusion tags for that matter) cannot be called from within `<CFSCRIPT>` blocks.

To instantiate a CFC object in a `<CFSCRIPT>` block, the `createObject()` ColdFusion function is used. This function acts in a manner similar to the `<CFOBJECT>` mentioned in the earlier section "Working with Components."

An object is accessed using dot notation, just as if the object were a COM+, Java, or CORBA object. Listing 5.9 shows the same code executed in Listing 5.8, but now done in a `<CFSCRIPT>` block.

Listing 5.9 **Invoking the Security CFC with *<cfscript>***

```
<cfscript>
   mySecurity = createObject("component","security");
   args = structNew();
   args.cfcUserName = "amcclure";
   args.cfcPassword = "password";
   bSecResult = mySecurity.authenticate(argumentCollection=args);
   args = structNew();
   args.cfcUserName = "amcclure";
   args.lAcceptedGroups = "administrators";
   bAuthResult = mySecurity.authorize(argumentCollection=args);
</cfscript>
```

Here, the `argumentCollection` attribute of CFC functions passes the required arguments. Results are returned to `bSecResult` and `bAuthResult`, respectively.

By using `<cfscript>` function invocation, *all* template business logic interaction can be completed within `<cfscript>` blocks. This not only cleans up the overall code (no longer mixing `<cfscript>` blocks and other tag calls), but it also results in the proven speed increases of `<cfscript>` usage.

Other Invocation Methods

To invoke CFCs by other methods than internal ColdFusion templates, a single change must take place to the `<CFFUNCTION>` tag. You must change the access attribute to `Remote`. This one small change allows invocation of that method by URL, form post, and by the Flash Gateway. No other changes are needed!

Web service invocation normally takes a couple of extra steps, but the inherent features of ColdFusion MX and CFCs make these painless as well. First, you must create the web service WSDL file for the CFC in question. Then you must register the web service in the ColdFusion administrator.

You can register the ColdFusion administrator and generate the WSDL file automatically by simply calling the CFC as if it were a web service all along. That's it—there's nothing more to it!

If you need to register a web service by hand, just go to the Data & Services heading in the ColdFusion administrator.

Component Introspection and Metadata

All CFCs can self-describe their individual functions, attributes (both required and optional), and return types at runtime. This information is known as the component's *metadata*. This ability is what allows for the auto-generation of the WSDL file in web service publication.

Developers can also use this metadata information during template execution through a process called *component introspection*. This might seem trivial when you initially look at CFCs and their design and development, but it can actually be a powerful and advanced mechanism to create custom persistence in applications. This CFC persistence will be an integral part of the dynamic publishing architecture and will be discussed in more detail starting in Chapter 8.

For now, know that the `getMetadata()` ColdFusion function is used to gain access to this metadata information. This function, when executed within a CFC, creates a structure that contains all of the pertinent information about the CFC for the developer to use. When used from a ColdFusion template, a CFC object can be instantiated and then "passed-in" as an argument of the `getMetadata()` function.

After this structure is returned, you can use it as any other ColdFusion structure.

The *this* Variable Scope

The `this` variable scope can be used to represent the instantiated object from the calling page within the code of the CFC. This concept is important when a second function (on the same instantiated CFC object) is called from within the CFC code. Instead of invoking an entirely new CFC inside of the current CFC, the call can be made with the `this.newMethodCall()` format.

In addition, you can access any data associated with that particular object in the second method call as well. This ability will come into play again when you're dealing with custom persistence using CFCs.

For information on usage of the `this` scope, see Chapters 8 and 9.

Component Design

Due to their object-oriented characteristics (properties, functions, and inheritance), designing components and their place within an application can be tricky without tools to help describe the system. Luckily, many tools have been developed since object-oriented programming started to help meet this demand. Early efforts by pioneering object-oriented developers evolved into modeling techniques such as the popular Unified Modeling Language (UML).

By taking advantage of UML, developers can design CFCs in context to each other, showing inheritance hierarchies and relationships in an effort to define a model of the entire application in advance of a single line of code being written. Changes to the model at this early stage of development are quick and easy to do without the prospect of changing vast amounts of code. In addition, UML has visual impact that can help technical managers to see how the architecture of the system begins to match up against design documentation.

UML also helps identify similar functionality that is needed throughout the application that can be abstracted into base CFCs and inherited universally.

> **Note**
>
> To learn more about the UML and its use in application development, try these resources:
>
> - Books:
>   - ***UML Distilled***, by Martin Fowler, Kendall Scott
>   - ***Sams Teach Yourself UML in 24 Hours***, by Joseph Schmuller
> - On the web:
>   - UML Resource Center—`www.rational.com/uml/index.jsp`
>   - UML Resource Page—`www.omg.org/uml/`

Figure 5.1, a CFC UML static diagram for the security.cfc, shows that a generic dataaccess.cfc can be used throughout the application and inherited to all other CFCs without code being duplicated.

By identifying and modeling a CFC hierarchy, the place of CFCs within the overall solution becomes obvious. The CFC makes up the bulk (if not total) business logic and data access levels of the MVC architecture.

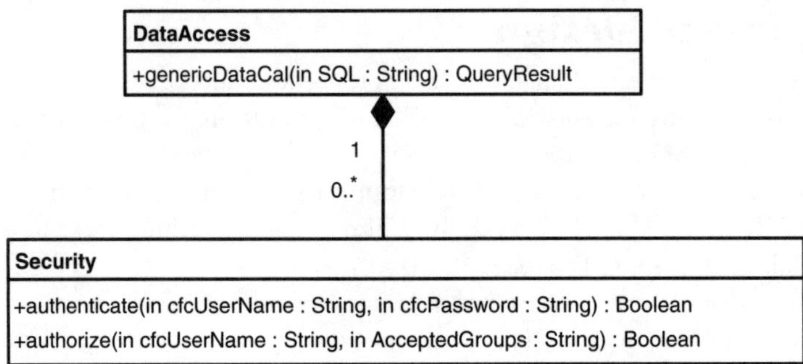

Figure 5.1 A UML example.

Conclusion

ColdFusion Components provide an amazing amount of code flexibility to the ColdFusion MX platform. With their myriad of invocation methods, introspection abilities, inheritance and package structure, built-in security, and function organization, a real revolution in ColdFusion development is on the horizon.

This chapter introduced CFCs and explained their code structure. In the most obvious of examples, it becomes easy to see the role that CFCs will play. In terms of the dynamic publishing system presented in this book, however, an even more advanced view of CFCs in application design will be examined.

6

Leveraging XML in ColdFusion MX

by Dan Blackman and Benjamin Elmore

EXTENSIBLE MARKUP LANGUAGE (XML) IS continuing to gain popularity in the global technology market. Its popularity stems from its ability to make the integration of applications a seamless task. XML allows developers to define their own specific markup languages, create self-describing data, and interchange data between disparate applications.

Why is this important? In recent years, XML has been highly touted as the standard format for sharing information between applications. In fact, XML is widely used to exchange information between many software products today. The Microsoft Office Products Suite (Excel, Access, Word, and so on), for instance, uses XML to share data between other Microsoft and non-Microsoft products alike. Excel, specifically, supports the use of Web Distributed Data Exchange (WDDX) in sharing information between it and the ColdFusion application server. The WDDX was introduced in the 3.0 release of ColdFusion and has opened doors for developers, providing an easier way to share data between applications. WDDX includes the key-value pairs, representing the data, as well as the elements datatype, to provide a well-formed, self-describing representation of the information at hand. Many applications outside of ColdFusion also have adopted WDDX as a mechanism to format and share data across applications.

Through subsequent releases, ColdFusion provided a way to build applications that support XML natively as well. However, this required additional knowledge of third-party XML parsing engines and required extended knowledge of XML parsing syntax. For the ColdFusion developer, ColdFusion MX makes the process of integrating data between disparate systems easier on the developer by shielding him from the administrative tasks of setting up the parsing engines. ColdFusion MX accomplishes this by inherently embedding the Apache Crimson parser for server-side XML parsing and Xalan for Extensible Stylesheet Language (XSL or XSLT) server-side operations within the ColdFusion application server.

Because this chapter focuses on leveraging XML in ColdFusion MX, the specific information related to the preceding products is outside the scope of this chapter. For more information on the Apache Crimson parser and the Xalan Parser for XSLT, you can go to the following web sites respectively: `http://xml.apache.org/crimson/` and `http://xml.apache.org/xalan-j/`.

This chapter explores the ins and outs of leveraging XML through ColdFusion MX. We walk through various templates demonstrating new tags and functions. We also look at how to use ColdFusion MX in wireless applications using WML and show how easy it is to extend web applications to clients other than common web browsers. This chapter assumes previous knowledge of both XML and ColdFusion. For more information on XML, visit `http://www.newriders.com`.

Working with XML Documents

To begin building our knowledge around XML and ColdFusion MX, we must first understand how to create, retrieve, and parse native XML documents. This chapter walks us through the creation of XML documents using tags and functions, retrieving XML documents using multiple techniques, and parsing XML documents into the XML Object.

To work with XML documents, we first must understand how the document is structured. Because XML is a meta-markup language, we can use it to describe virtually any type of data. In this case, we are using XML to describe a product catalog by a supplier. In Listing 6.1, we see a sample XML document called catalog.xml. This XML document serves as a base for most of the examples we use in this chapter.

Listing 6.1 **catalog.xml**

```
<?xml version="1.0"?>
<catalog>
  <supplier name="Exotic Liquids">
    <address>49 Gilbert St.</address>
...
    <product code="100">
      <name>Chai</name>
      <quantityperunit>10 boxes</quantityperunit>
      <unitprice>18.00</unitprice>
```

```
    </product>
  </supplier>
...
</catalog>
```

Our catalog.xml document contains elements that describe a supplier catalog. The outermost element, the <CATALOG> element, represents the root element of the XML document. By rule, each XML document must contain only one root element. The <CATALOG> element also acts as a parent to the <SUPPLIER> element, which in turn, acts as the parent to the <PRODUCT> elements. This is important to understand because of how ColdFusion MX exposes the document hierarchy through the XML Object. In other XML documents, the root element has a different name. If we were describing a product XML document, the root element might be called Products. This allows us to describe the data in the file at the highest level, or the *root level*.

Another important consideration in working with XML documents is the inherent adaptability. XML documents take many shapes. The most common form of an XML document is a text-based file with an .xml extension. The file usually resides on a file server or web server and serves as one way to exchange information using XML. This method usually results in a higher amount of network traffic because the XML files require retrieval. This can be mitigated with a persistence strategy. Data manipulation takes place by simply reading the file and making changes to the data. After the changes are made, we simply save the file back to the file server and the data is persisted. Another common way to store XML files is within a relational database by creating a new XML document and storing the results in a database entry. This method requires less network traffic, but it increases the load on the database server. Again, this can be mitigated through the use of a persistence strategy. Chapters 8, "ColdFusion Components with Persistence," 9, "Centralized Data Persistence," and 10, "Persistence with Localization," focus on persistence and how to make use of it within web applications.

Creating the XML Document Object Using ColdFusion

With an understanding of the XML document, we have a foundation to create XML documents using ColdFusion MX. ColdFusion MX offers several ways to create XML document objects:

- <CFXML> tag
- `xmlNew()` and `xmlElemNew()` functions
- Using existing XML documents

Using the *<CFXML>* tag

The easiest and most straightforward way to create an XML Object is through the use of the new <CFXML> tag (see Listing 6.2).

Listing 6.2 **<*CFXML*> Tag**

```
<cfxml variable="catalog">
  ...
  XML and CFML code
  ...
</cfxml>
```

In this example, the `<CFXML>` tag uses a single attribute called variable to create an XML Document Object stored under the name provided (see Table 6.1).

Table 6.1 **<*CFXML*> Attributes**

Attribute	Required	Data Type	Description
`Variable`	Yes	String	This attribute acts as the name of the structure that the `<CFXML>` tag produces.
`casesensitive`	No	Boolean	This attribute sets the case sensitivity of the XML elements and attributes within the XML document object

The `<CFXML>` tag uses a start tag and an end tag to build the XML document object. Much like writing a nested custom tag, the code inside is processed between the start and end tags. In many cases, the code inside is a combination of CFML and XML. CFML provides the dynamic data output, and XML provides the structure of the document that is output.

> **Note**
>
> The XML tag structure within the start and end tags must be well formed. If a tag is misspelled or missing, ColdFusion throws the following error:
>
> ```
> Expected "" to terminate element starting on line xx
> ```

The code in Listing 6.3 demonstrates the `<CFXML>` tag using a real-world example. Here, we build a product catalog grouped by supplier.

Listing 6.3 **<*CFXML*> Example**

```
<!--- fetch the Catalog information --->
<cfquery name="qCatalogGet" datasource="DynPub">
Select s.CompanyName, s.Address, s.City, s.State,
Zipcode, p.Code, p.Name as productName,
p.Quantityperunit, p.Unitprice
  From suppliers s, products p
  Where s.supplierid = p.supplierid
  Order By s.CompanyName, p.Name
</cfquery>
```

```

<!--- Create the XML document object --->
<cfxml variable="catalog">

 <!--- Root Element --->
  <catalog>
    <cfoutput query="qCatalogGet" Group="CompanyName">
      <supplier name="#CompanyName#">
      <address>#address#</address>
      <city>#city#</city>
      <state>#state#</state>
      <zipcode>#zipCode#</zipcode>
      <cfoutput>
      <product code="#qCatalogGet.Code#">
          <name>#productName#</name>
          <quantityperunit>#quantityPerUnit#
</quantityperunit>
          <unitprice>#unitPrice#</unitprice>
          </product>
      </cfoutput>
      </supplier>
    </cfoutput>
  </catalog>
</cfxml>
```

All code is processed between the `<CFXML>` start and end tags, and an XML Object is returned and assigned to the variable name that is used as a reference.

After the XML Object is created, we use the ColdFusion `toString()` function to transform the XML Object back into an XML string. This allows us to write the string to a file server, database, or other storage facility and in another transaction.

Using XML Functions

Although the `<CFXML>` tag provides a useful way of creating XML Objects, the `xmlNew()` and `xmlElemNew()` functions provide a new look at creating the XML document object. The `xmlNew()` and `xmlElemNew()` functions provide a more dynamic way of building XML documents (see Table 6.2).

Table 6.2 ***xmlNew( )* and *xmlElemNew( )***

Function	Description
`xmlNew()`	This function creates new XML Object. By setting a variable as a reference to the object (catalogXml = xmlNew();), we can continue to refer to it by name.
`xmlElemNew()`	The `xmlElemNew()` function is used to build each element within the XML Object hierarchy.

In the catalog2xmlfunction.cfm code, we build the catalog XML Object using a complex data type (an array of structures), as shown in Listing 6.4.

Listing 6.4 ***xmlNew( )* and *xmlElemNew( )* Functions**

```
  // Create a new document and root element
  catalogXml = xmlNew();
catalogXml.xmlRoot = xmlElemNew(catalogXml, "catalog");
```

Using the `xmlNew()` function, we initialize catalogXml as an XML Object. After the XML Object is initialized, we can create the `xmlRoot` element and assign its new value ("`catalog`"). Using the catalog2xmlfunction.cfm document, we can see how easy it is to create a new XML document and elements using the `xmlNew()` and `xmlElemNew()` functions. Listing 6.5 demonstrates their interactions.

Listing 6.5 **catalog2xmlfunction.cfm**

```
// Let's create the supplier element
supplier = xmlElemNew(catalogXml, "supplier");
//Set the attribute [name] to the supplier name
  supplier.XmlAttributes["name"] = aSupplier[i].name;
.
.
//Loop over the products array and set up each element
  for(x=1; x lte arrayLen(aSupplier[i].product);x=x+1)
  {
    product = XMLElemNew(catalogXml, "product");
    product.name = XmlElemNew(catalogXML, "name");
    //Set the text value for the product
    product.name.xmlText = aSupplier[i].product[x].name;.
    .
    //Append the products to the supplier
ArrayAppend(supplier.XmlChildren, product);
  }
    //Append the array supplier to the root catalog
    ArrayAppend(catalogXml.XmlRoot.XmlChildren, supplier);
```

Retrieving XML Documents

As mentioned earlier, XML documents come in many shapes and sizes. To pull the documents into memory, we must leverage certain tags and functions within ColdFusion.

Using the *<CFFILE>* Tag

Because many XML documents are presented in a text file format, the first thing we must do is read the file into memory. In Listing 6.6, we see how to retrieve the file using the `<CFFILE>` tag.

Listing 6.6 ***<CFFILE>* Tag**

```
<cffile action="READ" file="e:\cfusionmx\wwwroot\xmlapp\includes\ products.xml"
   VARIABLE="ProductsXml">
```

The `<CFFILE>` tag reads the document into memory using a variable called ProductsXml. After the XML document is in memory, it can be parsed into an XML Object.

Using the *<CFQUERY>* Tag

Another form of XML storage is as a database entry. Many times, the data is used to store complex data, such as XML, which allows rapid access to the XML document. The ColdFusion `<CFQUERY>` tag reads the XML document from storage in the same manner that it retrieves fields from the database server. Because the XML document is stored as a string, the data type is common to all database servers (see Listing 6.7).

Listing 6.7 ***<CFQUERY>* Tag**

```
<cfquery name="qCatalogGet">
  Select catalogXml
  From catalog
  Where supplierId = 100
</cfquery>
```

Here, we leverage the `<CFQUERY>` tag to query the catalogXml data entry for supplier 100. We then can simply refer to the `qCataloGet.catalogXml` variable name to parse the XML content.

Using the *<CFHTTP>* Tag

A popular way to syndicate content is by using the `<CFHTTP>` tag. Using this technique, we execute a `get` operation on remote XML files using the `<CFHTTP>` tag to retrieve the XML data within. This allows us to display the information on a local web page. Listing 6.8 demonstrates the `<CFHTTP>` tag executing a `get` method on the news0402.xml file.

Listing 6.8 ***<CFHTTP>* Tag**

```
<cfhttp method="Get" url="http://www.xyzcompany.com/news/news0402.xml"
.
.
<cfscript>newsXml = cfhttp.fileContent</script>
```

After the `<CFHTTP>` tag is executed and the `newsXml` variable is created, we can use the `xml` variable as a local XML document. A number of syndication web sites are available for content syndication. SlashDot.org and Moreover.com are two companies that allow syndication of content, such as news stories and stock quotes.

Parsing XML Documents

After the XML document is in memory, we use the new `xmlParse()` function to parse it into an XML Object. In Listing 6.9, we read the XML file into memory. We then use the `xmlParse()` function to parse the document into the XML Object. Listing 6.9 shows the XML Object represented by the variable `productsXml`.

Listing 6.9 **Parsing XML Documents: products.cfm**

```
<!--- Read the XML file --->
  <cffile action="READ"
    file="e:\cfusionmx\wwwroot\xmlapp\includes\products.xml"
    variable="Products">

  <cfscript>

  //Parse the productsXml
  productsXml = XmlParse(Products);
```

> **Note**
>
> The XML document that is passed to the `xmlParse()` function must be well formed. If a tag is misspelled or not present, ColdFusion throws the following error:
>
> `Expected "" to terminate element starting on line xx`

ColdFusion exposes the element node types in each element structure. The `xmlParse()` function's sole purpose is to parse XML documents and create the XML Object. However, even though it's a relatively simple approach, the `xmlParse()` function opens doors to the world of Document Object Model (DOM) objects, properties, and methods and can handle and perform complex operations. ColdFusion MX allows you to use the DOM and built-in ColdFusion functions to create powerful XML applications.

XML DOM Driven Through the New XML Object

If you have used XML in the past, you are probably familiar with XML DOM. This portion of the chapter looks at the XML DOM and the ColdFusion XML Object and ascertains the differences between the two.

Overview of the XML DOM

The W3C defines the XML DOM as "a programming interface for XML documents." It contains a vast amount of properties and methods for use in navigating the XML document hierarchy and adding, modifying, or deleting any of its elements. The DOM is built to work with many programming languages and XML parsers. Programmers use an XML parser to load the document into memory and then use the DOM's properties and methods to navigate the hierarchy, retrieve data, and manipulate the XML document.

Listing 6.10 demonstrates a basic example of the DOM's capabilities. To learn more about the DOM and its capabilities, visit the W3C web site at `www.w3c.org`.

Listing 6.10 **JavaScript DOM Example**

```
<script>

  //Create the DOM Object using the createObject function
  xmlDoc = CreateObject("Microsoft.XMLDom");
  xmlDoc.async = false;
  // Read in the XML file
  xmlDoc.load("note.xml")

  // Loop over the childNodes and display them using HTML
  for each x in xmlDoc.documentElement.childNodes
    document.write(x.nodeName & "<br />")
  next
</script>
```

Node Types

Within the DOM, object elements are broken down into nodes, represented as a hierarchical tree. When we look at the tree as a whole, we see that it is made up of nodes with different types. We can see in Table 6.3 how the node types help describe the elements and provide more descriptive access to the node objects.

Table 6.3 **Node Types***

Node Type	Node Name	Example
element	tagName	`<name>Tea Time Biscuits</name>`
attribute	name	`<product code="100">`
text	#text	chai
cdatasection	#cdatasection	character data not parsed by XML parser
entityreference	entity reference name	`<!entity copy02 "Copyright 2002">`
entity	entity name	`& < >`
processinginstruction	target	`<?xml version="1.0"?>`
comment	#comment	any string comment

continues

Table 6.3 **Continued**

Node Type	Node Name	Example
document	#document	name of document element
documenttype	doctype name	`<!doctype products SYSTEM "products.dtd">`
documentfragment	#document fragment	
notation	notation name	`<!notation MF SYSTEM "myfile.exe">`

* Table from w3schools.com

The ColdFusion MX XML Document Object

The ColdFusion XML Document Object (XML Object) is a ColdFusion structure that contains the DOM node names and values. The structure of the document allows for a full representation of the nodes. To view an XML Object in ColdFusion, use the <CFDUMP> tag and specify the name of the XML Object variable assigned at creation.

> **Note**
> Not all nodes are present when the <CFDUMP> displays the XML element structure. For example, xmlDocType node, xmlParent, and the xmlNodes array are not present with the dump. To view nodes that are not represented, use <CFOUTPUT> to display the values.

The top level of the XML Object is represented by three properties: xmlRoot, xmlComment, and xmlDocType, as shown in Table 6.4.

Table 6.4 **Document Object Structure**

Property	Description
xmlRoot	Contains the top-level element in the XML Object.
xmlComment	Identifies the comment space within the top-level root element.
xmlDocType*	Identifies the Doctype attribute. Allows the entry of a document type declaration.

*The xmlDocType does not exist if the entry is not specified.

The basic element structure is represented by the properties shown in Table 6.5.

Table 6.5 **Element Structure**

Property	Description
XmlName	The name of the element.
XmlNsPrefix	The prefix for the XML namespace, such as xsl for the XSL namespace.
XmlNsURI	The URI of the namespace, such as http://www.w3.org/XSL/Transform/1.0 for the preceding xsl prefix.

Property	Description
`XmlText`	The text value of the XML element. The string value between the start and end tags of the element.
`XmlComment`	The string representation of comments within the element.
`xmlAttributes`	A ColdFusion structure containing name-value pairs of the attributes within the element.
`XmlChildren`	A ColdFusion array representing the child elements of a parent element.

Not all the values are used at once. It merely provides the ability to store information about an element using nodes and values. Nodes are individual values along the DOM tree structure that make up an element. For instance, the catalog XML root element is made up of several nodes describing the XMLName, XML text, any comments, and so on related to the element.

Assigning Values

Because the elements within the XML Object are represented by ColdFusion structures and arrays, ColdFusion programmers will find working with the XML Object quite familiar. Programmers can simply use the familiar dot notation syntax (.) to set properties values. Table 6.6 shows the differences between using a function and using an assignment.

Table 6.6 **Adding, Modifying, and Deleting Values**

Using a Function	Using an Assignment
`StructInsert(supplier.xmlAttributes,`	`Supplier.xmlAttributes["name"]`
`"name", "Specialty Biscuits, Ltd.")`	`= "Specialty Biscuits, Ltd."`
`arrayAppend(catalogXml.XmlRoot.`	`catalog.xmlRoot.xmlChildren[i]`
`XmlChildren, supplier);`	`= supplier`
`structUpdate(supplier.city,` ➥`"xmlText", aSupplier[i].city);`	`supplier.city.xmlText =` ➥`aSupplier[i].city;`

In Table 6.6, we set an attribute within the supplier tag to the value `"Specialty Biscuits, Ltd"`. We also append a group of elements (`supplier`) and its children (`product`) to the catalogXml.XmlRoot element and update the xmlText of the `supplier.city` element to the value of the city key in the `aSupplier` array. ColdFusion allows us to use standard functions or simple assignment syntax to accomplish this task. A ColdFusion developer who is familiar with this syntax should have no problem assigning values to the XML Object.

Modifying the XML Object

Along with retrieving information and assigning values, ColdFusion allows us to manipulate the XML Object using built-in tags and functions.

Adding Elements

Adding elements to an existing XML Object is a straightforward task. In Listing 6.4, we saw how to use the `xmlElemNew()` function to create a new element within a newly created XML Object. Using the `ArrayInsertAt` function along with the `xmlElemNew()` function, we are able to insert an element into an "existing" XML Object. We also can use `arrayAppend` to append a new element to the `xmlChildren` array of an existing element (see Listing 6.11).

Listing 6.11 **Adding an Element to an Existing XML Object**

```
<cfscript>
ArrayInsertAt(catalogRoot.supplier.xmlChildren, 1,
xmlElemNew(catalogXML,
"Contact");

ArrayAppend(catalogRoot.supplier[1].xmlChildren,
xmlElemNew(catalogXML, "Contact Title");

</cfscript>
```

Copying Elements

Because each set of element nodes is exposed as a ColdFusion structure, we can copy the entire element using the built-in `Duplicate()` function. The `Duplicate()` function copies the entire structure along with any nested child elements. After the elements are copied, we can modify them to build a new XML document or use ColdFusion functions to assign and modify values.

Listing 6.12 demonstrates the use of the `Duplicate()` function to create a new copy of the catalogXml Object.

Listing 6.12 **Copying the Existing XML Object**

```
<cfscript>

  // Copy the entire XML structure and initialize to newCatalogXML
  newCatalogXml = Duplicate(catalogXml);

  // Set the attribute "name" to the value "Salty Dog"
  newCatalogXml.supplier[1].xmlAttributes["name"] = "Salty Dog";

</cfscript>
```

Removing Elements

Removing elements from the XML Object is as simple as adding them. Removing an attribute(s) from the xmlAttributes structure is a straightforward task that uses the `structDelete()` function. The `structDelete()` function removes the attribute and its associated value from the element that is specified. To remove a specific element from the hierarchy, we use the `arrayDeleteAt()` function. This function removes the element at the position specified within the function. We also can use functions, such as `arrayClear`, to remove multiple elements from an element structure.

Listing 6.13 demonstrates the use of `struct` and `array` functions in removing attributes and element structures.

Listing 6.13 **Removing an Element from an Existing XML Object**

```
<cfscript>

  // Removes the attribute name from the supplier element
StructDelete(catalogXml.supplier[1].xmlAttributes, "name");

// Removes the three product elements from the supplier parent element
ArrayDeleteAt(catalogXml.supplier.xmlChildren, 3);

// Removes the product elements from supplier parent element
ArrayClear(catalogXml.supplier.xmlChildren);
</cfscript>
```

Using Direct Assignment

We also can use direct assignment to accomplish many of the modifications to elements. Using the preceding examples, in Listing 6.14 we accomplish many of the same tasks using direct assignment.

Listing 6.14 **Modifying Elements Using Direct Assignment**

```
<cfscript>
  catalogRoot.supplier[1].xmlChildren[10] =
  xmlElemNew(catalogXML, "Contact Title");

catalogXml.supplier[1].xmlAttributes["name"] = "";

  catalogXml.supplier[1].address = catalogXml[2].address;

</cfscript>
```

However, we must follow specific rules when using direct assignment. When using direct assignment, it is a good practice to be aware of the rules:

- **Assigning elements to the `xmlChildren` array**—The index on the left side must be greater than the last child in the array.

- **Inserting elements into an array of elements**—You must use the `ArrayInsertAt()` function to insert these elements. You cannot use direct assignment.
- **Adding an element to the hierarchy**—The node name on the left side of the assignment cannot be the same as the new element on the right side of the assignment.
- **Copying element values from one key to another**—The node names must be the same on each side. The key holding the new value becomes a copy of the original, not a reference to the original.
- **Changing an element's name directly**—You cannot change an element's name directly because the XML DOM does not support the event. You must create a new element, reassign the value, and then remove the original.

> **Note**
>
> From a performance perspective, functions are optimized for faster performance through precompiled code. Thus, using functions to modify elements and their values is a better practice than using direct assignment.

Searching XML Documents Using XPath and xmlSearch

As part of the W3C XSLT standard (explained later in the section "Transforming XML Documents Using XSLT"), XPath is a syntax for defining and accessing data within an XML document. XPath syntax allows us to specify a path along the XML Object tree. The tree is a typical hierarchy, much like a directory hierarchy we use to organize web documents. Just as we specify the directory path in a URL, we begin with a single slash (/), which specifies the document. Because the root element is the first element in the hierarchy, we must specify the `"/products"` element as the first element in our path. As we continue down the hierarchy, we add child nodes of each element. This allows us to traverse the tree and pull the information we need from the XML document.

Listing 6.15 demonstrates these concepts using the products.cfm template.

Listing 6.15 ***xmlSearch()*—products.cfm**

```
<cfscript>

 // Use XML Parse to parse the XML document
 productsXml = XmlParse(productsDoc);

 // Check to see if the price has been passed in....
 if(structKeyExists(form, "price"))
 {

```

```
     // Search the form using the name attribute
aProducts = XmlSearch(productsXml,
"/products/product[unitprice>=#form.price#]");
  }else{

     //Set the Products to the Products array.

     aProducts = ProductsXml.XMLRoot.XMLChildren;
  }
</cfscript>
```

The template receives input from a form variable called `price`. If this `price` is passed in, we use the `xmlSearch()` and `XPath` syntax to find products with a price greater than the form variable "`price`" that is passed into the template.

In addition to using standard slashes and elements within our path, we also can use a series of expressions and functions to further delineate the information that is returned. We can use relational and Boolean operators to compare values. In addition, we can use functions to format strings and numbers to further extend capabilities. We accomplish this simply by entering multiple expressions within the brackets (`[]`) joining them using `and` and `or` operators. For instance, consider the following searches.

Find products by name:

```
/products/product[name="Chai"].
```

This returns all products with the name `"Chai"`.

Find product with id `"100"`:

```
aProducts = XmlSearch(oProducts, "/products/product[id="100"] Or

// here we use the @ symbol to specify an attribute.
aProducts = XmlSearch(Products, "/products/product[@id='#url.productId#'
➥and name="Chai"]");
```

The last example demonstrates how we can use ColdFusion syntax to create dynamic searches using XPath.

For more information and books related to the extensive XPath syntax, check out `www.w3.org/TR/xpath` and the XML books on the `www.newriders.com` web site, respectively.

Transforming XML Documents Using XSLT

XSLT provides a way for developers to transform XML documents into a new format. What does this mean? XSL, an XML language in itself, provides a separate, yet equally powerful, language for transforming and formatting XML documents. The transformation half of the language is powerful. Its ability to move data from one XML document to another is vital to many applications that are built around the technology. The formatting of half XSLT allows developers to specify a format for which to represent the XML document. One of the benefits of XML/XSLT used in conjunction with the other is the ability to separate the data from the formatting display.

To transform the catalog.xml document in Listing 6.1, we need to create a style sheet using XSLT. In doing this, we use XSLT intermingled with well-formed HTML to create the catalog.xsl document. This document contains the syntax we use to apply the transformation to the catalog.xml document. We see a portion of the XSL template in Listing 6.16.

Listing 6.16 **catalog.xsl**

```
<?xml version='1.0'?>
<xsl:stylesheet xmlns:xsl="http://www.w3.org/1999/XSL/Transform"
version="1.0">
// Output the results in HTML
<xsl:output method="html"/>

// Match the root element of the XML document
<xsl:template match="/">
  <table>
    <tr>
      <td>
// Fetch each of the Supplier elements and format in an HTML table
        <xsl:apply-templates select="/catalog/supplier"/>
      </td>
    </tr>
  </table>
</xsl:template>

// Match the name of the element named "supplier"
<xsl:template match="supplier">
...
  <tr>
    <td>
  // Get the value of the name attribute
<xsl:value-of select="@name"/>
</td>
    <td>
// Get the value of the address text
<xsl:value-of select="address"/>
</td>
...
  </tr>
  <tr>
    <td colspan="5">
      <table>
        <tr bgcolor="#DDDDDD">
          <td>Product Name</td>
          <td>Quantity per unit</td>
          <td>Unit Price</td>
        </tr>
        /// Fetch the product elements
        <xsl:apply-templates select="product" />
```

```
        </table>

      </td>
    </tr>
...
</xsl:template>
...
</xsl:stylesheet>
```

Now that we have an XSLT file to work with, we can use ColdFusion's new `xmlTransform()` function. This function helps apply the XSLT syntax against the XML document, creating a separate and new XML document. The `xmlTransform()` function takes two arguments:

- **XML Object**—Acts as the XML document to be transformed
- **XSL document**—Variable assigned to the path and filename of the XSL document

The transformxml.cfm template (see Listing 6.17) demonstrates how we use the `xmltransform()` function to apply the style sheet.

Listing 6.17 **Transforming catalog.xml**

```
<cfscript>
   // Parse the XML document
  catalogXml = xmlParse(xmlDoc);
 // Use the XML document and XSLT template to transform the document
   transformedXml = xmlTransform(catalogXml,xslDoc);
</cfscript>
```

The first step is to read the XML and XSL documents from the file system. We then must parse the XML document to pass the XML Object to the `xmlTranform()` function.

> **Note**
>
> Using contemporary methods, we attach the style sheet to the XML document and apply the style sheet to the XML document in that manner. In this case, we supply the documents separately because we are using two separate parsers. The `xmlParse()` function does not apply style sheet transforms to an XML document with attached XSLT documents.

The next step is simple. We use the `xmlTransform()` function to apply the XSL document to the XML Object. The newly transformed XML document is referenced by the variable named `transformedXml`. We can then use the `<CFDUMP>` tag to dump the variable and view the results.

Creating a Wireless Application Using ColdFusion MX

Wireless Markup Language (WML) was created to serve up Internet content to handheld devices, PDAs, and cell phones. Using ColdFusion MX, serving up dynamic WML documents has never been so easy. Using several approaches, we find that we can build powerful and interactive WML applications.

The first approach calls for using the techniques we learned in Listings 6.10 and 6.11. Within the \wireless\supplier.xsl document, we use HTML markup along with WML so that the XML content can work with wireless interfaces. Within the /wireless/supplierfind2.cfm document, similar to the /transformxml.cfm document, we add the`<CFCONTENT>` tag. This allows us to change the MIME type of the document served up at runtime—in this case, `"text/vnd.wap.wml"`. We also added an XML declaration and the `DocType` attribute for the WML DTD. The result of the transformation is a WML document that displays the suppliers in the catalog.xml document. See Listing 6.18.

Listing 6.18 **Using *<CFCONTENT>* to Build Wireless Documents**

```
<cfcontent type="text/vnd.wap.wml" >
<cfoutput>
  <?xml version="1.0"?>
  <!DOCTYPE wml PUBLIC "-//WAPFORUM//DTD WML 1.1//EN"
 "http://www.wapforum.org/DTD/wml_1.1.xml">
     #transformedXml#
  </cfoutput>
```

With few changes to existing files, we see that migrating dynamic, browser-based content to wireless content is a simple, straightforward process.

In a second approach, we use the `xmlParse()` function to create an XML Object. We then use ColdFusion and WML syntax to build a dynamic template that, at runtime, becomes WML content. Within the supplierfind.cfm page, we catch our first glimpse at how ColdFusion and WML work together to present XML data in a WML format. See Listing 6.19.

Listing 6.19 **Transforming catalog.xml**

```
<cfcontent type="text/vnd.wap.wml">
...
<cfscript>
  stCatalog = xmlParse(catalog);
  catalogRoot = stCatalog.xmlRoot;
</cfscript>
...
<?xml version="1.0"?>
<!DOCTYPE wml PUBLIC "-//WAPFORUM//DTD WML 1.1//EN"
"http://www.wapforum.org/DTD/wml_1.1.xml">
<wml>
    <card>
```

Again, we see the <CFCONTENT> tag that we used to define the MIME type returned to the current page requested. After we read and parse the XML document, we loop over the available nodes and display the data using WML. As you move through the document, you can see the integration of WML and well-formed HTML. This allows the user to interact with the document using an Internet-ready PDA or cell phone. Products on the market today make it easy to test WML applications. In this case, we used OpenWave's UP4.1 Simulator to test and validate the interaction the between the various technologies.

Conclusion

As we have seen, leveraging XML through ColdFusion MX is a relatively simple approach. We now understand that, through the use of ColdFusion MX, we can construct web applications that allow us to work with XML documents in ways that were difficult in the past. We covered how we can leverage XML to create XML documents, read and retrieve the document, and parse the XML documents to create a ColdFusion XML Object. We also explored how to use the built-in ColdFusion functions to work against the XML DOM Object within ColdFusion by assigning and updating values in the hierarchy and modifying the actual XML Object. Last, we explored how to leverage XML to build WML applications for Internet-ready PDAs and other handheld devices. Through this exploration, we should now have the knowledge to apply the concepts to our own real-world examples. This allows us to continue to build rapid application using ColdFusion, yet extend our capabilities by applying these concepts.

7

Java Interoperability with ColdFusion MX

by Allen Benson

ALTHOUGH JAVA WAS ORIGINALLY CONCEIVED as a platform-independent client-based programming language, it rapidly evolved into an extremely powerful and popular server-side application development environment. Through the introduction of a rich set of standard application programming interfaces (APIs), the Sun Microsystems-led Java Community Process has provided developers with the tools needed to build robust, reliable enterprise systems. Today, nearly every major corporation in the world has developed and implemented some form of Java-based applications to mainstream their business. These applications provide the backbone of many of our commerce, financial, insurance, and other systems today.

As we have discussed previously, it is rare that application development today can be done completely from scratch. Although new data repositories can be created and new processing systems can be programmed, a ColdFusion MX-based system, as well as other J2EE platforms, can utilize easily vast numbers of existing Java-based applications. This concept is known as *Java interoperability*. Previous versions of ColdFusion allowed limited interoperability with Java components through the `<CFOBJECT>` and `<CFSERVLET>` tags. ColdFusion MX, based on the Java 2 Enterprise Edition (J2EE) technology platform, takes this integration to a new level by providing native connectivity through the platform.

With ColdFusion MX Java interoperability, organizations can leverage many different skill sets. Java developers can build servlets, JavaServer pages, custom JSP tag libraries, JavaBeans, Enterprise JavaBeans, and many other components. ColdFusion developers can code in ColdFusion Markup Language (CFML). The Java components and the CFML components can then be combined into one or more applications. With this enhanced interoperability, a dynamic publishing system can utilize the best of both technologies.

This chapter briefly examines common Java components in web applications and describes how they work together in a typical system. It then examines the means by which these components can interoperate with ColdFusion MX.

Common Java Components in Web Applications

To understand the various ways in which you can achieve Java interoperability with ColdFusion MX, it is important to understand the many types of Java components that you can utilize in a web application and the roles that they play. These components are discussed in the following sections:

- Java classes
- JavaBeans
- Servlets
- JavaServer pages (JSP)
- JSP custom tags
- Enterprise JavaBeans (EJB)
- Java Message Service (JMS)

For more on the background of the Java language, an overview of the syntax and available APIs, and other introductory information, visit `http://java.sun.com`. The following links from that site are good for introductory overviews:

- **New to Java?**—`http://developer.java.sun.com/developer/onlineTraining/new2java/`
- **What Is Java?**—`http://java.sun.com/java2/whatis/`
- **Getting Started**—`http://developer.java.sun.com/developer/onlineTraining/ new2java/gettingstartedjava.html`

Java Classes

The simplest Java component is the *class*. Classes are programmed by writing Java source code and storing it in a text file with a .java extension. The code is compiled using a Java compiler into a binary class file with a .class extension. In a Java program, instances of different classes are created. You can structure classes so that these instances can contain their own unique data and perform operations. The instances send each other messages to request this data or to request that operations be performed. In a sense, a running Java program is an environment made up of these created instances, all functioning together to accomplish a set of tasks. Think of a Java class as the basic building block to all of the other different components discussed in this section.

Another important aspect about Java classes is that they are hierarchical in terms of organization. In fact, you can draw the entire Java class library as a tree structure, with the class object at the top. When a new class is programmed, it can inherit either from the class object or from another class in the hierarchy. If the new class inherits from another class (termed *extending* the other class,) it automatically inherits the ability to contain the same type of data and perform the same operations as the extended class and all classes above the extended class in the hierarchy.

JavaBeans

A *JavaBean* is a Java class that follows a particular specification for retrieval of the bean's data, called *properties*, and a request for the bean's operations, called *methods*. By following the JavaBean specification when coding, programmers allow tools and applications to easily use these components. Some integrated development environments, for example, allow developers to visually construct applications using JavaBeans by exposing the properties and methods in a graphical environment. Developers can connect these components together visually to build real applications.

Servlets

A *servlet* is a server-side Java program that you can access directly from a web client through a tag in a web page. As a single Java class, a servlet inherits the capability to open streams (communication channels) to and from the client, retrieve parameters passed from the client, and access session information. Through these streams, the servlet can receive a request from the client and also respond. The request might contain parameters passed from the web client, such as form input. The response is usually a string of characters containing HTML or XML. Because the servlet is written in Java, it can process between the time it receives the request and sends the response. This allows the servlet to send back dynamic information. A typical example would be a servlet that retrieves and writes back account information from a database based on user information passed to it in the request.

Because a servlet is written in Java, it has easy access to any other Java object on the server. In the architecture that this chapter discusses, the servlet typically does not perform actual business processing; instead, it calls other objects that perform that processing. When that processing is complete, the information is passed back to the servlet and then back to the client. We will explore the role of servlets in an entire application more in depth shortly.

JavaServer Pages

As Java programmers began to write more servlets, it became apparent that they needed to know more about creating web pages because the content had to be written into the code. In addition, web developers who created content typically were not Java programmers. Therefore, programming servlets to write back web content became onerous and error prone. Web content was tightly coupled with business logic, which made changes to content costly. It is important to separate (or *decouple*) the business logic layer from the Presentation layer. Using servlets to write information back directly did not allow that.

The Sun Microsystems-led standards consortium (now known as the *Java Community Process*) developed a new specification called the *JavaServer Pages*, or *JSP*. Based on Microsoft's "active server page" model, the JSP specification allows for an HTML-based web page to contain actual Java code and Java-based tags that call Java code. The page is named with a .jsp extension, signaling to a web server that it needs to send the JSP to an associated Java application server for preprocessing. The application server dynamically creates a new Java servlet behind the scenes, which writes the dynamic content back to the client based on the processing by the Java code. The huge advantage, obviously, is that web content designers can create HTML-like pages using tags to supply the dynamic content. This is the same way ColdFusion works. In this case, however, developers can supply the Java-based tags to provide the interface to the backend Java applications. Static content is separated from business logic, allowing designers to change the overall page layout without altering the dynamic content.

JSP Custom Tags

The JSP 1.2 specification provides nine standard tags for general types of tasks such as specifying a JavaBean, importing Java packages, and including files. In addition, syntax is provided for including Java code scripts and expressions in the page. Each of the standard tags has assorted attributes to provide information. Table 7.1 provides only a brief explanation for each tag. For more detailed information, see the JavaServer Pages 1.2 Specification, which is available at `http://java.sun.com`.

Table 7.1 **JavaServer Pages 1.2 Specification Standard Tags**

Tag	Purpose
`<JSP:USEBEAN>`	Associates an instance of a Java object with the page
`<JSP:SETPROPERTY>`	Sets the value of a property of the object
`<JSP:GETPROPERTY>`	Accesses the value of a property of the object and displays it on the page
`<JSP:INCLUDE>`	Includes other resources in the context of the page
`<JSP:FORWARD>`	Dispatches the request to another resource and terminates the execution of the page
`<JSP:PARAM>`	Provides key/value input for the `<JSP:INCLUDE>`, `<JSP:FORWARD>`, and `<JSP:PARAMS>` tags

Tag	Purpose
<JSP:PLUGIN>	Provides the capability to specify the download of a Java plug-in, applet, or JavaBean for execution
<JSP:PARAMS>	Provides parameters for the <JSP:PLUGIN> tag only
<JSP:FALLBACK>	Presents a message to the user in the event of plug-in failure

In addition to this, the specification allows for the creation of unique "custom" tags. This means that the Java developers can write specific applications for the server and then write custom tags for the web content designers to use to interface to these applications from the JavaServer Pages. This is similar to the ability that ColdFusion developers have of writing ColdFusion custom tags.

Enterprise JavaBeans (EJB)

Many times it is useful to use objects in a distributed manner. A good example is the ability to access a corporate data store in one location from many different applications in different locations. This allows greater reuse of code and better separation of the business, data, and presentation layers.

The EJB specification that the Java Community Process developed set out a set of standards for application vendors to implement. Every application server that supports the EJB specification provides all the services necessary for distributed communication. In this manner, developers can concentrate on creating the business and data access layer code, rather than worry about the underlying communication protocols.

The EJB 2.0 specification provides three types of beans:

- A session bean, which controls the programming and flow aspect of a particular session
- An entity bean, which encapsulates data it retrieves from a particular data source
- A message-driven bean, which allows easier access to messaging systems based on the Java Message Service (JMS) specification.

Entity beans in particular are interesting because they also provide the underlying data retrieval and store code themselves as part of the specification. Through a mechanism called *container managed persistence* (CMP), the programmer only needs to specify the database, tables, and rows associated with the properties of the EJB. When the EJB is compiled, the *container* (the part of the J2EE application server that handles the EJB) generates all the underlying code for reading and writing to and from the database. If the read/write function is more complicated (for example, data is stored in multiple databases or multiple tables), the programmer can write the underlying code if desired. This is called *bean managed persistence* (BMP).

More types of EJBs might be developed in the future as the specification evolves.

JMS

The JMS specification provides the standard for Java application server vendors in creating messaging systems. Messaging systems act very much like email. With email, another person (or system) can send a message to you anytime he wants, and it arrives at your server account. You do not have to be online and logged into email for the message to be sent. Then, at the time you desire, you can log in and retrieve your messages from the server. You and many others also can subscribe to a mailing list, and anytime the publisher of the list sends out a message, everyone on the list receives it. In software application messaging systems, applications can send messages to each other, providing information needed for processing. The best part is that they do not need to be connected physically. This allows for asynchronous communication, a greater decoupling, and distribution of software systems.

These two types of messaging (one-to-one and one-to-many) are called *messaging domains*. The current JMS specification calls for domains. Vendors must implement both domains to fully implement the specification and be certified as fully J2EE-compliant:

- **Point-to-point messaging**—This type uses message queues, producers (message senders), and consumers (message receivers). A sender places a message in a queue, and receivers retrieve messages addressed to them from the queue (see Figure 7.1).

Figure 7.1 Point-to-point messaging.

- **Publish/subscribe messaging**—This type uses producers, subscribers, and topics. Subscribers subscribe to a topic, and publishers publish messages to a topic. The system distributes published messages to the subscribers (see Figure 7.2).

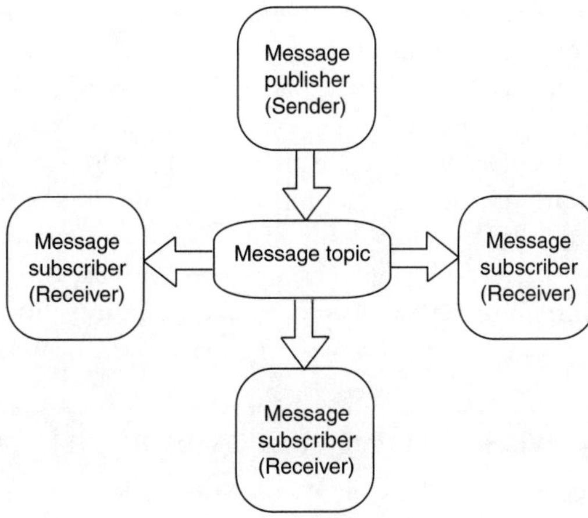

Figure 7.2 Publish/subscribe messaging.

Java Naming and Directory Service

The Java Naming and Directory Service (JNDI) is a standard extension to the Java platform that provides an interface to multiple naming and directory services in an enterprise. In the context of our discussion here, it is important to know that JNDI provides the naming and lookup services for EJBs and JMS.

The J2EE Specification

The Java Community Process, led by Sun Microsystems, provides specifications to describe all of the components we have mentioned here. J2EE combines the latest specifications for Java technologies relating to enterprise applications. This includes Servlets, JSP, EJB, JMS, and others. The J2EE specification also has versions. The current version is J2EE 1.3, which includes Servlets 2.3, JSP 1.2, EJB 2.0, and JMS 1.2.

Java Enterprise System Architecture

Most web-based, n-tier, Java-centric enterprise systems are built on what is known as the Model-View-Controller (MVC) architecture described in Part I. The *model* is the combination of the objects that work together to perform the business logic and access data sources. The objects can be regular Java classes, JavaBeans, Enterprise JavaBeans, or a combination of any of these. The *view* is the way the information is presented to the web client, generally through the use of JavaServer Pages. Often, one or more controller servlets help direct the flow of requests from the client in a logical manner. In some cases, a JavaServer page might act as the controller mechanism by being called initially by the client.

This model offers many advantages. First, functionality has a clear separation. Controlling servlets or JSP pages direct the flow. Model objects (classes, JavaBeans, or EJBs) perform the necessary business logic, including retrieving and storing data from databases and enterprise information systems (EIS). You can access databases with another Java API: the Java Database Connectivity (JDBC) API. You can access Enterprise Information Systems through proprietary connectors or through the J2EE Connector Architecture (JCA). When control is returned to a servlet, it can forward that control to a JSP to return the appropriate information back to the web client. By separating the model from the view, the same application can be used to display information in many different views, such as web browsers, PDAs, or WAP-enabled phones.

ColdFusion MX Java Interoperability Options

As we set out to design and build a ColdFusion MX application, we might discover that we need to leverage existing functionality in Java-based applications. In addition, with the MVC architecture in place, the individual components that make up these applications should be independently accessible. As mentioned previously, because ColdFusion MX is based on the J2EE platform, integration with these systems is now greatly enhanced.

Therefore, we can envision a scenario in which an application contains ColdFusion pages that call servlets; ColdFusion pages that utilize Java classes, JavaBeans, or even Enterprise JavaBeans; JavaServer Pages that call ColdFusion pages; and other similar mixtures. By designing a system in layers upon layers, we can leverage ColdFusion MX's Java interoperability methods to accomplish this goal.

Interoperability can be accomplished in the following ways:

- Including and forwarding to JSP pages and servlets from ColdFusion MX pages
- Including ColdFusion MX pages in JSP pages
- Sharing persistent scopes between ColdFusion MX and Java
- Using custom JSP tag libraries in ColdFusion MX
- Using Java classes, JavaBeans, and EJBs in ColdFusion MX

Including and Forwarding to JSP from ColdFusion MX

You can access a JavaServer Page or a servlet from ColdFusion MX using the `GetPageContext` function with the `include` or `forward` function. The `include` function puts the output from the included file in the outbound stream. The `forward` function actually dispatches to the new resource, effectively terminating the execution of the page. The following example shows a simple `include` of a JSP with no parameters:

```
<cfscript>
  GetPageContext().include("order.jsp");
</cfscript>
```

If the JSP requires parameters, include the parameters in the URL of the page. For example:

```
<cfscript>
  GetPageContext().include("order.jsp?total=#order.total#");
</cfscript>
```

To forward control to a JSP from ColdFusion MX, use the same `PageContext` object. Again, you can pass parameters with the URL if necessary:

```
<cfscript>
  params = "total=#order.total#&userid=#order.userid#";
  GetPageContext().forward(URLEncodedFormat("/jsp/order.jsp
  ?#params#"));
</cfscript>
```

Accessing a Servlet

If you are familiar with the <CFSERVLET> tag, keep in mind that this tag has been deprecated in ColdFusion MX. As with including and forwarding to JSP pages, you must use the `PageContext` object to invoke a servlet. However, remember these two important points:

- You must copy the .class file of the servlet to the serverroot/WEB-INF/classes directory under ColdFusion MX.
- In the ColdFusion MX page, refer to the servlet by class name in the URL given as a parameter for the `forward` function, as shown next. You can use the `forward` or the `include`.

```
<cfscript>
  GetPageContext().forward("/servlet/ProcessOrderServlet");
</cfscript>
```

Including ColdFusion MX Pages in JSP pages

Similarly to including JSP pages in ColdFusion MX pages, ColdFusion MX pages can be included in JSP pages. Because ColdFusiun MX is built on the J2EE platform, JSPs can be run on the ColdFusion MX server. You do not need to install a separate J2EE server. In the JSP, the tag `<JSP:INCLUDE>` is used to indicate the included file. Optionally, the `<JSP:PARAM>` tag can be used to pass parameters and their values:

```
<jsp:include page="displayOrder.cfm">
  <jsp:param name="orderNo" value="thisOrderNo" />
</jsp:include>
```

Sharing Persistent Scopes with ColdFusion MX and Java

A useful feature when mixing ColdFusion MX pages, servlets, and JSP Pages is sharing data in *persistent scopes*, which means that the same data can be shared between these components during the scope of a single request, for an entire user session, or for the duration of an entire application. Now it is possible to access data persisted in one environment (such as a ColdFusion MX page) from the other (such as a JSP) by setting variables.

JavaServer Pages only support the request, session, and application scopes. ColdFusion MX supports two additional scopes: client and form. These are not accessible from JavaServer Pages.

You can access JavaServer Pages in the following ways to share the data in the particular scopes (see Table 7.2).

Table 7.2 **Accessing JavaServer Pages**

Scope	Sharing Method
Request	`forward`, `include`
Session	`href`, `cfhttp`, `forward`, `include`
Application	`href`, `cfhttp`, `forward`, `include`

ColdFusion MX runs on a J2EE platform, which allows it to use either ColdFusion session management or J2EE session management. This becomes important when a developer wants to share session variables. When ColdFusion session management is used, session variables are not available in JSP pages or servlets that are called from ColdFusion MX pages. Therefore, to share session variables, you must specify the J2EE session scope management in the ColdFusion Administrator Memory Variables page. By default, session variables are enabled during installation. In addition, you must use the `<CFAPPLICATION>` tag in the ColdFusion MX page, with the `sessionmanagement` parameter set to `Yes`. This tag provides other configuration parameters, including time-out of the variables. The following tag enables session management for the MyApp application and sets session variables to time-out after a 30-minute period of inactivity:

```
<cfapplication
name="MyApp"
  sessionmanagement="Yes"
  sessiontimeout=#CreateTimeSpan(0,0,30,0)#>
```

With J2EE session management, the session and all session variables are deleted when the user closes the browser.

Note

Characters that you use for application and session variable names in unnamed ColdFusion MX applications that are accessed in JSP pages and servlets must be the same case as the created variables in ColdFusion MX. Variable names used in named applications are not case-sensitive.

The following are examples of the use of Request, Session, and Application variables in a mixed JSP and ColdFusion MX application. In the first example, we set the variables in ColdFusion MX and then call a JSP (see Listing 7.1).

Listing 7.1 **Setting ColdFusion Variables and Calling a JSP**

```
<cfapplication
  name="testApp"
  sessionmanagement="Yes">
<cfscript>
  Request.reqVariable="Here";
  Session.sesVariable="it";
  Application.appVariable="comes";
  GetPageContext().include("testVars.jsp?name=Jeremy");
</cfscript>
```

In this example of a portion of a ColdFusion MX page, we have named the application `"testApp"`, set session management to `"Yes"`, and set the values for a Request, Session, and Application variable. We have also included a JSP page named `"testVars.jsp"`, passing a parameter. In Listing 7.2, we will examine a portion of that JSP page.

Listing 7.2 **Setting the Values for Request, Session, and Application Variables**

```
1   <%@page import="java.util.*" %>
2   <%= request.getParameter("Name")%><br>
3   <%= request.getAttribute("reqVariable") %><br>
4   <%= ((Map)(session.getAttribute("testApp")))get ("sesVariable") %><br>
5   <%= ((Map)(application.getAttribute("testApp")))get ("appVariable") %>
```

In line 1, the `java.util.*` package is imported due to the use of the `java.util.Map` class for casting the session and application scopes. Line 2 is a simple parameter retrieval from the request. This parameter was passed in the ColdFusion MX `include` statement.

In line 3, you can retrieve the attribute `"reqVariable"` from the request object because the ColdFusion MX page stored it there.

In lines 4 and 5, you must obtain the session and application scopes first, and then you can cast them as `java.util.Map` objects. When that is done, the `get()` method retrieves by name the attributes that are stored in the ColdFusion MX page.

In Listing 7.3, we set the variables in a JSP, and then call a ColdFusion MX page:

Listing 7.3 **Calling a ColdFusion MX Page**

```
<%@page import="java.util.*" %>
<% request.setAttribute("reqVariable", "Here"); %>
<% ((Map)session.getAttribute("testApp"))put ("sesVariable", "it"); %>
<% application.setAttribute("testApp.appVariable", "is");%>
<jsp:include page="testVars.cfm">
<jsp:param name="name" value="Jeremy" />
</jsp:include>
```

In this case, we use a different method to set the session variable than for the request and application variables. This is purely for demonstration because either way is sufficient. For the request and application scopes, we use the `setAttribute()` method; it is clearly simpler than that used for the session scope. In the case of the session, we obtain the scope with the `getAttribute()` method, cast it to a `java.util.Map` object, and then use the `put()` method to set the variable. The casting is required because the object returned is not the specific type needed (the Map object) to utilize the `put()` method.

A portion of the included "testVars.cfm" page might look like that in Listing 7.4.

Listing 7.4 **A portion of the testVars.cfm page**

```
<cfapplication
    name="testApp"
    sessionmanagement="Yes">

<cfoutput>
    This is #URL.name#'s test<br>
    #Request.reqVariable#<br>
    #Session.sesVariable#<br>
    #Application.appVariable#<br>
</cfoutput>
```

Here, we are simply retrieving the named variable values from the passed parameter and the Request, Session, and Application variables.

Data Type Considerations with Scopes

It is important to consider data types when sharing variables between ColdFusion MX and Java scopes. ColdFusion MX does not use explicit types for variables. Java is a strongly typed language. In most cases, method names are not ambiguous, and ColdFusion MX can determine the appropriate type for the Java object in question.

Java method overloading, however, can cause ambiguous situations. *Method overloading* means that a Java class has multiple implementations of the same method, differing only in data type of the parameters. In this case, ColdFusion MX provides the `JavaCast` function. This function can specify the type of the parameter for cases of Boolean, int, long, float, double, and String. If possible, try to avoid method overloading with classes that will be used with ColdFusion. Sometimes, however, the classes already might have been created, and you cannot avoid it. In that case, utilize the `JavaCast` function.

For example, when you're calling an overloaded method on a Java object (which we cover in the section, "Using Java Classes, JavaBeans, and EJBs in ColdFusion MX") such as

```
<cfset temp = myObject.testMethod("100")>
```

use the `JavaCast` function to specify the type:

```
<cfset temp = myObject.testMethod(JavaCast("int", "100"))>
```

Using Custom JSP Tag Libraries in ColdFusion MX

Although it's possible to include JSP pages in ColdFusion MX and ColdFusion MX pages in JSP pages, it's not possible to use JSP syntax (including actual Java code) inside of ColdFusion MX. However, as we mentioned previously, Java developers can create custom JSP tags that execute Java code on the server, and these custom tags can be used in ColdFusion MX. You can also find JSP custom tag libraries at a number of web sites, such as `JSPTags.com`.

JSP custom tag libraries are usually provided in a Java Archive (JAR) file. The JAR file contains a tag library descriptor (TLD) file and a set of tag handler classes. These classes are the actual Java code that provides the implementation for each tag in the library.

To use a JSP tag library in a ColdFusion MX page, first put the tag library JAR file (and the TLD file, if provided) in the ColdFusion MX serverroot/WEB-INF/lib directory. The tag library is specified on the ColdFusion MX page using the `<CFIMPORT>` tag, as in the following:

```
<cfimport taglib="/WEB-INF/lib/random.jar" prefix="random">
```

The `<CFIMPORT>` tag must be in every ColdFusion MX page using the library, or in a header page included on every page. You cannot specify this tag globally in Application.cfm. The TLD file is sometimes provided in the JAR file, but sometimes it is not. If it is not included the JAR file, use the .TLD suffix in place of the .JAR suffix.

JSP tags are specified with a prefix to eliminate ambiguity. One common library from the Apache Jakarta project (an open-source Java community development project) is the Random library. This library provides various random number facilities. In this case, the prefix is random, followed by the particular tag name. So, for example, to use the random number tag in a ColdFusion MX page (following the `<CFIMPORT>` tag), use the prefix and the name as in the following:

```
<random:number id="randNum" range="00000-99999" />
```

Using Java Classes, JavaBeans, and EJBs in ColdFusion MX

Servlets and JSP pages are only part of an entire Java application. The real core of the application is the model. This is where the business logic processing actually takes place. For real Java interoperability with ColdFusion MX, it is important to be able to directly take advantage of those objects.

As mentioned previously, Java objects exist in varying forms: regular Java classes, JavaBeans, and distributed Java objects in the form of Enterprise JavaBeans. The basic method of calling these objects in ColdFusion MX, however, is fairly simple. The object is created or accessed with the `<CFOBJECT>` tag, and then the properties and operations (or "methods") of an object can be accessed with other tags, such as `<CFSET>`, `<CFOUTPUT>`, and `<CFSCRIPT>`. The method arguments and return values obtained by using a Java object can be any valid Java type. ColdFusion MX, as mentioned previously in the sidebar, "Data Type Considerations with Scopes," will perform the appropriate conversion to the valid ColdFusion MX type.

Accessing a Java Object

The `<CFOBJECT>` tag can access Java classes that are available in the following locations:

- In the JVM classpath
- In a JAR file (.jar) in the serverroot/WEB-INF/lib directory of ColdFusion MX
- In a class file (.class) in the serverroot/WEB-INF/classes directory of ColdFusion MX

The following is an example of the use of the `<CFOBJECT>` tag:

```
<cfobject type="Java" class="TestClass" name="testObject">
```

The name of the Java class is case-sensitive. You must match the case of the class name *exactly* in the ColdFusion MX page.

The `<CFOBJECT>` tag only loads the class; it does not create an instance of the class. Keep in mind that a class is like a car factory, and an instance is like a car. You cannot call instance methods (the operations) on the class—only static methods. Therefore, at this point, you can only access static methods and fields. If a public non-static method is called at this point, ColdFusion MX implicitly invokes the *default* constructor to create a new instance, which produces an instance with uninitialized properties. This is not a desirable result. Rather, you would typically prefer to invoke an *explicit* constructor, which can initialize property values and produce a stable object.

You can invoke an explicit constructor, however. To do this, use the `init` method after the `<CFOBJECT>` tag, passing any required arguments:

```
<cfobject type="Java" class="TestClass" name="testObject">
<cfset test=testObject.init(arg1, arg2) >
```

It is important to realize that the `init` method is a ColdFusion MX identifier that calls the `new` method on the object's constructor. If a Java object has an actual `init` method, there will be a name conflict and the object's `init` method will not be able to be called.

Any object created with the `<CFOBJECT>` tag or returned by other objects is implicitly released at the end of the ColdFusion MX page execution.

Accessing the Properties of an Object

You can access an object's properties if the properties are a) public, or b) the properties are not public, but the object is a JavaBean that provides public `getter` and `setter` methods for its properties in the form of `get`*`PropertyName`*`()` and `set`*`PropertyName`*`(value)`.

Use the following code to set the value of an object property:

```
<cfset random.id = "20912">
```

Use this to get the value of an object property:

```
<cfset RandomNumber = random.id>
```

For consistency, it is always best to use the same case with property and method names in ColdFusion MX that you do in Java.

Calling Methods on an Object

Some object methods require arguments and others do not. Similarly, some methods return values and others do not. When you're using a method with no arguments, follow the method name with empty parentheses. If a method requires arguments, put the arguments in parentheses, separated by commas.

```
<cfset returnValue1 = obj.method1() >
<cfset returnValue2 = obj.method2(x, "string") >
```

ColdFusion MX also supports nested object calls. Often, an object's method returns another object, and you need to access a property of the returned object. For example, a `Customer` object might contain an `Address` object, which contains a string representing the city. When you have nested method calls, you can use standard dot notation to access the returned objects:

```
<cfset city = customer.address.city >
```

Handling Java Exceptions

Often, the calling of a method on a Java object results in the need to catch a Java exception. Java exceptions are handled the same way in ColdFusion MX that ColdFusion exceptions are: using the `<CFTRY>` and `<CFCATCH>` tags. Specify the particular name of the exception class in the `<CFCATCH>` tag. At times, it might be necessary to try to catch any exception that an object might throw. In this case, specify java.lang.Exception for the exception type. In the following example, an object has been created to read a file, and the method throws a `FileNotFoundException`:

```
<cfobject type="Java" class="com.testing.TestFileReader"
  name="myFileReader" >
<cfset fileReader = myFileReader.init() >
<cftry>
    <cfset fileReader.readFile("c://testFile.txt") >
<cfcatch type="java.io.FileNotFoundException">
      <cfoutput>
        <br>Exception: #cfcatch.Message#<br>
      </cfoutput>
</cfcatch>
</cftry>
```

Uncovering what specific exception is going to be thrown is not always an easy task because it requires a copy of the Java API for the particular class that you are trying to use. Keep in mind that all Java API documentation is available at `http://java.sun.com`.

Most Java reference books have API documentation as well. At the very least, the class `java.lang.Exception` is the root of all exceptions, and `java.lang.Throwable` is the root of all errors including exceptions, so you can always use one of those. It is preferable, however, to use the most specific exception because it saves the Java virtual machine from having to traverse the exception hierarchy.

Using Enterprise JavaBeans in ColdFusion MX

ColdFusion MX can access Enterprise JavaBeans that are deployed on JRun 4.0 servers. You must ensure that the JRun Server JRun.jar file is the same version as the JRun.jar file in ColdFusion MX.

The `<CFOBJECT>` type is still Java, as with other types of Java objects. You must do the following prior to using an EJB:

- Deploy and run the EJB on the J2EE server.
- Register the EJB with the JNDI server.
- Obtain the following information:
  - EJB server name
  - EJB server's JNDI naming service port number
  - Name of the EJB as registered with JNDI
- Put the EJB JAR file in the serverroot/WEB-INF/lib directory of ColdFusion MX.

To call the EJB, do the following:

1. Use the `<CFOBJECT>` tag to create an object of the JNDI naming context class (`javax.naming.Context`). This class will help to find the EJB.
2. Use the `<CFOBJECT>` tag to create a `java.util.Properties` class object that will contain the properties of the context object.
3. Call the init method to initialize the Properties object.
4. Set the Properties object to contain the properties that are required to create an initial JNDI naming context. These include the `INITIAL_CONTEXT_FACTORY` and `PROVIDER_URL` properties.
5. Optionally, you also might need to provide `SECURITY_PRINCIPAL` and `SECURITY_CREDENTIALS` values required for secure access to the naming context.
6. Use the `<CFOBJECT>` tag to create the JNDI `InitialContext` (`javax.naming.InitialContext`) object.
7. Call the `init` method for the `InitialContext` object with the Properties object values to initialize the object.

8. Call the `InitialContext` object's `lookup` method to get a reference to the home interface for the bean that you want. Specify the JNDI name of the bean as the lookup argument.

   Call the `create` method of the bean's home object to create a new instance of the bean.

9. Call the bean's methods as required.
10. Call the context object's `close` method to close the object.

Listing 7.5 is a portion of a ColdFusion MX page calling and using an EJB.

Listing 7.5 **ColdFusion MX Page Calling and Using an EJB**

```
<!--- Create the Context object --->
<CFOBJECT action="create" name="ctx" type="JAVA"
class="javax.naming.Context">

<!--- Create the Properties object --->
 <CFOBJECT action="create" name="prop" type="JAVA"
class="java.util.Properties">

<!--- Call the init method on the Properties object --->
 <cfset prop.init()>

<!--- Specify the properties for the server --->
<cfset prop.put(ctx.INITIAL_CONTEXT_FACTORY,
JRun.naming.JRunContextFactory)>

<cfset prop.put(ctx.PROVIDER_URL, "localhost:2908")>

<!--- Note - These are optional
  <cfset prop.put(ctx.SECURITY_PRINCIPAL, "admin")>
     <cfset prop.put(ctx.SECURITY_CREDENTIALS, "admin")>
--->

<!--- Create the InitialContext  --->
 <CFOBJECT action=create name=initContext type="JAVA"
class="javax.naming.InitialContext">

<!--- Call the init method to pass the properties to the constructor. --->
 <cfset initContext.init(prop)>

<!--- Get reference to home object. --->
 <cfset home = initContext.lookup("SimpleBean")>

<!--- Create new instance of entity bean. --->
 <cfset mySimple = home.create()>

<!--- Call a method in the entity bean. --->
```

continues

Listing 7.5 **Continued**

```
<cfset myMessage = mySimple.getMessage()>

<cfoutput>
 #myMessage#<br>
</cfoutput>

<!--- Close the context. --->
<cfset initContext.close()>
```

JMS Considerations

Java messaging has become an important part of enterprise systems. Messaging is used to send notification of events and data between applications, providing an asynchronous communication mechanism that allows systems to interact without requiring them to be tightly coupled.

Although ColdFusion MX does not currently provide explicit functionality related to JMS, it is important to realize that JMS services are looked up through JNDI, similar to EJB lookup. Therefore, topics, queues, and other JMS features are accessed in much the same manner as the previous EJB example.

Conclusion

We have seen in this chapter how the integration of Java with ColdFusion MX has been significantly enhanced due to the ColdFusion MX foundation based on J2EE. ColdFusion pages can easily interoperate with Java servlets, JavaServer Pages, JavaServer Page Custom Tag Libraries, and all types of Java objects, including EJB. This gives development teams the power to leverage far more resources, both in software assets and in people. With the ease, elegance, and flexibility of ColdFusion MX as a powerful presentation layer accessing many different Java components, it must now be considered a vital part of the enterprise.

8 ColdFusion Components with Persistence

by Seth Hodgson

WE INTRODUCED COLDFUSION COMPONENTS (CFCs) and their role in revolutionizing ColdFusion application architecture and design in Chapter 5, "ColdFusion Components," but that was just the beginning of the story. CFCs are ideally suited to building out the business logic and Data Access layers of an application. This chapter introduces the role that CFCs play within the Data Access layer.

The foundation for a dynamic publishing system is the Content layer and the content repositories that store data for the application. At this layer in the application, CFCs are the model within the Model-View-Controller (MVC) architecture. They represent the core content within the system. A CFC can be developed for each type of content used in the application, such as products in an online store or news articles that are published on a web site. Every type of content that the system uses will require a corresponding CFC that contains properties and functions to represent the content type. We have already seen how to use CFCs to build single logical units and how the Unified Modeling Language (UML) can be used to design components and relationships between components for our application.

However, even after a solid design for the system is in place, it's still necessary to store the persistent state of many of these CFCs in a content repository. We need to be able to create instances of a CFC type, such as news articles, and save these instances in a database or some other persistent storage format. We can then publish these persistent CFC instances dynamically to the web site. To solve this challenge, we will look at the requirements for CFC persistence, the features that make it possible, and concrete strategies for building persistent CFCs.

What Is Persistence?

Persistence is the ability to save the state of CFCs used within an application to persistent storage, such as a database or flat XML file. The state of a CFC instance is represented by the values stored in its properties. With an instance of an article.cfc type with properties to store an author, article title, and article body, each persistent instance of this component type (each article) has unique values for these properties that are stored in the content repository. The content repository can take a variety of forms, but regardless of where and how content is stored, the Content layer of the application handles the programmatic interaction with the content repository that is required for saving and retrieving the state of persistent CFCs. The benefit of persistent CFCs is the ability to create instances of component types (such as online store products or articles), persist them to a content repository, and then dynamically publish them to a web site.

Modeling the System and Its Data

A key point is that persistent CFCs are used to model both the content that the system manages as well as the application. The first use for persistent CFCs is in modeling the content that the system publishes to its clients. A news article, with properties including a title, author, and body content, is an example of a content type that fits within this category. This type of content is well suited to be modeled and stored as a persistent CFC.

The less obvious but even more powerful application of persistent CFCs is found in modeling the system. Examples of this use for persistent CFCs include components that model application state or function, such as publishing rules for content, user profiles, or workflow state. This opens the door to building applications as a collection of services that use persistent CFCs to accomplish their tasks. A publishing service CFC can access the publishing data that is stored in persistent publishing rule CFCs to determine the content objects that should be displayed to the end user.

Persistent Storage Options

Persistent CFCs have a variety of storage options. They can be saved to database tables, XML documents, WDDX documents, or to other serialized formats. The storage location can be local or remote. An application can work with multiple content repositories simultaneously. In many cases, enterprises already have existing content repositories with which the application will interface.

Tying Persistence to Components

All persistent CFCs begin life as simple files containing the `<CFCOMPONENT>` tag set. The factor that sets persistent CFCs apart from static CFCs is the introduction of the `<CFPROPERTY>` tag. One `<CFPROPERTY>` tag is used to define each data value that must be persisted for the CFC. With a simple content type such as a news article, the CFC might have title, subtitle, author, and body properties. When a unique instance of this CFC type is persisted, the values of its title, subtitle, author, and body properties are stored in the content repository. That way, the article will persist in the content repository and can be accessed and dynamically published on the web site.

Instances of a CFC type, such as article.cfc, are instantiated using the `<CFOBJECT>` tag or the `createObject()` ColdFusion function. When a CFC is instantiated, ColdFusion creates an instance of the component type in server memory that returns a reference to this instance. Listing 8.1 demonstrates these two approaches to CFC instantiation using the example article.cfc.

Listing 8.1 **Instantiating article.cfc Instances**

```
<cfobject name="firstArticle" component="article">
<cfscript>
      secondArticle = createObject("component", "article");
</cfscript>
```

When the code snippet in Listing 8.1 is run, two instances of the article.cfc type are instantiated. It is important to note that the CFC type name does not include the file extension, .cfc, when used in `<CFOBJECT>` or `createObject()`. We simply use `"article"`. First, the `<CFOBJECT>` tag creates a new instance of the article.cfc type and returns a reference to the new instance in the variable, `firstArticle`. Second, the `createObject()` function call in the `<cfscript>` block creates a new article instance and stores a reference to the new instance in the variable, `secondArticle`. After an instance of a CFC type is created, you can call its functions, get and set its properties, and work with it until a response is returned to the client. This differs from the use of `<CFINVOKE>`, the ColdFusion tag that allows a function to be called on a component type directly.

Calling a CFC function by using `<CFINVOKE>` does result in the creation of an instance of the CFC type, but this instance only exists within the context of the `<CFINVOKE>` tag. When component instances are created using `<CFOBJECT>` or `createObject()`, each instance can contain its own set of instance property variables stored in the `this` scope, and the instance will exist across multiple function calls and interactions.

For each persistent CFC type, storage space needs to be created or configured within a content repository to persist the property values for instances of that type. This is where the magic of component introspection enters the picture. The ColdFusion function, `getMetadata()`, performs component introspection and returns a metadata structure for the CFC that is passed to it. This structure contains information about the component, its functions, and most importantly, its properties. You can use these property definitions to control CFC persistence in a content repository.

Persistent Component Structure

Now that we have a general understanding of components and persistence, we can move on to a detailed discussion of the structure of persistent CFCs, non-static CFC functions, and component introspection.

<CFPROPERTY>

The essence of persistent CFCs is the `<CFPROPERTY>` tag. You use this tag to create CFCs that are exposed as web services. For our purposes, the `<CFPROPERTY>` tag is instrumental in creating CFCs that can be persisted. It is used to define the properties for each persistent CFC that we want to be able to store in the content repository. The example article.cfc, which contains an author, article title, and article body, needs three `<CFPROPERTY>` tags to store each of these three properties. The attribute names and values that are defined in `<CFPROPERTY>` tags are available to us via component introspection. Component introspection was introduced in Chapter 5. It provides a way to examine a CFC at runtime so that you can view the properties and functions that are defined in the CFC. We will revisit component introspection in this chapter as it applies to CFC properties. The `<CFPROPERTY>` definitions within a CFC are inherited by components that extend the CFC. The `<CFPROPERTY>` tag attributes are listed in Table 8.1.

Table 8.1 ***<CFPROPERTY>* Attributes**

Attribute	Required	Data Type	Example	Description
`Name`	Yes	String	`myProp`	Name of the component property.
`Type`	No	String	`string`	Data type of the value stored in the property.

Attribute	Required	Data Type	Example	Description
`Display Name`	No	String	`My Property`	Friendly name for the property. Used in auto-documentation.
`Hint`	No	String	`This property stores a string value`	Comment describing the property. Used in auto-documentation.
`Required`	No	Boolean	`true`	Metadata indicating whether the property is required.
`Default`	No	String	`A default text string.`	Metadata indicating the default property value.

In addition to the built-in attributes that are available for the `<CFPROPERTY>` tag, any number of user-defined attributes can be added to the tag and used to drive custom data validation, initialization, or other handling of the property. User-defined attributes are simply added as name-value pairs in the `<CFPROPERTY>` tag, in the same fashion used to pass attributes to a custom tag or the `<CFMODULE>` tag.

You must place all `<CFPROPERTY>` tags directly after the opening `<CFCOMPONENT>` tag and before any executable code or `<CFFUNCTION>` tags within the body of the CFC. ColdFusion expressions are not permitted within the `<CFPROPERTY>` tag, so any values that are assigned to attributes must be simple values rather than variables, ColdFusion expressions, or functions. This only applies to values that are hard-coded into the `<CFPROPERTY>` tag. You can always update or set these values dynamically during runtime. Listing 8.2 shows a sample `<CFPROPERTY>` tag that contains all the attributes in Table 8.1 as well as a user-defined attribute.

Listing 8.2 ***<CFPROPERTY>***

```
<cfcomponent>
    <cfproperty
name="propertyName"
        type="string"
        displayName="The Property Name"
        hint="An exceedingly useful property!"
        required="true"
        default="A Default Property Value"
        myValue="This is a user-defined attribute"
    >
</cfcomponent>
```

The `<CFPROPERTY>` tags within a CFC do not exhibit any of the runtime data validation behavior seen with the `<CFARGUMENT>` tag that is nested within `<CFFUNCTION>` tags in a CFC. ColdFusion uses only the required and default attributes of a property to handle the CFC as a web service. This means that when a new instance of a persistent CFC is instantiated, its properties are not initialized as variables in the `this` scope of the instance by ColdFusion. Although we use CFC properties to represent the data for a persistent CFC type, it is up to the developer to initialize and validate these properties.

You can perform initialization of property values in a "constructor" code block within a CFC. Any ColdFusion code in the body of a component that follows all `<CFPROPERTY>` tags and is not contained within a `<CFFUNCTION>` is executed when the CFC is created or invoked. This code can perform setup for the component, such as initializing property values in the `this` scope for the component. To ease maintenance, it is best to keep all "constructor" code for your components in a single block of code immediately following `<CFPROPERTY>` definitions. The "constructor" code can initialize property variables in the `this` scope for your component and set them to their default values. To update these property values, however, we will use non-static functions.

Non-Static Component Functions

To interact with properties of persistent CFCs, non-static functions are required. The `<CFFUNCTION>` examples provided so far have been static functions. The client can access static functions by invoking them directly on a component type without first instantiating an instance of the CFC type. With direct invocation using `<CFINVOKE>`, an instance of the CFC is in fact instantiated behind the scenes, but it does not have its `this` scope populated with unique data. Therefore, the function can be regarded as static because it is called against a CFC type rather than a unique instance. You can find several good examples of static CFC functions in Chapter 5, in the discussion of a security.cfc component. This component contains a function for authenticating a user. A username and password are passed to the function, which performs a database query and returns a boolean indicating whether the user was authenticated. This function does not depend on property values of the component, and it is a perfect example of a static function because it is invoked against the component type instead of requiring a unique CFC instance.

Unlike static component functions, non-static functions deal directly with component properties. These functions are non-static because they are called on a CFC instance as opposed to being called against a component type. Public non-static functions can be defined for getting and setting the values of the properties defined for a component. These functions encapsulate the implementation details of the CFC and provide a public interface for clients to use when interacting with the component. Encapsulation allows for the internal data structure of the component to change without affecting other components or systems that interact with it. Another benefit of non-static functions for interacting with component properties is that runtime validation of the arguments passed to them is performed, ensuring that properties always have acceptable values. Remember that property values are set in the `this` scope for components. Listing 8.3 is a simple CFC to illustrate these concepts.

Listing 8.3 **Component with Non-Static Functions (article.cfc)**

```
<cfcomponent>
    <cfproperty name="title" type="string">
    <!--- Constructor --->
    <cfscript>
```

```
        this.title = "";
    <cfscript>
    <!--- End Constructor --->
    <cffunction
name="setTitle"
access="public"
>
        <cfargument
            name="theTitle"
            required="true"
            type="string"
        >
        <cfset this.title = arguments.theTitle>
    </cffunction>
    <cffunction
        name="getTitle"
        returnType="string"
        access="public"
    >
        <cfreturn this.title>
    </cffunction>
</cfcomponent>
```

In this example, a CFC with a single property, `title`, has been defined with public, non-static `get` and `set` methods for the property. The constructor code then runs when an instance of this CFC is created, initializing `this.title` and setting it to an empty string. The non-static `setTitle()` and `getTitle()` functions can be called on the instance to set or retrieve the value of the `title` property. The `getTitle()` function simply returns the current value stored in the `title` variable to the caller. The `setTitle()` function must receive a string argument; otherwise, ColdFusion throws an exception and sets the `title` variable to the new value. We could add further validation to the function, but this illustrates that non-static `get` and `set` methods can be used to encapsulate and validate component properties. Non-static functions work with unique property variables that exist in the `this` scope for CFC instances, whereas static functions provide a generic service and can be called on by a component type or instance because they do not depend on property variables.

Static methods also have a place within persistent CFCs. The process of retrieving a content object from a content repository requires that we first create an instance of the CFC type and then populate its property variables with data from the content repository. A static `get()` function can be defined for a CFC type that accepts an objectID as an argument and proceeds to retrieve instance data for a unique component instance that is stored in the content repository, assigns the persisted data to property variables in the `this` scope of the CFC instance, and returns the populated instance to the caller.

Component Metadata and Introspection

The ability to introspect CFCs is the glue that binds the properties of persistent CFCs to the content repository. This allows us to dynamically create storage space for unique instances of a CFC type, such as article.cfc, and save the property variables (`author`, `title`, and `body`) for each unique instance in our content repository for later retrieval. Any CFC can be introspected by calling the `getMetadata()` ColdFusion function and passing in an instance of the CFC as an argument. Listing 8.4 shows use of this function to view the component metadata for the article.cfc component we defined earlier.

Listing 8.4 **Viewing Component Metadata**

```
<cfscript>
    myComponent = createObject("component","article");
    componentMetadata = getMetadata(myComponent);
</cfscript>
<cfdump var="#componentMetadata#">
```

In Listing 8.4, an object of type `article` is created and a reference to the new object is stored in the variable `myComponent`. This is passed to the `getMetadata()` function, which introspects the component and returns the component metadata as a structure. The returned structure is stored in the variable `componentMetadata`, which is dumped to the screen using a `<CFDUMP>` tag following the `<cfscript>` block. Figure 8.1 displays the generated output.

For brevity, the functions for article.cfc have been omitted from the component metadata structure displayed in Figure 8.1. However, we can see that all three properties (`author`, `title`, and `body`) are listed as structures in the array stored in the Properties key of the metadata structure. Each of these properties has default, name, and type keys that correspond to the attributes in the `<CFPROPERTY>` tags of the article.cfc component. With components that exist at the end of a long inheritance chain, the returned component metadata structure can become quite large, but after you understand the layout of the returned structure, it is straightforward to navigate. Table 8.2 lists the component metadata structure.

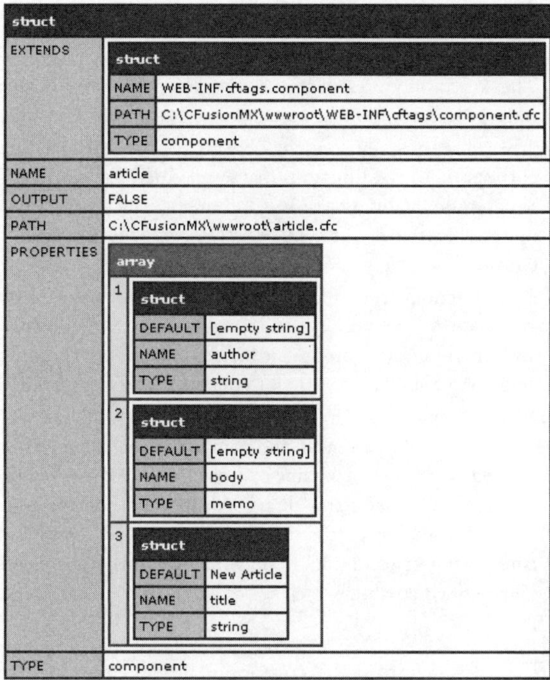

Figure 8.1 article.cfc metadata.

Table 8.2 **Component Metadata Structure**

Key	**Value**
Name	The name of the component.
Path	The absolute path to the CFC file.
Type	The type of object that is being introspected. CFCs are listed as type `component`.
Extends	This key contains the component metadata structure for the parent component that the current component extends. If the current component does not extend another component, this key is populated with the component metadata structure for `WEB-INF.cftags.component`. This is because a component that does not extend another component implicitly extends this base component. `WEB-INF.cftags.component` serves to root the inheritance hierarchy for CFCs, and it contains no property or function definitions.

continues

Table 8.2 **Continued**

Key	Value
Functions	This key is only present in the component metadata structure if the introspected component contains one or more `<CFFUNCTION>` tag. The `Functions` key contains an array of function metadata structures that correspond to the functions that are defined in the CFC. Each of these structures contains a `Name` key and might contain keys for the following optional attributes of the `<CFFUNCTION>` tag: `ReturnType`, `Roles`, `Access`, and `Output`. Each function structure also might contain a `Properties` key if `<CFARGUMENT>` tags are defined for the function. The `Properties` key contains an array of argument metadata structures. Each argument structure contains a `Name` key and might contain keys for the following optional attributes of the `<CFARGUMENT>` tag: `Type`, `Required`, or `Default`.
Properties	This key is only present in the component metadata structure if the introspected component contains one or more `<CFPROPERTY>` tags. The `Properties` key contains an array of property metadata structures that correspond to the properties defined in the CFC. Each property structure contains a `Name` key and might contain an optional `Type` key or other user-defined attributes.

Additional keys are displayed within the component metadata structure if user-defined attributes have been added to any of the tags in the introspected CFC. These additional keys are displayed exactly where you might suspect. Attributes that are added to the `<CFCOMPONENT>` tag become top-level keys in the component metadata structure, attributes that are added to `<CFPROPERTY>` tags are inserted as additional keys into the corresponding property metadata structure in the `Properties` array, and the same handling is true for attributes that are added to `<CFFUNCTION>` or `<CFARGUMENT>` tags.

The component metadata structure that `getMetadata()` returns enables the dynamic inspection of property definitions in any component, and this information can be used to drive the automatic creation or configuration of persistent storage. By recursively traversing the `Extends` key within the component metadata structure, a complete listing of properties along with all property attributes can be compiled for a given CFC. These property definitions can then be used to create a database table or an XML schema to persist instances of the CFC with constraints that are specified by property attributes (such as `required`, `default`, or other user-defined attributes).

Persistence Mechanisms

You can take several approaches to implement component persistence in a dynamic publishing system. These mechanisms are not mutually exclusive, and in most systems, it's likely that all will be used at some level.

Memory-Based Persistence

A short-term, high-performance persistence mechanism is storing component instances in server memory. You can use the session, application, and server scopes to implement memory-based persistence. Constructor code can initialize the properties for memory-based persistent components within the component upon instantiation, or the system can do it dynamically at runtime. After the component has been instantiated and stored in server memory, all client or user interaction with the component is persisted until the memory scope is reset or the component is destroyed.

Memory-based persistence is an ideal mechanism for components that have a short life span and are highly volatile, such as a customer shopping cart CFC in an e-commerce application. Keep in mind that a component can use several persistence mechanisms through its lifespan. With a shopping cart component, you can use a memory-based persistence mechanism while the customer is browsing the site and adding or removing items from her cart. This involves creating a cart component instance for the customer and storing it in session scope while the user browses the site. This can be substituted for a long-term database or XML-based persistence mechanism if the user decides to save her cart and return at a later date, in which case the cart component contents can be persisted to the content repository for later retrieval. As with any other use of shared memory scopes in ColdFusion, persisting component instances by placing them in one of these scopes should follow accepted best practices. Be sure to use `<CFLOCK>` when you're reading or writing to these scopes to avoid data corruption problems. Also be careful to avoid storing too much information in server memory, which can affect system performance and stability.

New Storage

As web sites develop and grow, new types of content are usually added to the mix. DuvalShock, our fictitious company, might need to add customer testimonials or product tutorials to their site. These are examples of new content types that have unique properties and will be published dynamically on the site. With new content object types, new CFCs are developed and new storage must be created or configured to store instances of the new types. The introduction of new content types into a system might require creating a new content repository or might take advantage of an existing content repository. For systems that are being built from the ground up, setting up new persistent storage requires defining the format and location for the content repository, such as a new content database running on a remote server or a local XML document file repository.

If an existing content repository, such as a database, is already in place, then creating storage for new content types might only require the creation of additional tables within the database to store the new content. Regardless of whether new or existing storage will be used, property metadata for the new content types can be used to drive the automatic configuration of new storage.

Existing Repositories

If existing content repositories are already in place, it is possible to use the content assets they contain. Existing content repositories that the developer might need to access include Spectra Content Object Databases, other content management or legacy databases, XML document repositories, and other content asset stores that are targeted for publication.

When you're dealing with existing repositories, CFCs can be written that mirror the attributes of existing content, serving as an adaptor between the dynamic publishing system and existing content. These CFCs can wrap existing content, providing the dynamic publishing runtime with a consistent CFC interface to all content assets, regardless of format or location.

Component Design

It is clear that all persistent components will share a common superset of functionality. The ability to save, update, retrieve, and delete instance data from a content repository is required of all persistent components. Because CFCs can extend other CFCs, it makes sense to abstract the functionality that handles component persistence into a base persistent component.

Building a Base Component for Persistence

Moving persistence code out of the persistent CFCs that will comprise a dynamic publishing application and into a base persistent component with a descriptive name like basepersistentcomponent.cfc provides the benefits of greater modularity and code reuse for the system. Making a component persistent simply entails extending the base persistent component. Changes to this base persistent component will automatically be propagated to all components that inherit from it.

The base persistent component needs to implement the following set of functions to support persistence. All CFC types that must persist only need to extend this base persistent component to inherit these functions:

- **Deploy**—Creates persistent storage for a CFC type.
- **Remove**—Undeploys a currently deployed CFC type.
- **Create**—Persists a new CFC instance in the content repository.
- **Update**—Updates the property values that are stored in the content repository for a particular CFC instance.
- **Get**—Retrieves property values for a particular object from the content repository and returns a CFC instance that is populated with the values.
- **Delete**—Deletes a CFC instance from the content repository.

These are not native ColdFusion functions and concrete implementations for these functions depend on the nature of the content repository. With `deploy()`, the function might create new tables to store instances of the CFC type if the content repository is a database, or it might generate an XML schema for the CFC type if XML documents are used for persistent storage. In Chapters 10, "Persistence with Localization," and Chapter 11, "Persistence with Versioning," we will see specific implementations for several persistent storage options.

Persistence Using an Abstraction Layer

Now that all functionality necessary to support CFC persistence has been abstracted into a base persistent component, other CFCs might extend this base component to become persistent. Converting the article.cfc component that was defined in Listing 8.3 to a persistent component is as simple as adding the `extends` attribute to the `<CFCOMPONENT>` tag, as shown in Listing 8.5.

Listing 8.5 **Inheriting Component Persistence (article.cfc)**

```
<cfcomponent extends="basepersistentcomponent">
     .
     Body omitted for brevity
     .
</cfcomponent>
```

By extending the base persistent component, the article.cfc inherits all of the persistence functions that are defined within the base persistent component. The article.cfc is free to override any or all of the functions it inherits from the base persistent component by defining a function with the same name. The static inherited functions such as `deploy()` can be invoked directly against the article.cfc type, and non-static functions such as `update()` can be invoked against article.cfc instances. Listing 8.6 shows an example of how the inherited persistence functions can be invoked directly on the article.cfc type and its instances.

Listing 8.6 **Using Inherited Persistence Functions**

```
<!--- Call deploy() on the article.cfc type using <cfinvoke>
     - This is a static function that creates storage space for
       article.cfc instances in the content repository --->
<cfinvoke component="article" method="deploy">
<cfscript>
     // Create an article.cfc instance, storing a reference to
     // this instance in the myArticle variable
     myArticle = createObject("component","article");
     // Build an arguments structure to store an author, title,
// and body for a new article
args = structNew();
args.author = "Mr. Duval";
```

continues

Listing 8.6 **Continued**

```
    args.title = "DuvalShock News";
    args.body = "...text for the article...";
    // Create the new article, and store a reference to it
    // in the newArticle variable
    newArticle = myArticle.create(argumentCollection=args);
    // Use the non-static setTitle() function to update the
    // article's title
    newArticle.setTitle("A New Hope");
    // Call the non-static update() function to persist the
    // updated article properties to the content repository
    newArticle.update();
</cfscript>
```

The static `deploy()` function is invoked against the article.cfc type, creating persistent storage for this type. This function is inherited from the base persistent component. Next, an instance of the article type is created, and the `create()` function is invoked with values for the new article's properties passed into the function in the `args` structure. The call to create returns an article instance that is populated with the property data of the newly created article, and this new instance is stored in the `newArticle` variable. Calling the `setTitle()` function defined in article.cfc updates the title property of the instance, and the final call to `update()` persists this change out to the content repository.

Persistence with Helper Classes and Delegation

A second strategy for designing persistent components is using helper classes and delegation. *Helper classes* are simply CFC types that help a separate CFC type accomplish a task. Rather than inheriting persistence functions from a base component, CFCs can use a persistence helper component to save their data. CFCs can pass their data to the helper component, and the helper component can handle storing the data in the content repository. This approach is particularly well suited to systems that must interact with a variety of content repositories that have different formats. Consider a situation in which one content type is stored in database A, and updates to content objects in this database are performed by executing a stored procedure. For a second type of content, which is stored in database B and lacks stored procedures, you must take a different approach to updating data. Clearly, a single `update()` function defined in a base persistent component class is not sufficient.

The solution is to define an abstract persistence helper component that provides empty implementations of the necessary persistence functions. This abstract persistence helper can then be extended as necessary by concrete persistence components that provide content repository-specific implementations of the persistent functions defined in the abstract persistence helper. All CFCs within the system that need to be persistent can store a reference to the correct persistence helper component. All persistence functions that are invoked against the CFC can then be delegated to the referenced persistence helper component that knows how to interact with the target content repository for the CFC.

Figure 8.2 shows how a CFC, in this case article.cfc, can use a persistence helper component that delegates responsibility for persisting article instances to the appropriate concrete databasePersister implementation.

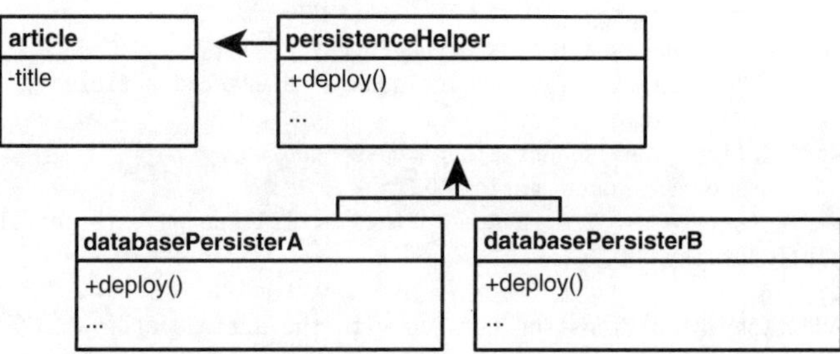

Figure 8.2 Persistence helper class and delegation.

Working with Components

Now that we have been introduced to the features of persistent components, discussed persistent storage options, and outlined strategies for persistent component design, we can touch on a few additional issues and strategies for working with persistent components before we move on to implementation details in Chapters 9, "Centralized Data Persistence," and 10, "Persistence with Localization."

Component Reference with URI

Alongside inheritance, another common technique for code reuse in object-oriented systems is composition. When applied to CFCs, the goal of composition is to take existing components and build or "compose" them into a new component with functionality that is greater than its parts. Component composition is achieved by storing references to other component instances within a CFC. This reference commonly takes the form of a uniform resource identifier (URI) that can locate the referenced component instance in the content repository. A URI serves to uniquely identify a component instance in the content repository. Therefore, when a component is referenced using a URI, this could simply be the objectID for the referenced component, or it could be a more complicated network or file path to the referenced data. A simple example of using component references is the creation of a multipage article CFC that stores internal component references to an individual article CFC instance for each page. Using composition, multiple article instances can be grouped together into a new component type that offers additional functionality. Listing 8.7 is a sample multipage article CFC that stores an array of article component URI references as strings.

Listing 8.7 **Component Reference Property (multipagearticle.cfc)**

```
<cfcomponent extends="basepersistentcomponent">
    <!--- The articles property stores an array of URI strings
          that reference individual article instances
  - one article per page --->
    <cfproperty name="articles" type="array">
    <!--- The addArticle() function adds a referenced article
  URI into the articles array --->
    <cffunction name="addArticle" access="public">
        <cfargument name="articleURI">
        <cfset temp = Σ arrayAppend(this.articles,arguments.articleURI);
    </cffunction>
    .
    Additional functions for working with the article array
    .
</cfcomponent>
```

This stripped-down component demonstrates how the `addArticle()` function is used to add article URIs to an array stored in the `articles` property of multipagearticle.cfc. The function accepts an articleURI argument as a string and appends it to the array of article URIs. You can use these component references to locate, instantiate, and work with the corresponding article instances. If the user is publishing a multipage article, he can page through the multipage article. For each page that is requested, we can look up the corresponding article that is referenced in the `articles` array property and load it from the content repository for display. This way, the work done to create the article.cfc type has been reused to create multipage articles rather than duplicate much of the code. Also changes to the article.cfc type will be automatically reflected in the multipagearticle.cfc type. Composition using component reference URIs is an excellent tool for achieving code reuse in place of direct component inheritance.

Granular Components

When you're modeling complex components, treating them as granular objects is an alternative to composition. Although composition provides the highest level of encapsulation and modularity, the instantiation of referenced components does incur higher processing overhead during system runtime. Consider a persistent component that represents a user of the system. If we store an address for the user, we can model a separate address CFC and store a component reference to this address component within the user component. This provides excellent modularity, but the inconvenience of instantiating and maintaining the additional component might well outweigh the modest benefit of code and data reuse in this case.

Rather then modeling the address as a separate component, you can treat it as a property of a granular component. To maintain component granularity, persistence-handling functions can store and retrieve complex embedded property values to separate database tables or XML documents apart from the main CFC property data. When an instance of the CFC is loaded from the content repository, it is stitched together from granular property values that are stored in unique locations. This approach simplifies working with the object at runtime and avoids the overhead of multiple referenced component instantiations. However, the developer should keep in mind that granular properties cannot be shared across multiple component instances because they are embedded within a particular CFC instance. The decision to use either granular components or composition will be driven by simplicity, reusability, and performance concerns, so don't be afraid to mix and match these approaches as the occasion requires.

Using Facade Components

Dynamic publishing systems are often composed of a variety of subsystems. A workflow service that is used to create content or a publishing service that provides content to clients and users are two examples of common subsystems within a dynamic publishing application. Subsystems are often composed of a collection of persistent components that work together to provide a service. If developers program directly against the components within a subsystem, and the public function interface for a component within the subsystem is modified, the developer must examine the entire code base of the application to ensure that all interaction with that component is updated to conform to the its new function interface. This approach leads to overly verbose code and makes maintenance extremely difficult.

The solution to this problem is to implement helper classes that serve as facades for subsystems within the application. These helper classes are implemented as static CFCs containing public static functions that provide a unified public interface to a subsystem. Clients should not have to worry about how the persistent components within a subsystem operate. Ideally, they should be able to invoke functions on a Facade component without worrying about how things are accomplished behind the scenes. It becomes the responsibility of the Facade component to interact with the various persistent components within the subsystem to perform any requested actions. This powerful and flexible methodology is well suited to systems of persistent CFCs. In Figure 8.3, we can see how a Facade component serves as a single gateway for interaction with a system of components. In the figure, a client calls functions on two components to perform an action in Case 1. The `doA()` function for Component A is called, followed by the `doB()` function for Component B. In Case 2, we see how a Facade component provides a simplified API for the client, which now only needs to call a single function, `doAction()`, on the Facade component to accomplish the same action as in Case 1.

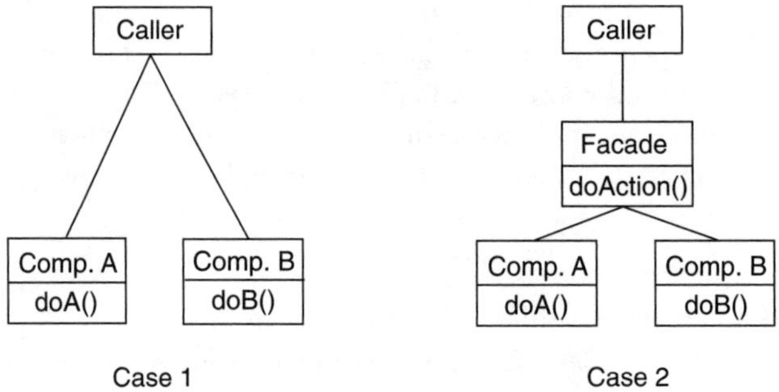

Figure 8.3 Facade component.

Figure 8.3 presents a simple interaction scenario, but with subsystems that involve a larger number of components, using a Facade component provides significant benefits. A Facade component insulates the client from the details of the subsystem. In Case 2 of Figure 8.3, we can see that even if the components in the subsystem are changed, we only need to update the `doAction()` function for the Facade component, and the changes will have no effect on the client. This ensures more stable, maintainable, and scalable applications.

Building Performance into Persistence

It is important to consider performance at every level of the application, and the Content layer is no exception. At a high level, performance in the Content layer is achieved by caching content and ensuring that the cache is synchronized with the underlying data.

Caching Frequently Accessed Content

You can use several strategies to cache frequently accessed content. Apart from built-in caching features in ColdFusion—including query caching and tags, such as `<CFSAVECONTENT>`—we also can implement custom content object caching within the Content layer. This is best implemented as an in-memory server cache using server scope. Content retrieval functions, such as the `get()` function that was defined for the base persistent component, can be designed to fetch object data and store a copy in the in-memory cache before returning the data to the caller. After this has run once, subsequent invocations of `get()` for that instance will use the data in cache rather than making a disk or database access. This greatly improves the response time for loading instance data from the content repository. When large amounts of data are being cached in server memory, it is important to ensure that sufficient physical memory is available to store the cached data. If sufficient memory is not available, more intelligent cache management will be necessary, such as a first-in first-out cache.

Synchronized Data Caching

For the cache to be useful, it must contain correct data. Upon any update to an instance, the Content layer will need to refresh the copy of the instance stored in cache. The cache refresh can occur along with the update, or a time span can be defined to specify the lifespan for the cached data. After the lifespan has expired, any access attempt can force a cache refresh for the instance. When an instance is deleted, the Content layer also needs to remove it from the cache. In a clustered environment, Java Message Service (JMS) can be used for messaging between servers to communicate changes in underlying data across servers in the cluster to keep in-memory caches synchronized.

Conclusion

This chapter introduced many of the issues and strategies surrounding component persistence. The ability to persist component instances in a content repository is the foundation for a dynamic publishing application built on ColdFusion MX. Component features including `<CFPROPERTY>` tags, non-static functions, and component metadata and introspection allow the data stored as component properties to be saved to the content repository. Interaction with the content repository can be implemented as a persistence API in a base component that all other persistent components extend to inherit the persistence API functions.

Alternately, interaction between component data and the content repository can be delegated to helper components that manage the process of saving component properties or retrieving these values from the content repository. Several approaches such as component references, granular components, and Facade components provide strategies for implementing more complex components or systems of components. Last, you learned about caching strategies at the Content layer of the application to build performance into this layer of the application. Chapter 9 will build on this high-level understanding of component persistence by presenting a concrete implementation of component persistence using a database as the content repository.

9

Centralized Data Persistence

by Anthony McClure

CHAPTER 8, "COLDFUSION COMPONENTS WITH PERSISTENCE," showed us that by using ColdFusion Components as a persistence mechanism, a standard application programming interface (API) might be exposed for use throughout a dynamic application. This API sets the stage for all interaction with various persistence repositories that we might use; therefore, it becomes the starting place for our Dynamic Publishing architecture.

Because of its importance as the foundation of the application architecture, it is paramount that you complete the API before production of any other code.

In this chapter, the CFC persistence API comes alive for the first time by showing CFC persistence against a database. We begin by designing and creating a Unified Modeling Language (UML) model of the persistence API based on the concepts presented in Chapter 8. Then we continue by taking that model and producing the foundation CFCs of the dynamic publishing system.

A finished API without the ability to use it is worthless. So, as a conclusion, we examine the API's usage going forward within the context of the dynamic publishing system.

Modeling the Persistence API

The process of creating a usable UML model can be a daunting one for any software architect or developer. A step-by-step approach would be best if we were in a perfect world; however, due to design constraints, changing requirements, tight development deadlines, and the general nature of modern software development, this is not always possible. Because of this improbability, we rely most often on an iterative process of examining the requirements, adding to or changing the object model, and then re-examining the requirements again until completion.

> **Note**
>
> To learn more about the UML and its use in application development, try these resources:
>
> - Books:
>   - *UML Distilled*, by Martin Fowler and Kendall Scott
>   - *Sams Teach Yourself UML in 24 Hours*, by Joseph Schmuller
> - On the Web:
>   - UML Resource Center—`www.rational.com/uml/index.jsp`
>   - UML Resource Page—`www.omg.org/uml/`

The importance of thorough requirements documentation (process models, user interface mockups, use cases, requirements documents, and so on) is extremely important for the production of this model. Without this, the architect will not be able to adequately determine the objects, methods, and properties needed to build the system.

Patterns of data and functionality begin to show through in completed models. For example, all users of the system might have addresses, but so do affiliate companies and authors of content. Rather than having the same properties duplicated in all objects that need it, we can extract the address information into its own object type that other objects might reference.

In addition, hierarchies of data might present themselves. In the preceding example, both a user object type and an author object type were mentioned. In reality though, isn't an author really a user with additional properties and methods? In this case, the author object type might extend a base object type of user. The author object type would automatically gain the properties and methods of a standard user, but it could expand upon these as necessary for author functionality.

The Persistence API UML

Examining the requirements shown in Chapter 8, we can begin the persistence UML model.

For the purposes of the persistence API, we know the standard methods that all objects need: `deploy()`, `create()`, `remove()`, `get()`, `delete()`, and `update()`. (See "Building a Base Component for Persistence" in Chapter 8 for more information.)

In addition to these methods, all persisted objects also need a set of properties that allow objects of varying types to be utilized in a standard way.

> **Note**
>
> It is important to note that the methods described here are not part of ColdFusion MX and CFCs by default. The individual developer must create and implement them as part of the development process.

For example, every article in the persistence repository must have a unique identifier. A single property that is available to all object types will fill this role. For this application, we shall call this special global property `objectID`. Other global properties, like this one, best belong along with the base persistence component, which all other objects then inherit.

Identifying object types, their functionality, and their properties in an object model allows production of a UML diagram for developers to work against. The proposed UML for the BasePersistentObject.cfc is shown in Figure 9.1.

BasePersistentComponent
-objectID : UUID -typeID : String -dtCreatedDate : DateTime -dtLastUpdatedDate : DateTime
+deploy() +remove() +get() +create() +delete() +update()

Figure 9.1 BasePersistentComponent UML.

The UML diagram shows all of the methods discussed and the new properties we want all objects to inherit. By creating a base persistent component of this nature, if additional global properties and methods are needed later during development, they are automatically available to all object types when they're added to the base component. This is possible because of the object-oriented nature of CFCs and the process known as inheritance.

The next step is to add the object types that inherit from BasePersistentComponent to the UML diagram. This shows a relationship of parent to child (in this case from BasePersistentComponent.cfc to all persistence objects). Figure 9.2 shows an object (the article type) added to the diagram and the aggregate relationship to BasePersistentComponent.

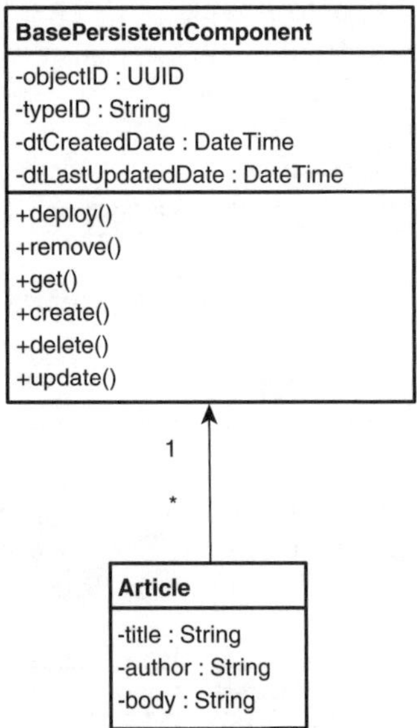

Figure 9.2 Article UML.

The article object does not need additional methods at this time; however, we can easily add methods on other iterative passes if the need arises.

From the requirements presented in Chapter 8, we know that the persistence API also needs to be able to access various types of object repositories (XML documents, SQL databases, and so on). To make the API more flexible to developers, we should add helper CFCs (helper functions) to the model to handle the various types of data access. The core method calls never change; only the implementation inside of BasePersistentComponent changes based on the type of access that is requested.

Ultimately, after the creation of the BasePersistentComponent and other object types inherited from it, the application developer only needs to focus on the actual development of the application, rather than worry about various types of data access. The complexity will be completely encapsulated inside of the CFCs and accessed via a simple method call.

This produces a black box type of effect to templates that access a persistence object (see Figure 9.3). The template could ask for an object update to a database or to an XML document without having to call differing methods to do so.

One helper CFC for every type of repository is required. This chapter deals with both database and XML access. To do this, we add two new CFCs to our model. As a side note, if your application does not require XML access, you do not need to implement that CFC.

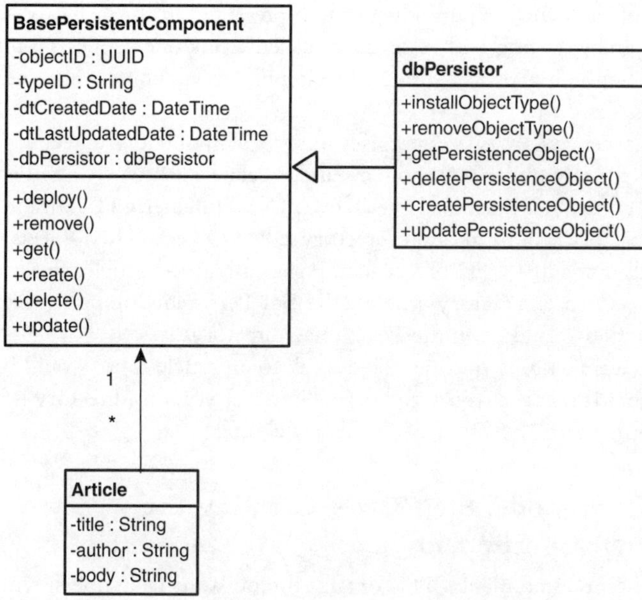

Figure 9.3 The Persistor CFCs.

The persistor CFCs contain the actual database/XML document interaction CFML code needed to implement the various persistence methods in BasePersistentComponent. At runtime, BasePersistentComponent creates a CFC property for each persistor type (persistor helper class) and places a reference to an instantiated appropriate persistor CFC within it. When a client calls a persistence method (`create()`, `get()`, `update()`, and so on) and wants database access, the BasePersistentComponent CFC calls the appropriate method within dbPersistor to carry out the database interaction.

Other than providing a consistent API to outside clients, placing the data interaction into individual CFCs provides logic encapsulation as well. Ultimately, this produces easier-to-maintain, faster-performing, reusable, and extensible code.

From UML to Code: Step One—Packing the Components

After the model is complete and the developers are ready to begin, you need to contain the components in an organized fashion. As discussed in Chapter 5, "ColdFusion Components," components provide for this organization by way of component packages.

Packages essentially map to the physical directory hierarchy that CFCs fall into.

> **Note**
> See Chapter 5 for more information on ColdFusion Components and component packaging.

For purposes of the dynamic publishing system presented in this book, we decided on a package hierarchy starting with a directory called Components. The Components directory will be the highest level in the hierarchy and will contain all other CFCs and CFC packages.

For the persistence API, two directories under Components are needed. The first comes in immediately under Components and is called Persistence. The Persistence directory will contain all persistence-related CFCs and helper CFCs. Inside of the Persistence directory will be another directory called Objects. The Objects directory will contain all individual CFC object files. For example, the article.cfc file would exist under the Objects directory, whereas the BasePersistentComponent.cfc and dbPersistor.cfc files would be in the Persistence directory.

In package terms, a fully qualified object call to an article CFC would be `components.persistence.objects.article`. The URI version (directory structure) would be \components\persistence\objects\article.cfc.

From UML to Code: Step Two—Creating the BasePersistentComponent.cfc

The BasePersistentComponent CFC contains the outward-facing persistence API. The standard API calls don't change, becoming a sort of contract that all other forms of client access can depend on. The architecture developers of the application first have to create the BasePersistentComponent to provide a starting place for the application and business logic developers to begin their work. Even with this component in place, until the helper CFCs for the various types of repository access are completed, the application developers are not able to test, but the standard API is known and ready to code against.

Using the UML object model as a guide, the BasePersistentComponent CFC is created. Properties and methods are defined using <CFPROPERTY>, and <CFFUNCTION> tags. In the end, a skeleton of the component is put into place. Listing 9.1 shows the BasePersistentComponent skeleton before the function code is implemented.

Listing 9.1 **BasePersistentComponent.cfc Skeleton**

```
<cfcomponent output="FALSE">
   <cfproperty name="objectID" type="UUID" default="">
   <cfproperty name="typeID" type="string" default="">
   <cfproperty name="dtCreatedDate" type="date" default="">
   <cfproperty name="dtLastUpdatedDate" type="date"
      default="">
   <cfproperty name="dbPersistor" default="">

   <!--- Initialize Persistors and Properties--->
    <cfscript>
      this.dbPersistor =
```

```
12          createObject("component","dbPersistor");
13        this.objectID = createUUID();
14        this.typeID = "";
15        this.dtCreatedDate = createODBCDateTime(Now());
16        this.dtLastUpdatedDate = createODBCDateTime(Now());
17     </cfscript>
18
19     <!--- Property Gets and Sets Start --->
20     <cffunction name="getObjectID" access="public"
21        returnType="UUID" output="FALSE">
22        <cfreturn this.objectID>
23     </cffunction>
24     <cffunction name="setObjectID" access="public"
25        output="FALSE">
26        <cfargument name="theObjectID" type="UUID"
27          required="1"/>
28        <cfset this.objectID = arguments.theObjectID>
29     </cffunction>
       *
       * Other Property Gets and Sets
       *
30     <!--- Persistence API Start --->
31     <cffunction name="deploy" access="public"
32        output="0"returnType="boolean">
          *
          * Implementation Here
          *
33     </cffunction>
       *
       * Other Persistence Functions
       *
34  </cfcomponent>
```

The code presented here should look familiar; it takes full advantage of the various CFC code techniques, including use of the <CFPROPERTY> tag discussed in Chapters 5 and 8.

There is a unique set of additions to this CFC that starts in the <CFSCRIPT> block at line 10 as well. This block runs when the component is first instantiated (acting like a constructor in object-oriented programming) and is important due to the nature of properties defined with <CFPROPERTY> tags in CFCs. Until a property is properly initialized by CFML code, ColdFusion does not assign it a memory location.

If the property were accessed before this initialization took place, ColdFusion would throw an error stating that it did not recognize the property.

The reason for this is that although <CFPROPERTY> tags are in place, they really do not do anything except the important job of making the properties available during component introspection.

> **Note**
>
> For more information on component introspection and component metadata, see Chapters 5, 8, and "From UML to Code: Step Three—Creating the dbPersistor.cfc and the Magic of Component Introspection" later in this chapter.

This block also contains the necessary code (lines 11 and 12) to create a component object of type dbPersistor and place that object into a property called `this.dbPersistor`. The `this.dbPersistor` property holding another object represents the helper CFC for doing database interactions mentioned previously and in Chapter 8.

With the skeleton CFC finished, normal CFML code is used to implement the function calls. `<CFSCRIPT>` blocks along with `switch()` and `if()` conditional statements are used to determine the type of persistence repository that the client wants to access (defaulting to database) and call appropriate functions of the requested persistor as needed.

Because database interaction is the first area to be covered in this code, the `switch()/case()` blocks only have the dbPersistor as an option (see Listing 9.2). Adding cases to this switch block and access to other persistence repositories is handled later in the chapter.

Listing 9.2 **BasePersistentComponent Functions Implemented**

```
1   <cfcomponent output="false">
       *
       * Starting Code and Gets and Sets
       *
2      <!--- Persistence API Start --->
3      <cffunction name="deploy" access="public"
4         returnType="boolean" output="0">
5         <cfargument name="dataStoreType" type="string"
6            required="1"/>
7         <cfargument name="dataSource" type="string"
8            required="0" default="testDB"/>
9
10        <cfscript>
11           switch (arguments.dataStoreType) {
12              case "database":
13              {
14                 returnVal =
15                    this.dbPersistor.installObjectType
16                    (this,arguments.dataSource);
17                 break;
18              }
19           }
20
21           if (returnVal)
22              return true;
23           else
24              return false;
25        </cfscript>
```

```
26    </cffunction>
      *
      * Other Functions
      *
27
28    <cffunction name="get" access="public" output="0">
29       <cfargument name="dataStoreType" type="string"
30          required="0" default="database"/>
31      <cfargument name="dataSource" type="string"
32          required="0" default="testDB"/>
30      <cfargument name="objectID" type="UUID" required="1">
33
34       <cfscript>
35          switch (arguments.dataStoreType) {
36             case "database":
37             {
38                returnVal =
39                   this.dbPersistor.getPersistenceObject
40                      (this,arguments.dataSource,
41                         arguments.objectID);
42                break;
43             }
44          }
45
46          if (returnVal)
47             return true;
48          else
49             return false;
50       </cfscript>
51    </cffunction>
52  </cfcomponent>
```

The consistency of the API is based on the arguments that are used throughout all of the calls. Every persistence function has the same two arguments: `dataStoreType` and `dataSource`. The `get()` function contains a third argument, `objectID`, because a single object reference is requested, and the `objectID` is the unique identifier of any object.

The code uses the data storage type as passed in by the client and executes appropriate code based on the `switch()` statement's outcome. Only if the data store type is a database is it necessary to also pass a data source name as well.

The real magic of the persistence API is inside of the case statements. This is where the actual database interaction, by way of calls to the stored persistor's methods, takes place.

Take, for example, the call starting at line 38: `returnVal = this.dbPersistor .getPersistenceObject (this,arguments.dataSource,arguments.objectID)`. Here, a local variable called `returnVal` is assigned the return value from a call to the `this.dbPersistor.getPersistenceObject()` method call. Remember that the `dbPersistor` property was initialized at runtime to hold a reference to a `dbPersistor`

CFC instance. This code uses that instance to load the properties of the currently initialized object with data from the database. Furthermore, it does not matter if the object type is an article, user, or any other type. The type just needs to extend the basePersistentObject CFC, and introspection takes care of the rest. How is this possible?

Passing a CFC Instance as an Argument to Another CFC

In Listing 9.2, starting at line 14, a method call to the `dbPersistor CFC` is made. Two arguments are passed into this method call. One argument, the second in the list, passes the data source name provided by the client, or the argument's default value for that property. The first argument passes a special reference to the `this` scope of the persistence object.

The `this` scope was first discussed in Chapter 5. It is in this variable location that all information about the component object is stored. By providing a reference to the instantiated object's `this` scope into another CFC, the developer is in essence allowing the CFC that the instance in being passed into access to the methods and properties of the passed instance. It is important to note that the passed instance is not a copy; it is a true reference to the instance.

This concept is easier to understand by diagramming what is happening. In Figure 9.4, we see the UML diagram of two CFC objects. The first is called `2dShape` and represents a simple two-dimensional shape (such as a square). This object contains no methods other than a property `set` and `get`, and one property called `shape` (stores the type of shape this object represents).

The second object is a `Shape_Changer` object; it acts as a helper CFC to the `2dShape` object. This object contains no properties itself, but does have a single method called `changeShape()`. The `changeShape()` method takes two arguments, the first is the new shape name to set into the `2dShape`'s shape property. The second needs a reference to the `2dShape` in which to act upon.

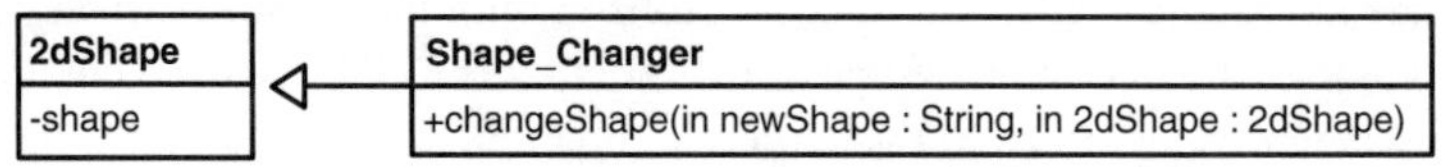

Figure 9.4 Shape example UML.

Figure 9.5 shows what happens when the `changeShape()` method is called and a `2dShape` object is passed into the `Shape_Changer` object.

Notice that in Figure 9.5 inside of the `changeShape()` method's code, a new object is not created for the `2dShape`. The instance of the `2dShape` object that is passed into the `Shape_Changer` object is what is being acted against. Also notice that the `newShape` object representation is what changes as a result of calling the `changeShape()` method.

A 2dShape is Created

```
newShape = createObject("component","2dShape");
newShape.setShape("rectangle");
```

A Shape_Changer is Created

```
newChanger = createObject("component","Shape_Changer");
```

The changeShape() Method is Called

```
newChanger.changeShape("triangle",newShape);
```

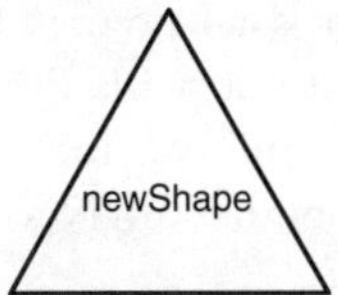

changeShape() method

```
<cffunction name="changeShape">
  <cfargument name="2dShape">
  <cfargument name="newShape">
  arguments.2dShape.setShape(arguements.newShape);
</cffunction>
```

Figure 9.5 Passing a CFC reference to another CFC.

Component Introspection Usage in Persistent Objects

Simply passing a reference of a persistence object into one of the persistor helper CFCs is not enough to make this a usable solution. Without a way to know what information about the CFC was passed into the persistor object, the developers have to have custom code for every type of persisted object in the system. Obviously, this is a bad solution, and it's likely to make developers quite upset at the thought.

It is at this point that component introspection saves the day. As pointed out in Chapter 8, by using the `getMetaData()` ColdFusion function call, all of the information we need about a CFC is at the developer's disposal.

Not only are the properties and methods of the child CFC available, but methods and properties from parent CFCs are available as well.

With access to a listing of properties, dynamic code can be written to take advantage of any object repository, and specifically, for a SQL database or XML document.

Building Data Storage and Dynamic Querying

Structured Query Language (SQL) is a development language used to interact with compliant databases. SQL statements issue commands to the database engine, allowing for database schema manipulation, data searching and retrieval, data creation, and data manipulation.

The most basic of SQL constructs is used in this dynamic publishing application. These constructs form the basis of any database interaction that might be needed. Please note that not all SQL is the same across databases. For this application, Microsoft Access is used as the database. If the database used to develop is different from this, the SQL code presented here might not work. Please consult the documentation that came with the database for specific information about SQL and that database, or check out Paul Dubois's *MySQL* (published by New Riders).

Here are the basic SQL constructs:

- **`CREATE TABLE`**—This SQL construct creates a new database table for data storage. In this system, each persistence object type will have its own unique table in the database. By having a unique table for each object type, the object instances are separated for easy and quick access from search interfaces and non-complex SQL queries. For easy visual recognition of object type tables, they are labeled with the obj_ prefix followed by the object type name. (You could, of course, name tables in any method appropriate to your environment). For example, the article.cfc object type would have a corresponding table called obj_article in the database. In addition to creating the table, this SQL call creates all of the columns in the table. For the persistence object types, each column in the table represents a different persisted property of the object.

Example:

```
CREATE TABLE obj_article (
objectID char(35) PRIMARY KEY,
typeID char(255),
dtDateCreated datetime,
dtLastUpdateDate datetime,
title char(255),
body memo,
author char(255))
```

- **DROP TABLE**—This SQL construct removes a table and all of its data permanently from the database.

  Example:

  ```
  DROP TABLE obj_article
  ```

- **SELECT**—The `SELECT` construct returns a recordset (data from the database) to the caller. This data can then be iterated through and used as needed. The asterisk (*) character is used to represent selecting all columns from a table.

  Example:

  ```
  SELECT * FROM obj_article
  ```

- **INSERT**—`INSERT` places data into the table.

  Example:

  ```
  INSERT INTO obj_article(
  objectID,
  typeID,
  dtDateCreated,
  dtLastUpdateDate,
  title,
  body,
  author
  )
  VALUES(
  '75BBFE35-1038-6549-968CB6B194604AED',
  'article',
  SQL Time Stamp,
  SQL Time Stamp,
  'Test Article',
  'This is a test…',
  'Anthony C. McClure'
  )
  ```

- **UPDATE**—The UPDATE construct is similar to the INSERT in that data is changed with its use. The UPDATE changes a specific record or set of records within the database by use of the SQL WHERE clause.

  Example:

  ```
  UPDATE obj_article
  SET (objectID = '75BBFE35-1038-6549-968CB6B194604AED'',typeID =
  'article',dtDateCreated = SQL Time Stamp,dtLastUpdatedDate = SQL Time
  Stamp,title = 'new title change',body = 'this is a changed body...',author =
  'Anthony C. McClure')
  WHERE 'objectID = a75BBFE35-1038-6549-968CB6B194604AED'
  ```

- **DELETE**—The final SQL construct, DELETE removes a record or records from the SQL table.

  Example:

  ```
  DELETE FROM obj_article
  WHERE objectID = '75BBFE35-1038-6549-968CB6B194604AED'
  ```

Static SQL constructs like those listed previously do not allow much functionality for a dynamic application like this one. With ColdFusion, however, developers are not limited to static SQL calls. By using the <CFQUERY> tag set and introspected properties from a passed-in CFC, we can dynamically create the SQL calls by implementing the functions of the dbPersistor CFC.

Persistent Objects

With all other aspects of the persistence API in place, all that remains is to implement the various persistors themselves.

From UML to Code: Step Three—Creating the dbPersistor.cfc and the Magic of Component Introspection

The first function of the dbPersistor is installObjectType(). Without this function, the deploy() method of the BasePersistentComponent CFC would not be able to execute and therefore no tables for persistence objects would exist to execute on. Examine the code for this function in Listing 9.3.

Listing 9.3 **The *installObjectType()* Function Implementation**

```
<cffunction name="installObjectType" returnType="boolean"
   access="public" output="0">
<cfargument name="cfcObject" required="1">
<cfargument name="dataSource" required="0"
   default="testDB">
<!--- Get the metadata for the object passed in --->
<cfset objectMetaData = getMetadata(arguments.cfcObject)>
<cfset
```

```
    cfcObject.setTypeID(listLast(objectMetaData.name,"."))>

<!--- Check for existing table --->
<cftry>
<cfquery datasource="#arguments.dataSource#"
   name="typeCheck">
   SELECT *
   FROM obj_#replace(cfcObject.getTypeID()," ","_","all")#
</cfquery>
<!--- If table exists return with a false result --->
<cfif typeCheck.recordCount GT -1>
   <cfreturn false/>
</cfif>
<cfcatch type="Any">
   <!--- Ignore on error, means no table exists --->
</cfcatch>
</cftry>

<!--- Place all properties into a single array. The inherited and local
properties are under two different structure keys; by placing all properties in
one area, we allow for easier Dynamic SQL creation. --->
<cfscript>
   aAllProperties = arrayNew(1);
   for(i=1;i LTE arrayLen(objectMetaData.properties);i = i
      + 1) {
      arrayAppend(aAllProperties,
         objectMetaData.properties[i]);
   }
   for(i=1;i LTE  arrayLen
      (objectMetaData.extends.properties);
      i = i + 1) {
      arrayAppend(aAllProperties,
         objectMetaData.extends.properties[i]);
   }
</cfscript>

<!--- Create a new table, using the property information -38 --->
<cftry>
<cfquery name="installTable"
   datasource="#arguments.dataSource#">
   CREATE TABLE obj_#replace(cfcObject.getTypeID(),"
      ","_","all")#
   (
<cfscript>
//loop object properties
for(i=1;i LTE arrayLen(aAllProperties);i = i + 1) {
//set property structure into currentProp
   currentProp = aAllProperties[i];

//if no type key, it is not a property
```

continues

Listing 9.3 **Continued**

```
if (structKeyExists(currentProp,"type")) {
//Determine if "," is needed
if (i GT 1)
   writeOutput(",");

//create properties
switch (currentProp.name) {
   case "objectID":
   {
      writeOutput("objectID char(35) PRIMARY KEY");
      break;
   }
   case "typeID":
   {
      writeOutput("typeID char(" & len("obj_" &
         cfcObject.getTypeID()) & ")");
      break;
   }
   default:
   {
      switch (currentProp.type) {
         case "string":
         {
            writeOutput(currentProp.name & " char(255)");
            break;
         }
         case "date":
         {
            writeOutput(currentProp.name & " datetime");
            break;
         }
         case "boolean":
         {
            writeOutput(currentProp.name & " byte");
            break;
         }
         case "memo":
         {
            writeOutput(currentProp.name & " memo");
            break;
         }
         case "struct":
         {
            writeOutput(currentProp.name & " memo");
            break;
         }
         case "array":
         {
            writeOutput(currentProp.name & " memo");
            break;
```

```
107                 }
108              case "UUID":
109                 {
110                    writeOutput(currentProp.name & " char(35)");
111                    break;
112                 }
113              }
114           break;
115        }
116  }
117  }
118  }
119  </cfscript>
120  )
121  </cfquery>
122  <cfcatch type="Database">
123  <cfthrow message="A database error occurred creating the
124     new object.">
125  </cfcatch>
126  <cfcatch type="Any">
127  <cfthrow message="An error has occurred creating the new
128     object.">
129  </cfcatch>
130  </cftry>
131
132  <cfreturn true/>
133  </cffunction>
```

This function is quite complex and uses all of the qualities of introspection and CFC instance passing. Starting at the beginning of the function, we see a new argument created called `cfcObject` (line 3). `cfcObject` is a required argument that holds the reference to the passed in CFC persistence object. With this reference, we can use the `getMetaData()` ColdFusion function to introspect the passed in CFC object.

This takes place in code at line 7. A local variable called `objectMetaData` is created to hold the CFML structure of data returned from the `getMetaData()` call. Notice that the `cfcObject` variable is passed into the `getMetaData()` call. This ensures that the structure returned is of the passed in CFC and not the dbPersistor.

On line 8, the first usage of the returned metadata structure takes place. To work against the correct database table, the code needs to know the `typeID` (that is, the object type name) of the CFC persistence object that is passed in. The "name" structure key within the `objectMetaData` variable holds this information, but it is in fully qualified package format. For instance, the article object's `objectMetaData.name` value would be `"components.persistence.objects.article"`.

Because of this, the code uses one of ColdFusion's built-in list functions called `listLast()` and calls the `set` method for the passed in object's `typeID` property. This works because the fully qualified package name is actually a string list with a period delimiter between values.

From this point forward (even in the calling template), the `typeID` is set in this object instance. For future reference of this property, a simple call to the `getTypeID()` (defined in the BasePersistentComponent) returns the needed information. With the `typeID` available, a call is made to make sure the table does not already exist. At line 16, the `typeID` is accessed to dynamically produce this table name.

If the table exists, the function returns with a boolean `false` result, which enables the calling template to know that the object type already exists in the database. If the table doesn't exist, then processing can continue and the building of the dynamic `SQL CREATE TABLE` statement can commence.

First, a slight bit of housekeeping takes place in the form of bringing all of the metadata property information under one array location. Within the instance metadata, properties of the child object are available by `variableName.properties` (as an array of property structures). The extended properties from the parent CFC(s) are not listed within this same array. They are first located under a structure key called "extends" and then followed by the Properties key as the standard properties are. By looping both sets of properties and placing them in one array, easier access is available for building the dynamic SQL. This process is noted in the code starting at line 30.

With the property arrays merged, the dynamic SQL building can begin. This is extremely important to keep from having a separate hard-coded SQL call for every type of object we want to create. The process is as follows:

1. Start the CFML `<CFQUERY>` with the `CREATE TABLE` statement (lines 45–48).
2. Iterate through the merged properties array.
3. On each iteration, place the current property into a structure called `currentProp` (line 54).
4. Check the `currentProp` structure for a key called "type." If this key does not exist, this is not a true property of the object to store in the database. For instance, the BasePersistentComponent CFC has a `<CFPROPERTY>` tag for the `dbPersistor` property, but because the code does not set a type value for this property, the code can check for this and not include it in the dynamic SQL building. Helper-type properties should never have a datatype associated with them, and conversely, all others should (line 57).
5. A switch statement checks the properties "name" key to see if it is the `objectID` or `typeID` property. Both the `objectID` and `typeID` are handled in a different way from standard properties, so a check is warranted here. (The `objectID` needs to be set as the table's primary key, and the `typeID` will have a fixed length.) If it is neither of these, then code continues by way of the default case (line 63).
6. If the switch statement does not match `objectID` or `typeID`, the default case occurs and a second switch statement takes place. This time, the switch looks at the "type" key that was tested for existence in step 4. SQL is a type full language, meaning that all data inside of a table has a specific data type associated with it. The type key of the property structure allows for the correct data type to be assigned to that new column (line 77).

7. After the iteration through the properties is finished, the dynamic SQL is generated and the call to the database is executed.
8. If no errors occur, a boolean `true` result is returned to the caller.

The other functions of the dbPersistor CFC work in a similar fashion to this one. The functions repeatedly use a basic pattern of looping the combined properties that come to the function via CFC passing and component introspection to build SQL statements. The main variance is only in the SQL statements.

One function in particular stands out as a little bit different in structure and bares further examination: `getPersistenceObject` (see Listing 9.4). The purpose of this function is to load the contents of an object record from the database into the properties of a CFC object. In other words, look up a specific object instance, loop its properties, and place them into the appropriate property variables of the CFC. Then allow the application developers to reference the properties directly instead of using the query used to get them.

Listing 9.4 **The *getPersistenceObject()* Function Implementation**

```
<cffunction name="getPersistenceObject" output="0"
   access="public">
   <cfargument name="cfcObject" required="1">
   <cfargument name="dataSource" required="0"
      default="testDB">
   <cfargument name="objectID" required="1">
   <cfset objectMetaData =
      getMetadata(arguments.cfcObject)>
   <cfset cfcObject.setTypeID(
      listLast(objectMetaData.name,"."))>

   <!--- Create the query --->
   <cfquery name="getObject"
      datasource="#arguments.dataSource#">
      SELECT *
      FROM obj_#cfcObject.getTypeID()#
      WHERE objectID = '#arguments.objectID#'
   </cfquery>

   <cfset queryProperties = getObject.columnList>

   <!--- Loop the query result and place into properties --->
   <cfloop query="getObject">
      <cfloop list="#queryProperties#"
         index="thisProperty">
         <cfset "cfcObject.#thisProperty#" =
            evaluate("getObject.#thisProperty#")>
      </cfloop>
   </cfloop>
<cfreturn true>
</cffunction>
```

This function call is much less complex overall in comparison to the `installObjectType()` function, but it has several interesting and key points:

- Similar arguments are used in this function, but a new one of `objectID` is required as well. In this case, the `getPersistenceObject()` function acts as the database implementation of the BasePersistenceObject CFCs `get()` method; therefore, it needs an `objectID` to tell it what object to "get" (line 6).
- Using the `objectID` that is passed in, a `SQL SELECT` statement is run and made to return all columns (the asterisk) where the `objectID` in the database matches the one passed into the CFC (line 17).
- Using a property of the ColdFusion query variable, a listing of the properties is set into a local variable called `queryProperties`. This is similar to what the `installObjectType()` function did, but now using information from the database instead of the object type CFC. It shows another way of accessing property information after a table is installed (line 20).
- Line 23 starts a loop of all records returned from the table. (For a `get` object, there should be only one.) Inside of this loop, a second iteration takes place. This iteration loops through the list of properties returned from the SQL query and placed into the `queryProperties` variable (line 24).
- Finally, at line 26, a `<CFSET>` is made against the passed in CFC `cfcObject` variable to set the properties for use by the client. The use of the ColdFusion `evaluate()` function allows for a generated string to be evaluated as a variable by the system and is in use here to retain the values of the recordset columns.

This starting point of BasePersistentComponent.cfc and dbPersistor.cfc forms the very foundation that the entire application will be developed from. You can use the same techniques used here for database interaction to access any other type of persistence storage or even an existing database.

Using CFC Persistence Objects with an Existing Database

Two methods are available to a developer who is using these techniques against an existing database.

The first method is fairly obvious. Create CFC persistence objects that have properties that match up to an existing database schema. Simply match columns to properties as needed. To handle interaction to these said databases, you can make a set of custom helper CFCs to facilitate the SQL calls just as we did in this application.

The second method is used for cases in which database data from several internal and external sources might be necessary. You could create a standard database structure using the process outlined in this book with pointers to table, database, and column names in external sources. Then you could store the primary keys to these sources as a property of the object in question.

The point is that with a little creative thinking, just about anything is possible using the architecture outlined here.

From UML to Code: Step Four—Creating the xmlPersistor.cfc

The addition of XML-based persistence is now a simple addition to the code already produced and creation of a new CFC called xmlPersistor.

We start by adding a new property to the BasePersistentComponent in which to hold the XML helper CFC. We do this inside of the initialization script (see Listing 9.5).

Listing 9.5 **BasePersistentComponent Initialization Updated with XML Persistor Code**

```
<!--- Initialize Persistors and Properties--->
<cfscript>
 this.dbPersistor =
   createObject("component","dbPersistor");
 this.xmlPersistor =
   createObject("component","xmlPersistor");
 this.objectID = createUUID();
 this.typeID = "";
 this.dtCreatedDate = createODBCDateTime(Now());
 this.dtLastUpdatedDate = createODBCDateTime(Now());
</cfscript>
```

Next, we add an additional case statement to the code from Listing 9.2, as shown in Listing 9.6.

Listing 9.6 **BasePersistentComponent XML Persistor Call Added**

```
<cfcomponent output="false">
    *
    * Starting Code and Gets and Sets
    *
    <!--- Persistence API Start --->
    <cffunction name="deploy" access="public"
       returnType="boolean" output="0">
       <cfargument name="dataStoreType" type="string"
          required="1"/>
       <cfargument name="dataSource" type="string"
          required="0" default="testDB"/>

       <cfscript>
          switch (arguments.dataStoreType) {
             case "database":
             {
                returnVal =
                   this.dbPersistor.installObjectType
                   (this,arguments.dataSource);
                break;
             }
             case "xml":
```

continues

Listing 9.6 **Continued**

```
            {
               returnVal =
                  this.xmlPersistor.installObjectType(this);
               break;
            }
         }

         if (returnVal)
            return true;
         else
            return false;
      </cfscript>
   </cffunction>
</cfcomponent>
```

This code allows a client to specify a dataStoreType of `"XML"`. When passed in this fashion, instead of accessing data via the database as before, a call is made to the functions of the xmlPersistor CFC. Notice that although the name of the function called within xmlPersistor is still called `installObjectType`, a datasource argument is not passed in; this is simply because an XML document does not need a database datasource to use. This code is shielded from the use of a persistence object; however, to the client, only a single function call of `"deploy"` is used.

After the BasePersistentComponent is updated, you can begin work on the actual xmlPersistor CFC. This component looks similar in design and scope to the dbPersistor, only using ColdFusion MX's built-in XML capabilities to access data instead of SQL to a database.

A full discourse on XML in CFMX is available in Chapter 6, "Leveraging XML in ColdFusion MX." Using these abilities, the `getPersistenceObject()` function of the xmlPersistor is shown in Listing 9.7. Notice that a similar flow to the logic is followed when compared to the `dbPersistor` function of the same name; only the implementation of storage changes.

The XML documents (for purposes of this example) are stored in the following location on the server's hard drive: c:\xmlObjects\objectTypeName\objectID.xml. With this directory/file name structure, like objects can be kept in a related directory (named after the object type), and all filenames match up to their respective `objectIDs`.

Although the files end in an .xml extension, they are in essence a flat text file that CFMX can easily deal with using `<CFFILE>`.

Listing 9.7 **The *getPersistenceObject()* Function Implementation**

```
<cffunction name="getPersistenceObject" output="0"
   access="public">
   <cfargument name="cfcObject" required="1">
   <cfargument name="objectID" required="1">
```

```
5       <cfset objectMetaData =
6          getMetadata(arguments.cfcObject)>
7       <cfset cfcObject.setTypeID(
8         listLast(objectMetaData.name,"."))>
9
10     <!--- Get the object XML from a file. --->
11      <cffile action="read"
12         file="c:\xmlObjects\#cfcObject.getTypeID()#\
13         #arguments.objectID#.xml" variable="xmlText">
14      <!--- Parse the xml text and create an xml Object. --->
15      <cfset xmlObject = xmlParse(xmlText)>
16      <!--- Loop the xml structure and place into properties --->
17      <cfloop collection="#xmlObject.objectID#"
18         item="thisKey">
19         <cfset "cfcObject.#thisKey#" =
20            xmlObject.objectID[thisKey].xmlText>
21      </cfloop>
22    <cfreturn true>
23    </cffunction>
```

Only the code used to read the XML file, parse it, and loop the properties is different from the SQL version of the function. Line 11 reads in the appropriate object based on the object type and `objectID` passed in as arguments to the function call. After the object is in memory, the text version of the XML is converted into a CFMX XML object using the `xmlParse()` ColdFusion function.

The resulting object is now in a form that you can manipulate as if it were a regular ColdFusion structure. At line 17, this structure is looped and the objects properties set.

The remaining functions are implemented in a similar way. They are identical to the SQL versions, but they use the ColdFusion XML functions instead of SQL calls to store, update, create, and get persistent object instances.

Persistence Objects Against Other Sources

Using the model outlined for SQL and XML data repository access, you could add any other repository to the system. This could include access to data through external objects such and COM+, Enterprise Java Beans (EJBs), or even a Microsoft Excel spreadsheet.

The pattern involves adding the appropriate persistor to the BasePersistentComponent's initialization script, adding a new case to the persistor switch statements for the standard function calls within BasePersistentComponent, and then creating a custom persistor CFC implementing the required persistor functions.

By only altering the implementation of the appropriate persistor helper CFCs, we allow for a consistent external API for all clients to use no matter what the internal storage method is.

Building Performance into Persistence

It is important to consider performance at every level of the application, and the Content layer is no exception. The general performance of CFCs is an advantage to general ColdFusion templates because of their compiled nature, but the slowest parts of any application involve trips to the data storage locations.

At a high level, caching content and ensuring that the cache is synchronized with the underlying data stored in the content repository achieve greater performance in the Content layer.

Caching Frequently Accessed Content

You can use several strategies to cache frequently accessed content. Apart from built-in caching features in ColdFusion, including query caching and tags such as `<CFSAVECONTENT>`, we also can implement custom content object caching within the Content layer. This is best implemented as an in-memory server cache using the server variable scope. Content retrieval functions, such as the `get()` function that was defined for the base persistent component, can be designed to fetch object data from the content repository and store a copy to the in-memory cache before returning the data to the caller. After this has run once, subsequent invocations of `get()` for that instance will be able to use the data in cache rather than making a disk or database access. This will greatly improve the response time for loading instance data from the content repository. When large amounts of data are being cached in server memory, it is important to ensure that sufficient physical memory is available to store the cached data. If sufficient memory is not available, then more intelligent cache management will be necessary, such as removing old or infrequently accessed objects from the cache.

Synchronized Data Caching

For the cache to be useful, it must contain correct data. Upon any update to a persistent component instance, the Content layer needs to refresh the copy of the instance that is stored in cache. The cache refresh can occur along with the update, or a time span can be defined to specify an expiration date for the cached data. When the cached content has expired, any access attempt can force a cache refresh for the instance. When an instance is deleted, the Content layer will also need to handle removing it from the cache. In a clustered environment, Java Message Service (JMS) can be used for messaging between servers to communicate changes in underlying data across servers in the cluster to keep in-memory caches synchronized.

Using the Persistence Components

With the persistence API in place, application development throughout the system can start in earnest. Developers who are using the persistence objects only need to know how to use the persistence API to get at the information they need.

The process for accessing and using any object in the system is a simple three-step process.

1. Create the object based on the appropriate CFC object type.
2. Call the `get()` method to load the properties, or set the properties and call the `create()` method to create a new object instance.
3. Call methods as needed.

Listing 9.8 shows a typical usage of a persistence object.

Listing 9.8 **Using an Article Object CFC**

```
1  <cfscript>
2     <!--- Get an article object from a database repository --->
3     myArticle = createObject("component",
4        "components.persistence.object.acticle");
5     <!--- With the new article object, load it with data --->
6     myArticle.get("database","testDB",
7        "75BBFE35-1038-6549-968CB6B194604AED");
8  </cfscript>
9
10 <!--- output the body to the user --->
11 <cfoutput>
12    #myArticle.getBody()#
13 </cfoutput>
14
15 <!--- change the author property --->
16 <cfscript>
17    myArticle.setAuthor("Anthony C. McClure");
18    //Update the object in the database
19    myArticle.update("database","testDB");
20 </cfscript>
```

This listing follows the standard three-step process and then goes a step further by setting a property and updating the object in the database.

At line 3, the object myArticle is created using the article CFC. At this point, we have reference to a blank article object, which is loaded with no data. Line 6 loads the blank object with data from a database and datasource called testDB. The particular loaded object has an `objectID` of 75BBFE35-1038-6549-968CB6B194604AED.

Because the object is now populated with data, to simply output a value from the object, we use simple CFML syntax. An example of this occurs on lines 11 to 13. The articles body is output to HTML by calling the `getBody()` property `get` method.

Starting at line 16, we change the `Author` property to `Anthony C. McClure`. At this time, the `object` property is loaded with the new data, but we have not instructed the object to update the database. If we were to reload the data for this object, the old Author would populate the `Author` property.

So that we can finish the process of updating the object, line 19 calls the object's `update()` method. Again, two arguments are passed, the first saying that we want to update a database, and the second determining the datasource name.

If we had instead wanted to create an XML copy of this object (assuming that we had fully implemented the xmlPersistor), the code could have stated `myArticle.create("XML");` instead.

From these examples, it should be clear that although some heavy code is necessary to start the persistence model, after it's completed, developers have a fast, efficient, and easy-to-code against API in which to develop the application and business logic.

Conclusion

In this chapter, database interaction with persistent components was explored in detail. A fully operational persistence API was generated from UML models to functional and extensible CFCs.

These CFCs take the underlying abilities of standard CFML (dynamic query generation using the `<CFQUERY>` tag) and new CFMX functionality (like the `xmlParse()` function and the `<CFXML>` tag) to abstract the complexities of data access from a variety of content repository types from the application and business logic developers.

You can now erect the application using the standard persistence API without creating additional code for data access.

10

Persistence with Localization

by Seth Hodgson

THE INTERNET FIRST EMERGED AS A TOOL for communication, entertainment, and commerce in the United States. As a result, many web sites and web-based applications were only available in English. But the online community is becoming increasingly global, and shifting online demographics are leading many companies and institutions to create multilingual web sites that speak to their assorted audiences in their native language.

International web use continues to grow at a rapid rate, and as more of the world comes online, the need to provide a familiar localized venue for communication and commerce across language boundaries will become an essential component of many online endeavors. Interacting with a global audience has great advantages as well as challenges, and this chapter will begin with an investigation of localization options. Following that will be a presentation of approaches for localizing content objects within the Content layer of a dynamic publishing application for global delivery.

What Is Localization?

Localization involves translating an application or a piece of content from one language to another. This is part of a larger process, and three terms are commonly used to describe the steps involved in creating an application that is targeted to a global audience:

- Globalization
- Internationalization
- Localization

You will commonly see these terms abbreviated to the first and last letters surrounding a number representing how many characters are between them.

Globalization (G11N)

This is the high-level process that describes the approach and preparations a company must undertake to participate globally in commerce and communication. Globalization is a blanket term that encompasses both internationalization and localization of a web site or application to make it globally available.

Internationalization (I18N)

This is the process of building applications in a fashion that allows them to adapt to various language and cultural requirements without extensive reengineering. Internationalization is the technical step of this process, and more specifically, it involves the following considerations:

- Support all relevant character sets and encodings. Most multilingual sites use the Unicode character encoding to store content in multiple languages in a single content repository. We will discuss Unicode and options for character encoding shortly.
- Refrain from using text within graphical elements, or keep text on a separate layer to allow for easier translation. In the case of Flash MX, text can be loaded into your movie dynamically or partitioned onto separate layers within the Flash movie to aid in localization.
- Ensure that locale-dependent details such as date, time, number, and currency formatting and display take the user's locale into account. You might also need to store or present other details, such as a customer name or address, differently depending on their locale.
- Build the Client layer, including templates and client-side programming, in a flexible fashion that allows for variable content lengths or content layout based on the user's locale. Certain applications might need to present content using a left to right layout, as is customary for Western languages, or a right-to-left layout for Arabic or Hebrew display. Designing the user interface to take these considerations into account is essential from the outset.

- A layered application allows content to be stored independently of display, which is important for localization. Storing the text displayed by the application in the content repository greatly simplifies localization by providing a centralized store of textual content, free from the clutter of design markup and business logic.

By taking these points into account, an application is well positioned to embrace the final step of the process: localization.

Localization (L10N)

Localization is the process of translating user interface elements and content into a target language. Because this chapter is focused on localizing the data stored within the Content layer of an application, a primary concern is providing enough space in our content repository and content type definitions to allow for text expansion. Content that is localized to some European languages might expand in size by 30% or more, whereas ideographic languages such as Chinese often decrease in size. If localization of content is even a remote possibility, take text expansion into account and be generous when configuring the content repository to allow for it.

Within the content repository, both primary and localized pieces of content need to coexist to be dynamically served to the users of the site. The solution for storing localized content within the content repository is to use a consistent character encoding. The encoding to use is Unicode.

What Is Unicode?

Over the years, all manner of character encodings have been developed to define character sets and map characters within these sets to numeric values with which computers can work. ASCII is one of the older, more common encodings that uses a single byte (seven bits, to be more precise) to represent each character in the Latin character set. The primary problems with earlier character encodings were that none of the available encodings could handle all of the multitude of letters, numbers, punctuation, and symbols in use in writing systems around the world today. In addition, the earlier systems often conflicted with each other by using the same number to represent different characters in separate character sets. This led to serious portability and localization problems that had no simple solutions.

In response to these problems, the Unicode standard arose. Its aim was to provide a unique number for every known character, regardless of platform or language. Unicode has broad industry support, and as the Internet becomes increasingly global, the use of Unicode is definitely picking up speed. In fact, ColdFusion MX and Java store all string data internally as Unicode. Also, many of the major operating system and database vendors now offer native support for Unicode. For any web site or application that needs to provide functionality and content for a variety of locales, the best path forward is to settle on storing all text using Unicode. Even though Unicode text requires more storage space than Latin encoding, it allows you to handle textual data consistently without worrying about separate character encodings per locale or platform.

Unicode Formats

Many specific formats are available within Unicode, including these:

- **UCS-2**—This is the encoding used internally for strings in ColdFusion MX and Java. It is a double-byte encoding that uses two bytes for each character. As the Unicode standard has expanded and more characters exist than can be stored using a straight double-byte encoding, UTF-16 has emerged as an updated double-byte approach to address this. UCS stands for Universal Character Set as defined by the international standard ISO 10646. Unicode corresponds to the level 3 implementation of ISO 10646, but it provides additional rendering information for characters in certain languages.
- **UTF-16**—UTF stands for Unicode Transformation Format. This is a double-byte encoding that originally could encode up to 65,536 characters. This limit has been shown to be insufficient, so a range of high-order values has been redefined as "surrogates" that provides 16 additional 16-bit "planes" for additional characters. Each plane contains 256 rows of 256 characters. These additional planes should provide the necessary space to store all of the world's writing systems and special characters.
- **UCS-4**—This is a 32-bit encoding, using four bytes for each character. It provides a far larger number space than a double-byte encoding, but for many languages that can be encoded with a single byte per character, this encoding wastes significant amounts of space and is not commonly used.
- **UTF-7**—This is a mail-safe transformation format that is compatible with mail gateways that require ASCII (7 bit) characters. This format is not a common general-purpose Unicode format as it was primarily intended for use with older email gateways, and its use will decrease as these gateways disappear.
- **UTF-8**—This is a multiple-byte encoding that uses 1 to 4 bytes to represent a character. Up to 6 bytes can be used to represent up to 31 bits of characters, but 4 bytes are sufficient to cover the "surrogates"—characters beyond the common Unicode range. This encoding has the strongest industry support due to its straightforward support for Latin characters that have traditionally been encoded using a single byte per character.

For web applications, the only encoding in this list that concerns us is UTF-8. The difference between UTF-8 and the other formats comes down to the way character data is stored at a byte level. UTF-8 uses a multiple-byte encoding approach, using a single byte for most Latin characters but requiring two to three bytes when encoding higher order characters, such as Japanese Kanji.

Because UTF-8 encodes Latin characters using a single byte, it provides legacy applications with a straightforward path to Unicode compliance. The UTF-8 format is well supported by modern web browsers, including Microsoft Internet Explorer, Netscape Navigator, Mozilla, and Opera. Because of this, the decision on what encoding to use is a simple one, and we can move forward knowing that all our text data will be presented using the UTF-8 format to ensure the broadest web browser support.

The Byte Order Mark

Unicode files contain a signature placed at the start of the file that indicates the encoding used for the file. This marker is called the Byte Order Mark (BOM). For plain text files, the BOM is instrumental in describing the encoding of the file to any application that might process it. In most editors, the BOM is not displayed to the user because it is only used to indicate the source file encoding to the editor, server, or any other program that might parse and use the file. The BOM is not something that the user must provide or type into the file. Dreamweaver MX supports creating files as UTF-8, and these files automatically have a BOM. On Windows NT/2000/XP, you also can create files with a BOM by opening the file in Notepad, editing it, and choosing to save as Unicode (UTF-8). ColdFusion Studio does not provide a way to generate a BOM, but you can edit Unicode files within Studio after they have been created elsewhere. In Hex, the BOM signature for UTF-8 files is EE BB BF, which is appended to the head of the file. If you edit a UTF-8 encoded file in ColdFusion Studio, you will see the BOM at the head of the file as the following three characters: ï»¿. If you do edit a UTF-8 file in ColdFusion Studio, simply save it back out without editing its BOM. The file will retain its encoding.

The ColdFusion MX application server first looks for a BOM at the head of the file when processing a template. If a BOM is not found, it will default to the encoding that has been specified for the Java Virtual Machine (JVM). You also can use the ColdFusion MX tag `<CFPROCESSINGDIRECTIVE>` to specify a page encoding. This tag generates the appropriate BOM for the page automatically. You can let ColdFusion MX know that a page to be parsed and compiled is in the UTF-8 format as follows:

```
<cfprocessingdirective pageencoding="UTF-8">
```

> **Warning**
>
> The encoding set by this tag needs to match an existing BOM for the template, or ColdFusion MX generates an error. Additionally, this tag is processed at compile time, not at runtime. Therefore, attempting to exclude this tag conditionally by placing it within a `<CFIF>` block has no effect.

Specifying Page Encoding

ColdFusion MX returns UTF-8 encoded pages to the user by default. If you need to return pages using a different character encoding, you must use the `<CFCONTENT>` tag as follows:

```
<cfcontent type="text/html charset=iso-8859-1">
```

In this example, ColdFusion MX sends the page to the user using the iso-8859-1 character encoding as specified within the `type` attribute of the tag. The iso-8859-1 character set contains all characters that western European languages require. ColdFusion MX uses the default UTF-8 encoding even if a different character set is specified in a metatag:

```
<meta http-equiv="content-type" content="text/html" charset="...">
```

Here, you specify a character set to be used to display the page. ColdFusion MX returns a UTF-8 encoded page to the user regardless of the setting in this tag because `<META>` tags are not processed by the ColdFusion MX Application Server. To override the UTF-8 default, you must use a `<CFCONTENT>` tag. `<CFPROCESSINGDIRECTIVE>` informs ColdFusion MX of the encoding of the source file it will parse and compile, and `<CFCONTENT>` sets the encoding for the page that is returned to the user.

The majority of the time, pages can be returned to your users in the default UTF-8 format. However, if you have legacy database content that is stored using a different encoding, such as Shift-JS (a common Japanese encoding) or EUC-KR (a common Korean encoding), you need to use the `<CFCONTENT>` tag to inform the user's browser of the character encoding in use.

Specifying URL and Form Variable Encoding

As you code global ColdFusion applications, it is helpful to keep everything UTF-8 encoded. You can accomplish this through the use of the `<CFPROCESSINGDIRECTIVE>` and `<CFCONTENT>` tags as detailed in the preceding section. An additional wrinkle when trying to keep everything in UTF-8 format is that you need to use the new built-in `setEncoding()` function to force ColdFusion MX to treat URL and Form variables as UTF-8 encoded text. The syntax for handling this is simple:

```
<cfscript>
  setEncoding("form","UTF-8");
  setEncoding("url","UTF-8");
</cfscript>
```

You can place this code near the head of a template, in a global include, or in your Application.cfm. We have seen how ColdFusion MX uses Unicode, but to learn more about the standard, visit the official web site at `http://www.unicode.org`.

Choosing What to Localize

Deciding what content to localize can be a daunting process. The extent of localization might fall anywhere along the spectrum of full localization to limited localization of only a few assets. Business requirements for target regions and locales drive both the level of localization and the set of languages for which the application is localized.

Available ColdFusion MX Locales

ColdFusion MX provides native support for 28 locales that cover most of the nations with the largest populations of Internet users. Table 10.1 lists the supported locales along with the standard Java locale—a combination of an ISO language code and an ISO country code—that each ColdFusion MX locale maps to.

Table 10.1 **ColdFusion MX Locales**

ColdFusion MX Locale Name	Java Standard Locale String
Chinese (China)	`zh_CN`
Chinese (Hong Kong)	`zh_HK`
Chinese (Taiwan)	`zh_TW`
Dutch (Belgian)	`nl_be`
Dutch (Standard)	`nl_NL`
English (Australian)	`en_AU`
English (Canadian)	`en_CA`
English (New Zealand)	`en_NZ`
English (United Kingdom)	`en_GB`
English (United States)	`en_US`
French (Belgian)	`fr_BE`
French (Canadian)	`fr_CA`
French (Standard)	`fr_FR`
French (Swiss)	`fr_CH`
German (Austrian)	`de_AT`
German (Standard)	`de_DE`
German (Swiss)	`de_CH`
Italian (Standard)	`it_IT`
Italian (Swiss)	`it_CH`
Japanese	`ja_JP`
Korean	`ko_KR`
Norwegian (Bokmal)	`no_NO`
Norwegian (Nynorsk)	`no_NO_nynorsk`
Portuguese (Brazilian)	`pt_BR`
Portuguese (Standard)	`pt_PT`
Spanish (Modern)	`es_ES`
Spanish (Standard)	`es_ES`
Swedish	`sv_SE`

Use the built-in `setLocale()` function to assign the current locale for your ColdFusion MX application. You can use the `getLocale()` function at any time to determine the current locale setting for the application. The locale setting is used to generate appropriate formatting for dates, times, numbers, and currency when using the various international functions in ColdFusion MX. Although ColdFusion MX only supports this subset of the world's available locales, you are free to use any locale. Note, however, that you must find or create your own user-defined functions to handle the formatting of dates, times, numbers, and currency for any locales that ColdFusion MX does not natively support.

Application Data Versus Content

The task of localizing an application and content displayed by the application can be viewed as two distinct processes. Application data includes all text and icons that are part of the application user interface. Localizing application data involves storing text strings, icons, and other elements that are separate from display templates and pulling them into the user interface dynamically based on the user's preferred locale.

Localizing content involves translating the text and any associated file assets for a content object into a target language. You can use several approaches to localize instances of a content object within the content repository, which we will see later in the chapter. After you have localized content objects and stored them in the content repository, the publishing layer of the application can access them by locale and present localized content to the user. We will investigate strategies for localizing application data and content throughout the rest of this chapter.

Choosing Selections of Content to Localize

Sometimes, full content localization does not make sense, such as the case of promotions or events that should only be presented to a specific region. However, it does make sense to selectively localize general application content that is presented to your users. Regional marketing and sales goals will drive the decisions behind what and where to localize. You can measure return on investment (ROI) for localization efforts by using a combination of marketing and sales metrics. You can tune this data further to tune the overall globalization approach for an enterprise.

Approaches to Localization

A dynamic publishing application will present both static assets—such as graphics, video, and sound—as well as dynamic text content to the end user. After settling on the portions of a site and its content to localize, you need to put processes in place to govern the localization of the application and its assets and content.

Static Assets

Static assets, such as HTML files, along with graphics and other media files require the simplest localization process. A good approach here is to create a directory structure that breaks out static assets per locale. If static assets for a United States site in English are stored under a document root, such as /assets/, simply create a new directory tree within the document root for each required locale. For example, create a new subdirectory, /assets/jp/, for static Japanese site assets that mirrors the directory structure for your primary locale. You can then translate content within this new localized directory tree into the target language as necessary.

The specific workflow process for updating static content and flagging it for localization depends on available resources and business requirements. Source code control systems such as CVS or Visual SourceSafe (VSS) are helpful in controlling and auditing changes to files. You can monitor changes to batch static files and content assets for translation and further processing.

Localization Vendors

You can translate a file asset or piece of content internally if the resources are available, or you can offload this task to a localization vendor. When you're working with a localization vendor, the general process involves sending the vendor a file or piece of content to translate. The vendor handles the process of translation and then returns the translated file or content for insertion into the file system or content repository of the application. Many localization vendors are available, but following are two of the most well-known vendors:

- **SDL International**—`http://www.sdlintl.com/`
- **Lionbridge**—`http://www.lionbridge.com/`

Custom-Built Solutions

Localizing dynamic content that is stored in the content repository of an application is more complex when you're dealing with dynamic assets. You must solve two issues. First, you must determine the party that is responsible for translating the content. As part of this first issue, you also must decide the process by which the party obtains content for translation and returns the translated result. Second, you must implement a framework for storing multiple languages for each piece of content in the content repository.

If translation is not performed internally for content that is stored in a content repository, then the best approach for localization is to tie interaction with a localization vender into the context of a workflow. For example, a workflow to create a new content object might offer the option to start localization workflows for a piece of content upon completion. These localization workflows could then interact with a localization vendor, sending the content object to the vendor for translation and inserting the translated content into the repository when the vendor returns it.

Regardless of whether the translation is performed in-house or by a localization vendor, you must store the translated content in the content repository. The full solution involves the Content layer for storing localized content. The Management layer controls the creation and translation of localized content via workflow and content management interfaces. The Publishing and Client layers handle localized presentation of the application and its content to the end user.

Challenges for Localization

Implementing a Content layer that is architected to handle content localization presents several challenges. The biggest challenge is how the various languages for a specific content object are related and how specific languages for given content objects can be retrieved from the content repository most easily.

Chaining Locales

In many applications, maintaining a relationship between the languages that a content item is translated into will be a requirement. This can be addressed in a variety of ways and will depend on the implementation route chosen for localizing content objects. If properties within a given content object are "doubled up," such that each property contains a structure of translations keyed by locale, there is only a single object to deal with, and chaining across locales is implicit. We will return to the disadvantages of this strategy later in the chapter.

On the other hand, if translations for a piece of content are stored as unique objects, you can use a helper component to chain these localized instances together, thereby maintaining a relationship between the available locales for a piece of content. With this strategy, each localized instance of a piece of content will have an identical set of properties, but the values stored in the properties will be translated into a target language. In the case of an Article.cfc instance discussing ColdFusion MX localization support, a Spanish localization for this article will still have `title`, `body`, and `author` properties, but the values stored for the `title` and `body` will be translated into Spanish. We will use a helper component to maintain the relationship between the various localized instances for a given piece of content.

Retrieval Constraints

The second challenge is to make the retrieval process for localized content objects as painless as possible. In the case of content objects that are localized by doubling up properties, only a single objectID is required for retrieval of the object regardless of the desired locale because it contains all necessary localized property data. After this rather heavy object has been retrieved, you can access and display the display properties according to the desired locale.

You can avoid the increased object size that doubling up properties causes if you instead store localizations as unique objects. It would be ideal if you could access the various localized instances of a piece of content using a single ID. Requesting various translations of the same content object using different IDs does not make sense because we are dealing with a single piece of content. We simply want to see the same content object in a different language. You can bridge this gap between a single content objectID and maintaining unique instances per locale by using the Single ID Locale Mask architecture.

Single ID Locale Mask

The aim of the Single ID Locale Mask architecture is to store each localized translation for a piece of content as a unique object, but still provide access to all available locales through a single objectID. This makes for a cleaner data model and simplifies the task of localizing content by encapsulating each locale for a given piece of content as a separate object. This architecture solves the challenges of finding a way to chain the various locales available for a content object together and control access to them through a single ID.

Addressing these issues is a two-fold process:

- First, we need a master ID for each piece of content regardless of locale.
- Second, we will use a helper component to maintain the list of locales that a piece of content has been localized into.

When a new content object—a new article, for instance—is created, this primary object will be the mask hiding the complexity of accessing its various localized instances. This mask object is an instance of a given content object type, such as an article, but it also maintains a reference to a helper component that stores the available locales for this individual piece of content.

The ability to localize a content object will be a common requirement for many component classes within a dynamic publishing application. We might need to localize articles, products for an online store, and a host of other possible component classes. As seen in previous chapters, it is a best practice to move shared functionality such as this into a base class that can be extended by any components that require this functionality. Because we are dealing with the localization of content, it makes sense to move this localization framework into a BaseContent.cfc component that will extend BasePersistentComponent.cfc to provide both persistence and localization to content components that extend it. A MaskInfo.cfc helper component is also defined that will store the localization information for a given content object. Note that our MaskInfo.cfc does not extend the BaseContent.cfc. This is because we need to be able to persist instances of MaskInfo.cfc, but these instances do not require localization. See Figure 10.1 for a UML diagram of this architecture.

In this architecture, each content type in our system extends the BaseContent.cfc component. This provides each content type with both the persistence API defined in BasePersistentComponent.cfc as well as the localization API that is defined in BaseContent.cfc. The primary locale instance for a piece of content also references a helper component of the MaskInfo.cfc type. There is a one-to-one correspondence in the system between a primary locale instance for a piece of content and a MaskInfo.cfc instance that will store localization information for the content. The Publishing layer of the application can load the primary locale instance for a piece of content directly, or it can ask the instance for other locales in which the content is available. The primary locale instance can look up this information in its referenced MaskInfo.cfc instance. Figure 10.2 shows the high-level relationships between the various locales for an example ColdFusion MX article instance.

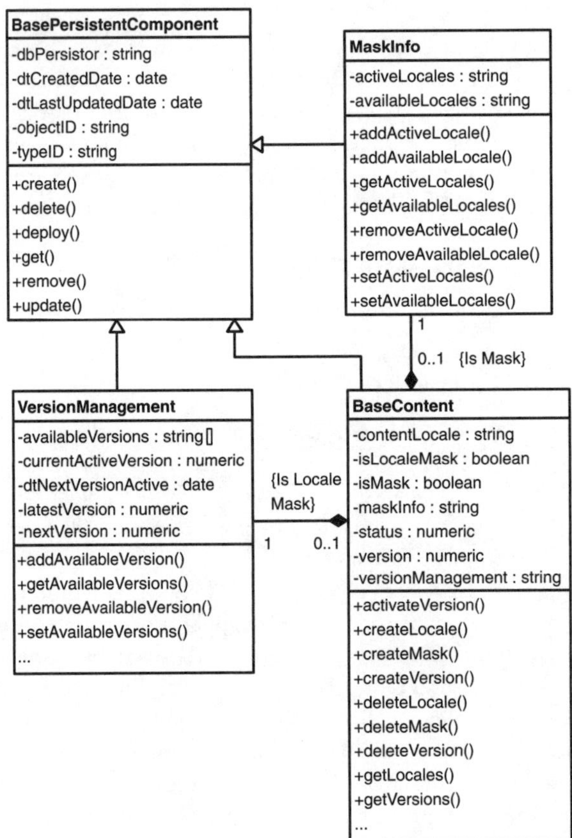

Figure 10.1 A class diagram for the proposed localization architecture.

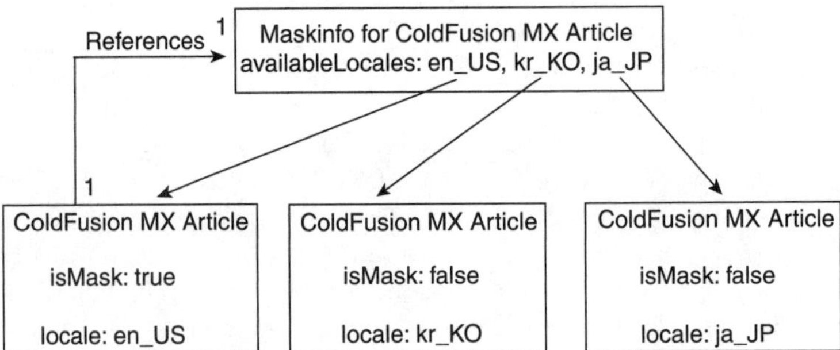

Figure 10.2 Localized article instance.

In Figure 10.2, we see that a mask object—in this case, the instance for the en_US locale—has a reference to a MaskInfo instance that keeps track of the various localized instances that exist for the specific piece of content.

Figure 10.1 raises some interesting points that we should cover before continuing. The BaseContent.cfc component extends BasePersistentComponent.cfc, so it will inherit the various properties and persistence functions that are defined in BasePersistentComponent.cfc. It also defines several new properties and functions, as shown in Tables 10.2 and 10.3.

Table 10.2 **BaseContent.cfc Properties**

Name	Type	Description
`contentLocale`	string	This is the locale for the component instance. The value stored for this property will be one of the standard Java locale strings. Therefore, an instance targeted to the U.S. will store a value of `en_US`.
`isMask`	boolean	This property is `true` for a content object instance that is the primary mask for a given piece of content. Localized instances of a piece of content will have this property set to `false`.
`maskInfo`	MaskInfo	This property is a reference to the MaskInfo for a given piece of content. Only a primary mask object, `isMask="true"`, will store a reference to a MaskInfo instance. The referenced MaskInfo instance is a helper component that stores localization information for the content object.
`status`	numeric	This property stores a simple integer to indicate the object state: 0 is inactive, 1 is active, 2 is archived, and 3 is deleted.

Table 10.3 **BaseContent.cfc Functions**

`createMask()`	The `createMask()` function creates the mask, or primary instance, for every new piece of content.
`createLocale()`	After the mask object has been created, the `createLocale()` function creates each required localized instance of the object.
`getLocales()`	The `getLocales()` function returns a list of locales that the content object has been localized to.
`deleteMask()`	The `deleteMask()` function deletes a content object entirely. This includes removing the mask object and any localized instances that exist.
`deleteLocale()`	The `deleteLocale()` function deletes a specific locale instance for a content object.

The additional `getter` and `setter` methods for each property of BaseContent.cfc have been omitted from Figure 10.1 and Table 10.3 but they follow the general pattern of `getPropertyName()` and `setPropertyName()`.

The MaskInfo.cfc does not extend BaseContent.cfc. It does, however, extend BasePersistentComponent.cfc. The reason for this is that MaskInfo.cfc must be persistent, but it does not represent a content object. Many utility components within a dynamic publishing application require persistence, but they might not require localization or versioning. Therefore, we can inherit persistence in our MaskInfo.cfc without cluttering it with unnecessary localization properties and functions. This component defines two properties that are type string and will store comma-delimited lists of locales. The `activeLocales` property contains a list of all localized instances for this content object that are currently active (status = 1), and the `availableLocales` property stores a list of all localized instances for this content object regardless of their status. This component also provides functions for getting and setting its properties as well as utility functions that add or remove locales from these two lists. Let's look at the implementation for MaskInfo.cfc (see Listing 10.1).

Listing 10.1 **MaskInfo.cfc**

```
<cfcomponent extends="BasePersistentComponent">
  <cfproperty name="activeLocales" type="string"
    default=""/>
  <cfproperty name="availableLocales" type="string"
    default=""/>

  <!--- Initialize properties --->
  <cfscript>
    this.activeLocales = "";
    this.availableLocales = "";
  </cfscript>

  <!--- Property getters/setters --->
  <cffunction name="getActiveLocales"
    access="public"
    returntype="string"
    output="false">
    <cfreturn this.activeLocales/>
  </cffunction>

  <cffunction name="setActiveLocales"
    access="public"
    output="false">
    <cfargument name="theLocales" type="string"
      required="true"/>
    <cfset this.activeLocales = arguments.theLocales>
  </cffunction>
  <!--- Get and set functions for availableLocales omitted --->

```

```
    <!--- Functions to add/remove locales --->
    <cffunction name="addActiveLocale"
      access="public"
      returntype="boolean"
      output="false">
      <cfargument name="theLocale" type="string"
        required="true"/>
      <cfscript>
        if( not listFindNoCase(this.activeLocales, arguments.theLocale) ) {
          this.activeLocales = listAppend(this.activeLocales,
            arguments.theLocale);
          return true;
        }
        else
          return false;
      </cfscript>
    </cffunction>

    <cffunction name="removeActiveLocale"
      access="public"
      returntype="boolean"
      output="false">
      <cfargument name="theLocale" type="string"
        required="true"/>
      <cfscript>
        listIndex = listFindNoCase(this.activeLocales, arguments.theLocale);
        if( listIndex ) {
          this.activeLocales = listDeleteAt(this.activeLocales,listIndex);
          return true;
        }
        else
          return false;
      </cfscript>
    </cffunction>
    <!--- Add/remove functions for availableLocales
          omitted --->
  </cfcomponent>
```

The MaskInfo.cfc component is fairly straightforward to implement, and the `getter`, `setter`, `add` and `remove` functions that deal with the `availableLocales` property have been left as an exercise to the reader. Every instance of BaseContent.cfc that is a mask object will store a reference to a MaskInfo.cfc instance. This MaskInfo.cfc instance is created along with the mask object, and a reference to it is stored in the mask object when the mask object is created. The BaseContent.cfc instance will use its corresponding MaskInfo.cfc to maintain a record of the locales it has been localized into and which of these locales are flagged as active.

Next, let's step through an implementation of BaseContent.cfc to see how it provides us with a single ID for access to any of the localized instances that might exist for a given content object, as well as controlling the creation of mask objects and localized instances. See Listing 10.2.

Listing 10.2 **BaseContent.cfc: Properties, *Getters*, *Setters*, and *createMask( )***

```
<cfcomponent extends="BasePersistentComponent">
  <cfproperty name="isMask" type="boolean"
    default="false"/>
  <cfproperty name="maskInfo" type="string"/>
  <cfproperty name="contentLocale" type="string"
    default="en_US"/>
  <cfproperty name="status" type="numeric"
    default="0"/>

  <!--- Initialize properties --->
  <cfscript>
    this.isMask = "false";
    this.maskInfo = "";
    this.contentLocale = "en_US";
    this.status = 0;
  </cfscript>

  <!--- Property getters/setters --->
  <cffunction name="getStatus"
    access="public"
    returntype="numeric"
    output="false">
    <cfreturn this.status/>
  </cffunction>

  <cffunction name="setStatus
    access="public"
    output="false">
    <cfargument name="theStatus" type="numeric"
      required="true"/>
    <cfset this.status = arguments.theStatus>
  </cffunction>
  <!--- Getters and setters for the remaining
        properties have been omitted --->

  <!--- Function: createMask() - This function creates
        a new "mask" content object instance --->
  <cffunction name="createMask"
    access="public"
    returntype="any"
    output="false">
    <cfargument name="contentLocale" type="string"
      required="true"/>
    <cfscript>
      this.isMask = "true";
      this.contentLocale = arguments.contentLocale;
      this.status = 1;
      // Create a MaskInfo instance to store the locale
      // information for all locales of this object
```

```
50        myMaskInfo = createObject("component","MaskInfo");
51        myMaskInfo.setActiveLocales(arguments.contentLocale);
52        myMaskInfo.setAvailableLocales(arguments.contentLocale);
53        myMaskInfo.create();
54        this.maskInfo = myMaskInfo.objectID;
55        // Now create this mask object
56        this.create();
57        return this;
58      </cfscript>
59    </cffunction>
```

Note

Following the definition of the properties that will be stored in BaseContent.cfc, there is a block of public `getter` and `setter` methods for working with these values. One interesting aspect to note is the use of `contentLocale` as a property name rather than the simpler `locale`. The reason for this is that if the property used the name `locale`, a `getter` method defined in BaseContent.cfc would need to be named `getLocale()`. The issue here is that `getLocale()` is a built-in ColdFusion MX function, and an error will be thrown when you try to run such a component. Avoid using variable and function names in your components that conflict with built-in variable and function names for ColdFusion MX.

Next, the `createMask()` function is defined beginning on line 38. This function is the basis for creating localized content objects, and it expects a locale to be passed in as a string. The locale that is passed in will become the primary locale for this new content object. First, the function marks this instance as a mask object by setting the `isMask` property to `true`. The function also assigns the desired locale to the instance and flags the object as active by setting its status to `1`. The function then instantiates a new MaskInfo.cfc object that will be used to store all localization information for this content object. Because this is the primary mask object, no localizations have been defined, so the MaskInfo instance is initialized using its `setter` methods to store this locale as both an active and available locale.

The `create()` function is called on the MaskInfo instance to persist it to the content repository. Its `objectID` value is retrieved and assigned to the `maskInfo` property of the mask object so that the mask object will have a reference to its associated MaskInfo instance. Now that the localization information has been saved to the content repository in the MaskInfo object and all necessary properties have been set for the mask object, it can be persisted to the content repository by calling `this.create()`. The function then returns the newly created mask object and its work is done. See Listing 10.3.

Listing 10.3 **BaseContent.cfc Continued:** ***createLocale( )***

```
<!--- Function: createLocale() - This function
      creates a new localized instance of the object
      using the mask object's ID and appending the
      locale for this instance --->
<cffunction name="createLocale"
  access="public"
  returntype="any"
  output="false">
  <cfargument name="contentLocale" type="string"
    required="true"/>
  <!--- Validate that this is the mask object --->
  <cfif not this.isMask>
    <cfthrow message="Validation error">
  </cfif>
  <!--- Load the MaskInfo helper class --->
  <cfscript>
    myMaskInfo =
      createObject("component","MaskInfo");
    myMaskInfo.get("database", "contentDB",
      this.maskInfo);
  </cfscript>
  <!--- Validate that no object has been created for the passed
locale --->
  <cfif listFindNoCase(
    myMaskInfo.getAvailableLocales(),
    arguments.contentLocale)>
    <cfthrow message="Validation error">
  </cfif>
  <cfscript>
    newLocale = createObject("component",
      getMetadata(this).name);
    // Copy props into this new locale object
    for( prop in this ) {
      if( not isCustomFunction(this[prop]) )
        newLocale[prop] = this[prop];
    }
      // Override necessary properties
    newLocale.setContentLocale(
      arguments.contentLocale);
    newLocale.setIsMask(false);
    newLocale.setStatus(1);
    // Set up the ID to use when creating this new
    // locale instance
    localeID = this.objectID & "/" &
      arguments.contentLocale;
    // Create the new locale instance passing in
    // the desired object ID
    newLocale.create(objectID=localeID);
    // Update the MaskInfo object
```

```
101         myMaskInfo.addActiveLocale(
              arguments.contentLocale);
102         myMaskInfo.addAvailableLocale(
              arguments.contentLocale);
103         myMaskInfo.update();
104         // Return the new locale instance
105         return newLocale;
106       </cfscript>
107     </cffunction>
```

The `createMask()` function is used to create the primary mask object for a content item, but the assorted localizations are created by calling `createLocale()` against the mask object. The mask object serves as a gatekeeper for all interaction between the client and the various locales the content object will be translated into. When this function is called against a mask object, several steps are taken to generate the new localized instance. First, a validation check is performed to prevent this function from being called against objects that are not mask objects. Second, the `maskInfo` property that references the associated MaskInfo instance for this mask object is used to load the MaskInfo instance from the content repository with the `get()` function on line 77. This function is a member of the persistence API defined in BasePersistentComponent.cfc, and it requires the data store type, the database name, and the objectID when loading an object from the content repository. Following this, we run a second validation check to ensure that only a single instance can be created per locale by testing whether the locale specified in the `contentLocale` argument is found in the list of `availableLocales` stored within the referenced MaskInfo instance. This list represents all locales that the content object has been translated into.

If it is safe to proceed, the next step is to create an empty instance of the content type that will become the new localized object. We do this on line 84 by calling the `createObject()` function and using the built-in `getMetadata()` function to introspect the type name of the current component and pass this value into `createObject()` dynamically. After we have our new instance, we loop over the properties stored in the current mask object and insert any non-function properties into the new instance. Several of these properties should not be acquired from the mask object, namely `isMask` and `contentLocale`, so we explicitly set these properties along with `status` using `setter` methods.

The magic of a single ID for the mask object and all localized instances occurs on line 96. We set up a `localeID` variable that is composed of the objectID for the primary mask object followed by a forward slash and the locale for this localized instance. Because locale strings are unique, the combination of the mask objectID and a locale string guarantee that every localization will have a unique ID. This provides us with a single objectID to use across locales. Accessing the various localizations for a given content object is now as easy as swapping out the locale specified on the end of the ID. Of course, the safer route is to request locales through the mask object, which we will see soon. If a request is made for a locale that does not exist, an error is thrown that the publishing or presentation layer must handle. However, accessing locales through the mask object ensures that we only get objects that are both available and active.

After the `localeID` for this new instance has been set, `create()` is called on line 99 to persist this instance to the content repository, passing in the `localeID` as an `objectID` argument. This requires that the `create()` function in BasePersistentComponent.cfc be coded to handle a user-defined objectID or default to a system-generated ID if none is specified. The final steps in this function are to update the MaskInfo instance for this mask object with the new active and available locale, and return the localized instance to the caller. See Listing 10.4.

Listing 10.4 **BaseContent.cfc Continued: *getLocales( )***

```
<!--- Function: getLocales() --->
<cffunction name="getLocales"
  access="public"
  returntype="string"
  output="false">
  <cfargument name="requestedLocales" type="string"
    required="false"/>
  <!--- Validate that this is the mask object --->
  <cfif not this.isMask>
    <cfthrow message="Validation error">
  </cfif>
  <cfscript>
    myMaskInfo =
      createObject("component","MaskInfo");
    myMaskInfo.get("database", "contentDB",
      this.maskInfo);
    // Set the localeType if not passed
    if( not
      structKeyExists(arguments,"requestedLocales") )
      arguments.requestedLocales = "available";
    // Return the locales the user wants
    switch (arguments.requestedLocales) {
      case "active":
        return myMaskInfo.getActiveLocales();
        break;
      case "available":
        return myMaskInfo.getAvailableLocales();
        break;
      default:
        return myMaskInfo.getAvailableLocales();
        break;
    }
  </cfscript>
</cffunction>
```

The `getLocales()` function is called against a mask object, and it returns a list of active or available locales for the object. Following initial validation that the function is being called against a mask object, the referenced MaskInfo object is loaded from the content repository. The `requestedLocales` argument allows the client to specify whether he wants the active locales or available locales for this object returned to him. If no preference is passed in, the function defaults to return all locales available for the content object. This function can prove useful within a management or workflow interface because it can drive the display of a listing of all locales that have been created for a content object and indicate which locales have been flagged as active and can be published to the site. We also can use this function at the Publishing and Client layers to provide the end user with access to other active, available, localized instances of a piece of content.

In Listing 10.5, the `deleteMask()` function deletes a mask object. Because the mask object is the one true representation of a content item, its deletion will cascade through all of the available locales that have been created as well. We can only call this function against a mask object, so the function performs the necessary validation before executing. The function begins by calling the `getLocales()` function (defined in Listing 10.4) to retrieve and store a list of available locales for the object. If this list has more than one element, localized instances have been created that need to be deleted as well. The function loops over the list of available locales and deletes any that do not match the locale of the mask object, stored in the `contentLocale` property. A single instance of the appropriate content type is created on line 152 before entering the loop. Each iteration of the loop results in the dynamic construction of an ID for one of the available locale instances to load it from the content repository using `get()` and subsequently deleting it. Following the termination of the loop, the mask object calls `delete()` against itself to remove its data from the content repository and returns a boolean value of `true` if it is successful.

Listing 10.5 **BaseContent.cfc Continued: *deleteMask( )***

```
139  <!--- Function: deleteMask() --->
140  <cffunction name="deleteMask"
141    access="public"
142    returntype="boolean"
143    output="false">
144    <!--- Validate that this is the mask object --->
145    <cfif not this.isMask>
146      <cfthrow message="Validation error">
147    </cfif>
148    <cfscript>
149       localesToDelete = this.getLocales();
150       numLocales = listLen(localesToDelete);
151      if( numLocales GT 1 ) {
152         tempLocale = createObject("component",
           getMetadata(this).name);
153        for(i = 1; i lte numLocales; i = i + 1) {
```

continues

Listing 10.5 **Continued**

```
        theLocale = listGetAt(localesToDelete,i);
        if(theLocale NEQ this.contentLocale) {
          theID = this.objectID & "/" & theLocale;
            tempLocale = tempLocale.get("database",
            "contentDB", theID);
          tempLocale.delete();
        }
      }
    }
    this.delete();
    return true;
  </cfscript>
</cffunction>
```

An implementation of the `deleteLocale()` function requires a slightly different approach. We need to call this function against the mask object, and we must pass in the locale to delete as well. To execute the function, the mask object loads its referenced instance of the MaskInfo helper class, stored in the `maskinfo` property, to verify that the locale to delete does in fact exist. If so, the mask object loads the localized instance that is targeted for deletion and calls `delete()` against it. It then calls `removeAvailableLocale()` and `removeActiveLocale()` against its MaskInfo instance to clear out the deleted locale, and finishes up by running an `update()` against the MaskInfo instance to persist the updated localization information to the content repository. The `deleteMask()` and `deleteLocale()` functions are most useful during development, or to completely remove content objects from the system rather than simply archiving them. In the case of workflow-generated content, a workflow can be terminated before reaching its conclusion. In that case, we should delete the content object that is being constructed from the system entirely.

The Single ID Locale Mask architecture provides an excellent framework for internationalizing and localizing the content layer of a dynamic publishing application. Content can be localized as needed, and the various locales created for a content object do not lead to object bloat while remaining accessible through a single ID. The combination of this framework with UTF-8 encoded text provides an astounding level of flexibility. The use of UTF-8 encoding for all localized text allows for uniform storage of any language within the content repository, as well as consistent delivery of this multilingual content to modern web browsers.

Doubled-Up Property Values

Another strategy for localizing data in the Content layer of an application is to double-up property values. This was touched on briefly earlier in this chapter, and we can now investigate this approach in more detail. Doubling up property values requires a different approach to modeling CFC properties. Rather than specifying a simple data type for the properties of a component, doubled-up properties reference property definition CFCs. Alternatively, these properties can be implemented as a complex ColdFusion MX data type, such as a structure. In this architecture, the properties become responsible for supporting localization. Listing 10.6 shows an example CFC containing a single complex property and some constructor code that initializes this property.

Listing 10.6 **Doubling-Up Properties**

```
<cfcomponent>
  <cfproperty name="title" type="struct">
  <!--- Constructor --->
  <cfscript>
     this.title = structNew();
     this.title["en_US"] = "The US English Title";
     this.title["ko_KR"] = "A Korean Title";
     this.title["es_ES"] = "A Spanish Title";
  </cfscript>
  .
  . Additional component code
  .
</cfcomponent>
```

The keys within the `title` structure are locale strings. The values are the localized title strings. Functions that display this property can use the correct translated string based on the locale key. An example would be, `myComponent.title[myDesiredLocale]`, where `myDesiredLocale` has a value such as `"en_US"`. This would return `"The US English Title"`, which is the localized title string for the en_US locale. Doubled-up properties that are implemented as referenced components follow a similar pattern.

The largest disadvantage in using this architecture for content objects is that most objects have a fair to large amount of content. For a two-page article that has been localized into five languages, every fetch of the object from the content repository returns 10 pages of content even though you are only likely to be interested in 2 of these. This can lead to performance and bandwidth issues between the Content layer and the Publishing layer. In the case of Flash MX and Flash Remoting, bloated objects also can adversely affect performance in the Client layer. However, for web sites or applications that use localization to a limited extent, doubled-up properties might prove to be a simpler solution to implement.

One excellent use of doubling-up properties is found in the construction of components that store text strings for use within the user interface of an application. You can define an AppStrings.cfc component to store and persist all of the localized text strings that an application uses. You can load this component from the content repository into server memory when the application starts up. The Client layer can then access localized strings for display as needed by requesting strings from this component. For example, if the Client layer were rendering a form for a user in the es_ES locale, it could use a reference to the AppStrings.cfc component stored in a variable named `appStrings` to output localized strings directly as follows:

```
<cfset pageLocale = "es_ES">
<cfoutput>#appStrings.formTitle[pageLocale]#</cfoutput>
```

The user would see the localized `formTitle` property output in Spanish. However, most content types are better handled using the Single ID Locale Mask architecture presented earlier. In the majority of cases, it makes little sense to load a content object containing data for all available locales if a user requests a single locale.

Separate Component Storage Structure

A third strategy for localizing the Content layer of your application is to use entirely separate component storage structures for the various locales in which a single content type might exist. Such an approach proves beneficial in many examples. Any scenario in which the defined properties within a content type vary by locale is a strong candidate for implementing the type using separate CFCs per locale.

A concrete example of when separate component storage makes perfect sense is storing information for global customers and users of your site or application. If you model customer addresses using a CFC and you intend to support global sales, you will quickly find that elements within addresses vary widely by nation. Take a Korean address as an example:

Mr. Lee

Seoul-si, Mapo-ku, Sekyeo-dong

461-1 bungi

121-210

We see that it starts with a personal name, but the second line contains a city (-si), district (-ku), and precinct (-dong), followed by a house number (bungi) on line three and finally, the zip code. There is no element for states, although a province is sometimes used. A street name is used only in the rarest of occasions. Formatting and validation rules for the various elements of addresses also vary significantly from nation to nation. In this case, it might make more sense to model each localized address format using a separate CFC, rather than attempting to force the many address formats used across the globe into a single type definition. Separate CFCs that represent the same content type can be stored within a directory structure, or package, that indicates the content type. For example, a /userAddress/ directory can store the various user address CFCs that are defined per nation or locale. Each localized type definition is then named using the nation code or locale it represents, giving us the following Korean and U.S. address components as an example:

/userAddress/ko_KR.cfc

/userAddress/en_US.cfc

These types that represent user addresses can be instantiated dynamically according to locale, where the final token in the component type name becomes the target locale:

```
address = createObject("component","userAddress.ko_KR")
```

If there is a shared set of functions that all addresses must implement, these functions can be abstracted into a base userAddress.cfc component that each localized userAddress component definition can extend and override as necessary. This provides the flexibility to implement component types with completely unique properties and functions per nation or locale when necessary. The case of user addresses is a simple example that provides a clear motivation for implementing separate component storage per locale but in a multitude of cases, implementing a type using separate component storage per locale makes perfect sense. Whenever you find yourself attempting to force properties and functions from one locale into property and function definitions for another locale that do not correspond exactly, consider implementing the type using separate CFCs per locale.

Warning

A point of caution when using separate CFCs per locale is that the architecture of the system becomes extremely fine grained. Fine-grained systems are more difficult to manage and maintain due to the high number of CFC types and the complex relationships that can grow between them. As a general rule, work to architect your systems at as course a granularity as possible to improve performance and maintainability. A course-grained system has fewer, more generic CFC types. However, sometimes you must bend or break the rules; keep this in mind and use fine-grained components if they fit the requirements.

Conclusion

This brings our discussion of persistence and localization to a close, but only temporarily. This chapter touched on many of the issues surrounding localization. We discussed the approaches to localizing static and dynamic assets, along with the Unicode standard that allows for consistent storage and delivery of textual data. We also explored concrete implementation details for building a Content layer that will support internationalization and localization using the Single ID Locale Mask architecture. Chapter 11, "Persistence with Versioning," will take content localization to the next level with the introduction of versioning persistent localized content objects.

11

Persistence with Versioning

by Seth Hodgson

As an application grows in complexity or moves from the departmental to the enterprise level, the ability to version content often becomes a requirement. This chapter focuses on the Persistence layer structure that needs to be in place to support versioning. We will also investigate a variety of specific approaches to take to implement content object versioning in the Content layer of a dynamic publishing application.

This chapter touches on versioning strategies for static file assets, but the focus of the chapter is on demonstrating how to implement a custom versioning solution for persistent content objects used in a dynamic publishing application. We will build a helper component that manages the multiple versions of an object even across various locales. Our discussion regarding versioning persistent content objects will begin by reviewing several of the primary motivations for versioning content, followed by an in-depth look into concrete strategies to implement a versioning framework for these persistent content objects. In this versioning framework, the content objects that are the data for the application are versioned independently of any templates or static files that the Presentation layer of the application uses.

What Is Versioning?

At a general level, versioning is the ability to create and manage different versions of the same document. This is true of all types of documents, whether they are web documents (HTML, PDF, GIF, XML, and so on), application source code (CFML, Java, C++, and so on), or even word processing documents. An inherent need exists to store versions of all kinds of documents in use today for audit, archival, and retrieval purposes. Saving multiple versions of a source document or file provides a way to audit the changes made to it over the course of time and allows you to view it in any of its previously saved states. An additional advantage of versioning is the ability to revert to a previous version of the source document or file if the need arises.

Versioning Content Versus Code

Most developers have encountered (or likely will encounter) a form of version control (VC) software at some point in their career. Most often, developers encounter VC software that is used to manage versions of source code. In smaller development efforts, this is often done to help prevent developers from overwriting each other's work. Large projects often have "builds" of applications, with one version existing on the development servers, another version locked for QA testing, a third version in regression testing, and a final version in production.

This chapter focuses on versioning content, rather than on versioning code. To version content, each time a piece of content is edited, the existing version needs to be stored, and a new version must be created and indexed with the new content. Updating the properties of a content object directly might be the simplest approach to editing the content that is used in a dynamic publishing application, but there is no record of what changed, who changed it, or when a change occurred. A better approach is to create a new version of the content object whenever it is edited. The following section will introduce several excellent reasons for doing this.

Why Version Content?

Although most developers can understand the value of versioning a code base, the reasons for versioning content are not always so obvious. Let's step through several of the primary reasons to version content objects within the Content layer of an application before diving into concrete implementation strategies.

Cyclical Content

One reason for versioning content is to support "cyclical content." This includes content that routinely changes from one form to another and then back to its original form. One such example of this type of content is a product in an e-commerce site that is temporarily on sale. With versioning, you can store the normal price and text for a content object representing a product in the online store, as well as store a separate version containing its sale price and sale description. This way, it is easy to switch between the Sale and Normal modes for the product without having to create duplicate objects or edit and re-edit a content object continually, requiring a high level of labor-intensive content revisions. Switching between the various versions of a content object only requires that the desired version to publish on the site is flagged as the active version for that piece of content.

Audit/Legal Requirements

Another situation in which you might need to version content is for enterprises that have stringent auditing/legal compliance issues. This is common in the finance industry, in which a lawsuit could force a company to reproduce the content for a certain page from their web site for some day in the past. Without versioning content, it would be impossible to satisfy this requirement. By versioning content objects, the dynamic data that the application uses, you can view the history of each piece of content and determine the period of time that each version of the content was active on the site. Versioning is crucial for maintaining a historical record of the state of content to satisfy audit or legal requirements. Specific strategies for re-creating past pages within the application depend on how content is rendered to the user by the Presentation layer of the dynamic publishing application. At the very least, you can query the content repository to generate reports to list content that was active on the site on a specific date.

Workflow

Versioning content also allows robust workflows to be built around the creation/editing of content. With a versioning component in place as a piece of content is edited, the original can remain in production, while the new version of the content can work its way through the workflow process. This way, no changes can be made to the live content until the appropriate participants have approved the changes. After the new version of a piece of content that is being passed through a workflow has been edited, reviewed, and approved, it can be set as the active version and published on the site. In this case, versioning content objects allows for a much higher level of control over the process of creating or editing content. Versioning also helps ensure a higher level of quality for the content that is published to the site by separating the work done on a new version of the content object from the live version that is visible on the site.

Determining What to Version

Now that we have seen the primary motivations behind versioning content, it is important to determine what to version more specifically.

Pages Versus Content Objects

When deciding on content to version, it is important to recognize that there are several levels at which versioning occurs. On the live site, pages determine how content displays to the end user. These pages pull in content from the content repository dynamically for display. The CFM pages in the Presentation layer of the site can be versioned using VC software such as Visual Source Safe or CVS. Static assets and HTML pages may also be versioned using this approach. Versioning can occur at the page level by versioning files as well as at the content level by versioning the content objects in the content repository. If you decide to version at the page level, you can roll the entire Presentation layer of your application back to a previous version.

The architecture and implementation chosen for versioning content objects in the Content layer depend in a large part on the format of the content repository.

- In the case of XML content storage, if content objects are stored as files, they can be versioned using VC software or through the use of a custom versioning application programming interface (API) for persistent CFCs stored as XML.
- For content objects that are stored in a database, you can build a custom versioning API (for persistent CFCs) that handles the creation of new versions for a content object in addition to the required interactions with the existing versions. In this chapter, we will implement a versioning API for persistent CFCs that is based on the database persistence strategies covered in Chapter 8, "ColdFusion Components with Persistence."
- Content in existing repositories might already provide a versioning mechanism, in which case the dynamic publishing application will need to interact with a versioning API for the existing repository or adapt to it by some other means to support content object versioning.

Versioning the CFM pages that are used in the Presentation layer of the application separately from the content stored in the content repository adds a great deal of flexibility in the management of a dynamic application. The CFM pages in the Presentation layer of the application serve primarily as templates that format and display content. The advantages of versioning content objects are the audit trail of changes made to the content and the ability to make any version of a piece of content active for publishing. Versioning the CFM pages in the Presentation layer of the application allows for the look and feel of the site to be managed. By versioning the assets in these two layers separately, you can make changes to one layer without affecting the other. If a new layout or design is implemented for the site, only the CFM pages in the Presentation layer need to be updated. The content can continue to be published without modification. Likewise, edits to the properties of a content object, such as a press release, will have no impact on the CFM pages in the Presentation layer. Versioning these layers independently makes them loosely coupled and eases maintenance by isolating the repercussions of a change to content or to presentation.

Selecting Types of Content to Version

How do we select content to version? Is it across the board or more selective? For any Enterprise-level dynamic publishing application, many content types will be used to store persistent information such as articles, products for an online store, or customer and user profiles. As the various content types that will be used to model content for the application are defined and developed, you must establish versioning requirements for each content type. As we saw earlier in this chapter, the motivations for versioning content include requirements to support cyclical content or to version content for audit or legal reasons. A custom shopping cart content type does not require versioning. Each new order requires a unique shopping cart instance. On the other hand, a financial press release type would benefit greatly from versioning for both audit and legal reasons. As you build the various content types used within the application, determining the content types that require versioning and those that do not should be straightforward.

How Is Versioning Done?

You can take a variety of approaches to implement versioning in the Content layer of an application. In the case of existing content repositories, content versioning might already be available. The Content layer of the application can be written to work with the versioning API that is in place for the existing repository. Apart from using an external versioning product, many options are available for implementing custom versioning in the Content layer. In the following sections, we will outline the process of integrating with external versioning products. We also will investigate several approaches to architecting a versioning framework for the content layer of the application.

Versioning Products

Several version control systems (VCSs) are on the market today, and many development teams have standardized on one of these for versioning their source code. In almost all cases, APIs are available for these products to allow for integration with external systems or applications. Through the use of these APIs, you can construct a set of tools to allow for versioning content within the same VCS that is in use for versioning code.

These APIs generally expose either a COM or a Java interface to the VCS. You can leverage these exposed APIs in ColdFusion MX by using the `<CJFOBJECT>` tag.

A good practice today would be to build a ColdFusion MX Component that abstracted the interface between ColdFusion MX and these APIs. That way, developers could use a standard set of methods defined for the adapter component to add content to the VCS and interact with it for localization and versioning of the content after it is there.

The specific nature of the adapter component depends on the VCS in use, but the general pattern is as follows:

1. Implement a ColdFusion MX Component that defines the functions that your application requires for interaction with content objects, such as creating a new object, creating a new version for an existing object, and selecting the currently active version or one of the non-active versions for the object.
2. After you have mapped out the necessary functions for the adapter component, you can implement these functions by using the `<CFOBJECT>` tag to instantiate the Java or COM interface for the VCS. You can program against the VCS API within the adapter component functions by calling methods on the instantiated Java or COM object.

Such an adapter component wraps the VCS and allows for relatively seamless use of its functionality within the realm of Macromedia ColdFusion MX. After the adapter component has been built, ColdFusion developers on your team can take advantage of the VCS without needing to program against it in Java, C++, or whatever other interface it might provide.

Custom-Built Solutions

Of the many options available to an enterprise for supporting content versioning within the Content layer of an application, custom versioning solutions might be the best approach for satisfying specific versioning requirements. Depending on the versioning requirements that the business owners of the application established, the architects and developers of the application can design and implement the versioning framework for content to suit the business requirements exactly, instead of modifying business needs to fit versioning software, which might force unwanted changes in business practices.

When you're architecting a custom versioning framework for content objects, you can take several directions. For example, versioning can be fully self-contained, in which each content object stores its own version history or versioned state.

One strategy for implementing self-contained versioning is to use a `versionHistory` property within content objects to store references to previously modified versions of the object. In this approach, a single active version of the object exists. As new versions are created, you can archive the current active version and add a reference to this archived object to the `versionHistory` property of the new active version. Figure 11.1 provides a simplified view into this approach using an instance of a DuvalShock article type. The active version of the article contains a `versionHistory` property that stores references to the previous archived versions of the article.

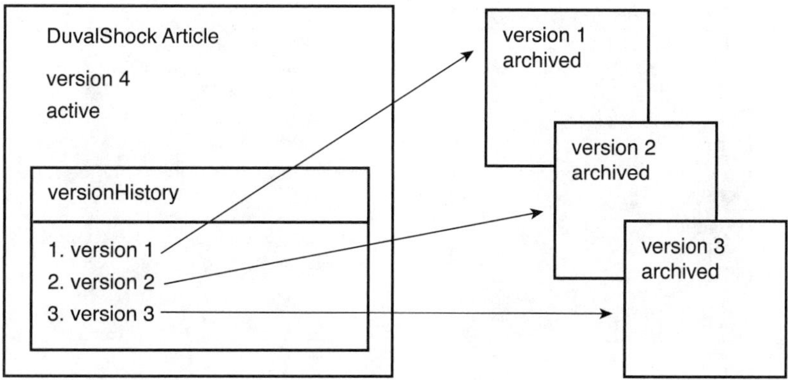

Figure 11.1 Self-contained versioning with `versionHistory`.

Instead of this self-contained approach, our implementation will store version history metadata outside of the objects and in a helper component. Baking version history and management into the content objects directly ties any implementation of versioning directly into the content model, leading to a fragile architecture that cannot be easily changed. Externalizing version management through the use of a helper component that will store version history for a content object allows for the versioning framework to be altered without directly affecting content objects that the system uses.

The strategy for content object versioning outlined in this chapter delegates version management to a helper component that keeps track of the various versions of a piece of content that exist in the content repository. For the code examples in this chapter, we will adopt the approach in which each content object only stores its own version number, and the majority of versioning data and processing is off-loaded to a helper component, VersionManagement.cfc. In this approach, when a content object is versioned, a new instance is created and made active. However, the list of available versions of the content object is stored in the helper component rather than in the content object.

Building on the content object localization framework presented in Chapter 10, "Persistence with Localization," the proposed versioning framework will support versioning content objects across any locales for which the object has been localized and provide a means of chaining content versions across locales or versioning content object locales independently. This framework provides a solution for all the versioning motivations listed earlier in this chapter, including cyclical content, versions of content stored for audit/legal requirements, or content versioning within the context of workflows to streamline the process of content creation and editing and ensure a proper approval process for all content within the application.

Let's begin with a Unified Modeling Language (UML) diagram of the proposed versioning architecture, as shown in Figure 11.2. (Check out *Designing Flexible Object-Oriented Systems with UML* and *A UML Pattern Language*, both published by New Riders.)

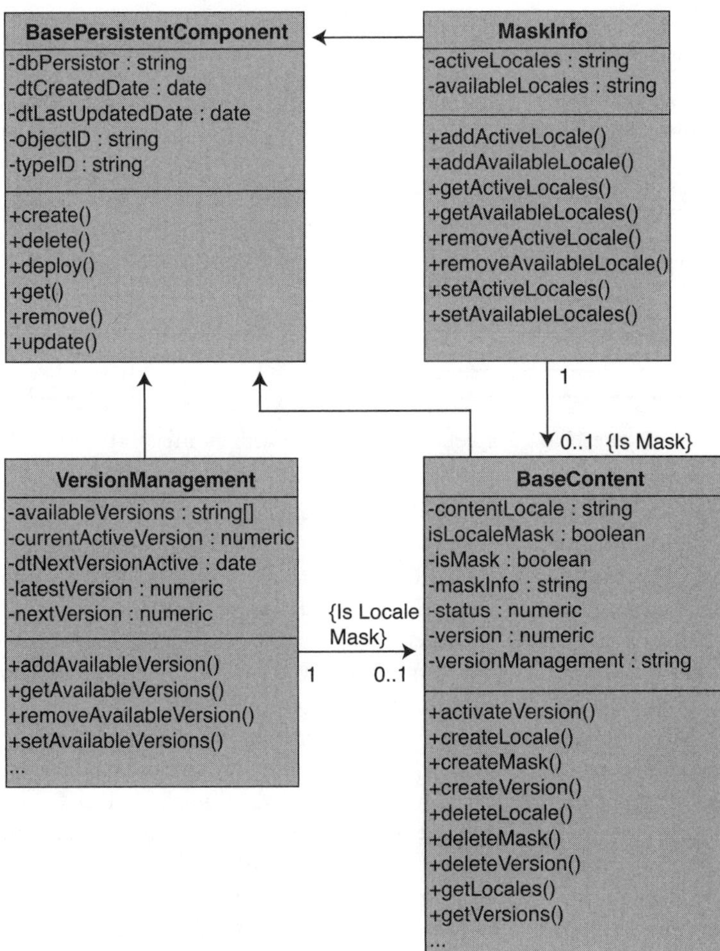

Figure 11.2 A class diagram for the proposed versioning architecture.

Investigating the UML diagram, we see that a new component, VersionManagement.cfc, has been added to the mix. Before we step through the properties and functions defined for this new component, it is important to note that a new property has been added to the BaseContent.cfc component. BaseContent.cfc now includes an `isLocaleMask` property, of type boolean, that specifies whether an instance of type BaseContent is a locale mask object. Recall from Chapter 10 that the creation of a localizable content object can be broken down into the following process:

1. Instantiate a new component instance of the desired type.
2. Populate this new instance with data and call the `createMask()` function, defined in BaseContent.cfc, to store the object in the content repository. This call implicitly sets up a MaskInfo instance to maintain localization data for this piece of content.

3. Create localizations for the content by calling the `createLocale()` function, also defined in BaseContent.cfc.
4. Repeat step 3 with multiple invocations of the `createLocale()` function, and store each localization for a piece of content as a unique object. All available localizations for a piece of content are accessed through the primary mask object and its associated MaskInfo helper instance that stores a listing of both active and available locales. Only mask objects, indicated by an `isMask` property set to `true`, store a reference to an associated MaskInfo helper instance.

Now that our content is being both localized and versioned, we also need to keep track of the primary instance for a piece of content per locale that will store the currently active version of the content. This allows content to be versioned for each locale it has been localized for. We specify that an instance of content is the primary object in a given locale by setting its `isLocaleMask` property to `true`. We need to add this property to the BaseContent.cfc type. Each of these locale mask objects (along with the primary mask object) for a piece of content stores a reference to a helper component of type VersionManagement.cfc. This allows each locale for a piece of content to have a unique set of cyclical versions or separate historical version history.

We see that the VersionManagement.cfc component type stores an array of references to versions that exist for a piece of content in a given locale in the `availableVersions` property. The type also stores the currently active version number in the `currentActiveVersion` property, as well as the version number for the most recently created version in the `latestVersion` property. The final properties for this type store the next version to be made active in the `nextVersion` property and the date and time that the next version is set to become the currently active version in the `dtNextVersionActive` property.

For a clear understanding of what is stored in these properties, let's look at an example VersionManagement.cfc instance for a DuvalShock article. A hypothetical article on a new DuvalShock widget is being published on the site. Its associated VersionManagement.cfc instance contains the following property values:

```
currentActiveVersion = 2
nextVersion = 3
dtNextVersionActive = "12/01/2002"
latestVersion = 4
availableVersions = 1,2,3,4
```

Based on the property data stored in the VersionManagement.cfc instance associated with this article, we can see that version 2 of the article is being published on the site currently. Version 3 is the next version of the article to be published and it has been created, completed, and is set to become the active, published version on December 1, 2002. Also, we see that an even newer version of the article, version 4, has been created, but it is still being edited and has not been set as the next published version of this content. If version 4 was set to be the next version to publish on the site, the `nextVersion` property would be set to 4 along with storing the date on which version 4 should become the active, published version of the article in the `dtNextVersionActive` property. The `availableVersions` property provides an overview of all the versions of this article that exist in the content repository.

In addition to the new `isLocaleMask` property in the BaseContent component, properties to store the version number for the object and a string reference, `versionManagement`, to an associated VersionManagement instance have been added. These properties allow a content object to store its version number and retrieve a VersionManagement instance that contains additional version information for a given locale of the object. A variety of new functions have been added to BaseContent that allow new versions of the object to be created, activated and deleted. Also added is a utility function, `getVersions()`, which returns version numbers for all available versions of the content object.

This versioning framework supports localized content within the Content layer of the application, but along with the ability to version the content. Each piece of content within the Content layer that requires localization and versioning now exists along two planes, one representing content locale and the second representing content version. See Figure 11.3, which shows the relationships between the various locales and versions for a single piece of content, to understand how this architecture is composed.

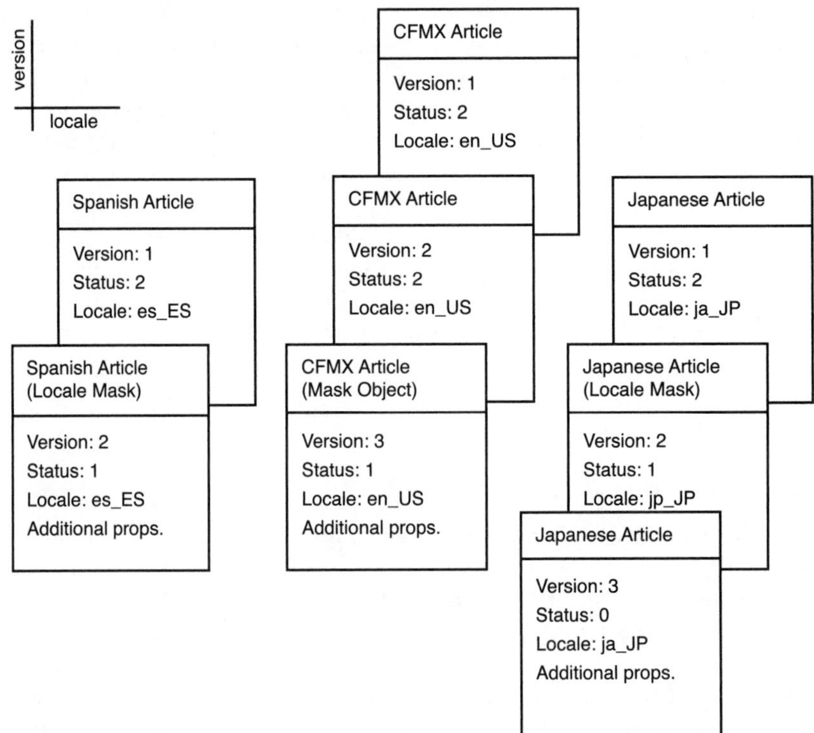

Figure 11.3 Structure of a single localized and versioned content object.

In Figure 11.3, we see a single piece of content, the CFMX Article content object. This is a hypothetical instance of a defined component type, such as Article.cfc. The horizontal axis in the figure represents the available locales for the content object, and the vertical axis represents the available versions for the content object per locale. This piece of content has been localized to the Spanish and Japanese locales. In the center, we have the primary locale for this content object, en_US, or English in the United States. The instance localized in Spanish is on the left, and the instance localized in Japanese is on the right. The primary mask object and locale mask objects are listed as Mask Object or Locale Mask, respectively. Extending above and below these mask objects, we see the various versions that have been created for this piece of content per locale. Each version contains a full set of property data. Storing a full set of data for each version of a content object allows for content auditing and comparison.

Beginning with the primary locale, en_US, version 3 is the currently active version (a status of 1) and two prior versions were created and are now archived (a status of 2). Recall that the status property within BaseContent.cfc specifies the state of any piece of content: 0–inactive, 1–active, and 2–archived. Within the Spanish locale, version 1 is archived and version 2 is the currently active version. For the Japanese locale, version 1 is archived and version 2 is active, but we also have a new version 3 in the works. The new version is currently inactive, having a status of 0.

The relationship between instances of a piece of content across locales is maintained through the use of a MaskInfo.cfc helper component, as discussed in Chapter 10. Now, with the new axis of instance relationships between versions, we add the VersionManagement.cfc helper component to keep track of these relationships. Each mask object, whether a primary mask object or a locale mask object, stores a reference to one of these version management helper components to manage the versioning for a particular locale of a content object. In the event that the content will never be localized, only the primary mask object will be required and will store a reference to a VersionManagement.cfc helper component.

For the various locales in Figure 11.3, versions are being created within each locale independently. The primary locale content, U.S. English, is currently at version 3. The Japanese locale for this content is in the process of being updated to version 3, and when this new version is set as the currently active version, the Japanese locale will be in synch with the English primary locale. The third version for the Spanish localized content has not yet been started.

Often, the process of editing a content object will take place within the context of a workflow process. The workflow can control access to editing content, and the various tasks in the workflow allow for the creation of a new version of a piece of content as well as make the new version active and publish it to the site. Workflows also can take advantage of the VersionManagement.cfc helper instance for each piece of content by completing the process of creating a new version of content in one locale by sending notifications to the other available locales informing them of the change. In the case of simultaneously publishing updates to content across multiple locales, workflows can use the VersionManagement.cfc to ensure that the active version of a specific piece of content is kept in synch across multiple locales. This chapter provides a strong framework for versioning content objects. However, your own business requirements for versioning dictate how this framework is used by workflows or through direct interaction with the versioning API modeled in Figure 11.2 and implemented in the sections to come.

Challenges of Versioning Content

Several challenges arise when you're versioning content objects in isolation or across a given set of locales. We will use the versioning architecture introduced earlier to present some concrete approaches to tackling these challenges. When we're integrating with a VCS, we must create an adapter component that addresses these challenges by interacting with the API for the system in use. We will discuss several alternative versioning architectures to emphasize the flexibility that custom versioning architecture affords.

Versioning Locales

To version localized content objects within the architecture that has been presented, we must implement a VersionManagement component. We can base its implementation directly on the class definition for this component type in the UML diagram of Figure 11.2. Each property for the VersionManagement class will become a <CFPROPERTY> within the VersionManagement component, and each method will become a <CFFUNCTION>. Listing 11.1 presents an example implementation of the VersionManagement component.

Listing 11.1 **VersionManagement.cfc**

```
<cfcomponent extends="BasePersistentComponent">
  <cfproperty name="currentActiveVersion" type="numeric" default="0"/>
  <cfproperty name="latestVersion" type="numeric" default="0"/>
  <cfproperty name="nextVersion" type="numeric" default="0"/>
  <cfproperty name="dtNextVersionActive" type="numeric" default="0"/>
  <cfproperty name="availableVersions" type="array"/>

  <!--- Constructor --->
  <cfscript>
    this.currentActiveVersion = 0;
    this.latestVersion = 0;
    this.nextVersion = 0;
    this.dtNextVersionActive = 0;
    this.availableVersions = arrayNew(1);
  </cfscript>
```

```
<!--- Property Setters and Getters --->
<cffunction name="getCurrentActiveVersion"
  access="public"
  returntype="numeric"
  output="false">
  <cfreturn this.currentActiveVersion/>
</cffunction>

<cffunction name="setCurrentActiveVersion"
  access="public"
  output="false">
  <cfargument name="theActiveVersion" type="numeric" required="true"/>
  <cfset this.currentActiveVersion = arguments.theActiveVersion>
</cffunction>

<cffunction name="getLatestVersion"
  access="public"
  returntype="numeric"
  output="false">
  <cfreturn this.latestVersion/>
</cffunction>

<cffunction name="setLatestVersion"
  access="public"
  output="false">
  <cfargument name="theLatestVersion" type="numeric" required="true"/>
  <cfset this.latestVersion = arguments.theLatestVersion>
</cffunction>

<cffunction name="getNextVersion"
  access="public"
  returntype="numeric"
  output="false">
  <cfreturn this.nextVersion/>
</cffunction>

<cffunction name="setNextVersion"
  access="public"
  output="false">
  <cfargument name="theNextVersion" type="numeric required="true"/>
  <cfset this.nextVersion = arguments.nextVersion>
</cffunction>

<cffunction name="getDtNextVersionActive"
  access="public"
  returntype="numeric"
```

continues

Listing 11.1 **Continued**

```
    output="false">
    <cfreturn this.dtNextVersionActive/>
  </cffunction>

  <cffunction name="setDtNextVersionActive"
    access="public"
    output="false">
    <cfargument name="theDtNextVersionActive" type="date" required="true"/>
    <cfset this.dtNextVersionActive = arguments.theDtNextVersionActive>
  </cffunction>

  <!--- Functions to add and remove versions
        from the available versions array --->
  <cffunction name="addAvailableVersion"
    access="public"
    returntype="boolean"
    output="false">
    <cfargument name="theVersionNumber" type="numeric" required="true"/>
    <cfscript>
      numVersions = arrayLen(this.availableVersions);
      for( i = 1; i lte numVersions; i = i + 1 ) {
        if( this.availableVersions[i] eq arguments.theVersionNumber ) {
          return true;
        }
      }
      arrayAppend(this.availableVersions, arguments.theVersionNumber);
      return true;
    </cfscript>
  </cffunction>

  <cffunction name="removeAvailableVersion"
    access="public"
    returntype="boolean"
    output="false">
    <cfargument name="theVersionNumber" type="numeric" required="true"/>
    <cfscript>
      numVersions = arrayLen(this.availableVersions);
      for( i = 1; i lte numVersions; i = i + 1 ) {
        if( this.availableVersions[i] eq arguments.theVersionNumber ) {
          arrayDeleteAt(this.availableVersions, i);
          return true;
       }
      }
      return false;
    </cfscript>
  </cffunction>
</cfcomponent>
```

The implementation for VersionManagement.cfc in Listing 11.1 begins with a `<CFCOMPONENT>` tag that specifies that this component extends the BasePersistentComponent. By extending this component, instances of VersionManagement can now be persisted to the content repository using the persistence API inherited from BasePersistentComponent. This is crucial because the versioning information that is stored in the properties of this component must persist along with the content with which it is associated. These properties include the currently active version for the content, the next active version, the date at which the next version is set to become active, the latest version, and a list of all versions of the content that are currently stored in the content repository.

Following the opening component tag, all of the necessary properties for this component are defined using `<CFPROPERTY>` tags. The property definitions are straightforward, but it is important to point out that the date property, `dtNextVersionActive`, is being stored as a numeric value. In ColdFusion MX, a date variable can be converted to a numeric value simple by adding 0 to the date, as follows:

```
<cfset numericDate = now() + 0>
```

Because different content repositories can represent dates using various formats, storing date properties as numeric values allows for consistent treatment of dates in the Management, Publishing and Client layers of an application. A numeric date can be output as a string using the `dateFormat()` function.

The block of property definitions is followed by a constructor `<cfscript>` block that executes when an object of type VersionManagement is first instantiated. This constructor code initializes properties defined for the object to default values in the `this` scope. Directly after the constructor block, `get` and `set` functions have been defined for retrieving property values from the `this` scope of the object as well as assigning values to these properties.

Two additional utility functions have been defined for maintaining the array of available versions for the object. As new versions are created or existing versions are deleted, we need to be able to add or remove version numbers from the `availableVersions` array property. The `addAvailableVersion()` function accepts a version number to add and searches the array for the passed version. If the version number is already present, the function simply returns to the caller. If the search through the array completes and the version number is not found, the number is added to the array and the function returns. Likewise, the `removeAvailableVersion()` function is passed a version number to remove. This function searches the array, and if the version number is found, it is deleted from the array and the function returns a boolean value of `true` to indicate that the version was successfully removed. If the version number is not found, the function returns a boolean value of `false` to indicate that the operation failed.

Adding Versioning to a Localized Content Type

Localized content types extend the BaseContent component that was presented in Chapter 10. With the VersionManagement component in place, we can move on to the modifications that BaseContent requires to support versioning. The BaseContent component is a persistent component that extends BasePersistentComponent and implements a localization architecture that allows a single objectID to access any locale that the content object has been localized for. We will step through modifications to make to BaseContent to support this versioning architecture in Listings 11.2 to 11.4.

Listing 11.2 **BaseContent.cfc Versioning Properties**

```
<cfcomponent extends="BasePersistentComponent">
  ... Current Properties omitted ...
  <cfproperty name="isLocaleMask" type="boolean" default="false"/>
  <cfproperty name="version" type="numeric" default="0"/>
  <cfproperty name="versionManagement" type="string" default=""/>
  <!--- Constructor --->
  <cfscript>
    ... Current Property initializations omitted ...
    this.isLocaleMask = "false";
    this.version = 0;
    this.versionManagement = "";
  </cfscript>
  <!--- Property getters/setters --->
  ... Current Property getters/setters omitted ...
  <cffunction name="getIsLocaleMask"
    access="public"
    returntype="boolean"
    output="false">
    <cfreturn this.isLocaleMask/>
  </cffunction>
  <cffunction name="setIsLocaleMask"
    access="public"
    output="false">
    <cfargument name="bIsLocaleMask" type="boolean" required="true"/>
    <cfset this.isLocaleMask = arguments.bIsLocaleMask>
  </cffunction>
  <cffunction name="getVersionManagement"
    access="public"
    returntype="string"
    output="false">
    <cfreturn this.versionManagement/>
  </cffunction>
  <cffunction name="setVersionManagement"
    access="public"
    output="false">
    <cfargument name="theVersionManagement" type="string" required="true"/>
    <cfset this.versionManagement = arguments.theVersionManagement>
  </cffunction>
```

The versioning properties that we must add to BaseContent are `isLocaleMask`, `version`, and `versionManagement`. The `isLocaleMask` property will be `false` for any nonmask object. Both the primary mask object and any locale mask objects for a given piece of content will have this property set to `true`. The `version` property stores the version number for a given content object instance. The third property, `versionManagement`, stores an objectID for a VersionManagement instance as a string. Only primary mask and locale mask objects will store references to VersionManagement instances. All nonmask objects will have their `versionManagement` property set as an empty string. In addition to the new `<cfproperty>` definitions, the constructor block for BaseContent has been expanded to initialize these properties in new instances, and necessary `get` and `set` functions have been defined for each new property as well.

Along with these updates, we need to modify the `createMask()` and `createLocale()` functions within BaseContent.cfc. These functions must now set the `isLocaleMask` property to `true` before creating a primary mask object or a locale object, which is now our locale mask object. These functions also need to set the `version` property to 1 because they are creating the first version of a given piece of content in the selected locale. In addition, they must create and initialize a new VersionManagement.cfc instance to maintain versioning for each locale of the object. The process required to initialize such an instance is shown in Listing 11.3.

Listing 11.3 **Initializing a VersionManagement.cfc Instance**

```
... Within createMask() or createLocale() ...
<cfscript>
  ... Mask object initialization ...
  myVersionManagement = createObject("component", "VersionManagement");
  myVersionManagement.setLatestVersion(1);
  if( this.status eq 1 )
  myVersionManagement.addAvailableVersion(1);
  myVersionManagement.create();
  this.versionManagement = myVersionManagement.objectId;
  ... Finish creating the mask or locale mask ...
</cfscript>
```

We begin by instantiating a new component instance of type VersionManagement. We can then use `setter` functions to populate this new instance with appropriate data. In the case of creating a new primary mask or locale mask, the version number is always 1, making the latest version 1 as well. When a new version of this object is created and scheduled to become the active version, this information will be stored in the `nextVersion` and `dtNextVersionActive` properties of the VersionManagement instance. The `lastestVersion` property is updated with the version number of each new version regardless of whether the new version is scheduled to become active. If the mask object is flagged as active, we can set version 1 as the current active version for this content object within the VersionManagement instance. After the VersionManagement instance has been created, its objectID is stored in the `versionManagement` property of its associated mask object that is being created.

Listing 11.4 **BaseContent.cfc—*createVersion( )***

```
... Top of BaseContent.cfc omitted ...
<cffunction name="createVersion"
  access="public"
  returntype="any"
  output="false">
  <!--- Validate that this is a locale mask object --->
  <cfif not this.isLocaleMask>
    <cfthrow message="Validation error">
  </cfif>
  <cfscript>
    // Copy current properties into a new instance
    newVersion = createObject("component", getMetadata(this).name);
    for( prop in this ) {
      if( not isCustomFunction(this[prop]) )
          newVersion[prop] = this[prop];
     }
    // Turn off props that should not be inherited
    newVersion.setIsMask(false);
    newVersion.setIsLocaleMask(false);
    newVersion.setStatus(0);
    newVersion.setVersionManagement("");
     // Load and update versionManagement
    myVersionManagement = createOject("component", "VersionManagement");
    myVersionManagement.get("database", "contentDB",
      this.versionManagement);
    newVersionNum = myVersionManagement.getLatestVersion() + 1;
    myVersionManagement.setLatestVersion(newVersionNum);
    myVersionManagement.addAvailableVersion(newVersionNum);
    myVersionManagement.update();
    // Create new version instance
    versionID = this.objectID & "/" & newVersionNum;
    newVersion.create(objectID=versionID);
     return newVersion;
  </cfscript>
</cffunction>
... Remainder of BaseContent.cfc omitted ...
```

You can only call the `createVersion()` function against a locale mask object to create a new inactive version of the content object. The function begins by instantiating a component instance of the correct type and copying over all the properties in the locale mask object into the new instance. It then uses `setter` functions to ensure that the new instance is not a mask object, that it has an inactive status, and that it does not contain a reference to a VersionManagement component instance. Next, the VersionManagement instance that is associated with the locale mask object is loaded from the content repository and the `getLatestVersion()` function is used to determine what version number to use for this new version. We set the new latest version number in the VersionManagement instance and add this new version number to the available versions stored in the instance. Then we call `update()`, which saves this version data to the content repository. To finish, we create the content ID for this new version by appending the version number to the end of the localized content objectID for the locale mask object, which is guaranteed to be unique. We create the new version in the content repository and return it to the caller. Each version of a content object has an ID in the following format: UUID/locale/version. In this way, every localization and version for a content object shares a single globally unique objectID (the UUID). Locales and versions are differentiated by appending the appropriate locale code and version number to the UUID, with each part of the full objectID delimited with a forward slash or some other character of your choosing.

The `activateVersion()` function is more involved than the `createVersion()` function, and in the interest of space and legibility, we will outline the actions for this function using pseudocode rather than a full code listing. The steps taken by the `activateVersion()` function are shown in Listing 11.5.

Listing 11.5 **BaseContent.cfc—*activateVersion( )* Pseudocode**

```
if( this is a locale mask object ) {
      Set the object status to 1 (active)
      if( this is the primary mask object ) {
            Add this locale to MaskInfo.activeLocales
      }
      else {
            Load the mask object from the database
            Add this locale to MaskInfo.activeLocales
      }
      Update the object
      Return the object to the caller
}
else {
      Obtain the locale mask id from this object's ID (parse out
         the "UUID/locale" only)
      Load the locale mask object from the database
      Archive the locale mask object (save out a copy using
         the full object ID, "UUID/locale/version" and set
         status to 2)
      Copy properties from this object into the locale mask
      Set the locale mask object status to 1 (active)
      Update the VersionManagement instance associated with
         the locale mask object
      Update the locale mask object
      Delete the current object (its data is now saved in
         the locale mask object)
      Return the locale mask object to the caller
}
```

The first half of the `activateVersion()` function is straightforward when dealing with an object that is a primary mask object or locale mask object. The complexity in this function occurs when a content object version that is not the primary or locale mask is made active. In this case, we must save out as an archival version, the locale version that is currently stored in the primary or locale mask object. From there, we must copy the version to be made active into the locale mask object and then delete it.

For example, if a single version of an article has been created and set as active, this object will have its `version` property set to 1 and its `isMask` and `isLocaleMask` properties set to `true`. If a second version is created and then set as active, the current mask object data will be saved out as a new object (version 1 of the content) with its `status` property set to 2 (archived), and the properties in the second version of the content will be copied into the mask object. Its `version` property will be set to 2 and `status` will be set to 1. After all the properties in the second version have been copied into the mask object, we can delete the second version. If a third version is then created and set as active, the second version (currently stored in the mask object) will be archived out and the properties of the third version will be inserted into the mask object before deleting the third version. The mask object operates as a container for the currently active version of your content. When a version is made active and transferred into the mask object instance, its version number is transferred as well. This allows us to archive the data back out as an archived object with the correct version number when a different version is made active and its data is transferred into the mask object instance.

The `getVersions()` function performs a simple retrieval of the available versions that are listed and stored within the VersionManagement instance that is associated with a given locale mask object. We should only call the `deleteVersion()` function against objects that are not a primary or locale mask object. This function performs some additional work following the deletion to clean up the available versions listed in the VersionManagement instance for the affected locale of the content. In addition to these two functions, we also must make minor changes to the `deleteLocale()` and `deleteMask()` functions to remove any associated VersionManagement instances when a primary or locale mask object is deleted.

Versioning Across Locales

Versioning content across locales when the version in any two locales does not need to be synchronized is straightforward. We can use a workflow or a simpler interface to allow users to create new versions of a content object in a chosen locale. When we can version the same content item independently within each locale that it has been localized for, no special considerations or notifications need to occur when we create new versions of the content.

A scenario in which this would prove useful is for product components in an online store. If separate site regions require unique sales or promotions, we can version a specific product to create unique sale or promotional instances per locale with no required correspondence across locales for the versions of the product content object. With editorial content, independent versioning across locales is a less common approach because this type of content usually requires that all locales be chained together to present the same content but in different translations.

Chaining Content Versions

When the various locales for a piece of content need to be aware of each other to present a uniform message, the versioning of content must be chained across the locales in which it is available. Chaining content versions across locales requires coordinated business practices to ensure that localized content will be translated and available in all target locales so that the content can be published simultaneously to all required locales. This might involve offline coordination between primary production staff and localization staff, or the process of versioning a piece of content can be governed by a workflow that ensures that the content is localized into all required locales, approved across the board, and pushed live in a synchronized fashion. Features of the versioning architecture presented in this chapter that make this possible are the `nextVersion` and `dtNextVersionActive` properties defined in the VersionManagement component. If we take a company press release that must be published in several locales at a specific date and time as an example, this can be coordinated within a workflow that takes advantage of these properties.

The workflow can ensure that synchronized versions are stored in the `nextVersion` property across the target locales and that they are set to become active at the same time. It is then the responsibility of the publishing system to retrieve the correct version of the content by checking when the next version is set to go active, and if necessary, making it the new active version of the content. Also synchronized publishing across locales might not force version numbers to be the same for synchronized releases. Content in a primary language often goes through more frequent updates than localized content; but for major updates to content, a synchronized push of the next version of a piece of content (regardless of version number) across all target locales can be coordinated by synchronizing the `dtNextVersionActive` property of the VersionManagement helper components for each locale.

We can configure a workflow to coordinate the creation, localization, and approval of the press release content for all required locales. Following content approval, the workflow can specify the next version of the content object to make active across all the required locales using the `nextVersion` property, and assign a uniform date and time for this to occur using the `dtNextVersionActive` property that stores a datetime.

After the workflow has accomplished this, the Publishing layer automatically retrieves the new version of the content object across all locales when the date and time to make this new version active have arrived. Workflow systems or offline coordinated processes can take advantage of the relationships that are maintained across locales and versions for a piece of content to chain together updates to a content object across all available locales for the content.

Self-Contained Versioning

The versioning architecture presented in this chapter adopted an external approach of storing minimal version information within content objects and relying on a helper component to store additional information that is required to support versioning. This is only one of many options available when implementing a custom versioning system. A different approach to the challenge of versioning is to build content objects in a fashion that allows for self-contained versioning. This was touched upon briefly earlier in this chapter with the discussion of a `versionHistory` property that is embedded within content objects and stores references to previous historical versions of the content. Embedding version history within the content object makes little sense from an architectural perspective because the `versionHistory` property does not represent data for the content object, such as a `title`, `author`, or `bodytext` property does. Additionally, we lose a great deal of flexibility by storing version metadata in this fashion. Storing version metadata externally in a helper component greatly simplifies version management and allows for simpler chaining of versions across locales and synchronized publishing for new versions of content.

With self-contained versioning, other options are also available. We can implement the method for storing version history in a self-contained fashion as full-embedded historical versions of the content object within the active object. We also can store updates to a content object as delta changes in properties from version to version. Storing delta changes requires the least amount of storage space within the content repository, but it complicates and slows the instantiation of versions for a piece of content because the state of a content object becomes a composite of the various versions of the object. None of these approaches provides the power and flexibility offered through the use of a VersionManagement helper component.

Conclusion

This chapter provided a glimpse into the many options available when tackling the challenge of versioning content within the Content layer of an application. These options range from integrating with existing versioning systems and VCS solutions to building custom versioning architectures for your content CFCs from scratch. The use of the architecture presented in this chapter for content versioning with ColdFusion MX provides a flexible, powerful, and rapid means of creating custom versioning frameworks for any Content layer.

12

Categorization of Content

by Jeff Tapper

ONE CHALLENGE THAT YOU MIGHT ENCOUNTER in dynamic publishing is organizing the data to make it easier to find and use. To solve this problem, you can use metadata. *Metadata* is simply data about data. In its simplest form, metadata can be a list of words that can be assigned to describe content. This way, you can find all content that has a particular word assigned to it. The act of assigning descriptive metadata to content is referred to as *categorization*.

This chapter explores the various methods of storing metadata and associating it with pieces of content, exploring various uses for categorization, and implementing a ColdFusion Component to ease the process.

Why Use Categorization?

Categorization is useful for finding content. This is a fairly broad statement because there are several different reasons for finding categorized content. Some of these reasons include the following:

- Dynamically building navigation
- Linking to related content

- Securing content
- Syndicating content
- Personalizing content

This list gives a few examples of how categorized content can be used. In short, any dynamically published application has a need to categorize its content in a logical, easy-to-find manner.

Challenges for Categorization

At its simplest, you can categorize content by allowing content creators to add words individually to every piece of content. However, this adds the risk that words will not be applied consistently. It becomes possible for similar content to be tagged with synonymous metadata, rather than identical metadata. If the intention is to be able to find all related content based on a keyword, such as categories of games, based on metadata, then it won't help to have some content labeled *Role-Playing Games* and have others labeled as *RPGs*. Likewise, using words with different suffixes can be dangerous, such as *game* versus *gaming* or *publish* versus *publishing* versus *publication*.

For metadata to be useful, you must apply it consistently. The best way to do this is to build lists of metadata and to allow content creators to choose metadata from the list. This way, you can guarantee that content is labeled uniformly.

Benefits of Hierarchical Categorization

A list of all possible words that can be used to classify content in an application is likely to become unmanageable quickly. If content creators need to search through 1,500 words to find the ones they want to assign to a piece of content, their job can become an extremely tedious task. To solve this problem, the words can be organized in a hierarchy. This allows the words to be grouped together based on how they are to be used. A simple example of a hierarchy is a company's organization chart. Imagine a company that employs Mr. CEO, Ms. CTO, Mr. CFO, Mrs. Developer, Mr. Networking, and Ms. Accountant. Although the employees can simply be listed, it's often more useful to list them based on who works for whom.

From this organization chart, we can tell who the boss of the company is, who the mangers are, and to whom each employee reports. Figure 12.1 shows such an organization chart.

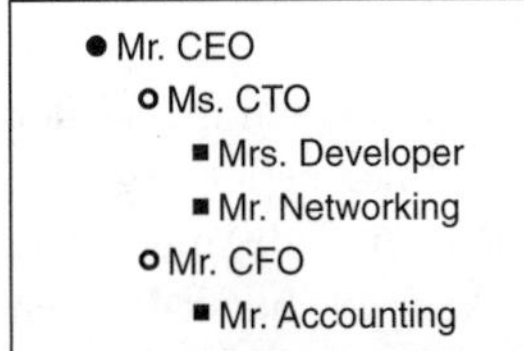

Figure 12.1 Organization charts offer a familiar example of a hierarchy.

Now imagine the same idea, but rather than describing an organization, it's describing software products, such as Figure 12.2 shows.

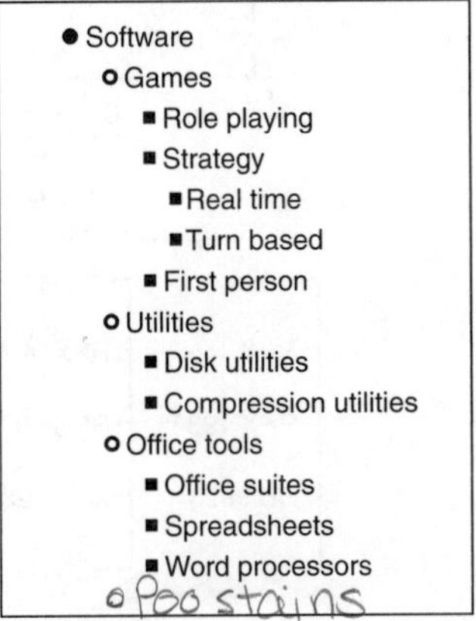

Figure 12.2 A product hierarchy.

By organizing metadata hierarchically, it's not only easier to find the keywords to assign them, but it also becomes possible to find content based on parents of a key. Using Figure 12.2 as an example, it's possible to find all content with the *Role Playing Games* keyword, or any content that has a keyword under *Games*. It's easy to see how a hierarchy can add to the power of content categorization.

Usages of Categorization

There is an endless supply of reasons that one would choose to categorize content. In this next section, a few of the more frequently encountered reasons are discussed.

Related Content

One of the most frequent features for which metadata categories are requested is for relating separate pieces of content. Imagine a category tree of products sold by a computer company. It could have a Printer node under the Hardware branch. Children of the Printer node could be Laser Printers, Inkjet Printers, and Multifunction. Each Printer model could then have its own node under the appropriate Printer Type category. Figure 12.3 shows such a hierarchy. You can use this hierarchy in several ways to relate these products.

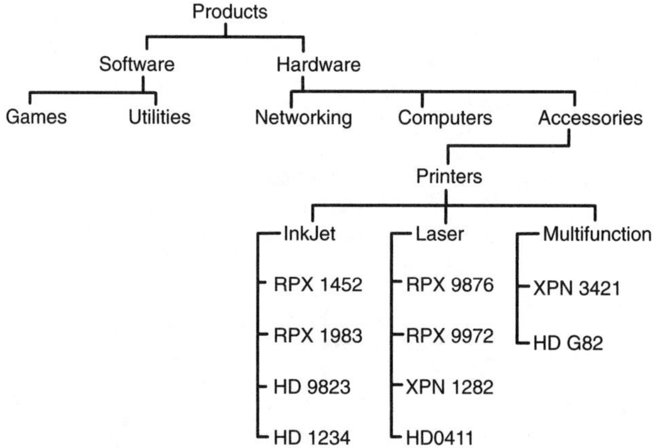

Figure 12.3 A visual representation of the Printers branch of the Products tree.

Navigation

One common use of such related products is for the construction of a navigation system that allows users to drill down the hierarchy, showing the children of each node. The home page would then have links to Hardware and Software. The Hardware page would have links to Computers, Networking, and Accessories. This linking would continue, allowing users to become more specific with each request until they arrived at a particular model.

Breadcrumbs

This same navigation scheme can be used to leave a "bread crumb" trail that allows users to navigate back up the hierarchy. With such a system, a user on the Product page of the RPX 1983 could have bread crumb links to the InkJet, Printers, Accessories, Hardware, and Products home pages. Figure 12.4 shows breadcrumbs in action.

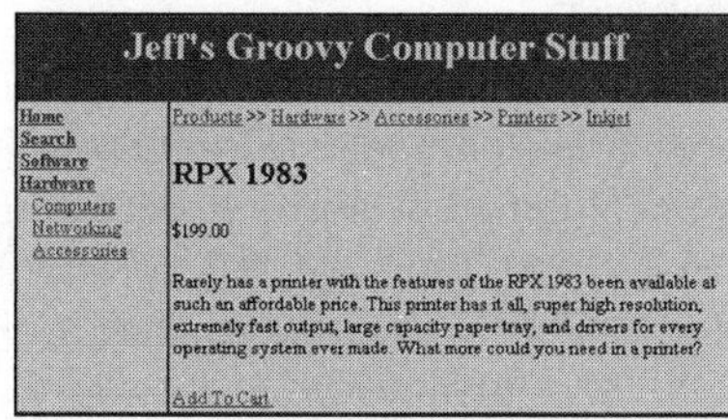

Figure 12.4 A product page that uses breadcrumb navigation.

Cross Sales

Many web sites today offer "related pages" as links from a particular page. One such example is using metadata to relate a product with accessories for it. In our preceding example, adding the ability to relate the specific print cartridges for each particular printer would add tremendous value to the customer as well as the merchant. Additionally, offering links to paper, cables, and so on could help drive even more sales. Relating content in this way is easy with metadata. It can be done by flagging the appropriate print cartridge with the keyword of the printer for which it is intended. Such a system can help customers find the information they need, while driving more sales.

Personalization

More and more sites today attempt to personalize the content of their sites for the individual users. This, of course, means that it is necessary to specifically identify users. This is usually accomplished by having users identify themselves through a login page, although it's sometimes accomplished more covertly, through cookies.

Regardless of how the users are identified, several types of personalization can be done, ranging from letting the users customize the look and feel of the page to their tastes, to the subtler method of presenting content (or products) that seems to fit their interests. This more subtle form of personalization is known as *implicit personalization* because it is done without the user specifically requesting it. Personalization in which users are specifically asked their preferences is referred to as *explicit personalization*.

Either implicit or explicit personalization can be aided through the use of metadata. For explicit personalization, users can be queried for the types of content that most interest them and can then be presented content in which the metadata matches their preferences.

Implicit personalization requires an analysis of a user's browsing history and uses that history to make decisions on the content most likely to interest him. This can either be achieved by relating a series of requests from that user through the web server's log files, or specifically logging information about users within your application. A simple example of this is storing the data that a particular user bought a specific brand and model of printer. On subsequent visits to the site, the user can "implicitly" be shown links to ink cartridges for his printer. For content-driven (as opposed to commerce) sites, analysis of the log files can indicate that on several visits to a site, a particular user always browsed to a specific type of content. This knowledge can be used to present the user with a home page link to this content on subsequent visits, enhancing the user's experience of the site, and hopefully encouraging him to return frequently.

> **Tip**
>
> Many products—including some freeware and some commercial—are available to help ease the log file analysis. These products can produce results varying from simple HTML reports to detailed database tracking of users. A bit of research can help you find the package that is right for your needs and budget.

Site Analytics

As mentioned in the previous example, relating the metadata of content on specific pages to the log files showing access to those pages can help drive implicit personalization models. Aside from this, it can also help the managers of a site understand what types of content are most appealing to their users, and therefore determine how to make their site as a whole more useful to their visitors. Often, web site managers get bogged down in their expectations of a user's desire and miss the clues given based on their actual users' histories. Associating the metadata in this way can help weed out content that users don't want, or perhaps help determine why a particular section of a site isn't performing as well, so that it can be improved. By knowing the "click-path" of an individual user, you can begin to make assumptions about an individual. By analyzing the trends of the "click-paths" of several users, it's easy to determine patterns about end users' impressions of a site's layout.

Challenges in Implementing Categorization

Although the concepts surrounding categorization and hierarchies are not difficult to fathom, the practicalities of implementing them are not as simple. The choices available for this implementation span several types of servers, and even have variations within each type.

Methods for Storing Hierarchies

Several types of software applications are suited for storing hierarchies, ranging from LDAP servers to object-oriented databases and even to relational databases. This next section examines some of the choices available for storage of hierarchies, as well as some of the strengths and weaknesses of each.

LDAP Servers

The Lightweight Directory Access Protocol (LDAP) is a software protocol that is designed to enable users to easily search across private and public networks to locate people and other resources (such as files and machines). LDAP gets its name because it is a "lighter-weight" (that is, smaller, faster, and simpler) version of the Directory Access Protocol x:500, a standard for directory services in a network. LDAP originated at the University of Michigan and has been endorsed by many industry leaders.

LDAP uses a simple tree hierarchy to relate elements through countries, organizations, organizational units, and individual nodes (such as people, machines, and so on). Because these relationships can be quite complex, the "depth" of a hierarchy created in LDAP is unlimited. This structure can be used to store relations between arbitrary keywords, although this is not what it was designed for.

LDAP servers are optimized for quick reading and suffer in performance when entering new data. At first glance, an LDAP server seems an ideal place to store our metadata categories, but upon deeper investigation, it is less adequate than initially thought. Few companies have the expertise needed to run LDAP servers as anything other than containers of user security information (such as Microsoft's Active Directory). In addition, the work involved in fitting keywords into the Country, Organization, Organizational Unit, and Node structure is not trivial.

LDAP implementations vary widely based on their configuration. Therefore, the hierarchy must be able to grow effectively with the organization. Often, this becomes a maintenance nightmare after sufficient additions to an LDAP directory and can cause headaches for anyone who manages it. A few good LDAP administrators know how to effectively plan for this, but many do not.

Experts in LDAP might consider it a worthwhile alternative for storing categorizations, although for most applications, it is not a good fit.

Object-Oriented Databases

The past few years have seen an increase in the "buzz" surrounding Object Oriented Database Management Systems (OODBMS, or sometimes OODB for short). An OODBMS database is one that supports the modeling and creation of data as objects. This allows for some interesting possibilities for modeling hierarchical data. You can find several object-oriented databases on the market today, including O2 (`www.o2tech.com`), Objectivity (`www.objectivity.com`), Objectstore (`www.odi.ocm`), and Versant (`www.versant.com`).

Sadly, OODBMS has no current industry standard, and OODBMS products are considered to be in their infancy. An object-oriented database interface standard is being developed by the Object Data Management Group (ODMG), which has already standardized an object-oriented data brokering interface between systems in a network.

Because OODBMSs are inherently more complicated than RDBMSs, it is difficult to find DBAs and developers who understand how to properly make use of such a system. Although one-day OODBMSs might offer the ideal means for the storage of hierarchical data, neither the software nor the developers to implement with it are readily available today.

Adjacency List Model

The Adjacency List Model (ALM) is the most frequently used method for representing trees in a Relational Database Management System (RDBMS). To represent a hierarchy this way, each element has an explicit reference to its parent. (Conversely, each parent can have a specific reference to its children, although this is less common.)

The ALM is nice because of its simplicity. It does not require a sophisticated developer to implement. Figure 12.5 shows a sample of our product hierarchy stored in this manner.

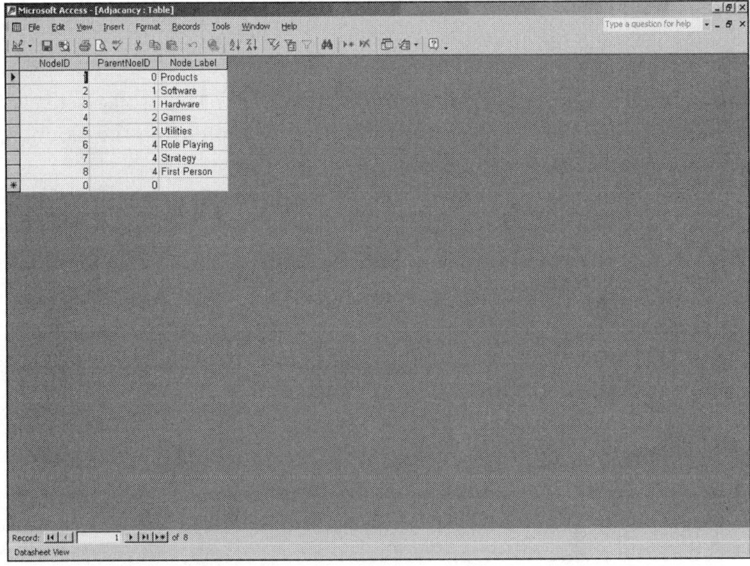

NodeID	ParentNoeID	Node Label
1	0	Products
2	1	Software
3	1	Hardware
4	2	Games
5	2	Utilities
6	4	Role Playing
7	4	Strategy
8	4	First Person
0	0	

Figure 12.5 A product hierarchy stored in the ALM.

Although this model is easy to create, it has unfortunate performance characteristics. In this simple example, trying to determine the parents of a particular node requires several recursive queries. The same would be true of trying to find all the children of a particular node. The one operation that the ALM performs efficiently is finding the parent or child of a particular node. Most other frequently performed operations require several queries.

Nested Tree Model

Another means to store hierarchical data in an RDBMS is to use the Nested Tree Model (NTM). The NTM is a more complex model to understand, but it's inherently more flexible. Using NTM, each node of the tree is assigned two numbers: a left and a right position. Children of a node have their left and right numbers within the range of their parents. Figure 12.6 shows a visual representation of a nested tree model, and Figure 12.7 shows the database implementation of it.

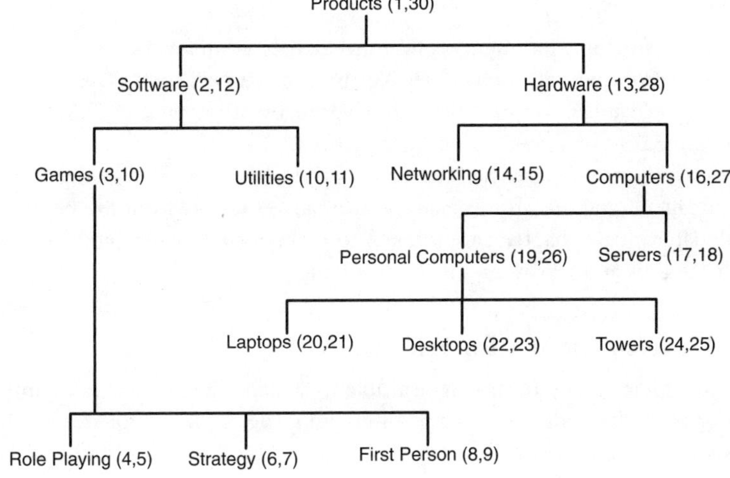

Figure 12.6 A hierarchy as nested sets of data. This helps visualize the structure for an NTM stored in an RDBMS.

Label	NodeID	lPos	rPos
Products	8E05D5FF-FB47-2DA4-17970EEF538DD5DE	5	30
Software	8E1E7D89-F238-B89E-1ED41EC54BC7D9BC	6	21
games	91821984-65BE-815F-7E76C4B18B93EE1A	7	16
Role Playing Games	91853D0D-65BE-815F-7775B1903D8591C5	8	9
Strategy	918F2BB1-65BE-815F-76E3BDC8B923AEE2	10	11
First Person	918F6059-65BE-815F-7422820A6938950D	12	13
Word Processing	918C4F0A-65BE-815F-7F2D0BE2FAABB765	19	20
Hardware	8E1F9DA5-9003-2CD9-7912D8152D7521E0	22	29
Laptops	918E2D4E-65BE-815F-76EC97398F9DC9F0	23	24
Desktops	918E5D43-65BE-815F-7BC9D8A438999919	25	26
Servers	918E84D0-65BE-815F-7E79F514EC52F6BC	27	28

Figure 12.7 The database implementation of the NTM displayed in Figure 12.6.

As you can see, it is easy to find all children of Software; simply select all records whose left value is between 2 and 13. Likewise, to find all categories under Computers, select all records whose left value is between 17 and 28, as seen in this SQL statement:

```
SELECT *
FROM obj_node
WHERE lpos BETWEEN 16 AND 27
order by lPos
```

This method of storing data might seem unnecessarily complex, but it's a truly efficient means of working with hierarchies. For more details on the NTM, see Joe Celko's *SQL for Smarties*. You can find another valuable resource on NTMs and their implementation at `http://www.codebits.com/ntm/`.

Of the various models discussed here, the NTM is the preferred choice for implementing our hierarchies because it takes performance to heart from the beginning. As we will see later in the chapter, care is taken to make room for new children and prevent duplicate lPos and rPos values from occurring.

Proper Development of a Hierarchy

As discussed earlier, several means are available in which a hierarchy can be implemented. For all the reasons given, we recommend using an NTM for storing the hierarchies in a relational database. Building such a hierarchy is discussed in detail later in the "Building Categories" section.

Management of Existing Categorized Content

After a hierarchy has been implemented, several challenges remain for allowing administrators to interact with the hierarchy. A few of the common tasks for maintaining hierarchies include assigning new children to a node, removing children from a node, and moving children from one parent to another. Challenges arise when administrators begin to delete nodes. A business decision needs to be made as to what to do with the children (if any) of the node to be deleted. Sometimes children of a deleted mode are reassigned to the parent of the deleted node. Other systems prohibit administrators from deleting nodes as long as children are still assigned to it. In these cases, administrators must reassign the child nodes before the parent can be deleted. Some applications require a workflow process before allowing a deletion. Whatever the requirements for your application happen to be, this same basic framework can be used.

Building Categories

Listing 12.1 shows an implementation of the NTM done with ColdFusion Components. This CFC extends the BasePersistenceComponent (a root component used for all persistent data throughout this book) created in Chapter 9, "Centralized Data Persistence." By extending the component in this fashion, we can concentrate on implementing the methods specific to this new component and leave the generic methods to the BasePersistenceComponent.

Listing 12.1 **ColdFusion Component Node Allows for Storage and Manipulation of a Hierarchy**

```
<!---
AUTHOR: Jeff Tapper
DATE: 5/1/2002
PURPOSE: Node Object. This is the core component for the creation of a
        Nested Tree Model for Metadata categorization. For more
        details on implementing Nested Tree Models, see
        http://www.intelligententerprise.com/001020/celko.shtml and
        http://www.codebits.com/ntm/
MODIFICATION LOG:
DATE        AUTHOR      MODIFICATION
====        =======     ============
5/1/2002    JST         Initial Generation

This CFC contains the following methods:
    createRootNode() - creates a root node (also known as a hierarchy)

    createChildNode() - creates a node as a child of another

    deleteNode() - removes a node from the database, checking to see if
    it has any children first. Elements with children are not allowed
    to be deleted.

    getParents() - returns an array of all of the parents of a node.

    getChildren() - returns an array of all of the children of a node.
```

continues

Listing 12.1 **Continued**

```
    getLabel() - returns a nodes label

    setLabel() - sets the label

    getlPos() - gets the lPos attribute

    setlPos() - sets the lPos attribute

    getrPos() - gets the rPos attribute

    setrPos() -  sets the rPos attribute
--->
<cfcomponent extends="components.persistence.basepersistentcomponent">

    <!--- set base properties --->
    <cfproperty name="Label" access="public" type="string">
    <cfproperty name="lPos" access="public" type="numeric">
    <cfproperty name="rPos" access="public" type="numeric">

    <!--- initialize properties --->
    <cfparam name="this.rpos" default="">
    <cfparam name="this.lpos" default="">
    <cfparam name="this.label" default="">

    <!--- specific methods --->
    <!---  create root node --->
    <cffunction name="createRootNode"
        access="public"
        returnType="UUID">

        <cfargument name="label" type="string" required="true">

        <!--- find max rPos --->
        <CFQUERY NAME="GETMAXRPOS" DATASOURCE="#REQUEST.DSN#">
            SELECT MAX (RPOS) AS MAXRPOS
            FROM OBJ_NODE
        </CFQUERY>

        <!--- if no nodes exist, use 0 for maxrpos --->
        <cfif not isNumeric(GETMAXRPOS.maxrPos)>
            <cfset GETMAXRPOS.maxrPos = 0>
        </cfif>

        <CFSCRIPT>
            /*
            create new node with an lpos one above the max rpos
            and an rpos 2 above the maxrPos
            */
```

```
            THIS.lpos = getmaxrpos.MAXRPOS +1;
            THIS.rpos = getmaxrpos.MAXRPOS +2;
            THIS.setLabel(arguments.label);
            this.create();
        </CFSCRIPT>

        <!--- return the node id --->
        <cfreturn this.nodeid>
    </cffunction>

    <!--- Create Child Node--->
    <cffunction
        name="createChildNode"
        access="public"
        returnType="UUID">

        <cfargument name="label" type="string" required="true">
        <cfargument name="parentNodeID" type="UUID" required="true">

        <cfscript>
        //get parent's l and r positions
        parent = createObject("component",
        "components.persistence.objects.node");
        parent.get(objectid=#arguments.parentNodeId#);

        parentL = parent.getlPos();
        parentR = parent.getrPos();

        //set this.lpos and this.rpos to top end of parent's range
        this.lPos = parentR;
        this.rPos = parentR + 1;
        this.label = arguments.label;
        </cfscript>

        <!---
        increment parent's r position, and every l and r
        position above it by 2
        --->
        <cftry>
             <cfquery name="updateTree1" datasource="#request.dsn#">
                UPDATE obj_node
                set rPos = rPos + 2
                where rPos >= #parentR#
            </cfquery>
            <cfquery name="updateTree1" datasource="#request.dsn#">
                UPDATE obj_node
                set lPos = lPos + 2
                where lPos >= #parentR#
            </cfquery>

            <!--- catch any errors --->
```

continues

Listing 12.1 **Continued**

```
            <cfcatch type="database">
                <cfreturn cfcatch>
            </cfcatch>

        </cftry>

        <!--- create child --->
        <cfscript>
        this.create();
        return this.objectID;
        </cfscript>

    </cffunction>

    <!--- getParents() --->
    <cffunction
        name="getParents"
        access="public"
        returnType="array">

        <!--- find all parent nodes --->
        <cfquery name="getParents" datasource="#request.dsn#">
            SELECT P2.*
            FROM obj_node AS P1, obj_node AS P2
            WHERE P1.lPos BETWEEN P2.lPos AND P2.rPos
            AND P1.objectid = '#this.objectid#'
            order by p2.lPos
        </cfquery>

        <!--- build an array of structures for parents --->
        <cfset stReturn = arrayNew(1)>

        <!---
        create a new structure for each
        parent with the label and objectID
        --->
        <cfloop query = "getParents">
            <cfset stReturn[currentRow] = structNew()>
            <cfset stReturn[currentRow].label = getParents.label>
            <cfset stReturn[currentRow].objectID = getParents.objectID>
        </cfloop>

        <!--- return the structure of parents --->
        <CFRETURN stReturn>
    </cffunction>

    <!--- function to get children --->
    <cffunction
        name="getChildren"
```

```
        access="public"
        returnType="array">

        <cfargument name="objectid"
            type="UUID"
            required="true"
            default="#this.objectid#">

        <!--- query all children from db --->
        <cfquery name="getChildren" datasource="#request.dsn#">
            SELECT *
            FROM obj_node
            WHERE lpos BETWEEN #this.lPos# AND #this.rPos#
            order by lPos
        </cfquery>
        <!--- build array of structure to return children --->
        <cfset stReturn = arrayNew(1)>

        <!---
        create a structure at each element
        of the array to hold child data
        --->
        <cfloop query = "getChildren">
           <cfset stReturn[currentRow] = structNew()>
           <cfset stReturn[currentRow].label = getChildren.label>
           <cfset stReturn[currentRow].objectID = getChildren.objectID>
        </cfloop>

        <!--- return array of structures --->
        <CFRETURN stReturn>

    </cffunction>

    <!--- function to delete a node --->
    <cffunction
        name="deleteNode"
        access="public">

        <cfargument
            name="NodeID"
            type="UUID"
            required="true"
            default="#this.objectid#">

        <cfscript>
            // determine if node has any children
            children = this.getChildren();
            if (arrayLen(children) gt 1) {
                // if any children, don't allow delete
                return "can't delete. Node has children";
```

continues

Listing 12.1 **Continued**

```
            } else {
                // if no children, allow delete
                this.delete();
                return "node deleted";
            }
            return children;

        </cfscript>
    </cffunction>

    <!--- generic get and set methods --->
    <cffunction
        name="getrPos"
        access="public"
        returnType="numeric">

        <cfreturn this.rpos>

    </cffunction>

    <cffunction
        name="setrPos"
        access="public">

        <cfargument type="numeric" name="rPos" required="true">

        <Cfset this.rPos = arguments.rPos>

    </cffunction>

    <cffunction
        name="getlPos"
        access="public"
        returnType="numeric">

        <cfreturn this.lpos>

    </cffunction>

    <cffunction
        name="setlPos"
        access="public"
        output="false">

        <cfargument type="numeric" name="lPos" required="true">

        <Cfset this.lPos = arguments.lPos>

    </cffunction>
```

```

	<cffunction
		name="getLabel"
		access="public"
		returnType="string">

		<cfreturn this.label>

	</cffunction>

	<cffunction
		name="setlabel"
		access="public"
		output="false">

		<cfargument type="string" name="label" required="true">

		<Cfset this.label = arguments.label>

	</cffunction>

</cfcomponent>
```

This starts like all the CFCs, with a header block describing the use of the CFC, followed by a declaration of the CFC name and the attributes to declare it as an extension of the BasePersistenceComponent. Next, the three properties that are specific to this component are declared with the `<CFPROPERTIES>` tag. Our Node Component has properties Label, LPos, and RPos. Label is self evident. LPos and RPos represent the left and right numbers that the NTM uses to determine the hierarchy.

Next, a number of Node-specific methods are declared. For this CFC, the methods are `createRootNode()`, `createChildNode()`, `getParents()`, and `getChildren()`.

The *createRootNote( )* Method

The `createRootNode()` method takes a label as an argument and uses it to create a new node at the root level. To create a new root node, the maximum rPos value is selected from the database. Then a quick validation function is performed after the selection to ensure that the value returned from the query is indeed numeric. If the nodes table had no entries, the `SELECT MAX(rpos)` would return a `NULL` value. Because we need to set our new value as one above the current maximum value, we want to be able to add one to this value, but ColdFusion will not allow us to increment a `NULL` value; therefore, if the value is `NULL`, we initialize getmaxrpos.MAXRPOS to a value of 0. With these tests in place, we can guarantee that no node is entered with an RPos or LPos value that already exists; that could cause serious problems for our hierarchy.

With a numeric variable now available for all cases, we assign an lPos and rPos value for our new node, set its label, and then write it to the database with the Create method inherited from the BPC.

The *createChildNode( )* Method

The `createChildNode()` method is similar in its purpose, but it's more complex in implementation. It takes two arguments: `label` and `parentNodeID`. The `parentNodeID` argument is the ID of the node that is to act as the parent for the newly created node. After the two arguments are provided, the next step is to retrieve the data about the parentNode. Specifically, we need to know the lPos and rPos of the parent. This is done by instantiating a handle to the parent object with the following code:

```
parent = createObject("component", "components.persistence.objects.node");
parent.get(objectid=#arguments.parentNodeId#);
```

Next, the parent's lPos and rPos are retrieved with the following calls:

```
parentL = parent.getlPos();
parentR = parent.getrPos();
```

The new node is given its lPos and rPos position. The new node will have an lPos equal to its parent's current rPos, and the new node's rPos will be one above its parent's rPos. Next, all nodes in the database that have lPos or rPos values above the rPos of the new node's parents have their values incremented to make room for the new nodes. This also handles renumbering the parent's rPos. This database interaction is surrounded with a CFTRY, with a CFCATCH block to catch problems in updating the database and prevent the database from being updated if errors exist. If errors are caught, the transaction is rolled back with a `CFTRANSACTION ACTION = "Rollback"` command. Otherwise, the new data is committed and the new object is added with the `this.create();` method.

The *getParents( )* Method

The next method is `getParents()`. It's a fairly straightforward method that uses the common NTM queries. No arguments are necessary because all the data we need to find a node's parents is contained within the node. The following query selects all nodes that have the current node's lPos and rPos values between their lPos and rPos values:

```
SELECT P2.Label, P2. objectID
FROM obj_node AS P1, obj_node AS P2
WHERE P1.lPos BETWEEN P2.lPos AND P2.rPos
AND P1.objectid = '#this.objectid#'
ORDER by p2.lPos
```

You can note the self join with the following statement:

```
AND P1.objectid = '#this.objectid#'
```

This serves to limit the query to just the object on which we want to act and provides a common key between the two tables. It's also interesting to note that because our objectID is a UUID (and therefore a string), single quotes are required around it. One feature of this query is that it also returns the current node as well as all of its parents.

Next, the recordset that the query returns is looped over and a new array is created, with each element of the array containing a structure holding each parent node's label and objectID. Each parent's lPos and rPos could easily be included by adding the following lines:

```
<cfset stReturn[currentRow].label = getParents.label>
<cfset stReturn[currentRow].objectid = getParents.objectid>
```

The *getChildren()* Method

Next, the `getChildren()` method is defined. It's similar to `getParents()`, but it has a more simplified query. The following query is used to find all nodes that have an lPos between the current node's lPos and rPos:

```
SELECT label, objectid
FROM obj_node
WHERE lpos BETWEEN #this.lPos# AND #this.rPos#
order by lPos
```

Note that lPos and rPos are integers and need no quotes around them. Because the NTM defines a child as having an lPos and rPos between that of its parents, this query must return all children of any particular node. After the recordset is returned, the rest of this method is identical to the `getParents()` method in that it creates an array and adds the child data to a structure within the array.

The *deleteNode()* Method

The next method we define is `deleteNode()`. For simplicity, we are not allowing users to delete nodes that have children assigned to them. It is certainly possible to build a method that would do something specific with the children, such as reassigning them to be children of the deleted node's parents. However, because the requirements for handling children of deleted nodes vary vastly from one project to another, we have left this with the least common denominator of preventing nodes with children from being deleted.

To accomplish this, we start with a `this.getChildren()` call. As discussed earlier, this method returns all children of the current node. Next, we test how many children the node has. If it has more than one, then there really are children; therefore, we will prevent them from removing this node. (Remember that `getChildren()` considers the current node to be a child of itself, so there will always be at least one child.) Otherwise, this node is deleted with the `this.delete()` method.

> **Note**
>
> It should be mentioned that we can extend this CFC easily with methods such as moveNode, among others. Because these methods require more advanced SQL programming than our Access database allows, we have not included them with the book. However, some stored procedures for accomplishing these tasks can be found at www.codebits.com/ntm.

get and *set* Methods

The remainder of this CFC is a series of generic get and set methods for each of the properties of the object.

To see a ColdFusion page that leverages this component, look at Listing 12.2.

Listing 12.2 **A ColdFusion Page Leveraging the Component**

```
<!---
nodeFunctions.cfm
AUTHOR: Jeff Tapper
DATE: 5/1/2002
PURPOSE: Page that calls various functions for creation
and maintenance of hierarchical nodes.

MODIFICATION LOG:
DATE         AUTHOR      MODIFICATION
====         =======     ============
5/1/2002     JST         Initial Generation

--->

<!--- add child to node --->
<cfif isDefined("form.addChild")>

    <cftry>
    <cfscript>

        // create handle to node
        x = createObject("component",
      "components.persistence.objects.node");

        // create a child node
        y = x.createChildNode("#form.ChildLabel#", "#form.parentID#");

     </cfscript>

         <cfcatch type="any">
             <cfdump var="#cfcatch#">
         </cfcatch>
     </cftry>
     Node Created.
```

```

<!--- add root node --->
<cfelseif isDefined("form.addRoot")>

    <cfscript>

        // create handle to node
        x = createObject("component",
         "components.persistence.objects.node");

        // create root node
        x.createRootNode("#form.ChildLabel#");

    </cfscript>

<!--- find nodes children --->
<cfelseif isDefined("form.getChildren")>

    <cfoutput>Children:</cfoutput>

    <cfscript>
        // create handle to node
        x = createObject("component",
        "components.persistence.objects.node");

        // get this instance
        x.get(objectid=#form.parentid#);

        // get children
        y = x.getChildren();

    </cfscript>

    <!--- output children --->
    <cfdump var="#y#">

<!--- find nodes parents--->
<cfelseif isDefined("form.getParents")>

    <cfoutput>Parents:</cfoutput>

    <cfscript>
        // create handle to node
        x = createObject("component",
        "components.persistence.objects.node");

        // get this instance
        x.get(objectid=#form.parentid#);

        // get parents
```

continues

Listing 12.2 **Continued**

```
        y = x.getParents();
    </cfscript>

    <!--- output parents --->
    <cfdump var="#y#">

<cfelseif isDefined("form.delete")>

    <cfscript>
        // create handle to node
        x = createObject("component",
"components.persistence.objects.node");

        // delete node
        y = x.deleteNode("#form.parentID#");
    </cfscript>

    <!--- output results --->
    <cfdump var="#y#">
</cfif>

<!--- query all nodes for pull-down menu --->
<cfquery name="getNodes" datasource="testdb">
SELECT
    child.label,
  COUNT(Child.lPos) AS lvl,
    Child.lPos,
  Child.rPos,
  Child.ObjectID
FROM obj_node as Parent, obj_node as Child
WHERE Child.lPos BETWEEN Parent.lPos AND Parent.rPos
GROUP BY Child.lPos, Child.rPos, Child.label, Child.ObjectID
ORDER BY child.lPos
</cfquery>

<!--- determine size of select box --->
<cfif getNodes.recordcount gt 10>
    <cfset size = 10>
<cfelse>
    <cfset size = getNodes.recordcount>
</cfif>

<!--- instantiate form --->
<cfoutput>
<form action="#cgi.script_name#" method="post">

<P>
<!--- build select menu --->
    <select name="parentID" size="#variables.size#">
```

```
    <cfloop query="getNodes">
        <option value="#getNodes.objectID#">
        #repeatstring("-", getNodes.lvl - 1)##getNodes.label#
        </option>
    </cfloop>
    </select></p>

<!--- name for new node --->
    <p>Node Name:<br>
    <input type="text" name="ChildLabel">
    </p>

<!--- control buttons --->
    <input type="submit" name="addChild" value="Add Child">
    <input type="submit" name="addRoot" value="Add Root">
    <input type="submit" name="getParents" value="Get Parents">
    <input type="submit" name="getChildren" value="Get Children">
    <input type="submit" name="delete" value="Remove Node"><br>
</form>
</cfoutput>
```

This page presents the user with a recursive form showing the entire current hierarchy in a select box. It also gives the user a text box to assign a name to a new node, and buttons that allow him to leverage any of the five nodes detailed earlier.

The select box is populated with the `getNodes` query:

```
SELECT
      child.label,
      COUNT(Child.lPos) AS lvl,
      Child.lPos,
      Child.rPos,
      Child.ObjectID
FROM obj_node as Parent, obj_node as Child
WHERE Child.lPos BETWEEN Parent.lPos AND Parent.rPos
GROUP BY Child.lPos, Child.rPos, Child.label, Child.ObjectID
ORDER BY child.lPos
</cfquery>
```

This query creates a self join on the obj_node table. The fields label, lPos, rPos, and ObjectID are returned in addition to a count of each node's parents, which is used to determine on which level this node resides (that is, how far it is from this node to the root).

The nodes level is used to create spaces before the node in the select box to indent child nodes below its parents. This gives a more accurate visual representation of the hierarchy.

The top of the page is populated with the specific code that is executed with the click of each of the five buttons.

Each of the five buttons starts with this:

```
x = createObject("component", "components.persistence.objects.node");
```

This gives the application a handle on the node object. Because the first two are not operating on existing nodes, but instead are for creating nodes, it's not necessary to follow this function with a `get()`. Instead, these simply call the `createRootNode()` or `createChildNode` methods with the appropriate arguments.

The other three blocks call methods on existing nodes, so it becomes necessary to augment the `createObject` line in the preceding code with this:

```
x.get(objectid=#form.parentid#);
```

This gives us a handle on the object that is chosen from the select menu. With this in place, we can call any of the specific methods on the object that correspond to the request from the user, such as `getParents()`, `getChildren()`, or `deleteNode()`.

Regardless of which method is called, the return value is displayed with the `<CFDUMP>` tag.

Although the user interface specified here is rudimentary, it offers a robust enough framework for building much richer interfaces, including exposing this to Flash via the Flash remoting technology discussed in Chapter 15, "Leveraging Flash Remoting in ColdFusion MX."

Assigning Content to Categories

To leverage these hierarchies for assigning categories to content that is created using the framework laid out earlier in this book, it's necessary to add a property to each content component that can hold metadata assigned to it. The best way to do this is to extend BasePersistentComponent developed in Chapter 9 to include a metadata property. This property should likely be an array, allowing for storage of multiple metadata keys for each content object. By adding this property to the BPC rather than to each content object, it is automatically included with each new type of content created in the system; therefore, system designers don't need to remember to include it manually. In addition to adding the property, methods should be added to `setMetaData()` and `getMetadata()`, which allow an interface such as that shown in Listing 12.2 (or an even more robust one that you create) to be used to assign nodes to individual objects of content. These functions should belong to the BPC CFC rather than the node CFC, because we want to be able to use them to classify individual objects rather than our nodes.

Retrieving Content with Categorization

After metadata has been assigned to individual pieces of content, we can search it by keyword. To do this, we need to add a method to the BPC, called `findObjectByMetaData()` that searches all the objects and finds matches. To improve performance, we can create a separate table that adds a cross reference between any nodes assigned to an object and the object itself in one central table. This way, to find any objects that use a particular keyword, you can search a single table rather than searching individually over all tables.

Building Performance into Categorization

The battle of making a categorization system is won or lost with the decision of how to implement it. As mentioned earlier, attempts to build such a system using the ALM are doomed to perform poorly from their inception. However, a system built with the NTM has a much greater chance of performing adequately. As with any component in which performance issues are paramount, a well thought-out caching strategy can mean the difference between a successful implementation and one that fails. Further performance gains can be derived by adding a table to index keywords, as mentioned in the preceding section.

Conclusion

Categorization of content can greatly improve an application's usefulness. Allowing for a hierarchy of categories allows for even greater flexibility in its use. You can store a hierarchy in a number of ways before settling on the NTM within a relational database for maximum performance and flexibility.

The Repository Management Layer

13 Basics of Managing Content

By Michael Mazzorana

FOLLOWING THE DESCRIPTION OF A CONTENT repository in Chapter 4, "Basics of a Content Repository," this chapter explores the next logical layer for a dynamic publishing solution. The Management layer is a major piece of your publishing application. It's the hub of your publishing application that relates most closely with your business process and is the tool that leverages timely content updates to your Client layer. This chapter provides an introduction to a dynamic publishing workflow. It describes the importance, necessary facets, and challenges of a workflow in your publishing system.

The workflow is important to how your business interacts with the content repository. It enables non-technical users to create and publish their own web content while enforcing necessary tasks to be completed on time. It also ensures that any internal audit or compliance rules are followed. This chapter examines how a workflow can compliment a business process and possibly improve efficiency. If built properly, a workflow can decrease the amount of errors made in a manual office process by defining clear roles and responsibilities in the creation of business communication or marketing material that you want to publish on your web site. A workflow that the business unit manages can also eliminate the interaction with IT groups to move content on web sites. This can prove to be a return on your development investment in both IT cost reductions and business process improvements.

To facilitate an automated publishing process, workflow features must meet the following basic requirements:

- They must be able to adapt to existing business processes, which improves the process. This is the return on investment (ROI) on the business end.
- They must seamlessly integrate with existing user authentication schemes like Active Directory, LDAP servers, or other user repositories.
- They must be configurable to enable different levels of security, such as creators or authors, editors, and approvers.
- They must be easy to use and require little or no training for the business user to complete a task.
- They must eliminate the developer, webmaster, and so on for basic content changes (Technical Unit's ROI)

It's important to keep asking yourself as you read this chapter, "How can I improve cost effectiveness with more efficient business and technical processes in my company?" Finding the most critical areas of your organization that need process improvement and decreased IT spending is important to your success with building automated business processes. Creating workflows can be complex, so keeping within the parameters of the requirements is important. You have a choice to create simple static workflows that can follow the same steps time after time, or more dynamic workflows that demand changes based on decisions made during the flow process. Choose the right business process to build a workflow and try not to over-complicate the development. Developing properly extends the components you have created to future requirements. Small or large organizations benefit from an automated workflow, and the complexity varies greatly based on the complexity of processes in your company.

Workflow Challenges

The challenges to creating the Management layer in your Dynamic Publishing solution mostly surround understanding the components of an automated workflow solution and clearly relating them to the business requirements. Getting your business area on the same page about terminology, roles, and automated tasks is important to the success of the outcome. Benefits to creating an automated workflow solution can come in several ways. The main reasons to create a workflow are probably these:

- An area or areas of your web site needs frequent updating.
- A multistep business process involves many individuals who are involved with the creation and approval of content that could benefit from automation to increase efficiency.

The greatest return on investment is where your requirements satisfy both reasons. Whatever your reason for building a workflow, hopefully it will have multiple results after it is in place. Your content repository that you architected should allow you to position your organization to leverage your Management layer in the most optimal way. Whether your content should show up on the web or on a wireless device, your workflow supports your business from inception to final approval for displaying a piece of content.

In the marketing department at DuvalShock, the employee roles can be looked at in three categories:

- A group of employees who receives tasks to initiate a piece of content material
- A group who validates or checks whether the material created is market-ready
- A third group who is accountable for final approval, or sending back the material if it is not market-ready

These roles are basically a generic description and translate to any office in any type of company. Let's break these roles down into a workflow system's roles:

- **Author or creator**—In a publishing system, this role can receive a task or initiate its own task for a piece of content to be created. It could be content in a repository from a digital asset, an upload of a PDF file, or new content to be created in a text editor.
- **Editor**—The responsibility of this role is to ensure that the content created is accurate. If necessary, this role might edit the content or add additional pieces. The Editor can also assign or reassign tasks and view the status of those tasks in the workflow system.
- **Approver**—A piece of content is created, edited, and complete. The next step is to send it to an approver to either approve the task or reject it. Rejecting it can reinitiate the task back to the Author or Editor queue with a reason why it was not approved for production. This group is typically a unit in your organization that approves material before releasing it to the public.

Figure 13.1 shows a basic flow of how roles and content would go through the process of a workflow interacting with the content repository.

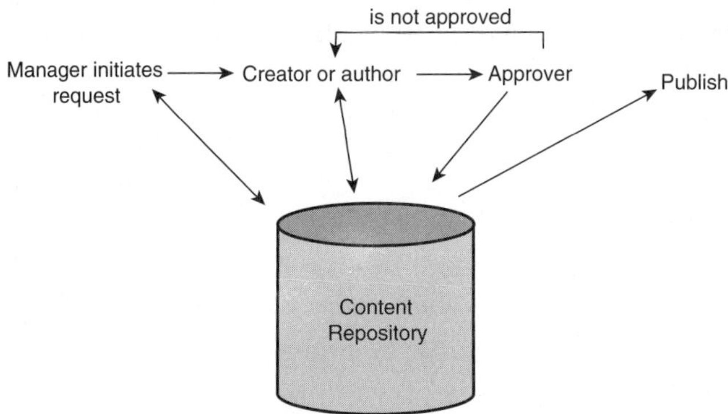

Figure 13.1 A basic automated workflow process.

Determining How Your Business Operates

To establish a successful workflow, you need to take the time to understand how your business operates. One of the main goals should not only be an automated way to deploy content, but also a way to improve the current business process on how a piece of content is managed. This can be a crucial ROI point when you're trying to fund a dynamic publishing solution project. An automated task process can also be an effective way to audit track how a piece of content made it or did not make it out to production. It allows you to track content that was published for viewing when it might not have been production-ready.

In determining potential areas to use an automated workflow, choose areas on your web site that could benefit from better management on both the IT side and on the business side.

On the business side, good content to consider using/implementing an automated workflow system has the following characteristics:

- Has no clear ownership. Sign off on today's manual process is inconsistent.
- Is important to your company's success.
- Could have a workflow that is a natural fit to a business unit.
- Needs to be shared in other areas of your site.
- Is shared with other sites and partners

From the technical side, using the business requirements as the priority benchmark, choose content that is characterized by the following:

- Has requirements for multiple views and formats (that is, PDF, print views, and so on)

- Has an area of your site that might be burdensome for a development staff to keep up-to-date because of frequent changes
- Needs to live in multiple template locations, other locations, and other devices, such as PDAs

Determining the ROI

Before you build a workflow application, determine your overall ROI. There are two major benefits for overall ROI when you're building an automated business workflow in your dynamic publishing solution:

- Increased business efficiency and performance. This includes improving, streamlining, and automating tasks that prove less redundancy, fewer mistakes, and more productivity to your supporting business environment.
- Cutting out the IT process after the solution is built. The IT staff focuses more on building these type of automated solutions and less time on managing static HTML templates. This increases site stability and consistency by automating how content is published.

Another benefit to expect is that when you have developed one or two automated solutions for a specific area, you often are able to reuse the same solution for other areas of your web site or within the company.

Factor in all the other benefits of what a workflow offers on top of a content repository. Your consumers, partners, and employees experience a richer client experience by being able to locate relevant, up-to-date content to make them and your company successful. Your web site can offer more client-rich experiences with the technologies explained in this book. Leveraging Flash Remoting with JRun 4 and ColdFusion MX becomes even more powerful now that you have established a solid Management layer foundation atop your content repository.

Determining the Business Requirements

By understanding your business requirements, you create a controlled process to manage content for your business units. The roles of a workflow system match the roles and the authority level of each employee in the workplace. Continuing in this chapter, we will use the example of the marketing department at DuvalShock. We will first look at the process in the marketing department before a Management layer was incorporated. Looking at Figure 13.2, we can examine how the office process flows. You can build a flow chart by simply sitting down with your business unit and mapping out how it goes about creating content that ends up on the web site. A flow chart like the one shown in Figure 13.2 can become your requirement for the workflow application.

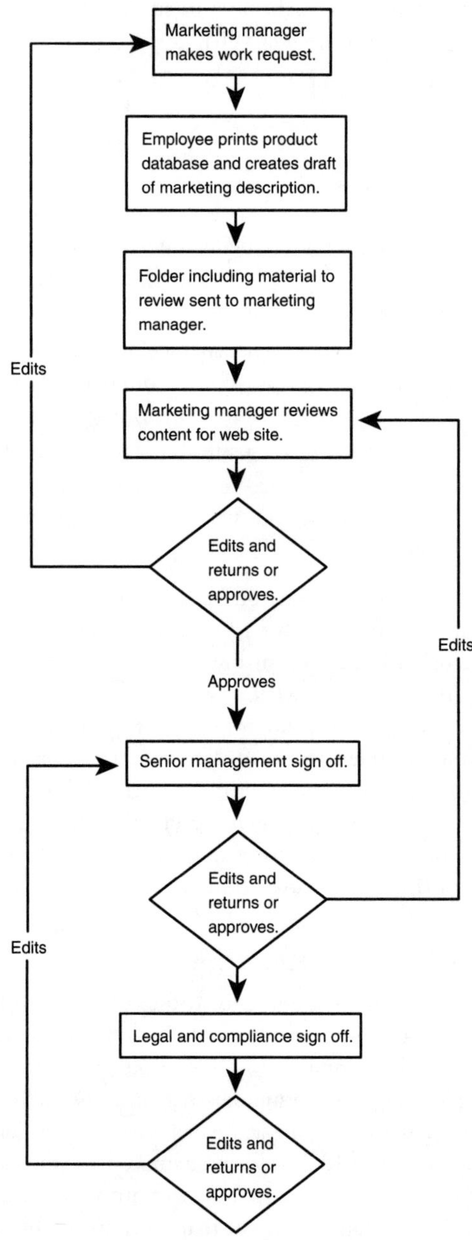

Figure 13.2 Example of a flowchart.

Note the following in Figure 13.2:

1. The marketing manager requests that a description of the new Big Spark 200 Generator needs to be created for the company web site to increase sales.
2. A marketing employee goes into the product database and prints product details for the generator. The content details from the product database are too dry for a product description and do not have all the necessary details to make the description marketable for a salesperson. The content is primarily specification details that do not appeal to a market campaign of the product.
3. A new word processing document is started. A first draft is created for the new product description and saved.
4. A working paper folder is created and includes the printout of the product database and a printout of the first draft of the marketing material for the web site.
5. The folder is walked over and placed into the marketing manager's mailbox for review.
6. The marketing manager averages five to six business days to review the draft and most likely returns with comments on the first go around. The edits are done manually on the paper copy and then returned to the marketing employee.
7. The marketing employee reopens the word processing file to make the edit requests.
8. A new copy of the file with the edits included is printed out and returned to the marketing manager with more urgency this time around.
9. At this point, either another round of edits takes place or the marketing manager routes the folder to his senior management, legal, compliance, and any other necessary groups that need to sign off on the marketing department's product description. Internal audit requires a signature from the appropriate individuals on a signoff sheet provided in the folder.
10. When all signatures are received, the marketing employee takes the final copy of the document and enters a request with the web development team's "project request" system.

This is a simple example of how complex a business process can get. What wasn't really captured are the many delays that can occur, the losing or misplacing of the folder, and the voice mails and other communications to complete this process. Continuing in this chapter, we break down the elements of this process and look at how to create a more efficient workflow with automated tasks that allow your organization to publish content on your company web site with no technology group intervention.

Translating the Business Flow into an Application

You now have an understanding of your business process in the back office. It meets most of the requirements as to why we would choose this as a perfect Management layer solution. Your next challenge is to translate the business flow into an application to support and improve upon this process. Before we begin to analyze it and break it down into a more automated solution, let's make some assumptions about the project approach.

Workflow Application Assumptions

The following are assumptions to determine how the DuvalShock requirements will be delivered in a workflow application:

- The workflow application will be built using a web interface. We need to keep in mind the limitations of the web as we design our application.
- DuvalShock uses Microsoft's Active Directory as the standard for intranet, extranet, Internet, and desktop authentication. Users and groups already exist in this repository. We will be expected to build our solution toward this security model.
- Understanding the development limitations of web technologies, the interface needs to be simple with little or no business training necessary to manage content.

Of these assumptions, the most important to understand is the challenges the web technologies present us. These challenges clash considerably with our desire to make the application easy to use, dynamic, and client rich, which is similar to traditional Client-Server applications that are written for a Microsoft Windows operating system. The web is stateless in nature, so a request-response model is dealt with in creative and not-so creative ways. Developers continually try to meet this challenge by extending web languages to their limits and sacrificing browser compatibility and performance of an application to get the most out of a better user experience.

If you have worked on a web application before, you most likely have been asked in the requirements to make your application perform a task that is not quite possible. The developer will come out with options for how to meet this requirement, but in all cases, the requirement needs endless explanation to your business group and many hours of a developer's time to meet expectations somewhere in the middle. Building a workflow application has many of these challenges. It will be tempting to try technologies like ActiveX Controls or Java Applets through a browser; ultimately, however, you will run into security, performance, and web browser compatibility issues. This is why most development teams have chosen to stick to simpler methods to build their web applications. This is also why building complex applications can be so difficult for the web.

Creating the Workflow Solution

With a basic understanding of the roles of an automated workflow and of the current business process for the content that needs to be managed, let's look at how this can be pieced together to create a workflow solution. Refer back to Chapter 1, "Overview of Dynamic Publishing," to refresh your memory of the elements that need to be managed on the DuvalShock web site. The content management process on the business end will compliment the publishing rules and user experience process on the company web site.

After reviewing this section, look at Figure 13.3. By using the Basic Workflow model earlier in this chapter, we expanded the requirements out to meet the business process.

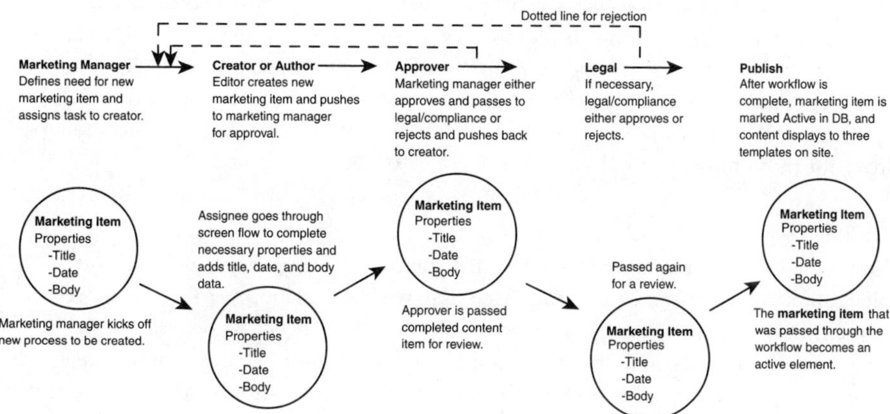

Figure 13.3 Example of a creation and approval process for DuvalShock marketing development.

Relating back to the business process earlier in this chapter, at this point we step through the illustration as a workflow application. Next, we describe the roles and authority of an automated workflow application.

> **Note**
>
> These are just some of the workflow application components that can be introduced. The possibilities are unlimited to meet the business processes that your organization follows. The goal is to simplify the business process when building this solution. When stepping through what a business unit goes through to create, approve, and publish content, you should be able to go back and compare your application design and show improvements to the process. You should be able to quantify where you are saving time, resources and cost by eliminating or streamlining certain manual tasks that took place. The requirements and design need to be well thought out before development begins. The architecture of the application should be considered for growth and change as additional requirements and business processes evolve.

Marketing Manager

In our workflow application, the marketing manager initiates a task requesting that his employee begin to create a product description for the Big Spark 200 Generator. After this is initiated, an automated task sends an email to the employee with a link to the task.

Creator or Author

The marketing employee receives the request and begins to create the content. If you built a feed from another digital asset into your content repository, you might have some of your content to work with to complete this task. The employee steps through a process of screens that ask for items such as title, date, and body description. You can also build in other items, such as metadata tagging and the target audience. In addition, you can provide tools like a word processing editor to format the content through this process, or you can require that a standard font size or style be used when the content is entered at this point. A WYSIWYG word processing HTML editor that includes features like spell checking can be an important piece of your workflow application. When this task is complete, the author submits the content into the repository for publishing approval.

Approver

In Figure 13.3, the requirements show that the marketing manager receives the completed task from the marketing employee. The role of the approver is to read over the content that is created for the new marketing news that needs to be released. If the approver decides the content is not complete or needs other changes, he can reject the content request and send it back to the author with information related to why it was not approved. If it is not approved at this point, it could be published to production or passed on to additional levels of approval.

Legal Approver

In this example, the requirements ask for additional sign off from the DuvalShocks legal department. This task can have the same characteristics as the marketing manager's approval. There is a key difference after the legal department approves the content. The end of this task is the final step before the content repository marks it staged for publishing.

Publisher

After the final approval occurs, the last task in this automated workflow is to publish the content to the DuvalShock web site. For the end user, this should be as easy as clicking a Submit button and having the content publish to the web site in the predefined format that is defined in the publishing requirements. Chapter 19, "Basics of Publishing," explains the publishing elements in detail as the next logical layer.

Increasing Efficiency and Accountability

We described the core components of an automated workflow, but now let's look at the other elements of your application that can assist in better business efficiency and accountability. The following components can add valuable functionality to your workflow application.

Authentication and Roles

Before you can enter a workflow application, you need to have a user login with an ID and password. Ultimately, they should authenticate against your organization's strategic user repository. By doing this, you have an opportunity to reuse groups that are already created for certain departments and granular roles that exist within the organization. Personalizing the workflow application becomes possible if a role is only allowed to manage certain categories in your web site. If your web infrastructure is mostly Microsoft IIS web servers, you are most likely going to be using an NT domain or Active Directory. Web infrastructures that use UNIX predominately go with a more open LDAP solution.

Email

Integration with your organization's email is a powerful facilitation and communication tool to assist the business process. It can be an automated event that can occur at certain points of the workflow. For example, if the marketing employee has completed a content contribution, an email event can send a message to the marketing manager notifying that a task is complete. In the email, can be a full description of the task along with a hyperlink to the content description that needs approval.

To take it a step further, if the task to approve or deny is not executed, then another email can be triggered to the marketing manager as a reminder that the task is still waiting for his action. Email can also be handy for senior executives who have read-only full-task descriptions and deny or approve important pieces of content via wireless devices.

Overuse of email can also be detrimental to your workflow application. Triggering emails at strategic points of a process ensures users that receiving an email from the workflow application is an important one and needs to be attended to.

Audit Tracking

Another feature that your internal audit or compliance unit might require in your workflow application is an audit tracking feature. This can be a utility that tracks completed tasks, dates completed, rollbacks, and, of course, which user is changing, deleting, editing, and approving content published to your web site. It can be a powerful reporting utility for a company that is concerned about the management activity of its web site.

Entry of Metadata, Keywords, and Categories

During the workflow, it is critical that the content being created is identified accurately and consistently. The workflow process can step a user through choosing the correct keywords for the category he is providing content for. Refer back to Figure 4.3 from Chapter 4.

The marketing employee can begin by choosing a category for which to edit content. In our business requirement case, the user might step through a screen flow to be certain that the category "Products" and the subcategory "Generators" is where the new keyword "Big Spark 200" is created. By forcing the user down a path on how and where the new content is created, you have ensured that the new content is located in the accurate taxonomy for proper searching and navigation.

Authoring of Content

Several options are available when a user needs to create or edit a content for font size, italic, bold, indenting, and so on. If you're creating a new keyword heading, or title that you can reuse in navigation, a page title, or a heading, you might not allow for full authoring capabilities and just provide a simple text box to enter the keyword "Big Spark 200." The body of text that describes the generator might have requirements to have full authoring capabilities.

Full authoring solutions in browsers allow for HTML and XHTML editing with most of the capabilities of a typical word processing interface. After a user completes editing using the tool, the content is submitted to the repository with the formatting intended for publishing to the web site.

Task Status

A business manager might request that he be able to view the status of content that is being created. As each task is completed, the status screen can show information like this:

- Date task assigned
- Date task completed
- User assigned for creating, editing, or approving a task
- Overall workflow status
- User comments field

Of course, task status should not be limited to just business managers. Occasionally, some components of a status will be available for all audience levels in your workflow application.

Conclusion

This chapter defined the Management layer, which is what most closely relates to your organization's business process. The workflow application is the center piece of this layer. The application you build for your dynamic publishing solution provides your business users with the ability to update and manage your company web site in a timely and efficient manner. We touched on the basic requirements for when you should build an application like this. It is important to keep asking yourself and your co-workers, "How can I improve cost effectiveness with more efficient business and technical processes in my company?" Finding the most critical areas of your organization that need process improvement and decreased IT spending is important to your success with building automated business processes.

The biggest challenges of building a workflow solution are getting your business to envision how this can benefit your organization and bringing the employees up to speed on a common terminology that should be used to define roles and tasks. Start with the basics. Educate your business to the basic roles of author, editor, and approver. Then build off of those basic roles and fit them to your organization. Walk through the daily manual process of how a piece of content is created, edited, and approved. Look for the inefficiencies in the current process and exploit them with an automated design model to bring cost savings and process improvements. Teach your business new ways to approach their business process and, by comparing the manual process, show an elimination of steps and improvements with automated tasks. Use business-familiar infrastructure tools like email to compliment your workflow application.

Most importantly, make sure the application you build to support the business process is intuitive and easy to use. Over-complicating the application does not win business acceptance, and users are less likely to use it effectively. Also consider taking advantage of "out of the box" solutions, such as Lotus Notes workflow components. It might not be necessary to build from scratch if requirements and your supporting technology allow for using a vendor workflow solution.

The ROI for building a workflow application can be seen on two fronts:

- Increased business efficiency and performance. Improving, streamlining, and automating tasks proves less redundancy, less mistakes, and more productivity to your supporting business environment.
- Cutting out IT processes after the solution is built. The IT staff focuses more on building these types of automated solutions and less time on managing static HTML templates. This increases site stability and consistency by automating the way that content is published.

The automated business process also enforces categorization and consistent input from a business user that results in better site structure, searches, and dynamic navigation. Creating a workflow application results in better business processes, technology resource efficiency, and a web site that meets or exceeds customer expectations for fresh content and usability.

14

Leveraging Security in ColdFusion MX

by Dan Blackman

KNOWING HOW TO IMPLEMENT SECURITY in web applications can mean the difference between a hacker's good day or bad year. At its highest level, security is a means by which we restrict resources from users of a system. By providing an ID and password to users, we require them to log in to our application and restrict them to certain areas of our site. We accomplish this by enforcing security permissions against data systems, sections of code, and entire pages within our applications. When developers used previous versions of ColdFusion, they lacked a standard way of implementing security within their applications. In general, organizations that use ColdFusion have attempted to standardize the approach of securing their applications. The problem with some of these "ad-hoc" security solutions is that they fail to solve some of the more complex problems that developers face today. Single sign-in environments, server fail-over, and unique security schemes are just a few of the complex issues we face in implementing security solutions.

Integrated into ColdFusion MX is a new set of security tags and functions that provide a standard solution for application level security. The tags and functions in ColdFusion's security toolbox provide an easier way to authenticate users against our applications. In this chapter, we explore how to implement the new security features and gain an understanding of their benefits.

The Security Playing Field

Identifying our users/roles and the resources you want to protect provides a solid foundation to secure our environment. Who are your users? A user can be external web browser that gains access to your site's resources, an external application that tries to extract data using syndication techniques, or a PDA or other WML device that accesses content. We must be aware of how users access the site so that we can protect our assets in the form of web content. Knowing our users helps us understand the type of security model that would be best to set up. Knowing our users and associated groups also helps us understand the roles they will play within the application.

Roles are application-level categories that are used to separate content into business-specific functions. Because users are categorized into groups (HR, Finance, Administration) in business, we assign users to roles based on the business function they perform within the application. These roles range from specific usage roles to more universal roles, such as "guest." This allows the security administrator to build a model that limits the users' access to application resources.

Resources make up our entire application at all levels. We start at the top with the application level and work our way down to the data level.

For more information on users, roles, and groups, see Chapter 13, "Basics of Managing Content," which provides a closer look at how these make up the security model.

Now that we have a high-level picture of the security playing field, the rest of the chapter demonstrates how to use the new security tags and functions within ColdFusion MX to authenticate our users, assign roles and permissions, and restrict access to our resources.

The Security Toolbox

To build the framework, we should become familiar with the tools we have at hand. In this release of ColdFusion, we work with a standard set of tools that we did not have in previous versions. The key here is *standard*. We now have a standard way of implementing a role-based security solution. The term *role-based security* refers to the use of role(s) within an application to group user access and permissions to a set of particular resources. The main tag that drives this process is the `<CFLOGIN>` tag. The `<CFLOGIN>` tag, in cooperation with other CFML tags, encapsulates the logic involved in authenticating a user into the system. In previous versions of ColdFusion, developers were required to create their own logic to implement security in their applications. This tag begins the natural progression of authentication, user registration, and authorization.

In the following sections, we will see how this progression flows to provide an entry barrier to our applications and enables us to identify our users and roles within our application.

Step 1: Detect User Authentication

The first step in the process is detecting whether the user is currently logged into the application. In previous versions of ColdFusion, we were required to write a set of logic that detected whether the user had logged into the application (usually a `<CFIF>` block). This logic was placed in our Application.cfm template as a way to detect the Login session each time a template was accessed. With the new `<CFLOGIN>` tag, we no longer have to write login detection logic; the tag handles this inherently.

Table 14.1 shows the `<CFLOGIN>` attributes.

Table 14.1 ***<CFLOGIN>* Attributes**

Attribute	Required	Datatype	Description
`idleTimeOut`	No	Integer	This attribute sets the login session expiration in number of minutes.
`applicationToken`	No	String	This attribute sets an optional token.
`CookieDomain`	No	String	This attribute sets the domain in which the cookie resides.

Listing 14.1 shows how the `<CFLOGIN>` tag wraps the authentication logic to detect a valid login session.

Listing 14.1 ***<CFLOGIN>* Tag**

```
<cflogin>
  ...
  Authentication Logic
  ...
</cflogin>
```

As the tag is encountered, it automatically detects whether the user is logged in to the application. After the user authenticates, the tag validates that the user's logged in session is active, skips the authentication step, and continues the application process. As we will see in subsequent sections, the `<CFLOGIN>` tag works in conjunction with the `<CFLOGINUSER>` tag to create a login session for the user. This login session persists until it times out (based on inactivity) or the user closes his browser. This allows each user to have a unique session identity within the application.

<CFLOGIN> Revealed

Beyond the basic functions of the `<CFLOGIN>` tag lies functionality that proves quite useful in securing applications.

In previous versions of ColdFusion, developers were required to use session variables to test the expiration of the user's login session. The session variables were created as the user logged in to the application. Upon each request, the variables tested the expiration of the user's login session. If the session variable(s) expired, the application would require the user to reauthenticate. With the new `<CFLOGIN>` tag, developers no longer have to write this logic and depend on session variable expiration because the tag handles this functionality inherently. As the login session expires, the `<CFLOGIN>` tag detects the expiration and permits the execution of the logic within the `<CFLOGIN>` block.

The domain attribute of the `<CFLOGIN>` tag also sets the value of the domain where it executed. This sets the domain the cookie used to authenticate against. An example of this could be `intranet.devalShock.com`. This is useful when you have multiple applications hosted on different servers that all need to be associated to the same security authentication and domain.

The `<CFLOGIN>` tag has an internal scope called cflogin. It is populated with the name and password used at the time of authentication. The scope is set from a cookie, URL/form variables, or HTTP Basic Auth Package. Take, for instance, a Challenge/Response Security model. The username and password are passed as part of an HTTP header as the request is received. The cflogin scope is populated with the username and password from the header. It is then used in authenticating the user into the application.

One of the underlying problems in web security is maintaining state across multiple servers. In the case of a server failure, the `<CFLOGIN>` tag allows users to remain authenticated from one server to the next. This is accomplished through the creation of a cookie on the client's machine. The cookie, named CFAUTHORIZATION, holds the login session information for the user, including the CFID and CFTOKEN. Figure 14.1 displays the output of the <cfdump var="#cookie#"> instruction.

Struct	
CFAUTHORIZATION_WkfPub	ZGFuOmFkbWlu
CFID	1301
CFTOKEN	32789305

Figure 14.1 CFAUTHORIZATION Cookie

The cookie is in a form of a ColdFusion structure with three keys. The structure sets the first key to the name CFAUTHORIZATION_ plus the name of the application named using the `<CFAPPLICATION>` tag. If the `<CFAPPLICATION>` is not present, then the first key of structure is named CFAUTHORIZATION_ with no name following. The value of the named key is the encrypted username and password that were used for authentication against the security scheme. This information becomes important to the server that the request failed over to. The server uses this information to reauthenticate the user into a new session.

> **Note**
>
> We must understand the clear distinction that the login session (created using the `<CFLOGIN>` tag) and session state management (within our application) are separate entities. For instance, we can use `<CFLOGIN>` to manage the login session for a user, and we can create session variables during authentication. When the user logs out, however, the session variables that were created as part of the application remain in the session scope. Session state management (session scope variables) is unaffected by ending the users' login session with the `<CFLOGOUT>` tag.

Step 2: Authenticate User Against Security Scheme

Within the <CFLOGIN> code block, developers write logic that is used to authenticate users. This logic can assume various forms depending on the security model the developers choose to implement. Following are three common ways to authenticate users:

- A Listing Directory Access Protocol (LDAP) server
- Challenge/Response
- A common RDBMS against relational database tables

Note

Each of the following methods has benefits and drawbacks that you must take into consideration. It's best to research which authentication model is right for your application before you build the logic into your application.

RDBMS Authentication

The third approach uses a common RDBMS server to simplify the process of application level authentication. Developers use RDBMSs, such as SQL Server and Oracle, to establish a set of relational tables for use in authenticating users. Because this approach relies solely on the relational database as its foundation, it is the more common approach in securing ColdFusion applications.

Within the <CFLOGIN> block, the developer uses the <CFQUERY> tag to fetch the user information for the person who is logging in. Listing 14.2 demonstrates how we use the <CFQUERY> tag in authentication.

Listing 14.2 **Using *<CFQUERY>* to Authenticate Users**

```
<cflogin>
  ...

<cfif structKeyExists(form, "username") and structKeyExists(form, "password")>

<CFQUERY NAME="GET_USER" DATASOURCE="#application.dsn#">
  SELECT U.FNAME, U.LNAME, UID, ROLES
FROM USERS U
  WHERE USERNAME = '#form.NAME#'
  AND PASSCODE = '#form.PASSWORD#'
</CFQUERY>
  </cfif>

  Additional authentication logic...

</cflogin>
```

The <CFQUERY> tag passes the results back in the form of a variable. The result set can then be used to log the user in and set the user's roles and name using the <CFLOGINUSER> tag.

LDAP Authentication

Organizations that manage users internally using an LDAP server might find it a logical approach to use the <CFLDAP> tag during authentication. This tag provides an interface between the ColdFusion application and the LDAP servers. In a large organization, this type of authentication requires a fair amount of upfront time and effort. Listing 14.3 demonstrates the use of the <CFLDAP> tag within the <CFLOGIN> block. Developers who have used this approach in the past will find the approach familiar.

Listing 14.3 **Using the *<CFLDAP>* Tag**

```
<cflogin>
  ...
<cfldap server="ldap.myserver.net" name="myresult"
username="#form.username#" password="#form.password#" ...>
Additional authentication logic...
</cflogin>
```

The <CFLDAP> tag queries the LDAP server for the requested user. The LDAP server returns the results to the ColdFusion application through the `name` attribute. We have a variety of options for supplying the username and password to the <CFLDAP> tag. Using the <CFLDAP> tag in a single sign-on environment, we can catch the username and password from the internal CFLOGIN scope because it is passed as part of the HTTP header. The more simplistic approach we use is to pass the variables into the <CFLOGIN> block and use them to populate the <CFLDAP> tag.

Challenge/Response Authentication

Within the Windows environment, developers might be more familiar with the Challenge/Response approach. In this approach, the security model is built into the Windows environment. Administrators establish user accounts and set restrictions on specific directories and files with the web application. Because the Challenge/Response approach is operating-system centric, setting up this security approach requires interaction with O/S UI tools to set it up. System administrators select directories or specific files editing their security permissions along with granting access to users. As the files are accessed from a remote client, the server displays a dialog box requiring the user to authenticate against the security model.

When authentication is established, the server passes the username and password as part of the CFLOGIN scope to the ColdFusion application. We then use these variables within our <CFLOGIN> block to log the user into the application. Listing 14.4 demonstrates this type of authentication. (The <CFLOGINUSER> tag will be described later in this chapter.)

Listing 14.4 **Using Challenge/Response Authentication**

```
<cflogin>
  ...
    <cfif isDefined("cflogin.name">
    Additional authentication logic...
cfloginuser name="#cflogin.username#
password="#cflogin.password#" roles="#roles#">
    </cfif>
</cflogin>
```

Populating the CFLOGIN scope variables is not a Microsoft Windows/IIS only concept. Within the UNIX environment, the popular Apache server uses a set of files to restrict access to resources. The .htaccess file works with a username/password file to restrict access to those listed in the file. As we interact with the security files using our web application, the Apache server also can populate the CFLOGIN scope username and password variables. We can then use the variables to log the user into the application.

Mapping Roles to Groups

In Chapter 14, "Leveraging Security in ColdFusion MX," we explore setting up users, user profiles, and groups to provide a foundation for our web application security model. As users interact with our application, we must decide what role they will play within the context of the application. In the context of a simple application, we merely assign users a role or a set of roles in a list format ("Manager, Assistant"). The list is then dropped into a security table along with the user's username and password. That way, when the user authenticates, we can set the roles using the `<CFLOGINUSER>` tag.

In dealing with a more complex security model, users are assigned groups that help describe the business group they fall under within the real world. How then do we describe the role the user will play within the application? Using the RDBMS approach, we map the user's role(s) to his group(s) by building an additional set of tables to support that relationship. We create a Roles table and a table called GroupRoles that describes the relationship between the groups and the roles within the application. The GroupRoles table acts as an associative table between the Groups and Roles table. When we join the tables in a query, we can then fetch the roles for the users based on the group to which they are assigned.

During authentication but before calling the `<CFLOGINUSER>` tag, we query all the roles for the authenticated user and use the `queryList(qryName.roles)` function in setting the `<CFLOGINUSER>` roles attribute list. Listing 14.5 illustrates this concept.

Listing 14.5 **Mapping User Roles**

```
<cflogin>

Authentication logic...

  <cfquery name="qFetchRoles" ...>

SELECT  role.roleid
  FROM  user,
   usergroup,
   group,
   role,
   grouprole
 WHERE  user.userid = usergroup.userid
     AND
     group.groupid = usergroup.groupid
        AND
        role.roleid = grouprole.roleid
     AND
        group.groupid = grouprole.groupid
     AND
     user.userid = #qFetchUser.username#



  </cfquery>

  <!--- Log on user --->
<CFLOGINUSER name="# qFetchUser.username[1]#"
password="# qFetchUser.password[1]#" roles="#
querylist(qFetchRoles.roles)#">

Additional authentication logic...

</cflogin>
```

Setting User Permissions

Another tag that proves useful to the authentication of users is the `<CFLOGINUSER>` tag. This tag compliments the `<CFLOGIN>` tag by handling the actual login of the user into the application. The `<CFLOGINUSER>` tag is embedded inside the `<CFLOGIN>` block. After the authentication has taken place (LDAP, RDBMS, and so on) and a set of roles is retrieved, the tag has the necessary items to perform the authentication. Listing 14.6 demonstrates the complete `<CFLOGIN>` block using an RDMS for authentication.

Listing 14.6 **Complete Login Block Using RDBMS**

```
<cfset bGoodLogin = false>

<cflogin>

<cfif structKeyExists(form, "username") and len(request.username)
and structKeyExists(form, "password") and len(request.password)>

<!--- fetch user info, passing username and password --->

<CFQUERY NAME="qFetchUser" DATASOURCE="#application.dsn#">
    SELECT U.FNAME, U.LNAME, UID, ROLES
FROM USERS U
    WHERE USERNAME = '#form.NAME#'
    AND PASSCODE = '#form.PASSWORD#'
  </CFQUERY>

<!--- If the user is found and is valid; Login em in --->
<cfif qFetchUser.recordCount and len(qFetchUser.roles[1])>
    <cfset bGoodLogin = true>

  <cflock scope="SESSION" type="EXCLUSIVE" timeout="5">
    <cfset session.User_Id = stUser.userName>
  </cflock>

  <!--- Log on user --->
<CFLOGINUSER name="#qFetchUser.username[1]#"
password="#qFetchUser.password[1]#" roles="# qFetchUser.roles[1]#">

  <cfelse>
<!--- Send an error message back to the login form --->
  <cfset errMsg = "Invalid Username or Password">
  </cfif>

</cfif>

<cfif not bGoodLogin>
  <!--- Display Login Form --->
  <cfinclude template="loginform.htm">
  <cfabort>
</cfif>
</cflogin>
```

The `<CFLOGIN>` tag detects the status of the user's session and allows the rest of the code block to execute. The username and password are passed into the authentication block. The form variables are used in authenticating the user against the RDMS security tables. After the query returns the record and roles are assigned to the user, the bGoodLogin flag is set to `true` and the user is considered authenticated against the RDBMS. The last step is the actual authentication of the user to the application. The `<CFLOGINUSER>` tag logs in the user and sets his roles for use in the application. The roles act as permissions to various resources within the application.

Identifying the User

Now that we have authenticated the user, how do we know whether he is logged in? Going back to previous versions of ColdFusion, we simply created a `<CFIF>` block to test the session variable we set during authentication. ColdFusion MX provides a function that allows us to test the login status of a user. The function `getAuthUser()` returns a string representation of the user's name passed into the `<CFLOGINUSER>` tag. Listing 14.7 demonstrates how easy it is to test user authentication.

Listing 14.7 **Using *getAuthUser()* to Test Authentication**

```

<cfif len(getAuthUser())>

  Code Goes Here...

</cfif>
```

If the `getAuthUser()` function returns an empty string, the user has not been authenticated using the `<CFLOGINUSER>` tag.

Securing Resources

Although authentication sets the foundation to securing your web site assets, the ability to secure resources plays an integral role in limiting user access to resources.

Restricting Access to Resources

As described earlier, role-based security refers to the use of role(s) within an application to group user access and permissions to a set of particular resources. With this in mind, we must take a step back and carefully determine the security model we will use and the roles each user will play within the application. Chapter 16, "Securing the Application and User Management," explores the concepts of user management and the application of a security framework to manage security within our applications.

The `roles` attribute within the `<CFLOGINUSER>` tag becomes an important part of the application's security. It allows us to restrict users based on the roles given to them by the application's administrator. We can restrict users within our ColdFusion MX applications in two ways. The first way is through the use of the `isUserInRole("")` function. This function requires a single attribute, which represents the name of the role the function is testing. Listing 14.8 demonstrates using `isUserInRole("")` to test whether the user has been assigned the Admin role.

> **Note**
>
> Use discretion when you're setting up roles in your application. We use the role name in the `isUserInRole("")` function to restrict users. Although using the numeric ID might prevent errors from typos, the administration of IDs in your application code is not recommended.

Listing 14.8 **Using *isUserInRole("")* to Test Role Access**

```
<cfif isUserInRole("Admin")>

  Code Goes Here...

</cfif>
```

If the user logged in and is assigned the "Admin" role, access to the code block will be granted. We can use the isUserInRole("") to secure UI pages within our application. By simply placing the `<CFIF>` block at the top of the page we can restrict access to the page by requiring the user to possess the role. We also can use the function to secure blocks of code or portions of HTML forms by placing the `<CFIF>` block around the form element(s). This is illustrated in Listing 14.9.

Listing 14.9 **Securing Code Using *isUserInRole("")***

```
<cfif isUserInRole("Admin") or isUserInRole("Manager")>

  <!--- Page is secure --->

<form name="myForm" Action="" method="post">
   <cfif isUserInRole("Manager")>
<input type="text" name="empSSN" value="#emp.SSN#>
   </cfif>
   <input type="text" name="firstName" value="#emp.fname#>
</form>
</cfif>
```

The second method of restricting access within ColdFusion MX applications is through the use of the `roles` attribute of the `<CFFUNCTION>` tag. In building the application framework, we must consider the use of the `roles` attributes in restricting access to some or all of the methods (see Listing 14.10). Restricting access to the component's method offers another layer of protecting our application.

Listing 14.10 **Roles Attribute in the *<CFFUNCTION>* Tag**

```
<cffunction name="maintainEmployee" roles="Admin" ...>

  <!--- this function is restricted to the Admin Role --->

</cffunction>
```

By restricting access to the methods within a component, we can assign users to perform specific tasks within an application.

If a `roles` attribute is encountered while you're invoking a function, the following actions take place:

1. The method detects user authentication.
2. The method checks the user assigned roles against the value of the `roles` attribute within the `<CFFUNCTION>` tag.

If the user's assigned roles do not match the values of the `roles` attribute, an error is thrown similar to that shown in Figure 14.2.

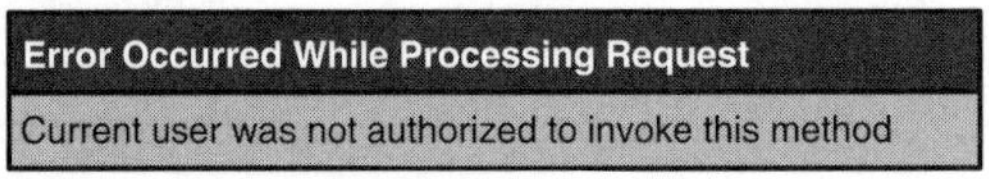

Error Occurred While Processing Request

Current user was not authorized to invoke this method

Figure 14.2 Error that appears when the user's assigned role doesn't make the value of the `roles` attribute.

Logging Out of the Security Session

ColdFusion MX makes it easy to end the user's security session. A new tag, aptly named `<CFLOGOUT>`, logs the user out of the security session. In Listing 14.7, we illustrated the process of authenticating a user. Within the authentication process, we set a flag called bGoodLogin equal to a `false` value. By simply placing the following code above the `<CFLOGIN>` tag, we extend the capability of the login process and allow the bGoodLogin code block to execute (see Listing 14.11).

Listing 14.11 **Logging Out with the *<CFLOGOUT>* Tag**

```
<cfif isDefined("request.logout")>
  <cfset structDelete(session, "User_Id")>
  <cflogout>
</cfif>
```

If we pass a variable, in this case `"request.logout"`, we can process the code required to log a user out of the application. The first step that takes place is the removal of any session variables that are created during authentication. The second step is to invoke the `<CFLOGOUT>` tag. Executing the `<CFLOGOUT>` tag logs the user out, removes the CFAUTHORIZATION cookie, and removes/deletes user/role information from the cflogin scope.

Centralize Your Security

As we learned in Chapter 5, "ColdFusion Components," ColdFusion Components allow us to encapsulate business logic into single, cohesive units. We now can package our security logic into a CFC that allows us to reuse the logic across multiple applications. To package the security logic into a CFC, we simply wrap the logic with a `<CFFUNCTION>` tag and place it inside a ColdFusion Component (see Listing 14.12).

Listing 14.12 **Embedding Security Logic into a CFC**

```
<cffunction name="authenicateUser" returnType="any">
   <cfargument name="userName" type="string" required="yes">
   <cfargument name="password" type="string" required="yes">
```

```

   Security Logic goes here...

<cfreturn result />
```

To invoke the CFC, we simply use the `<CFINVOKE>` tag to authenticate the user (see Listing 14.13).

Listing 14.13 **Invoking the UserManagement Component**

```
<cfscript>
  stParams = structNew();
  stParams.username = request.username;
  stParams.password = request.password;
</cfscript>

<cfinvoke component="rs.usermanagement" method="authenicateUser"
argumentCollection="#stparams#" returnVariable="stUser">
```

Within CFCs, we can combine all the aspects of security into one place. We can build methods for authentication, security schema access, and security schema management. By encapsulating security logic in CFCs, we leverage the power of both ColdFusion Components and ColdFusion's new standardized security features.

Conclusion

The ColdFusion MX security tags and functions provide a new approach to an old problem. By encapsulating functionality into each of the tags and functions, collectively, they provide an easier, more straightforward approach to securing ColdFusion MX applications.

As we explored, developers can now use a standardized approach for detecting, authenticating, and restricting users within their applications. This improves the time to market for applications by lending more time for developers to tune/optimize their applications.

With that said, we must not minimize the extent to which we secure our applications. If we fail to use these and other methods of security, we fail in the effectiveness of the application. Remember: We not only are trying to protect ourselves from unauthorized users gaining access to resources, but we also are protecting ourselves from ourselves.

By restricting our authorized users to certain roles, we minimize the risk of accidental copying or deletion of our data. This is often overlooked as a reason for securing our applications. This proves we must take care in setting up and maintaining our security environment.

The bottom line is to make effective use of the new security features within ColdFusion MX. If we don't, the security holes might be more prevalent than you think.

15

Leveraging Flash Remoting in ColdFusion MX

By Jon Briccetti and Benjamin Elmore

FLASH REMOTING IS THE FIRST TANGIBLE EVIDENCE of the merger between Macromedia and Allaire and the shared vision of bridging the gap between rich web clients with powerful server technologies. Flash Remoting lets Flash clients communicate with server technologies, allowing seamless transmission of data into and out of Flash movies through native integration with web services, XML documents, server recordsets, and server-based authentication.

Flash Remoting integrates with Web Services, ColdFusion MX Components, .NET Components, EJBs, and ColdFusion and ASP pages. Easy to configure, Flash Remoting requires no installation on the server when you're running ColdFusion MX or JRun 4. Development shops that choose to leverage the .NET architecture or the WebSphere J2EE platform need to run an installation on their server for the required Flash Remoting server components. Flash developers must download the Flash Remoting components for the Flash MX Studio. You can download these free of charge from Macromedia's web site by visiting Flash Remoting at `http://www.macromedia.com/software/flash/flashremoting/`. This installation adds needed tools to the Flash MX Studio, enabling Flash developers to call upon the server components.

After Flash Remoting is installed, a Flash developer can simply include the Flash Remoting scripts in his Flash files and become familiar with a single, simple API. Browsing clients only need to have the Flash 6 player. Although Flash MX provides the ability to publish for the Flash 5 player, Flash Remoting functionality in a Flash movie only executes properly if the publishing format is Flash 6. Thus, clients need to have the latest Flash player, which can be downloaded for free from Macromedia's web site at `http://www.macromedia.com/shockwave/download/index.cgi?P1_Prod_Version=ShockwaveFlash`. Of course, you will be able to build your applications to determine the version of the client's Flash player and enable the download of the latest version.

Historically, implementing a Flash front end with a dynamic publishing system has required advanced ActionScript coding techniques and forced experienced Flash developers to really stretch the native functionality of Flash. ActionScript WDDX serializers and XML parsing routines were developed and shared among the Flash community, but they were difficult to use and performed relatively poorly. Development and maintenance cycles were often hefty, so in many cases, a Flash user interface on a data-driven web application was too labor intensive to be feasible. Additionally, implementing such an application required ActionScript-savvy developers who were able to cross the gap between designer and developer.

With the release of Flash MX and ColdFusion MX, this gap is bridged by the technology, not the technologists. Flash developers are able to access data easily and efficiently. ColdFusion developers can focus on what they do best: building server-side business logic components to provide data services to multiple user interfaces—Flash MX included. However, because the Flash Remoting process is so easy to code in the Studio MX environment, ColdFusion developers will find an easy migration to Flash now that they have simple methods for communicating with the server. And Flash developers, who leverage Dreamweaver MX's capability to create CFC web services in ColdFusion MX, will find that they too can build data-driven Flash front ends with ease. This flexibility allows both ColdFusion shops, as well as Flash shops, to leverage their talents across technologies. The end result is better, more flexible use of development resources and faster development cycles.

All this comes at no cost to application architecture. In fact, the Flash Remoting architecture, together with improved functionality of ColdFusion MX, thrives in our Model-View-Controller (MVC) environment, enabling the optimum development and maintenance benefits of true application partitioning: encapsulated architectural layers for presentation, business logic, and transaction management. Be sure to visit the Flash Remoting web site (`http://www.macromedia.com/software/flash/flashremoting/`) to look further into the possibilities of Flash Remoting, obtain any needed downloads, or check the FAQ. Flash Remoting for .NET has its own site at `http://www.macromedia.com/software/flash/flashremoting/net/`.

How Does Flash Remoting Work?

The term *Flash Remoting* refers to the process of leveraging these new technical features of the MX platform. Conceptually, the process of incorporating data into a Flash user interface is not unlike the dynamic Flash of old. The basic process is as follows:

1. The Flash player makes an HTTP request back to the server, asking for some data.
2. The server executes a script to obtain the requested data.
3. The server delivers the data to the client Flash player.
4. The Flash player executes some ActionScript code to reformat or display the information to the user as needed.

ColdFusion developers can liken this process to ColdFusion pages that utilize `<CFHTTP>` to go out, get some data, process it, and return the information in a dynamically created web page.

Since Flash 4, this process has been able to successfully deliver dynamic content to a Flash client. What's new in the Flash Remoting environment is that the addition of the following components has streamlined the process:

- **The Flash Gateway**—This is a "virtual" server—really just a common URL that acts as a broker for managing all of these Flash Remoting requests. The gateway is a Java servlet that listens for Flash Remoting requests and delegates the request to the proper server-side component, or acts as a proxy to make calls to other web services anywhere on the web.

  Behind the scenes, this broker also is a translator between the Flash client and a variety of supported server communication formats. Flash Remoting "talks" to this servlet using a special binary format (ActionScript Message Format, or AMF) that travels over HTTP. So, for example, when a Flash Remoting request is made to a web service, the gateway servlet translates the request from AMF to Simple Object Access Protocol (SOAP), the "native" format of web services. It then translates the SOAP response back to the Flash format when returning data to the Flash client. This is the process when requests are made to web services either across the web or created in technologies other than ColdFusion. When calls are made to CFCs, this servlet is aware of how to invoke that component without having to convert to SOAP. Thus, calls to CFCs might perform better than those to other web services hosted on machines that do not directly support Flash Remoting. This is achieved by routing such requests through this gateway servlet. From a developer's standpoint (in Flash), the process is virtually transparent because the servlet always handles the work. Of course, on the .NET architecture, this gateway is not a servlet; it's a dll, but the process is identical.

- **Flash Remoting Components**—These Flash Authoring tools consist of a series of non-visual ActionScript classes and scripts that provide connectivity, server component invocation methods, and debugging functionality. Also included in these classes is a data structure class, Recordset, which provides intuitive methods for managing server-based query resultsets in the Flash client. Finally, the service class DataGlue provides a means to plug in recordset objects with the new Flash UI Components (see Figure 15.1).
- **Flash UI Components**—Although these ActionScript visual objects are usable without Flash Remoting, their ability to quickly and easily work with server data completes the round-trip process from server data to interactive, intuitive interfaces.

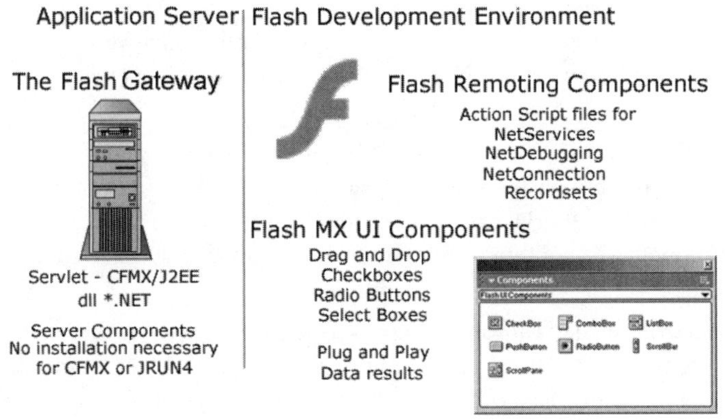

Figure 15.1 Flash Remoting Components.

It might not seem that the addition of these features would significantly improve the development of data-driven Flash, but one look at the techniques of old, and you can see the design pattern emerge that called for just these components.

Prior to the MX platform, a Flash developer had to build special pages in ColdFusion to deliver data as either of the following:

- **Name/value pairs**—Much like URL parameters, they provide a data feed to the Flash movie.
- **XML documents**—Many developers leveraged the WDDX format to represent complex data structures. In fact, XML was the *only* way to work with complex data types prior to Flash MX and Flash Remoting.

Therefore, Flash designers either had to know ColdFusion and spend time building these pages, or they had to pull in ColdFusion developers to assist them. More importantly, every time Flash designers developed a new interface component, they likely needed to have another server page created to deliver the data. With the addition of web services to the ColdFusion platform, it made sense that a single URL could provide a brokerage service between Flash clients and server components.

In addition to the efforts involved with preparing data on the server for Flash data feeds of old, a significant effort was required *within Flash* to parse and convert the data into ActionScript data structures and then, of course, to display the data as needed. Included within this effort was the development of UI controls to allow user interactivity. These interfaces were often constructed from the ground up and bore little resemblance to the UI controls that are intuitive to the average user: select boxes, check boxes, option buttons, and so on.

These challenges represented the most significant stumbling blocks that prevented the union of a Flash UI with a data-driven application. Or, at least, they were the most obvious. Looming in the background were performance problems, which often didn't materialize until applications were brought to production, with *real data*. The combination of complex ActionScript on a client machine with potentially limited resources—along with the server processing that needed to restructure data in an acceptable Flash-feed format—would ultimately overshadow any hopes of a robust environment for dynamic Flash. With the Macromedia MX platform and Flash Remoting, the delivery of data to Flash is powerful, efficient, and easy to develop.

> **Note**
>
> A key initiative for Macromedia has been the incorporation of the Flash player in micro devices. This has been successful, and already, many devices support the Flash player. Many development shops have embraced Flash as a means to solve cross-browser support issues, which is an enormous hurdle in DHTML development. What many developers have yet to realize is that by implementing a Flash front end, they are able to create a single user interface not only across browsers, but also across devices. This can be a significant improvement in application development cycles and can expand a business application to many new clients. For more information on the Flash player support for micro devices and other mobile device development, visit Macromedia's Mobile Device Development Center at `http://www.macromedia.com/desdev/mobile/`.

Flash Remoting substitutes these traditional methods with a far more streamlined process. Flash developers can now designate a single entry point to the server: the Flash Gateway. Next, API calls to Flash Remoting objects provide simple ways to request server data from within Flash. Finally, avoiding clunky code to transform data, we can use other service classes to plug data into reusable, intuitive user interface components.

Note

Keep in mind that the availability of web services is also a core aspect of Flash Remoting. In most implementations, your server needs to have web services built and available to the Flash Gateway. See Chapter 5, "ColdFusion Components," to see how to create these services in our ColdFusion MX environment.

Web Services, Flash Remoting, and Server-Side ActionScript

Flash Remoting can invoke ColdFusion MX Components (CFCs), ColdFusion and ASP pages .NET Components, and web services created using other server technologies. The Flash Gateway server is the abstraction layer between the Flash client and all of these supported formats. Our brokerage service will manage all requests from Flash to server and back again and in doing so handle any needed "translation" between the varieties of supported server technologies. In addition to ColdFusion Components, another server-side format is new to ColdFusion MX and specifically geared toward Flash Remoting. An alternative syntax to ColdFusion Markup Language (CFML), called Server-Side ActionScript (SSAS), executes on the server to deliver data to Flash requests. SSAS allows Flash teams to leverage the benefits of Flash Remoting without knowing ColdFusion, Java, or ASP. SSAS files are deployed to the server and contain ActionScript-like code, with a few special commands to perform typical server behaviors. For example, there is a query object to communicate with the database and an HTTP object to make URL requests.

As if this weren't enough, these SSAS "server behaviors" are really just instances of Java objects; therefore, you can expand SSAS by writing new functions that encapsulate common Java APIs. If a development shop has Java and Flash Resources and little ColdFusion knowledge, the Java developer(s) could customize the SSAS capabilities on the server to build an easy-to-use server scripting environment that provides business-specific data services to the team of Flash developers. This maximizes the return on investment for IT managers who want to leverage the resources they currently have, without having to outsource or bring in consultants. Although ColdFusion shops will likely not need SSAS, it offers a viable option to the right development team. This kind of flexibility delivers a rich client toolset with powerful server technologies. This was the vision of the Macromedia-Allaire merger, and that vision has truly come to life with the Macromedia MX platform and Flash Remoting.

Step-by-Step Flash Remoting

In the next section, we will take a hands-on walkthrough and create a small application using Flash Remoting. This application will consist of a single ColdFusion Component and a single Flash movie. Using Flash Remoting instead of a traditional ColdFusion application, we can provide a drill-down interface without having to send the client to multiple "pages" in our application. As a result, our code is easier to maintain, and the user can go through a better user experience.

Step 1: Setup

To move forward with this example, you need to have the following software:

- ColdFusion MX.
- Flash MX Studio.
- Flash Remoting Components for Flash MX.
- The example applications installed with ColdFusion MX. (We'll specifically use the ExampleApps datasource.)
- Dreamweaver MX, ColdFusion Studio, or Notepad.

You can download all the resources you need from the Macromedia web site. For the Flash Remoting Components, you can go to the Flash Remoting site at `http://www.macromedia.com/software/flash/flashremoting/`.

Any installation of Flash Remoting is already taken care of after you have ColdFusion MX installed. No extra steps are involved in installing Flash Remoting on the server. Remember this, however: For the .NET Framework of other supported J2EE platforms, you need to perform a server-side installation.

As mentioned, you can use Flash Remoting to access web services (CFCs) as well as ColdFusion Markup Pages (CFMs). For the most part, this process is identical in Flash, but ColdFusion pages communicate with the Flash Gateway a bit differently.

Although it might make sense to utilize the Flash Gateway's communication capabilities with standard CFM pages in some cases, most applications that use Flash Remoting make calls back to web services because this fits best the Model-View-Controller architecture. Architecturally, CFCs in ColdFusion MX find themselves in the service tier—functional components that are developed to act as a service to other software entities in the Presentation layer. A CFC by nature is an encapsulated component that is designed to know little about what is invoking it. Other components simply make requests to a CFC via its API. Well-designed CFCs have little concern for the Presentation layer, which enables quick and easy development of alternative user interfaces without having to redevelop business rules and transaction logic. Thus, our Flash movies will, in most cases, communicate with CFCs. Of course, ColdFusion Components that need to communicate through the Flash Gateway are identical to CFCs built for consumption from other *remote* environments. For Flash to invoke methods on these components, those methods only need to specify "remote" access in the signature. In our example application, we'll use a CFC with a function with the following signature:

```
<cffunction name="getDepartments" access="remote" returnType="query">.
```

For more information on the `<CFFUNCTION>` tag, see Chapter 5.

Sometimes CFM pages will be acting as routers or controllers to delegate processing. Thus, you might need to invoke these pages from Flash Remoting. These functional CFMs will be a rarity in most architectures that leverage CFCs because CFM pages in ColdFusion MX will most often serve to deliver dynamic content, such as HTML, CSS, and JavaScript. This step-by-step walkthrough will make use of a CFC, but we will look briefly at calling both CFM pages and other web services immediately hereafter.

The steps that follow will make use of a ColdFusion Component (CFC) that provides access to data in the ExampleApps data source to delivery resultsets from a company department table and an employee table. You should name this CFC EmployeeServices.cfc and deploy it to a folder called FlashRemoting under the web root of your ColdFusion MX server.

Listing 15.1 shows the code for this component.

Listing 15.1 **ColdFusion Component Code to Access Employee Data**

```
<cfcomponent>
 <!--- :::Function: Retrieve List of Departments --->
 <cffunction name="getDepartments" access="remote" returntype="query">
    <cfquery name="qGetDepartments" datasource="exampleApps">
        SELECT  DepartmentID, DepartmentName
        FROM tblDepartments
        ORDER BY DepartmentName
    </cfquery>
    <cfreturn qgetdepartments>
 </cffunction>

 <!--- :::Function: Retrieve List of employees EITHER ALL OR FOR A DEPT
ID --->
 <cffunction name="getEmployees" access="remote" returntype="query">
    <cfargument name="DepartmentID" type="UUID" default="">
    <cfquery name="qGetEmployees" datasource="exampleApps">
        SELECT FirstName,LastName,EmployeeID
        FROM tblEmployees
        <cfif len(trim(departmentid))>
           WHERE DeptIDFK = '#DepartmentID#'
        </cfif>
           ORDER BY LastName, FirstName
    </cfquery>
    <cfreturn qgetemployees>
 </cffunction>

 <!--- :::Function: Retrieve List of employees EITHER ALL OR FOR A DEPT
ID --->
 <cffunction name="getEmployeeDetails" access="remote" returntype="query">
     <cfargument name="EmployeeID" type="UUID" required="yes">
     <cfquery name="qgetEmployeeDetails" datasource="exampleApps">
        SELECT FirstName,LastName,EmployeeID,Title,IsTemp,Email,Phone,
 StartDate
```

```
            FROM tblEmployees
            WHERE EmployeeID = '#EmployeeID#'
            ORDER BY LastName, FirstName
        </cfquery>
        <cfreturn qgetemployeedetails>
    </cffunction>
    </cfcomponent>
```

This web service will supply the functionality for an employee drill-down, providing at first a list of departments and a method to deliver the employees for any selected department. Finally, as an employee name is selected, the final method, `getEmployeeDetails`, will send back information specific for that employee. After this web service is installed on the server, you're ready to begin creating a rich, interactive user interface in Flash using Flash Remoting. I've created a basic layout in Flash that looks like Figure 15.2.

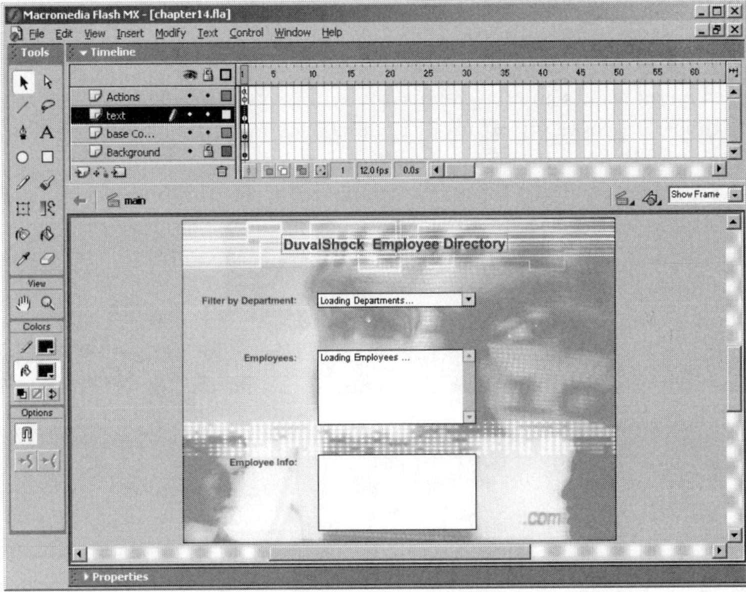

Figure 15.2 Employee directory UI layout in Flash MX Studio.

> **Note**
>
> Figure 15.2 shows a screen shot from Flash Studio. If this is new to you, the MX family of products will help you become familiar with other MX products. Like Dreamweaver MX and Fireworks MX, tools are organized into dockable panel windows. In this figure, we see a Timeline panel, the Tools panel, and the main graphic work area, called the Stage. In the Timeline panel, you can see layers named Actions, Text, BaseComponents, and Background. These layers allow you to add content to the Flash movie in both physical and logical layers. The standard for coding ActionScript, the programming language for Flash, is to put all code in a separate layer called Actions. The other layers are for physically stacking and organizing the visual items seen on the stage.

Aside from the static text and the background image on the Stage, there are only two components (from the Flash UI Components set) and a dynamic text field. The combo box will be used to allow the user to select a single department from the Employee Directory database. After it's selected, the other component, the list box, will contain a list of multiple employees who work in that department. To access these components, use the Flash menu and select Window, Components. Then you can simply drag and drop these controls onto the Stage.

When the user selects an employee in the list box component (only one is selectable at a time), employee information is pulled back from the Flash Remoting Gateway and displayed in the dynamic text area. Instance names for the UI components are `departments_cb` (cb for combo box), `employees_lb` (lb for list box), and `employeeDetails_txt` (txt for text field). Instance names are assigned through the Properties panel. (This is a new panel window in Flash MX; Flash 5 used an Instance panel.)

Like both Dreamweaver 4 and Dreamweaver MX, the Properties panel "morphs" itself to provide easy editing of properties for whatever item is currently selected. Thus, the Properties panel will look like Figure 15.3 after the combo box is selected.

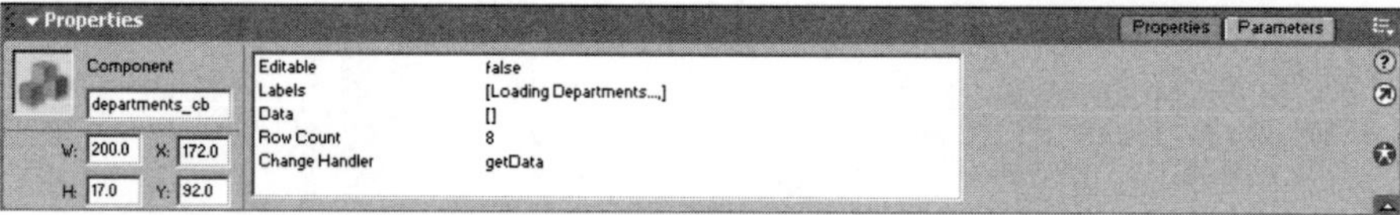

Figure 15.3 The Flash Properties panel when combo box `departments_cb` is selected.

Note

New in Flash MX is the use of variable and instance name suffixes (hence the _cb, _lb, and so on extensions added on to the end of each instance name in our example). Using these suffixes enables coding tips to these types of component methods and properties in the ActionScript editor. These tips are provided exactly the same way that tag insight and function insight are provided in ColdFusion Studio and Dreamweaver MX, so ColdFusion developers should feel right at home with this concept. This feature works for Flash components, movie clips, and many other native data types in Flash. For more information on this practice, see the Macromedia white paper on Flash coding standards at `http://www.macromedia.com/desdev/mx/flash/whitepapers/actionscript_standards.pdf`.

At this point, everything that needs to operate in this movie will occur from ActionScript, all contained right in the first frame of the movie.

Step 2: The ActionScript—Including Flash Remoting Components

When you install the Flash Remoting Components for Macromedia Flash MX, you're really just installing files into your Flash installation folders. (Remember: You won't need to install server components if you're using ColdFusionMX or JRun 4, but you will need to install the Flash Remoting Components for Flash Studio.) These files provide a collection of ActionScript files that are available in the [*Flash MX installation root*]\configuration\include\ folder, as depicted in Figure 15.4.

D:\Program Files\Macromedia\Flash MX\Configuration\Include

Name	Size	Type	Modified
DataGlue.as	3 KB	AS File	4/4/2002 10:17 PM
NetDebug.as	1 KB	AS File	3/20/2002 5:03 PM
NetDebugConfig.as	5 KB	AS File	3/20/2002 5:03 PM
NetDebugEvents.as	9 KB	AS File	3/20/2002 5:03 PM
NetDebugHelpers.as	8 KB	AS File	3/20/2002 5:03 PM
NetDebugImpl.as	4 KB	AS File	3/20/2002 5:03 PM
NetDebugLocalConnection...	7 KB	AS File	3/20/2002 5:03 PM
NetDebugNetConnection.as	8 KB	AS File	3/20/2002 5:03 PM
NetServices.as	12 KB	AS File	3/20/2002 5:03 PM
RecordSet.as	18 KB	AS File	3/20/2002 5:03 PM
RsDataProviderClass.as	3 KB	AS File	3/20/2002 5:03 PM

11 object(s) 71.6 KB My Computer

Figure 15.4 ActionScript files available after installation of Flash Remoting Components for Flash Studio.

These ActionScript files contain various variable and function declarations that provide all of the core functionality we'll need in Flash to access the Flash Remoting server components. To use these scripts in your Flash movie, you simply use the compiler directive `#include` *`filename`* to pull these scripts into your movie. Many of the

ActionScript files listed in the figure are actually included by others, so you won't need to know about all of them directly. In fact, developers only explicitly include three files in their code:

- NetServices.as
- NetDebug.as
- DataGlue.as

The NetServices file provides object definitions for us to specify the URL of our Flash Gateway and obtain reference variables to services on the server. The DataGlue.as file includes a single object definition in your Flash movie. It will act as a controller class for associating data that is returned from the server, with User Interface Components (or other custom developer Flash Components that work with recordsets). The `dataglue` class makes it easy to fill a UI component with data without having to loop. In fact, you can usually "stick" data to a UI component with a single line of code.

NetDebug provides access to debugging utilities. Flash Remoting brings many new challenges with regards to debugging; errors can occur either on the server, in Flash, or perhaps in the communication between. Although many ColdFusion and Flash developers have been successful without using debugging tools, the NetDebug utilities offer helpful tools. At the end of the step-by-step, we'll take a brief look at this powerful debugging tool.

After these files are included in your ActionScript code, they establish aptly named reference variables: NetServices, NetDebug, and DataGlue. Listing 15.2 shows all of the ActionScript code we will build in this step-by-step (coded in the first frame of the Actions layer). Lines 1 to 4 show the coded needed to include the Flash Remoting Components in the movie.

Listing 15.2 **ActionScript for Step-by-Step Flash Remoting Example**

```
1   // Include the Required NetService class files
2   #include "NetServices.as"
3   #include "DataGlue.as"
4   //#include "NetDebug.as"
5
6   // Flash Gateway Connection init
7   if (bGatewayOpen == null) {
8    bGatewayOpen = 1;
9     // Make the Gateway connection
10   NetServices.setDefaultGatewayUrl("http://localhost:8500/flashservices/
gateway");
11   gatewayConnnection = NetServices.createGatewayConnection();
12   empService = gatewayConnnection.getService
("FlashRemoting.EmployeeServices", this);
13  }
14  empService.getDepartments();
15
```

```
// CHANGE HANDLER FOR UI Components departments_cb and Employees_lb
function getData(changedObj) {
 if(changedObj._name == "departments_cb")
    empService.getEmployees(changedObj.getValue());
 else
    empService.getEmployeeDetails(changedObj.getValue());
}

//RESPONDER FUNCTIONS WILL BE CALLED BY DEFAULT FROM FLASH WHEN THE FLASH
REMOTING CALL IS COMPLETE
function getDepartments_Result(result) {
 DataGlue.BindFormatStrings(departments_cb, result, "#DepartmentName#",
"#DepartmentID#");
}
function getEmployees_Result(result) {
DataGlue.BindFormatStrings(Employees_lb, result, "#LastName#, #FirstName#",
"#EmployeeID#");
 Employees_lb.setSelectedIndex(0);
}
function getEmployeeDetails_Result(result) {
employeeRow = result.items[0];
var details = '<p align="center"><b>' + employeeRow.Title + '</b></p>';
var temp = "Permanent";
if(employeeRow.isTemp) temp = "Temporary";
details +='<p align="center"><b>Status</b> ' + temp + '</p>';
details +='<p align="center"><u><a href="mailto:';
details += employeeRow.email +'?subject=Flash Remoting">'
+ employeeRow.email + '</a></u></p>';
details +='<p align="center">'+ employeeRow.phone +'</p>';
employeeDetails_txt.htmlText = details;
}
stop();
```

Note

The NetDebug.as file is for development only and should be commented out or removed before moving to production.

Note

You must code compiler directives, such as `#include`, in a frame. They cannot appear in ActionScripts for movie clip instances or other non-frame actions. Also, do not add a semicolon (;) character after the `#include` or you will get an error.

Step 3: NetServices—Specifying the Flash Gateway

The `NetServices` object delegates all communication between the Flash client and the Server components invoked via Flash Remoting. This service object creates reference variables (of type `NetConnection`) to specific gateway servers and can be initialized to specify the URL to the Flash Gateway. You can make this specification in three ways.

The most common way to set this up is to call the `setDefaultGatewayUrl("URL")` method of the `NetServices` object. This essentially makes a global setting for the movie to specify the URL as the single gateway server to be used by default for any `netconnection` reference variables created through the `CreateGatewayConnection()` method. It provides a mechanism for setting the gateway server URL in one place. Our example will take this approach. Line 10 in Listing 15.2 shows the code we'll use to specify our Gateway URL.

A second approach is to pass a variable into the Flash movie called `GatewayURL`. You can do this by adding a querystring to the SWF file specification in the `<OBJECT>` and `<EMBED>` tags, or you can specify a `flashvars` parameter to the movie using a *`key=value`* format. The latter would look like this in the HTML `<OBJECT>` tag:

```
<param name="flashvars" value="gatewayUrl=http://localhost:8100/
➥flashservices/gateway">
```

These parameters that are sent to the Flash movie really just become global variables in the movie; alternatively, the developer could set `"_global.gatewayUrl"` *before* including NetServices.as.

Finally, the third approach is to specify the gateway URL when creating individual instances of the `netconnection` object through the `createGatewayConnection` method of the `NetServices` object. This approach is the only way to set multiple Flash Gateways to use in a single movie.

> **Note**
>
> A search hierarchy will be used if the `gatewayURL` is specified in multiple locations.
>
> When setting a `gatewayURL` as the optional argument in a `CreateGatewayConnection()` method call, that URL will always be used for the returned `netconnection` reference variable, regardless of any global settings. Therefore, you can set a default gateway and then specify other URLs on a service-by-service basis by providing them as arguments in other `creategatewayconnection()` calls.
>
> However, the `gatewayURL` argument of the `createGatewayConnection()` method is optional. If this argument is omitted, Flash looks for the `_global.gatewayURL` argument first; then it checks whether a `defaultgatewayURL` was set using the `setDefaultGatewayUrl()` method. Although this might seem odd, it actually solves a nice deployment issue that might arise when moving a large Flash Remoting project out to production. The FLA/SWF files do not need to be modified to specify the production Flash Remoting `gatewayURL`; the HTML or ColdFusion developers can simply specify the `flashvars` parameter to the Flash movie through Dreamweaver MX dialog boxes, or by hand-coding in HTML. The Flash movie will resolve to use the production Flash Gateway server instead of the development server. This is considered a Flash Remoting best practice as specified by the Flash Remoting white paper.

Step 4: Connecting to the Gateway and Web Services

After included, the netservices.as file creates a global variable called `NetServices`, which is just an ActionScript object with a couple of properties and some methods that return reference variables to objects of type `NetConnection`. These `NetConnection` objects are the actual worker ants that communicate back to the server, whereas the `NetServices` object is just the delegating service object. Therefore, to communicate with the Flash Gateway or with multiple gateways, we'll need to instantiate instances of `NetConnection` objects through the `CreateGatewayConnection()` method of the NetServices object. Line 11 in Listing 15.2 shows the code as this:

```
gatewayConnection = Netservices.createGatewayConnection();
```

Because this method call omits the optional `gatewayURL` argument, this connection will utilize the `gatewayURL` specified in the `setDefaultGatewayUrl()` call we made in the previous step.

The result of this `createGatewayConnection` call is an instantiated variable, *`gatewayConnection`*, which provides service functionality to connect to web services via the `getService()` method. Line 12 in Listing 15.2 shows that code as follows:

```
empService = gatewayConnnection.getService("FlashRemoting.EmployeeServices",
this);
```

Now, a new reference variable, often referred to as a service object, is created to provide the ability to call methods on the web service designated by `"FlashRemoting.EmployeeServices"`. This web service maps to the employeeServices.cfc file, packaged in the FlashRemoting folder under the ColdFusion MX web root. We'll see later that the `EmployeeServices` web service doesn't really have to be a web service or a CFC page. We can invoke a regular .cfm page using the same Flash syntax.

> **Note**
>
> The `this` argument in the `getservice` method call is the argument for what Flash object will handle the response back from the services on the server; in this case, this refers to the parent Flash movie, although one could code this to manage the responders in other Flash objects besides the root movie object. In fact, responders can be custom objects; they don't have to be of type `movieclip` so that one could leverage the object-based nature of ActionScript to build re-usable responder objects. Responders will be discussed in step 7.

Step 5: Creating the Connection

So far, we have performed the following:

1. Set up a default gateway URL path specification by using the `setDefaultGatewayURL()` method.

2. Set up a connection to the gateway using the `createGatewayConnection()` method. Our example only uses a single gateway server, and because we have specified a default gateway URL, we don't need to provide a gateway URL to our `createGatewayConnection()` call.
3. Create instances of service objects to communicate with each of our web services by using the `getService()` method. Remember: If we were hooking up to several services, we would call multiple `getService` methods, each setting up reference variables to a corresponding service. In our example, we use a single web service, and our reference variable is `empService`.

In most cases, the Flash Remoting services will be needed throughout the movie, so we'll want to code these initial steps to only fire once. In addition, we'll want to ensure this is done immediately when the movie loads. Because we have to put compiler directives, such as `#includes`, into frame scripts, the best place for all of this code is in frame 1 of an Actions layer, in the first scene. To prevent the code from firing multiple times (such as if the Flash playhead were to be reset back to frame 1 due to an animation), we'll want to set a global flag variable to indicate the script has fired once already and all needed services have been initialized. Of course, you can build a Flash application that needs to connect to service objects based on some events occurring in the application. Therefore, in some cases, this code might be on a frame other than frame 1. However, you need to have these connection routines coded in a frame, and not, for example, on an instance of some object on the stage. Coding in frames on the Actions layer is also part of the documented best practices for ActionScript coding (see `http://www.macromedia.com/desdev/mx/flash/whitepapers/ActionScript_standards.pdf`). Putting all the code together so far, our code will look like lines 1 to 13 in Listing 15.2:

```
// Include the Required NetService class files
#include "NetServices.as"
#include "DataGlue.as"
//#include "NetDebug.as"

// Flash Gateway Connection init
if (bGatewayOpen == null) {
bGatewayOpen = 1;
// Make the Gateway connection
NetServices.setDefaultGatewayUrl("http://localhost:8500/flashservices/
➥gateway");
gatewayConnnection = NetServices.createGatewayConnection();
empService = gatewayConnnection.getService("FlashRemoting.EmployeeServices",
➥this);
}
```

At this point, all of the initialization work is complete for our ActionScript. From here on, developers can leverage calls to the server and work with resultsets through a simple API. Combined with the DataGlue service class and Flash UI Components, discussed hereafter, plugging data into Flash movies is a snap.

Step 6: Calling Service Functions (Methods)

When connections to server resources are established, you can begin to make use of those services from ActionScript. The `getService()` method returns a reference variable to a service object. This object is actually of type `NetServiceProxy`, appropriately named because it will act as a proxy to the corresponding server's service. And as a proxy should behave, it acts just like it is the service. Therefore, if the web service has a method called `"getDepartments()"`, you can call that web service method on your proxy object. In our code example, `empService` is the proxy object to the `"FlashRemoting.EmployeeServices"` web service. EmployeeService.cfc has defined within it a method, `getDepartments()`, so we would code the following to invoke that method on the web service:

```
empService.getDepartments();
```

This call invokes Flash to make the request back to the Flash Remoting gateway server to invoke the `getDepartments` method in the `EmployeeService` ColdFusion Component.

Line 14 in Listing 15.2 shows this code. This will be the initial call to the web service, so our departments_cb combo box can initialize with the department data.

Now that our initial service is called, our next step is to obtain the results from that service and populate our ComboBox control. Architecturally, it is important to recognize that these service calls from ActionScript are asynchronous. This means that Flash will not wait for the web service to deliver its results before continuing on to execute the next lines of ActionScript code. The flow of the ActionScript firing to invoke these server calls is completely independent of the server request and response. Although this adds a layer of complexity to our environment to get results, because it is an incredibly powerful feature.

Step 7: Getting Results from the Server

Asynchronous processing and multithreaded environments are sometimes difficult to conceptualize. It's even more challenging to write code that is robust enough to hold up under such conditions. Fortunately, the `NetServiceProxy` object defined in the NetServices.as file and created by the ActionScript gurus at Macromedia was designed to shield this complexity from developers wanting to take full advantage of Flash Remoting. The good news is that handling the results from the calls to the server is easy! The simplest way to handle results is to write a single ActionScript function using a naming convention.

In the example code, we called the `getEmployees()` method on the `empService` `NetServiceProxy` object. To handle the results, we'll simply define a function called `getEmployees_Result(returndata)`. That function will fire when the Flash movie receives the data back from the `getEmployees` server call. The argument, *`returndata`*, will contain the result data from the service. That's easy enough!

Keep in mind that when we first created the `empService` object using the `GetService()` method call, we specified the argument `this` as the responder to results. In this case, `this` refers to the main movie. When results are returned from the server to the Flash movie, Flash looks for the result handler function to be defined in the main movie (and not, for example, defined in a movie clip). For most Flash Remoting implementations, you should use the main movie as the responder to service calls and then simply define a function in frame 1 of the movie to handle the results. Of course, more experienced ActionScript developers who are comfortable using other object to handle results can do so, but in this example, we'll just put these response handlers in the main movie.

You might find that defining all these functions becomes tedious, especially when you're working with many web services. Conveniently, Flash Remoting provides a solution to streamline the responder code development. In the responder object (in our case, the main movie), a developer can designate a single result handler function, named `onResult()`, and the Flash movie will invoke that handler for every service response when it can't find a specific named handler. Again, we have a hierarchy that allows us to handle results for specific service returns, and when no specific handler is found, the generic can work as a catch-all. For example, if we were to invoke another method, called `getPayrolls`, on the `empService` object, Flash would first look for a function defined in the main movie, called `getPayrolls_Result`. If Flash didn't find that function defined, it would then try to pass the results to a function called `onResult()`. Last, when you're in development mode of Flash Studio (when you're previewing your movie internally), if no result handler is found, the results are traced to the output window.

> **Note**
>
> There is quite a bit more flexibility in place with handling results. When you're creating the `NetServiceProxy` object with the `getService()` method, the second argument, `responder`, is optional. When omitted in the `getService()` call, all method calls to the `NetServiceProxy` object require a responder object to be specified as a second argument. This provides granular control over which Flash objects respond to a single service *on a* method-by-method basis. Combined with some advanced ActionScript, perhaps creating custom Flash objects, using the new `object()` constructor, or defining a new function with a nested onResult() handler, you can create highly customized responder objects that are business-specific, ActionScript entities.

Virtually identical to result handlers, error handlers are available by building method-specific functions with `_Status` appended to the name. Thus, the example service call `empService.getEmployees()` might throw an unexpected error (such as if the database is down for maintenance). In such a case, if a defined function `getEmployees_Status()` were defined in the movie, that function would fire to allow soft handling of the error. Like the Results handling hierarchy, Flash will look up a chain of appropriate responder objects from `onStatus()` or `functionName_Status()` functions. Unlike the Results hierarchy, however, all errors can be managed in a global error handler in the Flash movie. This global error-handling function must be named `_global.System.onStatus()` and can act as a last line of defense for managing all errors softly. Alternatively, it can allow generic error handling processing to alleviate the need to handle all errors individually. This is similar to the error-handling hierarchy in ColdFusion; it offers a powerful and flexible system for managing exceptions.

Continuing with our code example, we'll add a responder function to trap the results from our `getDepartments` service call:

```
function getDepartments_Result(result) {
```

We'll add the code for this in the next step. Lines 24 to 27 of Listing 15.2 shows the complete code.

Step 8: Flash UI Components

Another new feature of the Flash MX authoring environment is components. Flash Components are completely independent of anything that is server related and will find their place on many Flash movie stages that do not use server data. However, conceptually, many components are visual manifestations of data. As a result, they are perfectly suited for integration into Flash Remoting. The most obvious example of components that fall into this category is the Flash UI Components, which are installed by default with Flash MX Studio. Figure 15.5 shows a Flash movie with Flash UI Components. These well-encapsulated, intuitive interface components are built to mimic the appearance and behaviors of standard windows controls: buttons, option buttons, check boxes, list boxes, and so on. By providing drag-and-drop usage of complicated visual components, built with simple APIs to customize and "fill" with data, these components drastically cut Flash development cycles, while easily implementing a system of controlled usability into the Flash interface design. In addition to the Flash UI Components, graphing components and other slick components are available, including tree views and sliding panes. Highly encapsulated for maximum re-use, these components, like extensions, install easily. Undoubtedly, the Flash community will start cranking out Flash Components and making them available for fee and for free at the Macromedia exchange. You can find Flash Components on the exchange at `http://dynamic.macromedia.com/bin/MM/exchange/main.jsp?product=flash`.

Also check out `http://www.flashcomponents.net/` for some good free components. If you are interested in building your own, you can find a good tutorial at `http://www.macromedia.com/support/flash/applications/creating_comps/index.html`.

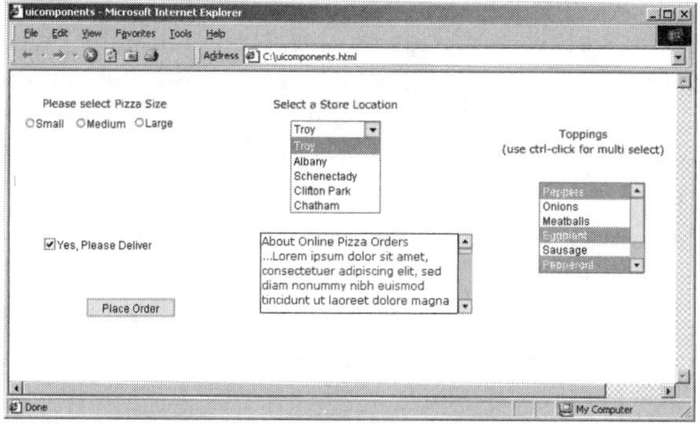

Figure 15.5 Flash UI Components.

In Flash Remoting, components offer visual objects into which we can plug server data. This provides easy design implementation (drag-and-drop) for non-designers and application development (plug-and-play) for non-programmers. Again, we see Macromedia MX tools bridge the designer-developer gap.

In our example, we'll use the most intuitive data-centric UI Components: the combo box and the list box. Conceptually, these are really the same kind of entity; however, from a visual standpoint, they are distinct and have been developed as separate Flash UI Components. A combo box provides a select list style interface displaying only one option at a time, with no multiselect capability. A list box provides single or multiple selections and displays three or more selections at a single time.

These components can be introduced to the stage by dragging and dropping them from the Components panel window. Refer back to Figure 15.2 for the Flash movie layout. Our example requires a single combo box with an instance name of `departments_cb` and a single list box with an instance name of `employees_lb`. Finally, although not a UI Component, we'll add a multiline text field, with Render HTML checked, and instance name of employeeDetails_txt. Using ActionScript, we'll build up an HTML formatted string to set in this field when the user drills-down onto a particular employee by selecting one in the `employees_lb` list box.

Step 9: DataGlue

Flash UI Components, in many cases, can work directly with data structures. However, when we're using Flash Remoting, our resultsets are often query results from a database. A query is a rather specialized data structure, so Flash Remoting provides a special service class, called *`dataglue`*, to provide a simple way to "stick" the data into a UI Component. This service object is defined in the dataGlue.as file and is not terribly complex. When we're working with the combo box or list box components, we'll simple call a single method, `BindFormatStrings()`, which will take column values from our resultset and associate them with display (labels) and value (data) properties of the UI Components. In our example, we can now code our results handler to place the data from our results query directly into the `departments_cb` by adding this code:

```
DataGlue.BindFormatStrings(UIComponentInstanceName, queryResult,
"#displayColumnName#", "#valueColumnName#");
```

You'll note the pound signs, clearly brought over from the ColdFusion world of programming. These are simply treated as delimiters by the DataGlue parsing routine in the `bindFormatStrings` method call to provide a way to evaluate the value of that column name from the resultset. This method really just handles a call to the `setDataProvider()` method on the UI Component, but it handles it a little easier than if we were to invoke that method directly from our results handler. Using `setDataProvider()`, we would have to parse the result set each time we wanted to tie the data to the UI control. This is the work that the `DataGlue` object does for us each time the `BindFormatString()` method is called. We can now fill in the code for our result handler for the `getDepartments()` method call:

```
function getDepartments_Result(result) {
   // we'll add code to this handler in the next step!
DataGlue.BindFormatStrings(departments_cb, result,
 "#DepartmentName#", "#DepartmentID#");
}
```

Note

DataGlue offers further flexibility in that custom formatting functions can be assigned via the `bindFormatFunction()` method. This methodology allows a developer to define a generic function that returns labels and data back to the `dataGlue` object. In turn, the `dataGlue` object then sets the data into the UI Component. This can be particularly useful with formatting date column data in a recordset, although it is often better to do that either in the SQL statement or in server functionality before returning results to Flash. Although you might not find a lot of documentation about the `bindFormatFunction()`, don't be afraid to open up the dataglue.as file and look at the code!

Step 10: Putting It All Together

Another nice feature about UI Components is that they offer a simple way of trapping events. For example, when the user changes the selected item of a combo or list box, the UI Component checks to see whether it needs to call some developer-specified function or event handler for the `onChange` event. These events work similarly to DOM events in DHTML and JavaScript. When we drag and drop a component onto the Stage, the Properties panel provides a place for the developer to specify the function to call when the changed event occurs. This provides a simple way for us to trap this event and, inevitably, issue a Flash Remoting call to get more data or set a data element in another component. These events offer a location to code master-detail relationships between components. Figure 15.6 shows the Property panel for our `employees_lb` list box.

Figure 15.6 Specifying a change handler for the `employees_lb` list box.

In the sample code, when the user changes the department in the combo box, we want to get the employees for that department and populate the list box with employees from the selected department. Likewise, when the user selects an employee, we want to look up specific data about that employee and display it in our dynamic text area.

For UI Components, the `changehandler` function call passes a reference to the object that changed. When our `getData` function is called because the `departments_cb` combo box changes, that function has a function argument that is a reference to the `departments_cb` component. Therefore, we can build a single change handler to manage the changed event of both components because at runtime, the function will know (have an argument for) which component called the function.

Continuing with our code, use the Properties panel to specify `"getData"` as the function name for the changeHandler for both the `departments_cb` combo box and the `employees_lb` list box. As Figure 15.6 shows, the `()` are not included in the Properties panel; you simply need to provide the name of the function that will handle the event.

Lines 16 to 22 in Listing 15.2 shows the code for the `getData` function. Note the conditional logic to see whether the changed object was `departments_cb` or `employees_lb`. If the `departments_cb` component changed, the code will call the web service to get the employees for the department. In contrast, if the `employees_lb` component made the call, a web service call will be made to get the employee details for the selected employee.

Because we are now calling new Flash Remoting server calls in the change handler, we need to provide result handler functions to trap the return events of these asynchronous calls. Lines 28 to 42 in Listing 15.2 shows the code for handling the results of both the `getEmployees` service call and the `getEmployeeDetails` call:

```
function getEmployees_Result(result) {
DataGlue.BindFormatStrings(Employees_lb, result, "#LastName#, #FirstName#",
➥"#EmployeeID#");
Employees_lb.setSelectedIndex(0);
}
function getEmployeeDetails_Result(result) {
employeeRow = result.items[0];
var details = '<p align="center"><b>' + employeeRow.Title + '</b></p>';
var temp = "Permanent";
if(employeeRow.isTemp) temp = "Temporary";
details +='<p align="center"><b>Status</b> ' + temp + '</p>';
details +='<p align="center"><u><a href="mailto:';
details += employeeRow.email +'?subject=Flash Remoting">' +
➥employeeRow.email + '</a></u></p>';
details +='<p align="center">'+ employeeRow.phone +'</p>';
employeeDetails_txt.htmlText = details;
}
```

Note

The advantage to setting the HTML text by the instance name rather than associating the text field with a variable is that if the text area had a scrollbar, it would auto-refresh as needed. Also of note here is that the `getEmployees_results`, after using DataGlue to bind the data to the Employees list box, then selects the first item in the list box. The first item is element 0, not 1. This is a significant difference between Flash ActionScript (and JavaScript for that matter) and ColdFusion; arrays are 0 based in ActionScript and 1 based in ColdFusion.

Finally, the variables *`details`* and *`temp`* are declared in the `getEmployeeDetails_Result` handler with the `var` scope, which means they are local variables that will be destroyed when the function call is over. This is good programming practice because it will use less resources in the Flash client—especially because this function is likely to be called many times. Local variables should be used whenever possible, in both result handlers and change handlers. They also are considered a best practice and part of ActionScript development standards.

This ActionScript best-practice along with others is documented in the Flash whitepaper on ActionScript standards and can be downloaded from Macromedia's web site at

`http://www.macromedia.com/desdev/mx/flash/whitepapers/actionscript_standards.pdf`

At this point, you should be able to run your demo code for more details and to validate any code.

Your final code should look like Listing 15.3.

Listing 15.3 **Final ActionScript Code for Flash Remoting Step-by-Step**

```
// Include the Required NetService class files
#include "NetServices.as"
#include "DataGlue.as"
//#include "NetDebug.as"

// Flash Gateway Connection init
if (bGatewayOpen == null) {
  bGatewayOpen = 1;
  // Make the Gateway connection
 NetServices.setDefaultGatewayUrl("http://localhost:8500/flashservices/
gateway");
 gatewayConnnection = NetServices.createGatewayConnection();
 empService = gatewayConnnection.getService
("FlashRemoting.EmployeeServices",
this);
}
empService.getDepartments();

// CHANGE HANDLER FOR UI Components departments_cb and Employees_lb
function getData(changedObj) {
if(changedObj._name == "departments_cb")
    empService.getEmployees(changedObj.getValue());
else
empService.getEmployeeDetails(changedObj.getValue());
}

//RESPONDER FUNCTIONS WILL BE CALLED BY DEFAULT FROM FLASH WHEN THE FLASH
REMOTING CALL IS COMPLETE
function getDepartments_Result(result) {
DataGlue.BindFormatStrings(departments_cb, result, "#DepartmentName#",
"#DepartmentID#");
}
function getEmployees_Result(result) {
DataGlue.BindFormatStrings(Employees_lb, result, "#LastName#, #FirstName#",
"#EmployeeID#");
Employees_lb.setSelectedIndex(0);
}
function getEmployeeDetails_Result(result) {
employeeRow = result.items[0];
var details = '<p align="center"><b>' + employeeRow.Title + '</b></p>';
var temp = "Permanent";
if(employeeRow.isTemp) temp = "Temporary";
details +='<p align="center"><b>Status</b> ' + temp + '</p>';
details +='<p align="center"><u><a href="mailto:';
details += employeeRow.email +'?subject=Flash Remoting">'
+ employeeRow.email + '</a></u></p>';
details +='<p align="center">'+ employeeRow.phone +'</p>';
employeeDetails_txt.htmlText = details;
}
stop();
```

Using CFM Pages in Flash Remoting

Although ColdFusion Components (CFCs) are great candidates for performing the server responsibilities in a Flash Remoting application, at some point you might want to use a CFM page. This can be done when coordinating the development of a Flash front end to an existing application or when you don't want to have to re-create existing server functionality that has for other architectural reasons been built using a CFM page.

CFMs that deliver data to Flash clients closely resemble ordinary CFM pages. In fact, the standard CFML tag set is available, and much of the ColdFusion code is the same. However, unlike common ColdFusion pages that interact via form and URL parameters, pages that work by being called via Flash Remoting will work with a new variables scope in ColdFusion MX called Flash. Arguments that are sent to the page from Flash will be contained within a built-in variable, *`flash.params`*, that will be either an array or a structure. ActionScript arrays are converted to ColdFusion arrays on the server, and ActionScript objects (instances of custom classes), associative arrays (instances of the Object class), and mixed arrays are all converted to a ColdFusion structure. All native ColdFusion MX methods to these data types will work fine on the server, with the exception of `structCopy()`, which in most cases, you should avoid anyway (use `duplicate()`).

Also, unlike ColdFusion Components, which use the `<CFRETURN>` tag to send data back to the Flash client, ColdFusion pages simply set a "special" variable, *`flash.result`*. Of course, in both CFCs and CFM pages, this returned element can be a simple or complex data type. Therefore, if you have multiple data elements to return to the Flash client, you can send back a query, an array, or a structure.

Other than these differences, the ColdFusion code on the server is virtually identical. Similarly, the ActionScript to access CFM pages is only slightly different.

When we initialized the `NetConnection` object to a CFC web service in the previous examples (using the `GetService()` method), we specified the service using dot notation, as in `flashremoting. EmployeeServices`. This specification referred to the employees.cfc file, located in the flashremoting folder under the ColdFusion MX web root. When methods were called *within* that web service component, they were used as methods of the `netConnectionProxy` object—in our example, `empService`. Because ColdFusion pages don't have logically divisible methods within them, they are instead treated as a single method call, in and of themselves. Thus, the connection specification is to the folder that contains the CFM page, and the CFM filename is used as the method call. Of course, the .cfm extension will be dropped from the method name, so in our previous example, we could call a single ColdFusion page to get our departments by making the following modifications to our code:

1. Create individual pages named getDepartments.cfm and getEmployees.cfm. Code them to behave identically to the corresponding CFC methods in employees.cfc, and save them in the flashremoting folder.
2. Modify these templates to utilize the *`Flash.`* variable scope, pulling any needed parameters from the *`flash.params`* data structure.

3. Modify the `<CFRETURN>` tags to `<CFSET>` tags, setting the ***`flash.result`*** variable.
4. Modify (in the FLA file) the `getService` call to pass `"flashremoting"` as the service name

That's it!

Other considerations for Flash Remoting using ColdFusion pages might include how to build reusable pages to handle requests from both Flash and non-Flash clients. Because the params sent from the Flash movie are built into a special scope, called `Flash.`, a simple check with the ColdFusion expression is defined ("Flash") and can make a runtime determination whether the page is being invoked by Flash or some other user agent. Although the `cgi.http_user_agent` variable will be `"Shockwave Flash"` if the request is made from Flash, checking for the existence of the Flash structure is best to ensure that the request is being brokered via Flash Remoting.

Consuming Web Services Across the Web in Flash Remoting

Up to this point, we have discussed using either CFCs or CFMs to provide data to our Flash client. A powerful feature of Flash Remoting is the ability to call a web service anywhere on the web, regardless of whether the host server has the Flash Remoting server components installed. This is achieved by simply specifying the document Web Service Definition Language (WSDL) location in the `getservice()` method call from ActionScript. You still need to specify a valid gateway server URL when the gateway server receives the request from the Flash client. It sees a WSDL document specification for the service and knows to do the following:

- Translate the request from AMF to SOAP
- Make the request across the web for the service
- Receive and translate the SOAP response to AMF
- Deliver the AMF response to the Flash client

Thus, the only change to the ActionScript would be something like this:

```
EmpService = gatewayConnection.getService
("http://www.remotesite.com/Flashremoting/employees.wsdl",this);
```

Here, the gateway server will act as a SOAP proxy adaptor because Flash clients cannot directly issue SOAP requests in Flash Remoting.

A good example of this process is demonstrated in a tutorial (that's not so easy to find) on Macromedia's web site. This example makes use of the babelfish web service from AltaVista. You can access the tutorial at `http://www.macromedia.com/support/flash/flashremoting/consuming_ws_using_cfmx/index.html`.

Other Flash Remoting Features

Flash Remoting has several other features, including a powerful debugging tool and support for server recordsets, authentication, and session management.

You can access debugging services in Flash Remoting through the netDebug.as ActionScript file. Be sure to add the necessary `#include "netDebug.as"` directive (line 4 of Listing 15.3 shows this code commented out). After it's included, this file creates a global `netDebug` object on which you can invoke the `trace` method and pass any object you would like to debug. The results are similar to using the `<CFDUMP>` tag in ColdFusion; however, "dumping" data is only one thing this debugging tool can do. Add the following code:

```
NetDebug.trace(result);
```

between lines 25 and 26 in the `getDepartments_Result` function to see a "dump" of the recordset that returns from the server. Figure 15.7 shows the NetConnect Debugger window with the results. To view this panel window, you must select Menu, NetConnect Debugger from the menu before previewing the movie.

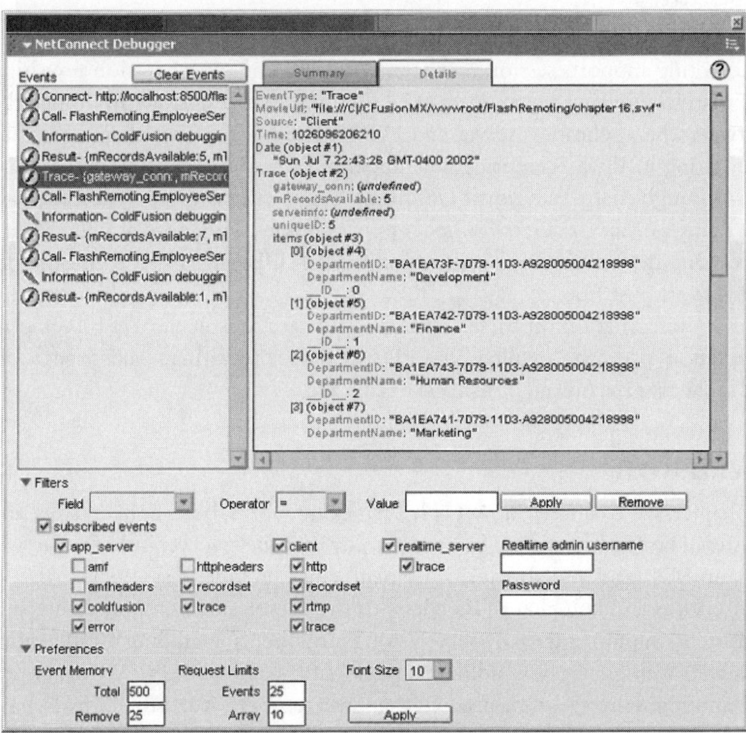

Figure 15.7 The NetDebugger in Flash Remoting.

One of the performance risks of dynamic data delivery—both in HTML and Flash—is the possibility of having large resultsets sent to the client. In a low bandwidth or minimal client RAM environment, an application can quickly become unusable. Flash Remoting provides built-in functionality to manage large recordsets on the server. Developers can invoke data delivery methods, including `setDeliveryMode()`, to instruct the gateway server to release recordset rows from the server either on-demand, paged (blocked in rows) or in their entirety (`"fetch all"`). On the server, when records are blocked in pages, the number of rows per page is set using a special variable, `"flash.pagesize"`. Behind the scenes, the gateway server will manage the data in a session object and provide more blocks of row data as requests are made back to the server.

Note

Both the recordset and data provider ActionScript classes in Flash Remoting provide a wealth of functionality. These class definitions are contained in the Flash Remoting Components installed in Flash Studio, in the recordset.as and RsDataprovider.as files. (See Listing 15.3 for the listing of installed ActionScript files.) Open these files directly to look at how these classes are defined. You'll find some interesting code!

Flash Remoting supports session management using cookies or session rewriting. Because Flash Remoting travels over HTTP, cookie-based sessions are implicitly handled between the application server and HTTP. The NetServices class, which supports URL rewriting in Flash Remoting, will append the session ID to all requests as needed. Although many traditional ColdFusion applications use cookie-based authentication, many portable devices do not support cookies. Therefore, if you are targeting these browsing devices for your application, a Flash UI using Flash Remoting for data access will work just fine.

For more information on these features and more, consult the Flash Remoting documentation. You can download the PDF at `http://download.macromedia.com/pub/flash/flashremoting/using_flash_remoting.zip`.

Conclusion

In this chapter, we have seen how Flash Remoting works, both conceptually and step by step. The Flash Gateway Server, our powerful new server-side feature with ColdFusion MX (and available for other platforms), provides fast, efficient data-delivery services to Flash clients. Requests to this server-side component are simple and consistent. Supporting many server-side components, including ColdFusion MX Components, Web Services, ColdFusion pages, ASP pages and .NET Components, Flash Remoting delivers a rich presentation layer, properly partitioned from business logic and transaction management.

Flash Remoting development in the Flash authoring environment is code centric. Therefore, ColdFusion developers will find migration to Flash relatively painless. A relatively simple language by nature, CFML in ColdFusion MX is similarly easy for Flash developers to pick up quickly; with tools such as Dreamweaver MX, the ability to develop ColdFusion MX code can often be done in a visual environment, again, offering rapid development and reducing developer learning curves. The incorporation of other Flash MX features, such as UI Components, not only enables less experienced Flash developers the ability to create rich interfaces, but also improves application usability, as the behavior of these components is consistent with standard web controls.

Flash Remoting is a powerful new feature of the Macromedia MX platform and will likely be taken into new and exciting directions. Driven by a need to improve the delivery of data to Flash clients, the Flash Gateway and the powerful authoring tools of Flash MX offer new hope for creating rich user interfaces on data-driven business applications. Development time has been drastically reduced to enable far more cost-effective solutions and maximize return on investment (ROI). Flash is the web's most popular rich-media technology, and the future looks brighter still. Initiatives are underway to unite communication and applications, providing data streaming between Flash clients. Imagine two-way audio, video, and graphic streams in applications that deliver sophisticated web casting, chat rooms and other multiuser interactions. The release of the MX platform and Flash Remoting has revealed Flash as a robust, data-centric application environment, intelligently wrapped in a lightweight, rich media technology.

16

Securing the Application and User Management

by Jeff Tapper

As you have seen in Chapter 14, "Leveraging Security in ColdFusion MX," a number of new tags and functions are available in CFMX for building security models. In this chapter, we will explore extending those models to allow for a robust application security framework.

Security Concepts

You must understand several basic concepts before we progress further into building security frameworks. A couple of these concepts include the following:

- Whether a user is valid in the system
- What that user can do to resources within the system

To restrict access to various items, you need to create security policies. Allowing individuals to be denied/granted access to these applications requires user management. These concepts are described in the following sections.

Authentication Versus Authorization

At the heart of any security framework are two concepts: authentication and authorization. These two concepts attempt to answer the following questions:

- Who is the user? (Authentication)
- What is the user allowed to access? (Authorization)

Authentication is the process of having a user identify himself to the system, usually through the use of a username and password. *Authentication* answers the question, "Who is this user?," but it does not answer the question, "What is the user allowed to access?" (Remember that in Chapter 14 we saw how the `<CFLOGIN>` and `<CFLOGINUSER>` tags can be used to authenticate users to an application.)

Many simple applications only use authentication and do not contain authorization methods. Imagine a simple web site in which most users come to the system and can browse the site, and a privileged few can access the administrative functions of the site. To build a system like this, the only users who would be asked to authenticate themselves would be those attempting to enter the administrative pages. If users have a valid login, they are authenticated and able to fully access the administration section. The ColdFusion administrator shows a great example of such a system. Any user who knows the password to the administrator can access it. An attempt is no longer made to selectively allow access to different aspects of the administrator for different users.

This type of security is fine for many smaller companies, which have small staffs and in which any technical employee is as capable of administering the system as any other. Such a scheme fails, however, if the administrative functions have different levels or if different privileges are available for individual sections of the site to be administered.

Imagine a company's intranet, which has human resources, information technology, marketing, and executive sections. It's quite possible in this case that different users will administrate the different sections. Presumably, you don't want the marketing administrator to change content in the technical support section.

This system might have a marketing administrator, an executive administrator, an IT administrator, an HR administrator, as well as a "super administrator" who is capable of administering anything on the site. In this case, it's not enough to know that the user is an authenticated user; it becomes necessary to know what the user is authorized to do.

The `roles` attribute of the `<CFFUNCTION>` tag can authenticate access to methods of any `CFCOMPONET` within the application. To limit access to individual instances of components, you will need to use the built-in `isUserInRole()` function after the user has been authenticated.

Resources

Our security framework will be concerned with two main types of resources: the methods of the ColdFusion Components (CFCs) and the individual instances of the PageNode component.

Securing methods is an obvious first security need because most users only need to access display methods and have no need to use a `Create`, `Edit`, or `Delete` method. Securing instances is a bit less obvious, but it becomes clear if you conceptualize content on a site that is intended only for specific users (subscription-only content, extranets, and so on).

> **Note**
> CFCs are discussed in detail in Chapter 5, "ColdFusion Components," and the PageNode component is defined in Chapter 22, "Assembling a Dynamic Application."

Securing Functions

Chapter 13, "Basics of Managing Content," defined the `roles` attribute of the `<CFFUNCTION>` tag and demonstrated how it can be used to restrict access to methods of a CFC to users belonging to a particular role. This will handle the majority of the security requirements for an application. Let's examine how this is so.

Each of our components has `Create`, `Get`, `Set`, and `Delete` methods, in addition to specific methods within the property. For most types of content, end users will be able to view the content, but not be able to change it, create it, or delete it. Users can do this by granting `GET` function access to the members of all four roles in our applications. Access to the `CREATE` functions is limited to the members of the content creators, editors, and administrators. `SET` functions are available only to editors and administrators, whereas `DELETE` and `DEPLOY` functions are available only to administrators.

You'll determine roles that can use various methods within components on a case-by-case basis.

Securing Instances of a CFC

A more complex concept is to secure instances of a component. One example of where this could be useful is with the PageNode component, which is described in Chapter 22. As you will see in that chapter, PageNode components represent individual pages in an application. These pages might be available for public consumption, or they might only be available as part of a subscription site or of an extranet. In these latter cases, it would be necessary to ensure that only authorized viewers could access these PageNodes.

The best way to be able to secure instances of a component is to have a property of the component that contains a list of the roles that are allowed to access it. If no roles are listed in this attribute, the instance is assumed to be available to all users. If roles are listed in the `roles` attribute, code can be added to any unsecured function to check whether the user has any of the roles listed for the instance. This check could look like the code in Listing 16.1.

Listing 16.1 **A Basic Authorization Script**

```
<cfscript>
      authorized = 0;
      for (x=1;x lt listLen(this.roles); incrementValue(x)) {
            if isUserInRole(listGetAt(this.roles, x)) {
                  authorized = 1;
                  break;
            }
      }
</cfscript>
<cfif not variables.authorized>
      Sorry, you do not have adequate permissions to access this.<cfabort>
</cfif>
```

If you find that your application requires securing access to instances of most types of components, you could add the `roles` property to the BasePersistentComponent and add the preceding code as a new function to this component. This would look like the code in Listing 16.2.

> **Note**
> You can find full information on the BasePersistentComponent in Chapter 9, "Centralized Data Persistence."

Listing 16.2 **Extending the BasePersistentComponent with an *isUserAuthorized* Method**

```
<cfproperty name="roles" default ="">

<!--- Initialize Persistors and Properties--->
<cfscript>
    this.dbPersistor = createObject("component","dbPersistor");

    this.objectID = createUUID();
    this.typeID = "";
    this.bActive = "1";
    this.createdBy = "";
    this.dtCreatedDate = createODBCDateTime(Now());
    this.dtLastUpdatedDate = createODBCDateTime(Now());
    this.lastUpdatedBy = "";
    this.roles = "";
</cfscript>
<cffunction returnType="boolean" access="public"
name="isUserAuthorized" output="FALSE">
    <cfscript>
        authorized = 0;
        if (not len(trim(this.roles))) {
            for (x=1;x lt listLen(this.roles); incrementValue(x)) {
                if (isUserInRole(listGetAt(this.roles, x))) {
                    authorized = 1;
                    break;
                }
```

```
        }
    } else {
        authorized = 1;
    }
    return authorized;
</cfscript>
</cffunction>
```

This code adds a new function to the BasePersistentComponent (BPC) called `isUserAuthorized`. You can call this function from any method of any component that extends the BPC, restricting access to instances of objects regardless of the roles assigned to a particular method. This allows you to encapsulate all of the security logic—regardless of the component type—in one central place.

User Management

Any application that applies authentication of users requires a module to manage users. A few different means are available to achieve these goals. These concepts surround the idea of security-specific information about users, such as application-specific information, referred to as a *user profile*, and authentication/authorization information, such as users and groups.

User Profiles

A *user profile* consists of information about a user other than the information required to authenticate/authorize him. This information can include user preferences, addresses, phone numbers, answers to questions, and so on.

By storing user profiles separate from user authentication information, many applications can use the authentication data without cluttering the database with information specific to other applications. It is still necessary to keep a common key between the user authentication data and the user profile so that their profile can be made accessible after they have authenticated themselves to the application.

If you know from the beginning that you will never need the user authentication information for other applications, you can intermix the profiles and authentication data.

Users

A core aspect of all security systems is the users who will be accessing the application. As mentioned earlier, a necessary component of security is user authentication—the ability to identify who the requesting user is. A basic data model for a security system will generally consist of three tables:

- A table that holds the information specific to the user
- Another table that holds information about the groups (a concept discussed later in this chapter)
- An intersection table that creates a many-to-many join between the first two tables

Because many applications might be able to use the user tables of a database, the users and groups often are stored separately from the application-specific data. They could be stored in a separate set of tables, or they could be in a separate namespace, database, or server.

It is equally possible to store this information in an LDAP server or MS Active Directory. The concepts hold true for these cases as well.

> **Note**
>
> See Chapter 13 for details on authenticating users who are stored in an LDAP or Active Directory.

Groups

Most often, user authentication data already exists before new applications are built with it. This can be a user directory from a company, subscriber information, and so on. Often, the users in such a directory are already classified into groups. These groups often relate a user's job within the company, applications to which a user has subscribed, and so on. As mentioned earlier, data about groups and the users who are part of them resides in the tables of the user authentication database.

Because groups often are independent of a specific application, it is not desirable to try to make them fit within an application's specific security framework. The types of users for a particular application are usually known (from use cases, in some examples), and it often makes sense to map groups to the application-specific types of users. The concept of roles, defined next, represents a description of the types of users that a specific application will have.

Roles

Just as we have discussed storing information about users that is specific to an application separately from information that is common across several applications, so will we introduce the concept of using application-specific roles for security, rather than groups that are common across several applications.

The main reason not to simply rely on groups within an application is that in today's corporate environment, groups that are based on departments in a company (a common theme for intranets/extranets) are subject to change as businesses consolidate departments, merge with other businesses, spin off division into separate companies, and so on. Because our `roles` attribute is coded directly into every CFFUNCTION call in an application, as well as included directly in instances of some components, it can become time consuming to change the application when a company goes through a reorganization of any kind.

It's often difficult for developers to understand the benefits achieved by introducing layers of abstraction, such as is seen here in the separation of groups from roles. Many developers with little application architecture experience see this as simply redundant and requiring more development upfront. Although it is true that the abstraction requires more development, it ensures the maintainability of the codebase. Without introducing immense complexity to the application, it is not practical to dynamically populate the `roles` attributes of CFFUNCTION calls, necessitating the hard-coding of roles. By introducing a layer of abstraction between the roles and groups, we can undo the damage to the application's maintainability.

To accomplish mapping groups to roles, we will create a table in our application database that will serve to map groups from our user authentication table to the roles that are coded within our application. This concept is discussed in detail in Chapter 14.

Managing Users

As mentioned earlier, it is recommended that you separate the user profile from the user authentication data. Although there are many upsides to such a separation, one downside is that there will generally need to be two user management modules. These two modules can contain a common interface and appear as one to the end user, but the separation is meaningful to developers and those who are maintaining the code base. This will initially involve more coding up front, but the benefit is that it will allow some users to be given permissions to maintain user profiles; only a privileged few will be allowed to maintain user security information. The benefits of letting highly skilled administrators focus on security issues instead of forcing them to manage user profile information is immediately apparent.

Managing Security

The security framework discussed throughout this chapter works on two levels. One level limits access to functions of a CFC to members of particular roles, and the other limits access to specific objects to certain users. The association of the role that is required to access a particular function is hard-coded within the ColdFusion Component. It is possible to design a framework that will dynamically populate the `roles` attribute and then recompile the classes that are generated from the components, but this solution—while offering flexibility—is unnecessarily complex. While roles are being hard-coded, a well-designed system will understand the roles of the "actors" who will be interacting with the system. The resources with which these roles will be allowed to interact are not likely to change. What is more likely to change is the users (or groups) who are occupying these roles.

For this reason, managing security will come down to two key aspects:

- Managing the relationship between users and groups
- Managing the relationship between groups and roles

The first of these two will be done in the User Authentication database. The relationship between users and groups can easily be stored in a database table, which achieves a many-to-many join between users and groups. A simple administrative screen can allow users to be assigned to groups, browsing of groups to which a user belongs, and browsing of users who are contained in each group.

Managing the relationship between groups and roles needs to be handled in the Application database. Because a groups table will not be in the Application database, it will be impossible to have the database provide the referential integrity for groups. For this reason, you need to take care in building the application's administrative screens to maintain that integrity. A common design of the administrative interface involves populating a multiselect menu with groups from one query and a simple select menu of roles populated from another query. This interface presents the administrator with the ability to choose any of several groups to relate to each role in the application.

Security Design Options

The ideas expressed throughout this chapter describe a lightweight, easy-to-implement framework for securing ColdFusion MX applications, but this chapter's ideas are certainly not designed to handle the security needs of every application. These ideas can work as the basis of a much more complex framework, if such complexity is required. As always, it is possible to purchase and integrate a third-party security framework to avoid the complexities of building advanced features into a security framework.

> **Note**
>
> A number of worthwhile off-the-shelf security framework applications are available, including Arcot (`www.arcot.com`), Tripwire (`www.tripwire.com`), and SiteMinder (`www.netegrity.com`).

Understanding Performance in Application Security

As with most pieces of an application, the greatest performance boosts are gained by appropriately caching data. If it becomes necessary to query the database for users' permissions on every request, performance will suffer. You can alleviate this problem by caching the username, password, and the roles of which the users are members. Fortunately, by leveraging the `<CFLOGIN>` and `<CFLOGINUSER>` tags described in Chapter 14, ColdFusion MX automatically caches this data and makes it available through the `getAuthUser()` and `isUserInRole()` functions.

Conclusion

Architecting and implementing a security framework that meets the needs of every application is a Sisyphean task. A phrase, sung by Joey Ramone in 1993, comes to mind each time I'm charged with such a task:

"Sometimes I feel like screaming

"Sometimes I feel I just can't win."

If you find yourself feeling this level of desperation when you're faced with such a task, focus on the basics. Are you creating a new repository for users or using an existing one? How are users going to be authenticated? What pieces of the application will have access restrictions? Will access be granted on an individual user basis, or will groups/roles be used to allow access to "classes" of people?

The system proposed throughout this chapter attempts to maximize on the maintainability of such a framework, creating a separation between users and user profiles, and a separation between groups and roles. These separations require a bit more coding during development, but they make the application inherently more maintainable.

17

Designing a Workflow System

By Benjamin Elmore, Seth Hodgson, and Dan Blackman

When we're dealing with a dynamic publishing application, the most critical challenge we face is maintaining a steady stream of fresh content to our site. Not only does the content need to be fresh, but it also needs to be driven through the organization's internal processes to ensure accuracy and relevance. This knowledge management concept is, first and foremost, a management discipline that treats intellectual capital as a managed asset. The primary tools applied in the practice of knowledge management are the understanding of organizational dynamics and responsibility, the process reengineering to break down the tasks that are involved and followed, and the technology implementation it is based in. These work in concert to streamline and enhance the capture, automation, and flow of an organization's data, information, and knowledge.

In addition to tracking the creation of content, a dynamic publishing application serves as an interactive interface to your client base. The primary manifestation of this interaction is content delivery, but it doesn't have to end there. Our applications also are a platform that allows our end users to communicate with or request an action from us. The way that we deal with these interactions is also core to our business. By automating the communication between the different points within our organization while providing an audit trail for tracking it, we see yet another management discipline emerge.

The technology concept that supports knowledge and process management is called *process automation*, or as it is more commonly known, workflow. This concept, at its core, is a series of automated steps mapping over and reflecting a business process within an organization. Collectively, these steps are organized within the workflow to deliver knowledge to individuals and groups that are engaged in accomplishing specific tasks. The concept also facilitates the dissemination of knowledge to those who make the day-to-day decisions that, in aggregate, determine the success or failure of the business. In this way, individuals at any level—either actors or monitors of the process—are satisfied.

Because the technology behind the workflow engine needs to support usage of process automation, this book is laid out in an abstract fashion working its way toward specific implementation. Therefore, the objectives of a workflow system and its base construction are presented without mention to specific usage. From there, we address how to tie the workflow into the specifics of dynamic publishing.

Key Objectives of a Workflow System

Many different requirements influence the design of a workflow system. These requirements range from one suggesting that business management needs to guarantee compliance all the way to outlining technical structural needs. The following subsections outline each of these objectives and what its purpose is. Although this is a list of objectives that a workflow system needs to consider, realize that the actual features that you use in your construction will be based on your particular needs. There is one exception to this: if the workflow system is deemed a component or service of a system framework. If this is the case, then it's probable that a majority of these features will need to be addressed or supported, even if just lightly.

Mapping to a Process

At the core of the workflow system is the automation of business processes. The objective is to include the ability to map over a process and all of its tasks. As we build the workflow, each element (tasks, rules, notification, and so on) is organized under a single name so that it can be uniquely identified. The collection of elements maps to the business process and acts as a vehicle for the interactions to occur.

This collection acts as a container to provide a blueprint or definition of a repeatable business process. The process most often results in some sort of data being produced. This data that is interacted with or affected strongly depends on what the purpose of the process is, which can range from content being approved for the web site to an audit trail of a user interaction. This piece of data is referred to as the workflow's *artifact*.

An example of a process that can be mapped is shown as Figure 17.1.

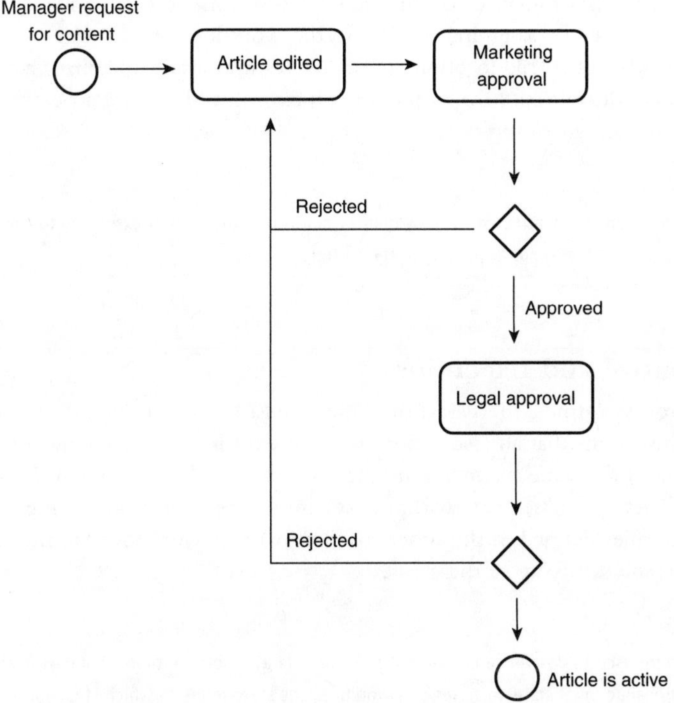

Figure 17.1 Example process that can be mapped.

Digital Artifacts

By its definition, process automation is the transition of a manual process that uses email, paper, and disparate documents to track and implement to a digital alternative. Thus, when you're defining an engine to track a process, it is important to define how you are going to handle the multiple different digital artifacts (database content, documents, audit trails, and decisions) that are generated throughout the process. Specifically, this objective needs to focus on how to manage, associate, and track these assets.

You have two options for doing that:

- Organize the collection of data into a more complicated content structure and associate that collection directly to the workflow. This has all the assets viewed as a single unit through the workflow.
- Actually allow the collection of tasks to check out and change individual pieces of content during the process by permitting each asset to exist by itself.

As a general rule, attachment of the artifact(s) is best done through a loose coupling. This is accomplished by assigning the IDs to the workflow. The ID can be anything from a primary key to a file location and name. It's important to realize that the digital assets you affect during the flow of the process exist outside of the process and are utilized by the remainder of the system.

Note

If the artifact needs to be affected by the workflow but also needs to exist externally to the system, then you need to use the versioning capability of the system.

State Control and Execution

With the process defined, the workflow system must be able to kick off the process at any time. This means that an association needs to exist between an active process and its definition. In the same manner, multiple processes can be running at the same time. For each of these processes, the workflow system must preserve and change the state based on the rules defined in the process definition. The workflow runtime satisfies the handling and satisfying of these rules.

Note

State is a term used to describe a current snapshot of data at a point in time. A change in the data results in a change in its state. In terms of a workflow, the state refers to which step(s) in the process the workflow is on.

Having a rich API, with which the developer or user can programmatically control the flow and state of workflow, is critical to creating a usable system. The reasoning has to do with the needs of certain steps within the workflow that allow the user to control the flow of the process. They rely on this rich API to make this requirement possible. The API acts as an interface between the user on the data, allowing each step to move forward or roll back to a previous state. Having these rules and user control over the flow of the process exposed only increases the flexibility of the workflow system.

Note

It is useful to capture the event of each of these transitions of state. This allows for the possibility of adding event-based functionality, such as notification or reporting. Looking at the example provided in Figure 17.1, we can identify a transition as the arrow between each of the different process steps.

Task Coordination and Versatile Execution

Each step of the process is mapped to a task in the workflow that performs some bit of logic. When you want to design a workflow system, the form in which these tasks can be executed is important. The goal is to provide the most extensive implementation base possible. Possible implementation options are independent task components, functionality encapsulated within content components, or another workflow. It also is important to realize that the tasks remain independent of the definitions to which they are associated. This allows for the maximum reuse of the tasks because many different business processes have common steps.

This mapping of tasks to the workflow takes place within the workflow's definition, and it plays a part in the actual workflow's state. As part of its association to its definition, a task mirrors the information specific to that association as well as the information that is specific to the way runtime works. The information can include the filtering of roles/users assigned to the task, the number of users required to complete the task before its state progresses, and the tasks that can be added dynamically to the task.

A distinct requirement of a workflow system is to be able to organize different tasks into separate flows and define their interrelationships. These interrelationships can be complex in light of the whole process. Take, for instance, a complex workflow that branches from one task into several tasks and then joins together again. The workflow system must support the branching of tasks at all levels. However, in the design, the only required dependency between tasks (that must be recorded) is the tasks' order of precedence. For example imagine a workflow for editing content. The first task allows the user to edit the properties for a piece of content. The second and third tasks required in the process are classifying content and reviewing the properties edits. The second and third tasks are handled separately, but they depend on the first task to complete. The fourth task in the process actually sets the dates for the content to "go live" or display on the site. In this flow, we can see how each task in the workflow depends on the other. We record these dependencies in our workflow system along with additional properties along the way. Through this, we provide the versatility to organize and manage our process.

User and Role Assignment

The members of the team collectively carry out a process within an organization. Therefore, a workflow system requires integration with the organization's user base and job functions. We accomplish this by assigning certain job functions to a user or a role. As tasks are worked with, validation can be made to guarantee that correct permissions are met. When this validation is in place, we ensure the integrity of our data, and the right users interact with the data as intended.

User and role usages extend throughout the entire workflow system. When the workflow is established, users and roles are created that reflect the usage of a process from beginning to end. Users and roles are validated at different points throughout the process. For instance, let's say a certain user begins the process as part of his job function. Within the workflow, the user is identified as the only user who is permitted to begin this particular process. At different points through the workflow, the user is given permission to interact with the content. User information and roles are mapped by job function so that the right user can be assigned to the proper tasks or functions.

A perfect business example focuses on the need for the legal department to review promotional material shown on the web site. Reengineering the process, you would note several tasks that had to be completed, one of which would be to submit the final material for legal review. The tasks leading up to legal review would be restricted to lines of business where the promotion is coming from. However, for the legal review, only members in the legal department would be eligible to perform this task, and in some cases, only a certain individual is allowed to.

Notification

When you are dealing with users, you inevitably need to communicate with them about events of the system. These notifications can include tasks in a queue, a task that has been rejected by another user, the disassociation of a task to a user, or the completion of a workflow or a pending decision.

Like tasks, notifications are specific to the actual implementation. They vary widely in form, verbiage, importance, delivery mechanism, and so on. Therefore, a workflow system not only has to support these different notification events, but it also must allow the actual notifications to remain detached from the workflow system. Notifications need to have a way in which they can be tied to the workflow definition or task directly.

Event Rules Engine

A workflow is characterized by a constant state of change as actions are taken and tasks are completed. This objective is to be able to capture and expose all the events that occur inside of the workflow engine. When each event is captured, the workflow service can perform some response action. The following are some possible response actions:

- Notification
- Task execution
- Audit logging
- Custom event handling

The start of the event rule engine is with the listing and then actual trapping of the events inside the workflow. Following are some possible events that can be trapped:

- Task completed
- Task began
- Task end
- Task executing
- Workflow end
- Time schedule
- External queue

The needs of the application determine the number of events that are trapped. After it is determined which events are to be trapped, the next step is how you are going to handle the event. You can use a couple of options to handle the action of the events. The first is to embed the action into the workflow runtime. To keep with the modularity of the workflow service, these embedded actions are limited to what the workflow can accomplish internally, such as state transition. The second option is to have the action handled outside of the workflow. You can do this by creating event handlers that are delegated.

Just as actions can be viewed as internally and externally implemented, the actual events that are trapped to make this happen can be caused by both forms as well.

User Auditing

Within a workflow process, a multitude of users are assigned to tasks throughout its life cycle. The workflow system's ability to keep an accurate audit trail of all user interactions is critical to effectively provide baseline legal requirements in certain situations. Take, for instance, a task that allows a user to edit a press release. After the user saves and completes his work, an audit log tracks the interaction with the content. If the edits are legally incorrect, but they were missed in the subsequent review and deployment tasks, then the audit log allows us to determine who interacted with the workflow and at what point the interaction took place. We have a couple of options for building an audit trail into our workflow system. One is to provide a global workflow log in which all actions are logged against. The other is to assign a user log to each task assignment that traps only the interactions for that task.

Reporting

Reporting against a workflow is arguably the most important user feature of a workflow system. Reporting gives users and managers a variety of information that helps them measure the effectiveness of their processes. This information includes the following:

- **Information about pending work**—The workflow gives workers, managers, and systems information about work to be done. The workflow system can be responsible for all or part of the connection to an entity carrying out the work.

- **Information about work completed**—The workflow obtains information from workers/systems to update internal representation of outside world work. This information is fed into reporting.
- **Information about defined approvals at any level**—This helps the managers to find out the status of the currently active processes and to take necessary action.

Workflow Packaging

Several occurrences call for multiple pieces of content to be made available in unison. This can be from the rollout of a new section of the site to a new product and its related marketing material. In addition to just rolling out multiple pieces of content it is important that we allow the processes for each piece of content to be unique if need be. Therefore, this objectives or features of the workflow system needs to deal with linking several unique atomically workflows together into one larger package in which they all complete and release the multiple pieces of content all at once.

We can accomplish this in a couple of ways. One way is to actually have a container workflow generated that relates the different processes and their respective artifacts together. Another way is to have the base definition defined in a way that allows it to relate itself to another process. One common bit of functionality that must be present in either situation is the ability for a workflow to have a state in which the workflow has completed all of its tasks but is not complete. This would allow us to complete the primary process (such as the creation of a new product) but not make it available to the site until the other secondary processes (such as the creation of the supporting marketing information) were complete.

Designing a Workflow System

At this point in the chapter, we have seen that a workflow system must meet a number of objectives to be successful. The key to successful implementation then surrounds how our design is laid out. To this effect, all designs—from the simple to the complex—center around there being two main components (workflow and task) that are required to build a workflow system. Figure 17.2 shows the baseline architecture in which all designs can grow.

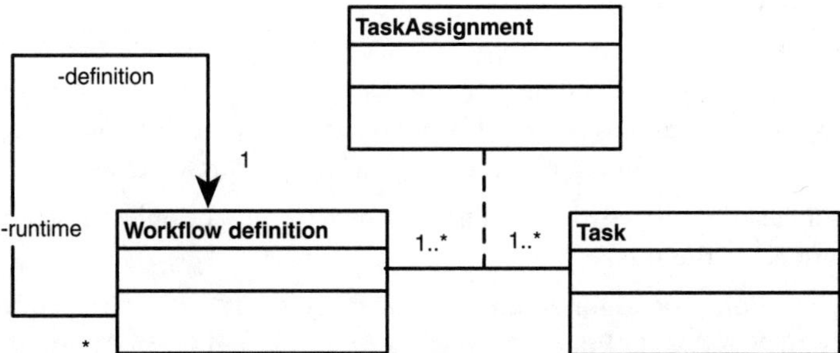

Figure 17.2 The base architecture for a workflow system.

Looking at the base design, we notice that we have set up the relationship between the definition of the workflow and the workflow runtime as a self relationship of the same type. Workflow runtime instances are derived from the underlying workflow definition, but they exist in the system as unique component instances. This allows us to create a workflow definition that models a business process (such as creating an article) and then proceed to create a new runtime instance of the workflow definition for each new article that we create. The workflow definition will store data related to the artifact, or work product, that the workflow generates. In this design, the instance and the definition are shown as one component. There are certain instances that you need to track more instance-specific information and to accomplish this you might need to break this because Workflow component into two components: WorkflowDefinition and WorkflowInstance. In this case, the same relationship would still be in place but this time shown between the two components.

A workflow definition can have many tasks assigned to it, and any defined task can be used in many different workflow definitions. That being said, every task needs to be treated completely externally from a workflow. For example, both Create and Update product workflows will most likely contain an Edit task that allows a user to edit the properties of the underlying content. Here, we can assign the same Edit task to both Create and Update workflow definitions. Likewise, each workflow definition most likely contains a sequence of tasks that model a business process.

Still, the workflow definition must have the tasks assigned directly to it. In this way, the actions that must be performed within a workflow will be modeled as task instances. Unlike the workflow component that can have two modes to it, a task component doesn't contain this dual behavior. Instead, it is an association between the workflow and task that actually contains the core process definition runtime information. In Figure 17.2, we see this as an association component named TaskAssignment.

Key Workflow Components

A *workflow component* is defined as an entity that realizes a piece of a business process, such as the high-level rules and information that govern a business process or the individual tasks within a business process. If we look at the process for creating a new article content object, as shown in Figure 17.1, the following points are evident:

- It is a creation process that results in an article content object instance being published to the site.
- The creation process for an article content object is further broken down into tasks, such as Article Edited, Marketing Approval, and Legal Approval.

Based on this brief analysis, it is clear that to automate this process, we need a workflow that models this process by keeping track of the tasks that are required along with the status for these tasks as each is started, completed, or rejected. Because this process results in the creation of an article content object, the workflow also needs to keep track of the content object instance that its assigned tasks operate against.

Workflow definitions and tasks are the key components used to model a business process. Together, these workflow components define both the structure and semantics of data exchanged through the course of a workflow, as well as the behavioral aspects of the process being modeled. The behavioral aspects of a process include the interactions that are allowed among the workflow components and the possible sequences of task interactions for a given workflow. The primary objective for workflow components is the coordination of these elemental components to achieve a business goal according to the business rules defined by the underlying process model. The state of a workflow component is defined by the state of the underlying process, rather than through the manipulation of operational business data. For example, if an article creation workflow has successfully proceeded to the final task, Legal Approval, then the state of the workflow is maintained within the workflow components by flagging the first two tasks in the workflow as complete and the last task as pending. Let's take a closer look at the two workflow components we need: tasks and workflow definitions.

Tasks

The primary component used in a workflow definition is the task, which represents the work to be done to achieve some objective. Editing an article instance and reviewing the edits are two actions that would be modeled as tasks. Both of these actions represent work to be done to complete a business process—in this case, the creation of a new article. We use multiple tasks to build sequences of actions, and each task can represent either an automated or manual activity. Each task is an action that an assigned (delegated) performer performs. The performer who carries out the specific task, such as reviewing an article, can be the task, or the task can delegate processing and handling of the activity to another workflow or external resource. We will return to task handling delegation shortly because we must discuss first one more aspect of tasks: processing rules.

When you receive change back on a purchase, you count it to make sure that it is correct before you put it in your wallet. This is a preprocessing rule that we have for receiving money. Vice versa, when we make a purchase, we count the money to ensure that we have sufficient funds before we hand it over to the sales clerk, and this is a preprocessing rule for making a payment. The concept of processing rules for actions is a simple idea, but it is often overlooked. It makes sense to have both pre- and post-processing for tasks in our workflows. To ensure that a task will function properly, ensure that you have all of the artifacts you will need for the task and that the system is ready for you to continue before running the task. These checks are preprocessing rules for the task. Likewise, you should have post-processing rules to ensure the task did what it was supposed to do, especially if you are sending data to external sources. In addition to processing rules, tasks also can delegate the handling of the activity to another component, external system, or workflow.

The delegation of processing for a task allows for a great deal of flexibility and interoperability within a workflow system. We can take three primary paths when task handling is delegated. These are delegation to components, delegation to generic management, and delegation to another workflow. In the first of these three approaches, the task can delegate to another component for the specific implementation of the task-handling logic. If we take an Edit task as our example, ideally, we should be able to reuse the Edit task in multiple workflows. However, editing an article might have a very different interface and set of business requirements than editing a product or some other content type. In this situation, it makes more sense to delegate the instance editing for each type to another component rather than to place all of the various edit-related business logic within the task. This allows the Edit task to work with a variety of different content types or to be reused in multiple workflow definitions. The Edit task can store a reference to a helper component, or it can delegate task handling to the artifact for the workflow by calling a method against it.

Task delegation to generic management allows a task to hand off processing to a completely external system. In this delegation strategy, the workflow system relinquishes all control over the particulars of task handling after the task has begun. A clear example of this form of task delegation is found in localization workflows for content. In a localization workflow for an article, rather than editing the content, the existing content often is sent to a localization vendor for translation. Localization vendors frequently require that content be transferred to their systems for translation, and the completed work is returned to you. In a content localization workflow, the Translate task would delegate all specific task handling for translation to the external vendor and its system. The task would package up the piece of content for translation and send it to the localization vendor. The post-processing for this task would be to retrieve the translated content and insert it into the content repository. This is a clear example of a task delegating to generic management—in this case, the localization vendor's systems—to handle the particulars of its processing.

The final task-handling delegation strategy that we will discuss is delegation to another workflow. We can use a task within one workflow to instantiate a nested or chained workflow within the context of the currently running workflow. Returning to the business process for creating an article, as shown in Figure 17.1, if the underlying business process for legal approval actually involved several actions, it would make more sense to model legal approval as a unique workflow. In this case, the Legal Approval task in the Create Article workflow can start a new, nested legal approval workflow. The task is delegating its action, legal approval, to another workflow. After the nested legal approval workflow has run its course, the Legal Approval task in the Create Article workflow is complete and the article becomes active. These various forms of task handling delegation allow complex business processes to be modeled successfully. Task components allow us to model individual actions within a business process, but to complete the picture, we must aggregate these tasks into full workflows, using workflow definition components.

Workflow Definitions

Workflow definitions place less emphasis on the internal workings of tasks, and instead focus on the relationships between the various tasks that comprise a business process. Their aim is to capture the coordination requirements for performing the set of tasks for a given process. They do, however, capture some information about the execution of tasks that is needed for coordination. The workflow definition also stores information related to the artifact, if any, which the workflow produces or alters.

To coordinate the flow of tasks within a workflow, the workflow definition stores information for the tasks that must execute to complete the workflow. This information includes the status for the various tasks so that the workflow system can perform appropriate logging and notification as a workflow proceeds through its member tasks. As each task in the workflow is completed, the runtime workflow instance keeps track of that information and notifies or starts any later tasks in the flow that can be executed. The workflow definition might also contain information related to ad-hoc tasks that could be dynamically inserted into the workflow task sequence in more advanced systems. The implementation of ad-hoc tasks that can be dynamically added to a running workflow is non-trivial, but they can provide a far higher level of flexibility to a workflow system that will improve process efficiencies and encourage business user acceptance.

Task Execution

Task execution really deals with the way that the workflow instance monitors the coordination between when the tasks are executed. The tasks in a workflow instance go through three stages. The first stage is the initial creation in which the workflow definition, which includes the related tasks, creates the workflow instance. At this point, nothing other than creation has happened and the tasks are in a resting state. The next state is when the tasks are being interacted with. At this point, the tasks are made available to execution based on whether or not they were up in the sequence of firing. The final stage is when the tasks are all complete and the workflow instance is complete. By focusing in on these three stages, we can see that both the leaving of the first and the entering into the last stage depend on what the individual tasks are set up to deal with.

To monitor the task execution, the workflow instance must first understand when it is appropriate to fire each of the tasks. Looking at Figure 17.1, we see that the task of Legal Approval should only occur after the other two tasks have completed successfully. We also note that the Marketing Approval task was waiting on the first tasks.

From an implementation standpoint, it is possible to set up a definition of a task's instance to know about all of the tasks that are to come before it. However, from a technical perspective, this can be difficult to maintain. Instead, just keeping track of what the immediate preceding tasks are to a specific task allows us to create a ordering through the cascading effect. In our example, letting the Legal task know that it is dependent upon the Marketing task is enough because the Marketing task knows that it needs the first tasks. This path for execution also allows for the possibility of multiple tasks to fire concurrently. If we wanted to add a task to our earlier example that fired in sync with the Marketing task, we would simply have to note that the task was waiting on the first task to complete. The workflow instance would then make both the new task and the Marketing task available as soon as the first task was complete.

The actual storage of the data that would track this would belong as part of the assignment of the task to the workflow definition. In addition, if we want to allow the workflow to be able to revert back to a previously completed task, we need to keep track of not just what tasks have fired to date, but what the original task ordering was.

Integrate Workflow into Dynamic Publishing

When we're integrating the workflow system into the dynamic publishing environment, it is important to gain first an understanding of the environment we're integrating into. This section highlights these considerations and serves to help us understand the benefits and drawbacks.

Content Approval

When we're designing workflows for content approval, we must recognize the dynamic that takes place when humans become involved. As we begin to look at workflows a bit deeper, we find several options for directing humans who are involved in a workflow. These options include the following:

- Different ways to allocate workload within the workflow
- Different methods of user notification of work in a queue
- Launching of a task-specific UI from the dashboard with the necessary context

- Launching of a task-specific UI from the workbench with all necessary context (artifacts)
- The manner in which people tell a workflow that the step is complete
- Reporting

We first consider the allocation of our workload among the workflow participants. In an automated workflow system, the process can easily become complicated. The system must take into account caveats such as employee leave and holidays. To manage this complexity, it is smart to have a human team lead managing and allocating the workload. With a team lead in place, informed allocations and reallocations can balance out the process and minimize the number of bottlenecks that occur. The team can manage the entire workflow by forcing interactions to take place or reassigning users to new and different tasks.

Another important option in directing human interactions is use of notification helpers. The workbench/dashboard is a useful tool for notifying users of tasks that require interaction. A portion of the dashboard can include a list of active tasks waiting in a queue for the user to respond. As the user logs into the system, the dashboard displays a list of the tasks notifying the user. The user can begin work by choosing the appropriate task and then executing it.

User Interaction Modeling

The other alternative to using a workflow in a dynamic application is having the workflow assist in coordinating any response that the user requests. For example, a business sells products online. If the product fails, the customer can go to the web site and request a return request shipping label. In effect, this allows the customer to return the purchase without having to pay the costs of shipping it back.

The simple course of action would be just to have the form (or whatever the interface was written in) validate that the product number the user entered does indeed exist and just allow the user to print the shipping label from the screen. However, a more valuable avenue would be to actually have this tied to a process that would start a series of steps to get back in touch with that customer to gain further knowledge about the situation.

The only difference between the first and second option is that one coordinates a set of background tasks to make sure the customer is followed up with, and the other simply satisfies the immediate need for the customer. Unlike content approval, the information used to track during the process doesn't result in anything visible to anyone outside of the customer service organization. However, this sort of workflow will tend to associate more digital artifacts to itself to provide the folks involved in the business process the necessary information. Returning to our example, the digital artifacts associated to the customer follow-up could be the customer record, related products to what the customer returned, and the history of this product in the market.

Conclusion

This chapter walked through the multiple objectives needed to create a successful workflow system. The needs that drive the fundamental usage of the workflow system are quite varied. Each viewpoint that is taken—whether it is technical, business, content, or straight process automation—brings out the fact that workflow integrates itself into our application at the core.

As complex as it is, understanding the base structural design of the components provides us the flexibility to grow our system to meet the demands of our application.

18

Enhanced Business Experience for Managing and Presenting Content

by Seth Hodgson

THE INTRODUCTION OF THE MACROMEDIA MX PRODUCT line provides a dynamic publishing application with amazing new opportunities for content creation, management, and presentation. ColdFusion MX Components revolutionize the Data and Business Logic layers of a ColdFusion application, allowing for the clean and effective modeling of system content and functionality as reusable, encapsulated components. The management and presentation of content also takes a dramatic step forward with the introduction of Flash MX and Flash Remoting.

In this chapter, we will investigate the impact that Flash Remoting has on the creation of rich applications and site management tools. We also will study several design patterns that prove especially useful for integrating CFCs on the server with Flash MX movies in the Client layer. Design patterns are well-defined best practices for software development and architecture based on past experience, and they embody the collective wisdom of the development community. This chapter will provide you with a solid introduction to building rich interfaces for content and site management systems. It also will demonstrate how to architect your application so that your Flash MX Presentation layer can take advantage of several popular design patterns.

Communication Models

Dynamic publishing applications can now take advantage of the current HTML page request/response communication model or the new communication model facilitated by Flash Remoting. Let's look at the characteristics of each of these models and their respective strengths and challenges.

Current Communication Model

The current communication model of web applications consists of data and business logic for the application residing on a server, and an HTML/DHTML Presentation layer delivered in a web browser. User interactions are sent to the server for processing, and the server returns an HTML page response to the user. The current communication model treats the user's browser as a thin client that provides access to applications and functionality on the server. The web browser, as a thin client, does not contain your web application's core logic or functionality apart from limited in-page scripting. The current communication model requires a full-page request for any user interaction with the application on the server.

Traditional rich clients, such as Java applets or ActiveX controls, allow for a far richer graphical and interactive Client layer experience for your end users. However, these approaches suffer from various levels of browser and platform compatibility, making them difficult to develop, support, and maintain. In addition, Java applets and ActiveX controls often require large downloads to install necessary code on the client system before running, and this negatively impacts the user experience by forcing the user to sit through a long download process to use the application. Consequently, the promise of these technologies for improving user experience on the web has never been fully realized.

Aside from the lack of viable client-side alternatives, a second primary reason for the heavy use of the current communication model in web applications today is that business logic resides on the server, rather than being spread across both the server and client tiers. Rich Client layers using Java applets or ActiveX contain application logic. Therefore, code maintenance and upgrades are simplified because updates can be applied to the code base on the server, and few updates or changes are required on client machines. As long as users have a suitable web browser installed, they can use the web application.

Shortcomings of Thin Clients

Although an HTML/DHTML Presentation layer has become the de facto standard for web applications, this approach leads to several serious problems that stand in the way of building the next generation of web applications. A major issue with the current model is poor responsiveness, in which every user action results in a full-page load or refresh. This becomes evident when you're performing form-based interactions in a web application. Take a shopping cart on an e-commerce site as an example. The actions of an item being added to a cart, the quantity for an item in a cart being adjusted, or an item being removed from the cart require a round trip to the server to interact with the server-side business logic code or components that implement the user shopping cart. The result of this round-trip interaction is an extremely jarring user experience, in which even the simplest interactions lead to a full-page refresh that might take several seconds or more. The wait time following each action is jarring for your users, and it places a high processing burden on web and application servers and server-side code and components.

Due to the round-trip nature of user interaction in which every action requires a request to and response from the server, rich Internet application user interfaces are not possible with thin clients. When a thin client is used, many form-based interactions are broken out into a sequence of steps with each on a separate page. In most cases, a more intuitive interface can be developed using a rich client that surfaces all of the necessary data and input fields to the user within the context of a single consistent interface. However, this is not a viable option when you're using HTML/DHTML and common HTML form elements given their low level of interactivity and inconsistent scripting support across browsers and platforms.

Thin clients also suffer from inconsistent support for audio and video. Inclusion of media within an HTML Presentation layer relies on separate plug-ins or proprietary browser tags. Providing audio or video often requires that the user download additional plug-ins that might also suffer from browser and platform inconsistencies. Complex interactivity with this media is difficult to implement when you're using a thin client, and it often relies on an additional layer of JavaScript of VBScript code within the page to allow the user to interact with the media.

A thin client is fully dependent on its connection to the server. If that connection is closed, the thin client is completely nonfunctional. Take, for example, a web application that provides the sales team of DuvalShock with regional sales targets, current client information, and a queue of sales leads to follow up on. If this web application uses a thin client, then a constant connection to the server that is hosting this application is required even though a better strategy would be to build a rich client that could support a disconnected operation model. In that case, a sales associate could view the most recently retrieved data on his local machine even in the absence of a network connection. A disconnected operation is simply not an option with thin clients. A disconnected client places a higher load on the application when it first retrieves a set of data to store and work with locally, but after it has loaded this data, no additional requests need to be made against the server until the local data is once again synchronized with the server.

New Communication Model

Flash Remoting ushers in a new client-server communication paradigm for developers who are working with the Macromedia MX family of technologies. Although we could build highly dynamic and interactive interfaces to web applications using prior versions of Flash, these endeavors suffered from poor integration between the Flash Player and server-based resources and components. Data transfer involved passing simple variables or resorting to XML transfer between the Flash movie and server components or scripts. The serialization and deserialization of these XML documents at both ends of the connection added an unnecessary layer of code complexity to this approach and negatively affected application performance.

Flash MX solves these problems with Flash Remoting, which was introduced in Chapter 15, "Leveraging Flash Remoting in ColdFusion MX." Flash Remoting offers a vastly superior communication model for client-server interaction between Flash MX movies and server-side components and resources. Loading variables or exchanging XML documents has been replaced with a binary data transfer format between the Flash MX movie and the server. Refer to Chapter 15 for a complete discussion on building a Flash MX movie that communicates with ColdFusion MX Components on the server via Flash Remoting. When you're using Flash Remoting, the Flash Player on the client and Flash Remoting on the server handle *marshalling* (formatting and transferring) data between the client movie and server-side components. Flash MX movies can invoke methods against ColdFusion MX Components on the server, introducing an entirely new communication model utilizing server-side business logic and resources implemented as ColdFusion MX Components and a rich client interface implemented as a Flash MX movie.

Benefits of a Flash MX Rich Client

Flash MX excels as a rich client and addresses the failings of the traditional thin client HTML/DHTML Presentation layer for web applications. With perceived responsiveness, Flash MX provides a superior user experience to traditional thin clients. In Chapter 15, a Flash MX movie was built that allows the user to drill down through a DuvalShock employee directory, filtering by department and presenting detailed employee information for any selected employee. Behind the scenes, multiple Flash Remoting calls were made to a ColdFusion MX Component that implemented the business logic for the application. The remote function calls invoked methods on the ColdFusion MX Component on the server, and the server-side component then performed database queries and returned the results to the movie for display.

A process that would theoretically require two or more page requests (selecting a department followed by choosing an employee to view) can be presented as a single unified interface in Flash MX that is both easy to use and avoids jarring full-page reloads. A rich client interface revolutionizes the end user experience by masking requests to the server, leading to a higher perceived responsiveness for the application, but there are additional concrete benefits as well.

The act of selecting a new employee to view requires that you use the current communication model to rebuild the full page on the server and send it back over the network to the client browser. In the case of the Flash MX movie, you must return only the data for a newly selected employee to the client. Not only has the amount of data being transferred per request dropped dramatically in the case of a Flash MX interface, but using a rich client layer also offloads significant load from the application server in the case of complex pages that require multiple database hits and other server processing to construct dynamically. This means that requests are handled more quickly and place lighter load on the server using the new communication model, allowing for higher traffic and reduced bandwidth requirements for the application.

In addition to these benefits, Flash MX provides excellent support for audio and video media along with an object-oriented scripting environment to support complex user interaction with the media. The Flash Player now provides native support for embedded video using the Sorenson Spark codec (a high-performance video compression/decompression algorithm), and it can dynamically load MP3 audio files for playback or external JPG files for viewing. You can use media such as audio and video files within a content management interface to provide interactive help or training for your business users.

Finally, the ability to publish Flash MX movies as standalone projectors enables the creation of disconnected web-based applications. In the presence of a network connection, a projector movie can interact with a remote server using Flash Remoting to retrieve data for local use. You can store this data on the client machine as a shared local object and then view the data or edit it offline. The many possible applications of this for web applications are exciting. Disconnected distributed web applications can now be built and require nothing more than the client machine running the Flash Player 6 and appropriate components and resources configured on the application server.

Improving Efficiency

Flash MX and HTML have advantages and disadvantages, and improving the business experience for managing a web application and its content needs to play to the strengths of both. HTML shines when you're displaying text data and markup with hyperlinks. Flash MX excels when complex user interactions or rich interfaces are required.

Breakdown of User Thought

To leverage the benefits of Flash MX, it is important to begin by breaking down the various user actions that an application interface must support. Within the realm of traditional HTML-based web applications, the application will direct the user through a sequence of steps (actions) implemented as a separate page. These steps can present information to the user or require the user to enter form data. In the world of Flash MX, this interaction model can be turned on its head, allowing user-determined interaction with the application rather than a canned sequence of steps. You can implement each step, or user action, within a traditional web application as a Flash MX Component that provides the necessary functionality. You can then compose these Flash MX Components that support specific user actions into a unified interface by embedding them within containers on a single page, or attach and display them as components within a full Flash display, to provide access to all available actions that the application supports.

Exposing all of the various actions that are available in an application gives the user control over his experience. In a Flash MX application, the user can be given direct access to any of the actions that are supported by the application within the same interface. With each action implemented as a Flash MX Component, the user can perform actions on an as-needed basis. This frees the user from the locked-in interaction model of traditional web applications, but it also requires a clear and modular design for the Flash MX Components used to build an application. Modeling each user action in the application as a Flash MX Component in a modular fashion to support a single user action ensures that the component can be combined with others to create complex unified interfaces or used individually as necessary. Another strategy for modularizing your Flash MX Components is to externalize as much ActionScript as possible into AS files to be included in your movies as needed using the `#include` directive.

Leveraging Flash into Your Design

Flash MX provides the developer with a highly interactive and capable programming environment, and it excels in the realm of rich client interfaces. For user interfaces that benefit from a more dynamic and application-like UI than HTML/DHTML can provide, Flash MX is an excellent solution. With new support for dynamically loading JPG and MP3 files from the server, as well as supporting video natively within the Flash player, there are few limits to what a creative developer can accomplish at the Presentation layer of an application with Flash MX. In addition, it is important to consider the possibilities that Flash Remoting introduces to web applications to fully leverage the capabilities of Flash MX.

The object model within Flash MX, along with ActionScript, provides a powerful development environment. Classes, inheritance, and polymorphism are all easily implemented in ActionScript, and within Flash MX, nearly everything has become a scriptable object. You can dynamically create, size, and populate text fields with textual data. You can use text format objects to achieve a level of formatting control over text within Flash that has never before been possible. You can now treat movie clips as buttons and extend them to create your own custom movie clip subclasses.

Perhaps most exciting of all the feature additions in Flash MX is the introduction of Flash MX Components. These descendents of Flash 5 smart clips are configurable, reusable intelligent movie clips. The first batches of components that Macromedia offered have included two UI Component sets and a Charting component set. In addition, you can find many third-party components on the Macromedia Exchanges or elsewhere on the Internet. The UI Components provide a collection of common form elements, such as list boxes, push buttons, and tree controls, which you can use to easily create forms in your Flash movies.

These components bring drag-and-drop simplicity to the process of creating Flash forms. APIs for these components allow the developer to support complex user interactions and event handling, and as we saw in Chapter 17, "Designing a Workflow System," you can use the DataGlue ActionScript class to bind data that the server provides to UI Components, such as the list box within your movie. This provides a simple but powerful technique for dynamically driving the information presented by form elements to the user. The power and ease of developing complex forms and content management interfaces in Flash has improved significantly with the introduction of Flash MX Components, coupled with ActionScript.

You can use the new features in Flash MX to create compelling movies for content presentation and management. However, fully leveraging Flash in the design of an application requires a clear understanding of how it can be used in concert with HTML and how to modularize the Flash movies that your application uses. In the next several sections, we will investigate how to enhance HTML content delivery with Flash and how you can build Flash MX Components as independent or multi-step components to meet your various application design goals.

Flash MX Component Structure

Components within Flash MX are the descendents of smart clips in Flash 5. They are movie clips containing additional scripting that allows you to easily instantiate and configure them. For components that are dragged onto the Stage, the Properties panel provides the developer with quick access to set available properties for the new component instance. Components also can provide an API to allow for dynamic ActionScript interaction with them while a movie is running.

Developing your own custom Flash MX Components is beyond the scope of this chapter, but sometimes a custom Flash MX Component is the best solution to the problem at hand. Although many of the currently available Flash MX Components are form elements or UI widgets, components can be far more complex. As movie clips, they might have multiple states or contain other embedded components. You can even implement a generic multi-step process as a reusable component. You can write a data provider class to pull configuration data from an XML document or database via Macromedia Flash Remoting, and it can drive the construction and display of each step within the multistep component. Imagination is the only limit to what you can implement as standalone Macromedia Flash MX Components or full-blown component systems, such as rich text editors or complete UI layout managers.

Leveraging HTML

One area in which you will often use HTML instead of Flash MX is for the presentation of large blocks of textual content. In many cases, existing content might contain presentation formatting and will be best displayed as straight HTML text. However, you must make the decision on where to leverage Flash MX and HTML for content display on a case-by-case basis. In most situations, either presentation technology can be used, or you can adopt a hybrid approach in which an HTML page is augmented with Flash MX movies that provide enhanced site navigation or present micro-applications within the page.

The hybrid delivery of HTML content and Flash movies is a powerful approach for leveraging both Flash and HTML in the Presentation layer of an application. A hybrid approach really shines when Flash movies add value to the HTML content that is presented in a page. In a hybrid design, the movies that are used can take the form of components for user polls, user comments, content rating, or a multitude of additional possibilities keyed off of the content. If we take the example of a page that displays an article on the DuvalShock web site, the primary page content will be the article, displayed using HTML. However, the page also can contain Flash movies that allow the user to rate the article, comment on it, or send it to a friend.

The power of Flash MX allows components to offer a rich user interface that cannot be matched using browser scripting and DHTML. Now with Flash Remoting, these movies can interact with server resources independently of the page. If the article display page contains a Rate Content component, the user could rate the article using the in-page movie, which would pass the new rating to the server and receive an updated rating score for the article back from the server for display without requiring a page refresh. The same would be true for a User Polling component or a User Comments component. You can implement any of these components to interact with the server independently, providing a means for the user to interact with content on the site without forcing a page refresh.

To effectively leverage both HTML and Flash in this way, it is important to develop highly modular components and movies that can be reused easily throughout the site. Modular components are designed for use as either independent or multistep components, and they have as few dependencies on other Flash Macromedia MX Components as possible, allowing for flexible reuse. The distinction between these two approaches lies in whether the component provides a single user interface or a traditional multistep interface, such as a form-based process or workflow, to the user. Regardless of the implementation strategy chosen for a component, developing it to operate in a self-contained fashion allows it to be reused in a hybrid HTML and Flash MX Presentation layer or within a full Flash MX interface.

Independent Components

By breaking down the user thought process surrounding interaction with an application, we can model each desired user action as an independent Macromedia Flash MX Component. Returning to the case of an article display page in the DuvalShock web site, the user is presented with content and might want to perform a variety of actions related to the content. Possible actions that the user might want to perform include the following:

- Rating the content
- Discussing the content
- Sharing the content with a friend

For each of these actions, you can design a corresponding Flash MX Component to facilitate the action. Let's examine the strategy for turning a proposed user action into a modular, independent component by looking at the case of rating content.

To implement a Content Rating component, you must develop a Flash MX Component that will receive a content objectID and pass the ID to a server-side ColdFusion Component to retrieve the current ranking for the selected piece of content. The Macromedia MX Component also must allow the user to submit his own ranking for the content. Flash Remoting is the best approach for handling the communication that will take place between the Flash MX Component and a server-side ColdFusion MX Component to retrieve ranking information and to submit the user's ranking for the content. Our user can rate the piece of content without causing a page refresh.

In a simple implementation, you can use a single database table to store ranking information for content objects in the system, as shown in Table 18.1.

Table 18.1 **contentRanking Database Table**

ObjectID	User	Rank
article1234	Jason	4
article1234	Chuck	2
article5678	Jonah	3
article1234	Robert	5

You should set the first two columns, ObjectID and User, as a composite primary key for the table. This ensures that a single user can only rate a given piece of content once; the composite primary key constraint ensures that no objectID/user combination can be repeated. You can develop a ColdFusion Component, contentRankingService.cfc, for example, that implements two functions that work with this database table. The first function returns the ranking for a given piece of content. This requires a database query to sum the `rank` values for a given piece of content and to divide that amount by the number of records that exist for the content object in the table. The second function inserts a new ranking submitted by a user for a content object. If the user had already ranked the content object, an error message might be returned. Otherwise, a new record is inserted into the table that contains the objectID, user, and the rank he gave the content. These functions need to specify the `access="remote"` attribute in their opening `<CFFUNCTION>` tags to be accessible to Flash Remoting, and you must place the contentRankingService.cfc component into a directory within web root.

When the page to display an article first loads, the objectID for the article and the currently authenticated user are passed to the Rate Content component using the `flashvars` attribute for both the `<OBJECT>` and `<EMBED>` tags for the Flash movie. After the movie is loaded, it can pass these values to the Rate Content component that makes a remote call to the server-side ColdFusion MX Component to retrieve the current ranking for the article and displays this information. Within the component, you can develop a set of option buttons, icons, or some other custom interface to allow the user to select a ranking for the piece of content and submit it. When the user submits a ranking, a second remote call to the ColdFusion MX Component on the server is made to store the user ranking in the database or return an error if the user has already ranked this content.

This simple approach for implementing a Rate Content Flash MX Component outlines how a Flash MX Component can interact with the server or with other resources independently of anything else on the page. The benefit of independent and modular components is that you can reuse them easily in pages that present HTML content or as a member component within a larger movie.

Multistep Components

You can develop independent Flash MX Components to model multistep processes. Some user actions, such as rating content, might only require a single interface to meet business requirements. However, certain user actions are more involved, in which case a multistep wizard might be necessary. A variety of implementation approaches for presenting a multi-step process in Flash MX are available, spanning the spectrum of frame-based steps on the movie timeline to creating internal movie clips that can be shown, hidden, or animated for each step in the process. The Flash MX UI Components provide a simple solution for building the forms that will most likely comprise the various steps in a multistep component.

Regardless of the implementation approach you choose for a multistep Flash MX Component, the component should be fully independent, performing its tasks via Flash Remoting calls to server-side components and resources independently of other components on the page. This way, you can slot multistep components easily into an HTML presentation or use them as a component within a larger movie. One important benefit of multistep components is that they open the door for a user to work with and configure data on the client rather than interacting with the server at all times. This translates into improved performance of the application for the user and lower load on the application servers. Modeling a multistep process as a Flash MX Component versus the traditional HTML approach allows for a vastly improved user experience that avoids page reloads between steps along with simplified and improved data validation across the various steps of the process. In addition, working with data within Flash avoids the issues associated with maintaining the state of the data across multiple HTTP requests in a traditional multistep HTML process.

Communication Between Flash Player 6 and the Server

Flash MX movies communicate between the player to the server using a NetServices ActionScript class. Both the NetServices class and Flash Remoting were introduced in Chapter 15, but in the next two sections, we will take a brief look again at these two essential pieces to uncover additional functionality to leverage when you're building out site management tools with Flash MX.

Net Services

The NetServices.as ActionScript class provides the API for managing the connection to Flash Remoting on the server. In addition to the functionality covered in Chapter 15, the NetServices class also provides security and session support that is essential when developing site management tools for business users with Flash MX. The first of these functions allows us to set user credentials for a given NetConnection, allowing user authentication to occur on the server. The general format for this function is as follows, where NetConnection has already been created with a call to `NetServices.createGatewayConnection()`:

```
netConnection.setCredentials("username","password");
```

You should call this method before any protected server-side component methods have been invoked. This method sets user credentials to send to Flash Remoting by packaging the username and password into a custom header that is sent along with the rest of the data when a remote function call is made to Flash Player 6.

If a function within a CFC on the server is protected using the `roles` attribute, then only a user who belongs to one of the listed roles can access it. To invoke this function from a Flash MX movie, we need to set proper user credentials for any user who belongs to a listed role. This is straightforward, and it is accomplished with the single `setCredentials() function call` as listed earlier. On the server, the username and password that are set in this function call are available within the `cflogin` scope as `cflogin.username` and `cflogin.password`. In your Application.cfm or any other template you use for login control, you can authenticate the user against a user directory using these variables. If the user can be successfully authenticated, use the `<CFLOGINUSER>` tag as follows:

```
<cfloginuser name="#cflogin.username#" password="#cflogin.password#"
➥roles="#userRoles#">
```

In this snippet, `userRoles` is a list of roles that was selected from your user directory when the user was authenticated. Now that the user has been authenticated, the protected function is successfully invoked and the results are returned to the movie.

The second feature of NetServices that we need when we're building site and content management tools or public applications such as a shopping cart is a persistent session between the client and the server. This is maintained transparently for us. The browser automatically passes back cookies that can be used for authentication, such as CFID and CFTOKEN, to the server when a Flash Remoting call is made. However, even in the case of users who have cookies disabled, their session is still maintained. Flash Remoting accomplishes this by sending a gateway connection URL, composed to maintain state, back to the Flash Player 6 if the user's browser does not support cookies. NetConnections automatically uses this URL for future Flash Remoting function calls to the server. This allows Macromedia Flash MX movies to interact with ColdFusion MX Components that use the `session` scope seamlessly.

Flash Remoting on the Server

Communication between Flash movies on the client and server-side ColdFusion MX Components or other resources occurs via Flash Remoting, which is installed automatically with ColdFusion MX and JRun 4. Flash MX movies send data or requests to the server by encoding the message into an HTTP-based binary protocol, Action Message Format (AMF). The Flash Player handles the serialization of ActionScript data into AMF transparently and sends the message to the server. When an AMF message arrives at the server, Flash Remoting automatically handles the process of discovering which server-side component the data is intended for, deserializes the data into a format that the receiving component can handle, and forwards the data to the component or invokes the appropriate method on the component. Flash Remoting captures the component response, serializes it back into AMF, and returns it to the Flash Player that initiated the process.

Communication between Flash MX movies and server-side components using Flash Remoting couldn't be simpler. The Flash Player on the client and Flash Remoting on the server handle all the serialization and deserialization of data between the client and server. Therefore, the old performance hit of parsing the text of transmitted XML documents at both ends of data transfer between a Flash MX movie and the server is no longer an issue.

ColdFusion MX Component Structure

Most Flash MX movies can use ColdFusion MX Components directly without needing to rearchitect their structure. As long as the ColdFusion MX Component defines functions that should be accessible via Flash Remoting with an `access` parameter set to remote, a Flash movie can use the component's remote functions. One caveat is that you must place remotely accessible components in a web-accessible directory path, either under the web root or in a directory that is web accessible. You also can place

ColdFusion MX Components in directories that are accessible via custom tag mappings, but these locations are not directly web accessible and will not be available via Flash.

With that said, you can apply several design patterns to ColdFusion MX Components to streamline interaction between these server-side components and a Flash MX rich client layer. A dynamic publishing application deals with a large variety of content objects as well as subsystems that manage workflows and content publication. We will investigate two design patterns that you can apply successfully to these two cases: the interaction between Flash MX and content using the Value Object pattern, and the interaction between Macromedia Flash MX and subsystems within the application that use the Facade pattern.

The Value Object Pattern and Flash MX

When we're working with persistent content objects in a Flash MX Client layer, we need a simple way to transmit the various properties of a content object between the client and the server. It is a good practice to create a content object instance and then get and set its assorted properties using non-static `getter` and `setter` functions when working with ColdFusion MX Components on the server. However, this is impractical in a distributed environment. The Value Object pattern, also known as the Data Transfer Object pattern, provides an excellent solution for moving data between layers in a distributed application.

The essence of this pattern is simple. A client, such as Flash MX, makes a request for an object or multiple objects from the server. In response, a component on the server returns a Value Object that contains all the data that the Client layer might need. The object that the server returns is referred to as a *Value Object* or *Data Transfer Object* because it contains copies of all the property values for the requested object(s) rather than a reference to the actual object(s). This allows the Flash Client layer to read property values directly from a local Value Object it receives from the server, rather than making additional requests to the server for other object properties or information. Therefore, Value Objects serve to reduce the number of remote calls that must be made from the Client layer to the server. A Value Object often contains more than a single object, and we have already seen this pattern in action in Chapter 15. When a Flash movie calls a function via Flash Remoting that returns a query, the returned RecordSet object that is available in Flash is a Value Object that contains many records of data.

Passing a Value Object to Flash MX

To pass a content object's data to the Flash MX layer as a Value Object, we can define a static function for the component type to provide this functionality. We can take the simple Article content type introduced in Chapter 8, "ColdFusion Components with Persistence," as our example. This content type only has a few custom properties including `Title`, `Author`, and `Body`. We will add a function to the end of Article.cfc to build and return a Value Object based on the Article objectID that is requested. This function is implemented in Listing 18.1.

Listing 18.1 **Article.cfc—*getArticle( )***

```
1   <cffunction name="getArticle"
2     access="remote"
3     returntype="struct"
4     output="false">
5     <cfargument name="articleId" type="string"
6       required="true"/>
7     <cfscript>
8       article = createObject("component",
          "components.persistence.objects.article");
9       article.get("database","testDB", arguments.articleId);
10      valueObject = structNew();
11      for( prop in this ) {
12        if( not isCustomFunction(this[prop]) )
13          valueObject[prop] = this[prop];
14      }
15      return valueObject;
16    </cfscript>
17  </cffunction>
```

We can invoke this simple static function directly against the Article type. The function begins by creating an Article instance, named `article`. Then it loads the requested article from the database into the instance based on the passed `articleId` argument. Next, we initialize a `valueObject` structure to serve as the Value Object that is returned to the caller. The Value Object is populated with data by looping over the loaded article instance and copying only simple property values into the Value Object. Finally, this Value Object is returned to the caller. You can implement function written to return a Value Object in a very specific fashion, where only the desired properties for an instance are copied into the returned Value Object on a per-property basis. In that case, rather than looping over the loaded instance, we could replace lines 11–14 in Listing 18.1 with the following:

```
valueObject.objectId = article.objectId;
valueObject.title = article.title;
valueObject.author = article.author;
valueObject.body = article.body;
```

This creates a Value Object with only these four properties to be returned to the client. We also could modify this function to accept a list of article IDs and to return an array of Value Object structures that correspond to the requested articles. The Flash client can then work with the various articles and their properties independently within the Client layer for display or management. We incur slight overhead with the initial request as we build the object, but moving the data into a Macromedia Flash MX movie means that no additional calls to the database need to be made.

To invoke this method from Flash MX, we could use the ActionScript in Listing 18.2 in frame 1 of an Actions layer in a manageArticle.fla movie. This code sets up the necessary Flash Remoting connection and service proxy, followed by invoking the method and displaying the result.

Listing 18.2 **Invoking *Article.getArticle( )* from Flash MX (manageArticle.fla)**

```
// Include the Required NetService class file
#include "NetServices.as"
// Init a variable to store the article Value Object
var valueObject;
// Create a responder class for getArticle()
function getArticleHandler() {
  this.onResult = function(result) {
    valueObject = result;
   titleBox.text = valueObject.title;
    authorBox.text = valueObject.author;
    bodyBox.text = valueObject.body;
  }
  this.onStatus = function(error) {
    trace(error.description);
  }
}
// Create Remoting Connection and Service Proxy
NetServices.setDefaultGatewayUrl(
"http://localhost:8500/flashservices/gateway");
var gatewayConnnection = NetServices.createGatewayConnection();
var article = gatewayConnection.getService(
  "components.persistence.objects.article");
article.getArticle(new getArticleHandler(), articleID:
  "A4574768-1022-EF4D-53A17C03089DCDEF"});
```

This script is placed on frame 1 of the Actions layer in our manageArticle.fla movie. We begin by including the NetServices.as class file, followed by defining a responder class, `getArticleHandler()`, for use in our Flash Remoting function call. This function actually serves as a constructor for a responder object that has two methods defined: `onResult()` and `onStatus()`. When a result for a Flash Remoting call returns to the player, the appropriate handler function is invoked on the responder object. On a successful result, the `onResult()` function is invoked. In this movie, the `title`, `author`, and `body` properties of the returned Value Object are output to corresponding text field objects that have been placed on a Display layer in the movie. In the case of an error with our Flash Remoting call, the `onStatus()` method of the responder object is invoked and the error message is sent to the output window using the `trace()` function.

After we have defined the responder object, we can set the default gateway URL and create a gateway connection. Next, we store a reference to the Article.cfc component on the server in the `article` variable, without specifying a responder object in the second argument passed to `gatewayConnection.getService()`. Rather than providing a single responder object to handle a single function or defining callback handler functions on the timeline, we will create a custom responder object to handle each distinct function we call against the ColdFusion MX Component. When we take this approach, we must specify a responder object for each remote function call we make. Therefore, the first argument to the `getArticle()` function on line 21 creates a new instance of our `getArticleHandler` class that is the responder object to handle the results of this function. We invoke the `getArticle()` function defined for Article.cfc in Listing 18.1 by passing in both the responder object and a hard-coded article ID. When the remote function call against the Article.cfc component returns a Value Object containing the properties for the desired Article content object, the `onResult()` function on our responder object is invoked. The `result` argument that is passed into the `onResult()` method is the data returned from our Flash Remoting function call.

Several points are worth covering regarding responder objects. Because the result object is only defined within the scope of the `onResult()` function, you must assign it to a variable in a persistent scope, such as a variable defined on the timeline, to inspect it in the debugger or interact with it outside of the `onResult()` method. Doing so allows you to view the returned object in the debugger. You will see that it is the Value Object returned by `Article.getArticle()`. In general, placing handler functions for Macromedia Flash Remoting function calls on the root timeline and specifying the responder object for service calls as `this` (indicating that handler functions have been defined on the current timeline) works in the case of using components that do not share function names. However, when you're working with ColdFusion MX components that model content and application services, multiple components might contain identically named functions. If this is the case, then creating unique responder objects, as was done earlier, is a requirement to support unique handling for identically named functions on a per-service basis within your Flash MX movie.

Updating the Content Repository with a Value Object

Using the Value Object pattern is a simple but powerful approach to transfer content object data from the Content layer of the application into a Flash MX Client layer. We can apply this approach to both content management and presentation. This pattern allows us to load content objects into a Flash MX Client layer to be edited within our movie and then sent back to the server to update the content repository with changes made to the content.

After a Value Object has been passed into Flash, we can display its properties for editing using the prebuilt Flash MX Components or custom-built components. Business users can update the object as necessary, and any updates that are made will only affect the Value Object within the Flash movie. To persist these changes, the Flash movie needs to pass the modified Value Object back to the server to update the content repository. In a similar fashion to the `getArticle()` function defined for

Article.cfc in Listing 18.1, we can add a static `updateArticle()` function as well that will receive an Article Value Object as an argument, and will handle saving this back to the content repository. At this point, we can see why `getArticle()` must create a Value Object that contains an objectID or some other unique identifier, so that when a modified Value Object is returned, we will be able to update the correct object in the content repository. We can insert this function at the bottom of Article.cfc, as shown in Listing 18.3.

Listing 18.3 **Article.cfc—updateArticle( )**

```
<cffunction name="updateArticle"
  access="remote"
  returntype="boolean"
  output="false">
  <cfargument name="articleProps" type="struct" required="true"/>
  <cfif not isDefined("arguments.articleProps.objectId")>
    <cfreturn false/>
  </cfif>
  <cfscript>
    // Load object to update
    article = createObject("component",
      "components.persistence.objects.article");
    article.get("database","testDB", arguments.articleProps.objectId);
    // Copy value object props into article instance
    for( prop in arguments.articleProps ) {
      article[prop] = arguments.articleProps[prop];
    }
    // Update content repository for this object
    article.update();
    return true;
  </cfscript>
</cffunction>
```

This function is relatively straightforward. It requires a Value Object structure to be passed into it as the `articleProps` argument, and it tests that this Value Object contains an objectID key. If this key is not found, the function returns `false` to indicate that the update failed. Otherwise, the article to update is instantiated and any properties that are defined in our Value Object are copied into the article instance. We then invoke `update()` on the article instance to persist any changes to the content repository and return `true` to indicate that the update was successful.

To persist a Value Object back to the content repository from within Flash MX, you can use the ActionScript in Listing 18.4.

Listing 18.4 **Invoking *Article.updateArticle( )* from Flash MX**

```
// Responder class for updateArticle()
function updateArticleHandler() {
  this.onResult = function(result) {
    if( result )
      statusBox.text = "Update successful!";
    else
      statusBox.text = "Update failed.";
  }
  this.onStatus = function(error) {
    trace(error.description);
  }
}
// Click Handler assigned to the 'Update Article'
// push button on our form
function updateArticleObject() {
  updatedValueObject = new Object();
  updatedValueObject.objectID = valueObject.objectID;
  updatedValueObject.title = titleBox.text;
  updatedValueObject.author = authorBox.text;
  updatedValueObject.body = bodyBox.text;
  article.updateArticle(new updateArticleHandler(),
    {articleProps:updatedValueObject});
}
```

We can place this code along with Listing 18.2 on frame 1 of the Actions layer in the manageArticle.fla movie. We first define a second responder object class, updateArticleHandler, to handle the results of calling the `Article.updateArticle()` function via Flash Remoting. This remote function was defined in Listing 18.3, and it expects to receive an `articleProps` argument containing an updated article Value Object. It returns a boolean value to indicate whether the update of the article instance in the content repository was successful.

After a user has viewed the article data in our form and made any desired changes to these values, he click an Update Article button to submit the changes back to the server for updating. The `updateArticleObject ()` function defined in our movie, in Listing 18.4, creates an empty `updatedValueObject` to store the updated article properties. After the objectID, stored in our timeline `valueObject` variable, and the article properties for `title`, `author`, and `body` have been retrieved from the form text fields, we can pass the updated Value Object back to the server using `article.updateArticle()`. Notice that we pass in an updateArticleHandler responder object as the first argument, followed by passing the `updatedValueObject` in the `articleProps` argument. Again, using custom responder classes allows for much finer control of Flash Remoting result handling and avoids issues surrounding services with identically named functions. Upon receiving data back from the server successfully, the updateArticleHandler responder object writes a message to the user indicating whether the update succeeded or failed. In the case of an error with the remote function call, the error message is written to the output window using `trace()`.

This provides a simple example of how we can apply the Value Object pattern to transferring content between the server and the Flash MX client layer for management and presentation. In a more robust implementation, the developer needs to take into account possible data synchronization issues surrounding updates. If multiple users load the same object for editing and then commit their changes, we run the risk of corrupted object data. A simple solution is to store a version number in the value object and compare this with the currently active version of an object on the server before running an update. If the value object passed in by the user is out of date, an appropriate error message can be displayed. Otherwise, the update can be committed.

In our example, we used several of the prebuilt Flash UI Components, including the Scroll Bar and Push Button components within the manageArticle.fla movie. However, we have only scratched the surface of what is possible. Armed with a clear understanding of how to tie the data tier of an application to a Flash MX Client layer, the possibilities afforded the developer are endless. Take time to work with all of the Flash MX UI Components, Charting components, and additional components available through the Macromedia Exchanges. With this rich stable of readily available and skinnable components, along with custom Flash MX Components you build and the rich ActionScript language and object model of Flash in the Client layer tied to ColdFusion MX Components in the Business Logic and Data layers, you have the tools necessary to take the process and interface for web content management to a completely new level.

The Facade Pattern and Flash MX

We have seen how to use Flash movies to interact with and manage content using Flash Remoting, but it is also possible to provide Flash MX management interfaces for subsystems of a dynamic publishing application. The Facade pattern is a great way to simplify development and reduce the number of remote calls that will be made from your Flash MX movie to server-side components when you're interacting with groups of ColdFusion MX Components on the server.

Many interactions with systems of interrelated components on the server, such as a workflow engine, require calling functions against a variety of components. If the Client layer is designed to access the individual server-side components directly, we end up with a fragile system that contains business and process logic related to the various server-side components inside the Client layer. This means that changes to the server-side components often have serious repercussions for the Client layer code. We can decouple the Client layer from the specific implementation of the server-side system of components through the Facade pattern. We can write a single Facade component that provides a remote interface for Flash MX movies to interact with a server-side system. Let's look at the role of a Facade component visually in Figure 18.1.

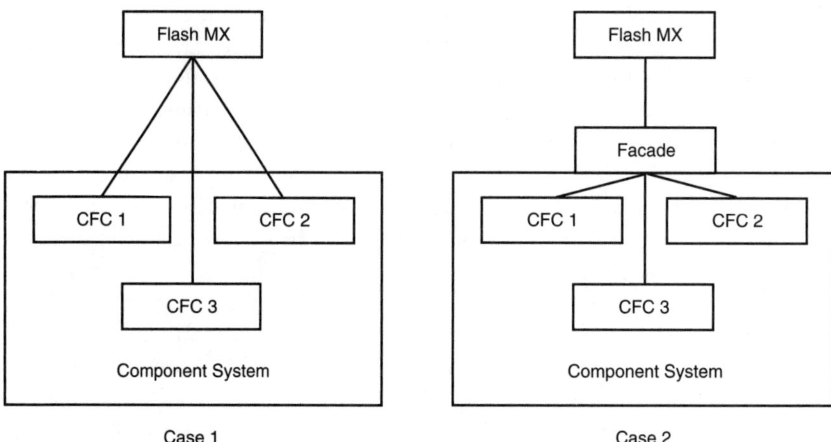

Figure 18.1 The Facade Pattern with Flash MX.

In Figure 18.1, we see a Flash MX movie interacting with a component system on the server. In Case 1, the Flash MX movie is interacting directly with each of the CFCs within the system on the server using Flash Remoting. From the figure, it is clear to see that changes to the components within the system directly affect the Flash MX layer. However, in Case 2, we see that the Flash MX layer only interacts with a Facade component that provides a single point of remote access into the system on the server. The Facade pattern solves the problem of Client layer code dependency to the server, and in this approach, changes can be made to the three components within the system without directly affecting the Flash MX layer. By directing all interaction with the server-side system through the Facade component, the client layer is unable to misuse the individual CFCs within the system.

An additional benefit to using the Facade pattern for interaction between Flash and server-side resources and systems is that we also improve performance by cutting down on the number of network calls to make. If a certain use of the system requires that the Flash MX layer calls a function on each of the three components, as in Case 1, then three separate remote functions calls are made via Flash Remoting. However, in Case 2, only a single remote function call must be made to the Facade component, which can then perform the necessary actions locally by invoking functions for components on the server. A performance characteristic of Flash Remoting is that all remote function calls within a single frame that use the same NetConnection are batched and sent to the server at once, with the assorted results sent back as a batch as well. Therefore, if all three remote functions in Case 1 are invoked on the same frame, we do not incur the overhead of three separate network connections. We do, however, have a better chance of improving performance across the board if the Facade pattern handles Flash Remoting function calls to the server.

Supporting Business Users

Using Flash MX to create a rich Client layer for the management of an application and its content opens up new means to support business users who will be using the system. Using ActionScript, you can implement custom movie clips or objects to provide context-sensitive help for your users. This can take the form of hover-over ToolTips for buttons or icons within your UI or interactive training applications for your end users employing embedded video and dynamically loaded audio assets.

Context-Sensitive Help

Context-sensitive help is a terrific way to improve the usefulness of site management tools for business users, and you also can apply it to the Presentation layer of the application that is accessible to public users. An important benefit of handling contextual help within a Flash MX interface is the simplicity with which non-textual help, such as streaming audio or video or traditional Flash animations and sound, can be incorporated and presented to the user. In addition to overt contextual help, a Flash MX interface also supports more subtle approaches for guiding a user through an application and promoting proper use of the application.

An infinite number of possibilities are available for crafting an application interface to provide contextual help to your users. Following are several options to consider within a Flash MX application interface:

- Selectively enable or disable form fields within the Flash interface based on user data entry and business rules. You can change other visual hints, such as the background color for form fields, as you enter data into a field or the user moves on to other fields. Doing so provides the user with a clear visual indication of what is active, what has been completed, and what remains for him to complete.
- Context-sensitive help components can be displayed for the user based on common events within the Flash movie, such as mousing over a button or clicking an interface element. You can implement Help components to provide something as simple as a ToolTip or as complex as an application tutorial to the user.
- Context-sensitive help also can take the form of error messages. You can display errors in user input in an Error component that is populated with an error message and shown and hidden dynamically based on user interaction with the application. You also can indicate data errors by using visual or audio cues associated with the form element or action that is in error.
- Be creative and remember that Flash MX components that provide contextual help, such as application tutorials or error display components, can be written in a modular, independent fashion and can interact with server-side components via Flash Remoting if necessary.

Audio/Video Support

The full story concerning Flash MX is revealed with the launch of the Macromedia Flash Communication Server MX. The Macromedia Flash 6 player contains support for this new server technology that allows for real-time audio, video, and data streams that can be simultaneously broadcast to multiple Flash players. This supports collaborative videoconferencing, chat, and even shared workspaces within a Flash movie. Clearly, these technologies hold immense promise for many web applications. In the case of customer support, a live videoconference with support staff that employs audio, video, and chat along with all of the features that are currently available to the Flash player is revolutionary.

Flash movies will also be able to provide support for recording video or audio streams for later playback, a feature that has no end of possible uses. Imagine recording a short video clip in which you provide details or comments when placing an order online. Collaborative workspaces for departments or employees within an enterprise are another area in which immediate benefits can be realized with these new technologies. One possible application is real-time collaborative content creation or review. The many new features of Flash MX, including Flash Remoting, are revolutionary, but they are only part of the story. The release of Macromedia Flash Communication Server MX completes the transformation of Flash from a simple animation tool for the web to an amazingly full-featured and robust client for rich Internet applications.

Conclusion

The release of ColdFusion MX, Flash MX, and Flash Remoting has ushered in an entirely new paradigm for building rich Internet applications. Flash MX and Flash Remoting provide the means to take the Presentation layer for content and site management to an entirely new level. You can create application interfaces entirely in Flash by using modular Flash MX Components that interact seamlessly with server-side components via Flash Remoting.

You can use Flash MX Components to create powerful hybrid HTML and Flash displays, in which the Flash movies interact with the server independently from each other and from the page or container they are embedded within. You can build these Flash MX Components to manage multistep processes, providing distinct performance and development benefits over a traditional multistep HTML process in a web application.

We looked at strategies that can streamline communications between Flash MX Components and server-side ColdFusion components. Namely, we looked at the Value Object pattern for passing data back and forth between the client and server tiers of the application and the Facade pattern that provides Flash movies or components with a single access point to complex server-side systems and functionality. The interactivity and rich media capabilities that are available natively in Flash MX are unmatched by any other client-side technology. They allow for the creation of amazingly rich user interfaces that can employ complex scripting, animation, and media (audio, video, and graphics) delivery to provide a world-class user experience.

IV

The Publishing Layer

19

Basics of Publishing

by Michael Mazzorana

IN THIS CHAPTER, WE WILL DISCUSS BOTH the Publishing layer and the Client layer. These two layers have a close relationship to one another and could be considered in some ways to be the same, but it's important to understand them separately for a better appreciation of the synergies between all the layers discussed in previous chapters.

You can think of a Publishing layer as the catalyst or leveraging point for content to be viewed by the end user. Content can live as a structure and evolve over time in a workflow, but to be able to retrieve content from the content repository for syndication, transformation, and presentation, the content needs to be exposed on a web site or other format, such as a word processing document or a wireless device. Content is contributed in a workflow with a business process, but a targeted audience views it with business rules. These business rules translate to publishing rules. Publishing rules are driven with a publishing engine that your developers develop based on your organization's requirements on how, to whom, and where your content is presented.

The second half of this chapter explains how your content is presented to your targeted audience. From a client/user experience perspective, we'll cover how your publishing engine can assist in the following areas:

- Enhance the web site visitor experience
- Drive users to navigate in a controlled manner

- Give personal experiences based on the individual or audience group
- Create publishing events to be triggered for timely information
- Keep content fresh/new because an engine is driving content

We will relate real-world examples of the business and technical impact of these layers by re-examining our fictitious company DuvalShock. We will look closer at how publishing behavior impacts the browser display for usability and how it relieves web development units of common mistakes and redundant maintenance tasks that are performed in a manual way in many organizations today. We also will show how a company can minimize embarrassing and business-harmful mistakes with clear and concise business rules that are applied across these layers.

By leveraging Publishing and Client layer solutions, your organization's return on investment (ROI) benefits in several key areas:

- Building a publishing API for reusability of your content repository
- Developers focusing on automated display functions that add better control and Client layer consistency
- Rules-based publishing
- Self-contained retrieval of content
- Guidelines becoming clearer for separation of business logic and client presentation

This chapter concludes with an understanding of why your organization decided to put this much effort toward building this infrastructure framework for your company content assets. The Client layer can offer many options for many audiences. The dynamic publishing solution you have in place allows your content to leverage wireless, web, and proprietary displays. Cell phones, Flash clients, and PDF documents are some of the ways that your content can display.

What Is Publishing?

In the traditional sense of the definition, *publishing* is thought of as the final step before content is grouped together in a deliberate format and then presented for a target audience or to reach an untouched audience in a strategic fashion. Whether publishing is targeted for print (such as a book) or an electronic format (such as the web), specific guidelines are needed for how the content displays for the end reader. This chapter looks at ways that publishing rules improve a development team's maintenance and the experience of users who are visiting your web site.

It's important to design a publishing engine to bring the benefits to your IT area and users. A publishing engine is a core application layer that assists the manipulation and presentation of the content stored in your repository. Let's look at the major elements of a publishing engine that you need to consider before developing one for your dynamic publishing application.

Where and in What Context Will Content Be Published?

Referring back to our fictitious company in Chapter 13, "Basics of Managing Content," DuvalShock, the marketing department goes through its workflow application to add content for DuvalShock's new Big Spark 200 Generator. After the department deems the content ready for production, a number of automated publishing actions can happen based on your requirements. These automated publishing occurrences replace the manual process that was first described in Chapter 1, "Overview of Dynamic Publishing." Please review Chapter 1 now. Let's also look at how these automated publishing rules can work for a web site.

After the content is marked approved in your workflow application, the content repository can respond to rules that are applied to the dynamic publishing application. Those rules can target different nodes on your web page. *Nodes* are any specific content element on your web site that can have cross relationships on how your page presents. Adding, removing, and introducing rule criteria to these elements on your web site can be referred to as *node management.*

Nodes can be any of the following on a web page:

- Basic text elements, such as titles and body of content
- Images and graphics
- Flash components
- Video clips
- Dynamic navigation

We can modify all these nodes via the workflow application or without the dependency of the workflow if a publishing rule event occurs without the need of a variable business decision. When we look at DuvalShock's home page that is targeted for its manufacturing representatives, we can identify several managed nodes highlighted on the illustrated web page in Figure 19.1.

We can define each highlighted area as individual nodes living in larger containers. These containers can have rules that define many design elements, such as what font should be used or how it should align when it is published.

Focusing on the New Products portion of the page, the container can be made up of the heading named New Products and the three bulleted titles below the heading. This container has defined the following publishing rules for how the content displays on this page:

- During the workflow, the title is contributed with a limited amount of characters allowed to fit properly on this page.
- The title appears as a hyperlink to the body of the new product description that the marketing department provided.
- Three titles are on the page at all times. The most recent title contributed always ends up above the other two titles. The fourth title is bumped off the home page.
- The font for the text in the title defaults to Arial at the same size at all times. It was decided in the requirements phase that the workflow would allow no flexibility for color, size, or font type in the title area.

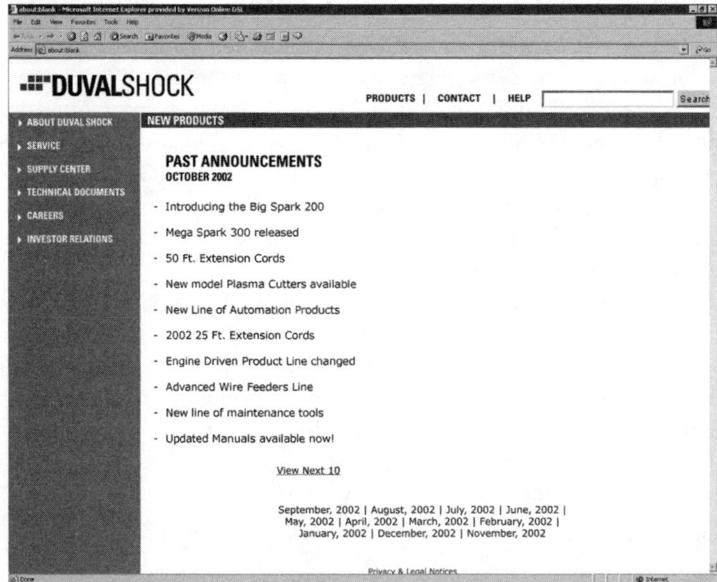

Figure 19.1 The home page with the managed nodes highlighted.

All these activities we just bulleted are automated publishing events that came out of requirements with the business area that we discussed in Chapter 1. Let's look at additional publishing rules on the two additional pages that are involved in this managed process.

Figure 19.2 shows us another publishing rule that occurs when the same piece of content is approved in the workflow. The publishing rule is programmed in such a way that the title hyperlinks to a secondary template that displays the related body of content. When the title "Introducing the Big Spark 200" is added to the home page, a designated web page template is dynamically generated so that the title can point to the body page shown in Figure 19.2.

In another step of the workflow application, a body of content is contributed. Here, the marketing department has a little more free-form ability to control font formatting. What is not editable is the title heading "Introducing the Big Spark 200." The same content that is contributed to the title on the home page is reused and made visible to this body page with a defined font size and color. This body page for New Products is predefined and designed so that it can be the template that will generate every time a new title and body are contributed in the workflow application.

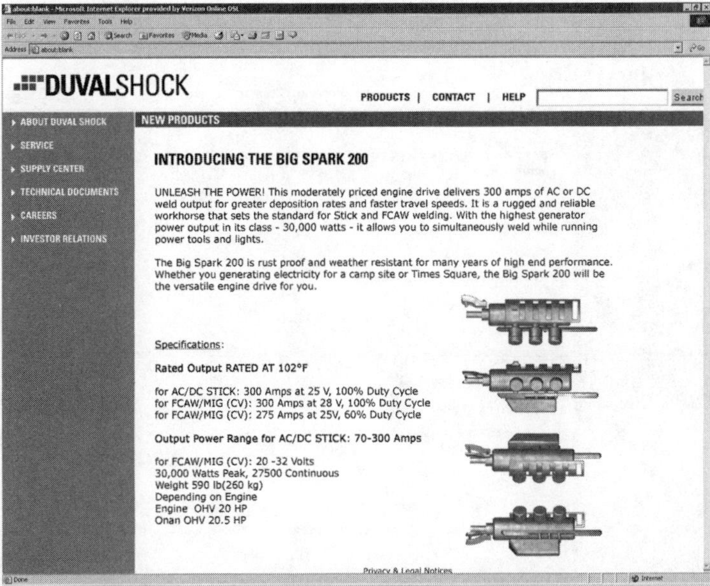

Figure 19.2 Introducing the Big Spark 200.

The final publishing rule that occurs on the workflow approval is for the archive template. As we pointed out, only three titles are allowed on the home page in the New Product container; a fourth that is added drops off. Another key business requirement is to collect all the titles and publish to a dedicated page so that the end user can refer back to older announcements. See Figure 19.3 for the archive web page.

This template has a few rules:

- All titles that are added for New Products end up on this template with the same font, size, and color as the home page.
- The titles are in chronological order with the most recent on top.
- Ten articles are allowed per page, and when the eleventh title occurs, a Next Page hyperlink is generated and a new page is dynamically created to handle the overflow as New Product titles are added.
- The archive template represents the current month's announcements. At the end of each month, a new template is automatically generated and last month's articles are available via a hyperlink shown on the bottom of the page for that particular month. Links to 11 previous months are shown at all times on the archive templates.

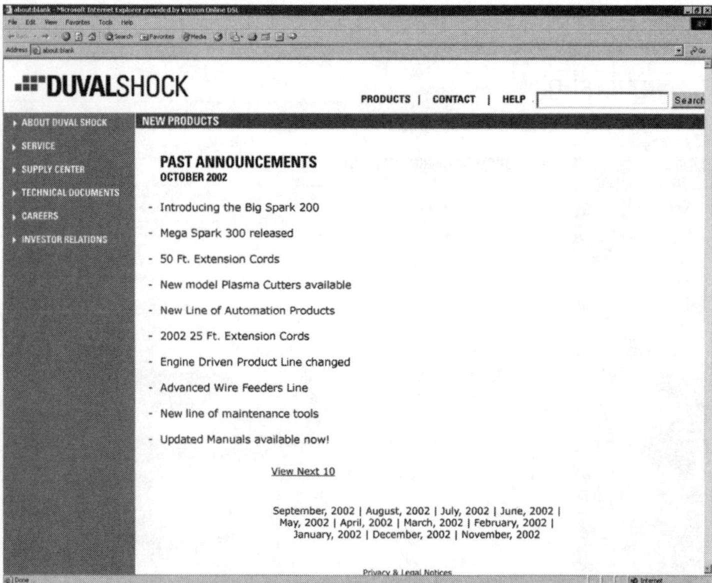

Figure 19.3 The past title/archive template goes here.

We have focused only on the elements of New Products. One idea to consider if similar properties exist in your requirements of other areas on your web site is using metadata to reuse workflow templates and publishing rules for end user templates. The properties are defined as "title" and "body." In our example, metadata has already played a role in categorizing the content as New Products. If we wanted to describe Company Spotlight, Sales Leaders, and Industry News as additional pieces of metadata, we could do this easily in our workflow application with something as simple as a drop-down box describing the categories. This would be an option before the title and body content were added. You can maximize the reusability if you convince your business to leverage the same publishing rules and properties.

The Return on Investment Advantages to Publishing Rules

When we again take a look back to the manual process described in Chapter 1 and compare it to the automation that our dynamic publishing application provided, it becomes obvious that publishing rules can save tremendous development time. Referring again to our return on investment (ROI) diagram in Figure 19.4, we can count the number of steps eliminated in the process.

Note

Note a few items in Figure 19.4. (These numbers do not include the business unit's time.)

- The average cost per hour for the IT team is $65.
- Marketing items per month average about 40.
- Each developer spends about 3 to 4 hours per article.
- The webmaster's time spent deploying and checking is about 1 hour.
- It costs the IT department $10,400 to $13,000 per month to manually publish static marketing items to the home page.

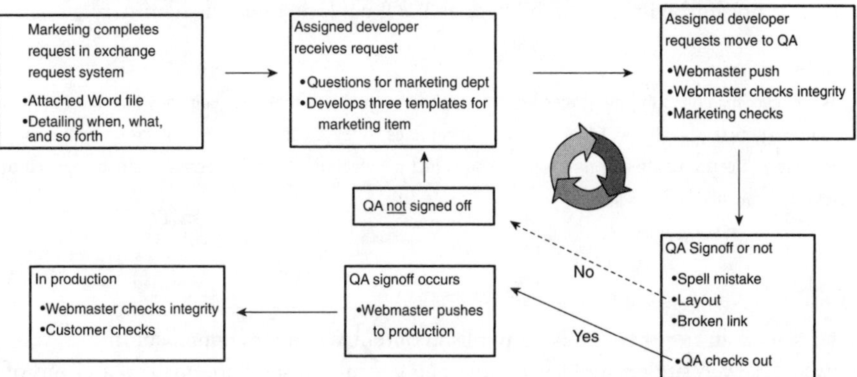

Figure 19.4 Change migration with cost analysis.

We have eliminated the redundant duties of the various roles mentioned in Figure 19.4:

- The change request system is no longer required to attach files and give an explanation of the change request.
- The developer no longer needs to touch and complete the three templates. He can focus instead on developing more strategic solutions, such as a dynamic publishing solution in another area of the web site.
- Communication between the developer and the business customer is not necessary now that the business unit has a more strategic tool to contribute and view content activity.
- The web administrator does not have to move template code through the various environments. Instead, he can focus on the pertinent activities to ensure stable development, QA, and production environments.

We have essentially built an application that supports a business process and is managed and controlled by the actions of the business unit in synergy to the automation applied.

Another major improvement in the process that might not have a strong ROI factor but could be considered important to business is consistency. By automating your publishing abilities to a dedicated set of templates, you have eliminated the possibility of content going out with the wrong font, size, color, order, and so on. Consider a developer's time in figuring out where content should be placed and how it should look. By introducing style sheets and other web development methods, you have found a powerful partner to the publishing rules your IT team created.

Other Ways to Expose Your Content Via Publishing

In the three templates reviewed, we explained some of the ways you could make automated publishing rules work for you on a web site. You can invent many other publishing rules for web site publishing and expose other methods so that your content is not limited to the web channel. We'll explore a few of them here.

> **Note**
>
> As you can imagine, publishing rules are only limited to the ideas that your company has and the technology that is available. Whether you're using rules to reuse content in multiple areas or to expose content at a certain date and time, publishing is just a collection of properties and methods applied to your dynamic publishing solution.

Email

Email can be an important way to publish content when it is approved. In our DuvalShock web site example, we could apply a rule to send an email to a group of manufacturing representatives when content is published to the web site. The email could contain a title hyperlink with the first few sentences of the body. This could be an important way to drive users to your site or keep users informed.

Printable Document

We might occasionally need content to become printable in a certain format. Unfortunately, HTML output of content is not always suitable for our audience. We could introduce a rule to publish a PDF version of the content on the web site.

Wireless and PDA Devices

In some areas of your web site, you might determine the need to expose the content via cell phones, Windows CE, or Palm OS handheld computing hardware. A publishing rule can be a great way to expose content in another format that is readable by the growing demand of various devices that are entering the market.

Content as a Web Service

You might have heard the term "syndication" from some of the content management hype. Exposing your content as a web service so that other companies or partners can retrieve your content for reuse on their sites is a perfect way to use some of the web service specifications available today. Our dynamic publishing application is an effective platform for pushing or pulling content data by exposing services for others to see.

Portals and Portlets

If your company is looking for more effective ways to expose content, applications, and branding to target client users, you undoubtedly have been evaluating portal vendor solutions. You will quickly find out that the portal solutions are only as good as the organization and categorization of your content. Publishing rules with the use of metadata should co-exist with any vendor product you're considering. This is an effective way to introduce personalization with targeting content to certain roles. Depending on your requirements, you might also find that a portal solution fits nicely in your infrastructure without the help of an additional product by creative publishing and role relationships.

Flash MX

The increasing popularity to expose content via Flash containers, such as advertisements and applications, gives publishing rules an exciting new dynamic. Flash gateways made available through Flash Remoting enable you to use ColdFusion MX and JRun 4.0 functionality within your Macromedia Flash movies to expose content. This technology option also can play into your portal requirements.

Challenges of Publishing

As with any application that you are building, good business requirements are the key to your success. It is important to explain what publishing rules do for your web site and other areas that you expose your content and business processes to. Hiding the technical complexity and sharing the possibilities of publishing rules in dynamic publishing can often be a challenge. Using visual diagrams or introducing screenshots like we have in this chapter can get business owners engaged in how they take advantage of the different components your development area is capable of building. Asking the right questions about how business owners want their content to behave is critical to how detailed elements of your site react when a visitor comes to a page. The goal is to get business areas to agree on the long-term effects of how your content is exposed and avoid having to rework publishing rules so that maintenance in the future is at a minimum. Also, have them understand the power of future reuse and the separation of content and presentation when requirements of publishing are agreed on.

The Client Layer

We will finish this chapter by exploring the last logical layer in a dynamic publishing application. The Client layer is no more complicated than your user experience of the content or data you want to present. It is "icing on the cake" and can be spread on as thin or as thick as you desire. It all boils down to a matter of taste. In this section, we will examine the Client layer and its role in a dynamic publishing solution.

In your requirements, you have determined how your publishing rules will expose your content. Publishing rules are not only business logic in the application server or middle tier, but they also can be leveraged in templates that present the user experience to the client. It is always best to contain your rules in a middle layer as much as possible. When this is not possible in web development, your templates will play a critical role in interacting with your content repository and Publishing layer. To expose your content with the layers we have described, you need a way for your content to be retrieved. Web templates can exist in two formats: static and dynamic. Your development team needs a dynamic method to call your components that you have written. You can accomplish this in several popular ways:

- **Active Server Pages (ASP)**—Pages with an .asp extension are usually running on a Microsoft web server and are written with a combination of VBScript, JavaScript, HTML, and other web scripting technologies embedded in them.
- **JavaServer Pages (JSP)**—Pages with a .jsp extension can run on any web server with Java running on it. JSP tags encapsulate object or database calls and can be used to expose your content or data. This type of template also handles the usual W3C.org standards.
- **ColdFusion Markup Pages (CFM)**—Pages that have a .cfm extension can also run on any web server that has Java running on it. CFM tags are similar in nature to JSP tags. The difference is that they use the ColdFusion Markup Language (CFML) with these tags and can also handle JSP tags.

In this book, ColdFusion MX is used for the coding examples. We can serve up dynamic content in many other ways, such as PHP and CGI, but ASP, JSP, and CFM are the most popular commercially supported methods in the market today. They come with the better developer tools available to construct and debug pages at different levels of development. In this book, the Macromedia Studio MX and coding examples should give developers an idea of how quickly ColdFusion MX can assist in building a dynamic publishing solution.

Client Layer Hardware Variations

The most obvious location that your content or data might be presented in is a personal computer. The PC contains a robust operating system with large amount of resources for optimal performance. Your options are nearly unlimited as to how you present your content.

You might consider the following other devices for publishing your content:

- Cell phones
- PDAs with small operating systems, such as Palm OS
- Blackberry's and paging/email devices
- Flat monitors in elevators or public locations
- Vehicles with navigation and interactive devices
- Windows CE handheld devices

Flash for Your Client Layer

Another component of Macromedia's Studio MX family is Flash MX. In the past few years, Flash has been popular in making web sites more exciting and dynamic. Flash is mostly used for an introductory or splash screen visual experience to a web site with a multimedia effect of moving objects and sound. Flash also has become an alternative to creating click-through advertisements because of a designer's ability to create low bandwidth, high impact visual effects. Some of the more adventurous designers and developers use Flash to create dynamic navigation and feed live data and dynamic content into Flash containers. The most recent versions of Flash are geared more toward a richer client experience that now includes more native solutions to application development. Also included in the ColdFusion MX and JRun 4.0 application servers is a gateway that allows you to stream content and data easily into a Flash component. This technology is called *Flash remoting*.

As we mentioned in Chapter 13, the limitations of HTML have made stateless web pages difficult to bring to an acceptable level of user expectations. Since the day that the web became an important vehicle for companies to do business, developers have been challenged to meet customer requirements that were often too complicated for the specifications released by the World Wide Web Consortium (W3C). Web browsers and the companies that have represented them have pushed the boundaries of standard and non-standard ways to satisfy the need of a richer client experience. These alternative browser technologies have either failed because they had lack of acceptance or failed because of architectural flaws and security holes.

As of the writing of this book, the Flash Player exists on more than 98 percent of web browsers on the Internet. Its wide acceptance is largely because of the minimal requirements needed to install the player. It often takes less than 30 seconds to upgrade to a newer version, and the base Flash Player is already included in the base installation of major browsers. Flash is not only in the browser, but it also is beginning to become mainstream in other hardware devices and operating systems. Microsoft announced that Flash Player would be included in their XP operating system. Some of the major cell phone companies such as Nokia have agreed to include Flash Player in their cell phone operating systems. A Flash application creates a low bandwidth, interactive, rich client experience. Flash components are created with vector-based graphics, which means that the same PC client version of your application can minimize in a smaller screen that runs a Windows CE version of the operating system and still hold the same shape and proportions.

Conclusion

In this chapter, we looked at the Publishing and Client layers. We also explained how building publishing rules can be a powerful area of a dynamic publishing solution. We showed how automating redundant tasks save development time and bring consistency to how your web site presents for ease of navigation and overall professionalism of your company reputation. Using DuvalShock as an example, we were able to show examples of publishing rules and contrast Chapter 1's explanation of the manual process. Tasks were eliminated and ROI examples were clear after we automated tasks that were previously maintained by all levels of a development team.

Publishing rules can come in all forms, such as these:

- Email
- Portals and personalization
- Web services or a document format
- Wireless and PDA devices

Tasks can be built in to have content:

- Added or removed based on date/time
- Placed in a specific category or multiple categories that dynamically drive your site

The Client layer was introduced with both solution options and challenges. The key is to architect your content repository to be handled by the Publishing layer for all current and future technology clients. Various devices and technologies are available to expose your content and data. We looked at Flash as an alternative to handling multiple client hardware devices and operating systems that might be limited to providing rich client experiences.

In Chapters 1, 4, 13, and 18, we have given you a technical manager or business manager view of a dynamic publishing solution. Using these chapters should help you relate to both the business problem you are trying to solve and the solutions that your development team is building based on your requirements. The most effective and successful solutions that are built are pioneered by the people in neutral territory who are trying to appreciate the goals and challenges in technology and business. If architects and developers alike read these chapters, they will be more effective in meetings and other interactions with the various people who make up the project team.

20

Web Services

by Jeff Tapper

ALTHOUGH WEB SERVICES IS ONE OF THE MOST talked about Internet buzz phrases of the past few years, it is really a simple concept. A web service is a framework that allows applications to expose their functionality and data to other applications over the Internet. Although conceptually simple, this framework offers an extremely powerful tool for the Internet application's architect and developer.

Web services extend the functionality of network software components to the Internet. Similar in function to software protocols such as COM/COM+, Common Object Request Broker Architecture (CORBA), and Remote Method Invocation (RMI); the Web Services protocols allow for discreet functionality to be abstracted into objects that are available across the web. This means that other applications can make calls to the methods of these objects to extend their functionality.

When we talk about Web Services, what we're really talking about is a platform-independent syntax for exchanging complex data. The data is exchanged as XML packets, meaning that virtually any platform (including Client/Server programs, other application servers, desktop applications, and so on) can easily make use of this technology.

Web services have the promise to revolutionize the software development industry because they allow a standard means to connect any application anywhere to consume Web Services from any other application that makes them available. Earlier, there were only proprietary means to achieve this, such as Remote Procedure Calls (RPCs),

RMI, CORBA, and so on. Application developers who wanted to expose functionality to outside applications had to choose a proprietary protocol and write the code to expose functionality manually.

Web Services Standards

At the heart of Web Services are two key standards: WSDL and Simple Object Access Protocol (SOAP). They are both open standards that enjoy broad support across the industry, including from Microsoft and Sun, as well as other industry leaders including IBM, BEA, Oracle, and Macromedia.

Web Services Description Language

One of the key standards that make Web Services possible is the Web Services Description Language (WSDL). This provides the syntax with which to describe the functionality of a web service. A WSDL file is an XML formatted document that includes information about the web service, including the methods that are available to be called, the attributes that are expected by each method, and the values that will be returned by each. Also included in the WSDL file is a description of what the web service does, as well as its location.

The WSDL file serves many useful purposes. It provides details for those who want to consume the web service. These details include the methods that are available to be invoked against the service. With this WSDL description, it is even possible to build "code-hinting" tools into integrated development environments (IDEs) to allow developers who are consuming the service insight into its methods and properties.

Note

With Web Services, *consuming* is how use of the service is described.

You can find the full specification of WSDL at `http://www.w3.org/TR/wsdl`.

SOAP

Another key standard at the heart of Web Services is SOAP. SOAP is the protocol that is used to send messages and data between applications. This serves to encapsulate the XML packet with the necessary descriptors for consuming the web service. SOAP contains the object name and method to be invoked, and the XML packet within it contains the attributes to be passed to the method.

The encapsulation of this information is accomplished using a SOAP envelope. A SOAP *envelope* is simply a hierarchical XML document. Listing 20.1 shows a sample SOAP envelope.

Listing 20.1 **A Sample SOAP Envelope**

```
<soap:Envelope xmlns:soap="http://schemas.xmlsoap.org/soap/envelope">
    <soap:Body>
        <!--actual SOAP content here -->
    </soap:Body>
</soap:Envelope>
```

SOAP is most often used across the Hypertext Transfer Protocol (HTTP), the protocol that web servers and web browsers currently use. This offers another key advantage to Web Services over proprietary protocols such as COM, RMI, and CORBA; all access can occur across port 80, the standard that is used to communicate with web servers today. As long as the company's firewall allows internal applications (such as browsers on the employees' desktops) to access the Internet across port 80, no modifications are needed to consume Web Services. Accessing remote objects with COM+, CORBA, or RMI most often requires specific rules to be added to a firewall, specifying the remote IP address, the local IP address, and the port to be used. Developers who have had to battle network administrators to get an additional port or IP address added to the access list for a firewall can certainly appreciate the benefits of avoiding such a battle. It also is possible to send SOAP messages across other common protocols, such as SMTP, FTP, or even a custom protocol, but this rarely is seen.

Universal Description, Discovery, and Integration

A third key standard that makes Web Services possible is Universal Description, Discovery, and Integration (UDDI). UDDI is a directory of Web Services, with descriptions of what each service provides. This directory allows for producers of Web Services to share their services with the world and for clients to find a service that meets their needs. A UDDI query is used to locate a service provider offering the functionality that the client requires. UDDI queries are answered with a response that contains the necessary details to consume the matching Web Services. At this time, ColdFusion is not a UDDI registry, nor does it provide ties to the UDDI SDK; however, Web Services that are built with ColdFusion can be registered and found through UDDI. A number of publicly accessible UDDI registrars are available, including IBM's (`https://www-3.ibm.com/services/uddi/protect/registry.html`) and Microsoft's (`http://uddi.microsoft.com/`).

Benefits of Component-Based Web Software

With the introduction of component-based web development, Internet architects can now leverage the same benefits that the traditional software industry has enjoyed for years. Encapsulation of application logic into discreet components provides tremendous power to an application. It allows for a truly clean separation between client, presentation, application, integration, and data tiers. With such a separation, application maintainability increases exponentially. You can make changes to the look and feel of the application on the client tier alone, without needing to touch application, integration, or data access components. Adding the capability for other types of clients (that is, providing a WML interface in addition to the HTML interface) can be done on the presentation tier without changes to the other tiers. Additionally, by separating business logic from the other application tiers, any changes to the business logic need not impact the code for the rest of the application.

With component-based software, it becomes easier to scale applications to handle increased load. For years, web applications have been distributed over several web servers, with a load balancing mechanism spreading the requests across a cluster of servers, rather than directing it all at a single server. Because Web Services are discreet applications that respond through a web server, it will be possible to distribute individual Web Services across a cluster of servers, rather than having to distribute an entire application. This way, if an individual web service is garnering excessive traffic, you can scale requests to it.

Another benefit of component-based software is the reusability of components that are exposed as Web Services. After a piece of functionality has been made into a web service, it can be instantly reused on other projects, even if the other projects are built on top of a different technology. Imagine the case of an employee search component. Many different applications could be intranet, extranet, or public Internet, which could leverage this functionality. Now, as happens in many corporations, one development staff builds and maintains the intranet in one technology, whereas another staff takes responsibility for the public Internet, and perhaps a third (or fourth or fifth) staff maintains various extranet activities. Regardless of how the employee search mechanism is used, all applications use the same basic logic: provide some detail (department, last name, skill, and so on) and return all matching employees. By building functionality as a web service, it will be possible for all these applications to call this function in a single place, passing in only the parameters it requires and manipulating the results as it sees fit.

Current State of Web Services Technologies

Although Web Services offer a tremendous future for Internet applications, critics rightly charge that the technology is not yet fully baked. The largest shortcomings of Web Services today are the issues surrounding security. For Web Services that are intended for free and open access to the world, the SOAP and WSDL standards offer a great framework. However, the issues surrounding security—specifically, around encrypting access to Web Services and guaranteeing the integrity of message sent to and from them—are still being worked out.

To help solve these issues, IBM and Microsoft have recently proposed an initial specification for the WS-Security standard. The initial specification, WS-Security, addresses three key aspects of securing SOAP requests: authentication, encryption, and message integrity. The road map proposes to build on this foundation with additional specifications for configuring trust relationships and for handling complex security situations. (Heffner, Randy; "Secure Web Services: WS-Security Is a Formidable Proposal," Giga Information Group: April 2002.)

To date, only VeriSign has joined with Microsoft and IBM in this standard, although there is reason to believe that the WS-Security standard will thrive. Industry leaders don't support any other Web Services security standards, and this is the first Web Services security standard that addresses both the .NET and J2EE platforms.

Web Services and ColdFusion MX

At the heart of ColdFusion MX's ability to support Web Services is the Apache Axis, an implementation of the SOAP specification. Axis handles underlying functionality that is necessary to support Web Services, such as generating WSDL files. Complete information on Axis is available at `http://xml.apache.org/axis`. Fortunately, the folks at Macromedia have abstracted Web Services, so as ColdFusion developers, we do not need to be familiar with SOAP or perform SOAP actions to produce and consume Web Services.

Figure 20.1 shows how a client interacts with Web Services that are built in ColdFusion.

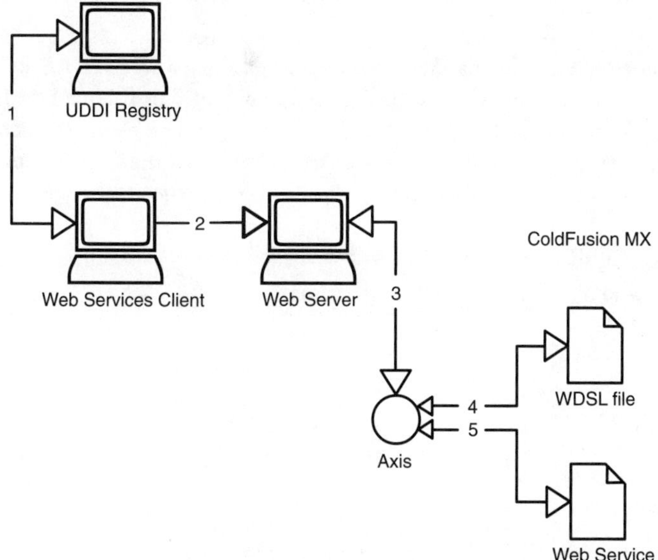

Figure 20.1 Consuming a ColdFusion web service.

The client finds the desired service using a UDDI registry (1). The client calls the WSDL file for the service to discover its syntax (2). The web server then hands the request to the ColdFusion application server (3).

In processing the request, ColdFusion uses Axis to return the WSDL information (4). This Axis is then sent back to the web server (3) and then back to the client (2). Now armed with the web service syntax, the client makes a call to one of the methods of the service (2). This request is again handed from the web server to the ColdFusion server (3). ColdFusion uses Axis (5) to parse the SOAP request, call the method, and return the data (3) to the web server. The web server then returns the requested information to the client (2).

Producing Web Services in ColdFusion MX

The act of creating a web service and making it available for others to use is referred to as *producing* a web service, whereas the act of using a web service is referred to as *consuming* it. As mentioned earlier, Web Services that are produced on one platform can be consumed by applications on the same or any other platform that supports Web Services.

To produce a web service with ColdFusion MX, you make use of ColdFusion Components (CFCs).

> **Note**
> For complete information on producing CFCs, see Chapter 5, "ColdFusion Components."

The major difference between a CFC intended to produce a web service and any other CFC is the attribute that allows it to be accessed remotely. This is done by adding `access="remote"` to the `<CFFUNCTION>` tag. It is a good practice to use the `<CFARGUEMENT>` tag to specify a data type for all parameters. Table 20.1 shows the WSDL data type, which corresponds to the ColdFusion type specified in a `<CFARGUMENT>` tag.

Table 20.1 **ColdFusion Data Type to SOAP Data Type Mapping**

ColdFusion Data Type	WSDL Data Type
Numeric	SOAP-ENC:double
Boolean	SOAP-ENC:boolean
String	SOAP-ENC:string
Array	SOAP-ENC:Array
Binary	xsd:base64Binary
Date	xsd:dateTime
Guid	SOAP-ENC:string
Uuid	SOAP-ENC:string
None	(Operation returns nothing)
Struct	tns2:Map
Query	tns1:QueryBean
Any	Complex type

In Listing 20.2 you can find a simple web service called arrayReverse. It takes one parameter: inputArray (an array of strings). As you might have guessed by the name, this web service takes an array and returns it in reverse order.

Listing 20.2 **ArrayReverse.cfc: A Web Service That Takes an Array and Returns in Reverse Order**

```
<!--- /webservices/arrayReverse.cfc
created 4/25/02 by Jeff Tapper
Remotesite Technologies
Jeff.tapper@remotesite.com

Change History:

Usage:
Web service that takes an array of strings as an argument and returns the array in reverse order
 --->
 <cfcomponent>
     <cffunction
         name = "reverseArray"
         returnType = "Array"
         access = "remote">

     <cfargument name = "inputArray" type = "array" required="yes">
       <cfset returnArray = arrayNew(1)>
       <cfloop from="#arrayLen(inputArray)#" to="1" index="i" step="-1">
             <cfset arrayAppend(returnArray, inputArray[i])>
       </cfloop>

       <cfreturn returnArray>
   </cffunction>
 </cfcomponent>
```

As you can see, this is a simple web service that takes an array as an argument and returns the array in reverse order. It starts by declaring that this is a ColdFusion component by using the `<CFCOMPONENT>` tag. Next, a method is declared on this component, with the `<CFFUNCTION>` tag. Because this is a web service, the function is set with the `access` attribute equal to remote. The method name of this function is declared as `reverseArray`, and the `returnType` is listed as Array. A `<CFARGUMENT>` tag is used to declare that this method will accept an argument named `inputarray`, which must be provided and must be an array.

The middle of the component is simple CFML. It declares a new array to hold the results and then loops over the input array from the last element to the first, setting the first element of the return array equal to the last element of the input and so on.

Finally, the return array is sent back to the consumer, with the `<CFRETURN>` tag, and the `<CFFUNCTION>` and `<CFCOMPONENT>` tags are closed.

You can see an immediate benefit of using ColdFusion to produce Web Services when it comes to generating a WSDL file. Rather than having to manually create this file, ColdFusion creates it for you. Calling your new web service in a browser with ?wsdl appended to the URL returns the full XML packet, which is the WSDL file. In the case of the web service previous, it looks like Listing 20.3.

Listing 20.3 **The WSDL File Automatically Created for the ReverseArray Web Service**

```
<?xml version="1.0" encoding="UTF-8"?>
<wsdl:definitions targetNamespace="http://DefaultNamespace"
xmlns:wsdl="http://schemas.xmlsoap.org/wsdl/"
xmlns:xsd="http://www.w3.org/2001/XMLSchema"
xmlns:wsdlsoap="http://schemas.xmlsoap.org/wsdl/soap/"
xmlns:intf="http://DefaultNamespace" xmlns:impl="http://
DefaultNamespace-impl" xmlns:SOAP-ENC="http://schemas.xmlsoap.org/soap/
encoding/"xmlns="http://schemas.xmlsoap.org/wsdl/"><types><schema
xmlns="http://www.w3.org/2001/XMLSchema"
targetNamespace="http://schemas.xmlsoap.org/soap/encoding/"><element
name="Array" nillable="true" type="SOAP-ENC:Array"/></schema></types>
  <wsdl:message name="reverseArrayRequest">
    <wsdl:part name="inputArray" type="SOAP-ENC:Array"/>
  </wsdl:message>
  <wsdl:message name="CFCInvocationException">
  </wsdl:message>
  <wsdl:message name="reverseArrayResponse">
    <wsdl:part name="return" type="SOAP-ENC:Array"/>
  </wsdl:message>
  <wsdl:portType name="array">
    <wsdl:operation name="reverseArray" parameterOrder="inputArray">
      <wsdl:input message="intf:reverseArrayRequest"/>
      <wsdl:output message="intf:reverseArrayResponse"/>
      <wsdl:fault name="CFCInvocationException"
message="intf:CFCInvocationException"/>
    </wsdl:operation>
 </wsdl:portType>
  <wsdl:binding name="array.cfcSoapBinding" type="intf:array">
    <wsdlsoap:binding style="rpc" transport=
"http://schemas.xmlsoap.org/soap/http"/>
    <wsdl:operation name="reverseArray">
      <wsdlsoap:operation soapAction=""/>
      <wsdl:input>
        <wsdlsoap:body use="encoded" encodingStyle="http://
schemas.xmlsoap.org/soap/encoding/"namespace="http://DefaultNamespace"/>
      </wsdl:input>
      <wsdl:output>
        <wsdlsoap:body use="encoded"encodingStyle="http://
schemas.xmlsoap.org/soap/encoding/"namespace="http://DefaultNamespace"/>
      </wsdl:output>
    </wsdl:operation>
```

```
  </wsdl:binding>
  <wsdl:service name="arrayService">
    <wsdl:port name="array.cfc" binding="intf:array.cfcSoapBinding">
      <wsdlsoap:address location="http://localhost:8100/array.cfc"/>
    </wsdl:port>
  </wsdl:service>
</wsdl:definitions>
```

Although this isn't a terribly large XML packet, it certainly is larger than you would want to have to produce by hand for each of your Web Services.

Later in this chapter, in the section titled "Registering Web Services Through the ColdFusion Administrator," we will see how to register Web Services as a data source in the ColdFusion Administrator.

Consuming Web Services

You can consume Web Services from a ColdFusion template, a Flash file, or from any other platform that supports Web Services.

Consuming Web Services from ColdFusion

After you know the location of a web service that provides a service you would like to use, it is a simple matter to call it from ColdFusion. In fact, you have several options as to the syntax you can use in calling Web Services from ColdFusion. In this section, we will create some Web Services "clients" to call the web service we created earlier, as well as to consume an external web service. Listing 20.4 shows the creation of an array, which is passed to our arrayReverse web service in Listing 20.5.

Listing 20.4 **An Array to Be Included in Our Web Services Clients**

```
<!--- /aPresidents.cfm
created 4/25/02 by Jeff Tapper
Remotesite Technologies
Jeff.tapper@remotesite.com

Change History:

Usage:
A page that builds an array of the first 16 presidents of the United States.
--->

<cfscript>
aPresidents = arraynew(1);
aPresidents[1] = "George Washington (1789-1797)";
aPresidents[2] = "John Adams (1797-1801)";
aPresidents[3] = "Thomas Jefferson (1801-1809)";
aPresidents[4] = "James Madison (1809-1817)";
aPresidents[5] = "James Monroe (1817-1825)";
```

continues

Listing 20.4 **Continued**

```
aPresidents[6] = "John Quincy Adams (1825-1829)";
aPresidents[7] = "Andrew Jackson (1829-1837)";
aPresidents[8] = "Martin Van Buren (1837-1841)";
aPresidents[9] = "William Henry Harrison (1841)";
aPresidents[10] = "John Tyler (1841-1845)";
aPresidents[11] = "James Knox Polk (1845-1849)";
aPresidents[12] = "Zachary Taylor (1849-1850)";
aPresidents[13] = "Millard Fillmore (1850-1853)";
aPresidents[14] = "Franklin Pierce (1853-1857)";
aPresidents[15] = "James Buchanan (1857-1861)";
aPresidents[16] = "Abraham Lincoln (1861-1865)";
</cfscript>
```

Listing 20.5 **Consuming a Web Service with the *<CFINVOKE>* Tag**

```
<!--- /Client.cfm
created 4/25/02 by Jeff Tapper
Remotesite Technologies
Jeff.tapper@remotesite.com

Change History:

Usage:
A web service client that uses CFINVOKE to consume a web service
--->
<cfinclude template="aPresidents.cfm">

InputArray:
<cfdump var="#apresidents#">

<cfinvoke
webservice ="http://localhost:8100/arrayReverse.cfc?wsdl"
  method ="reverseArray"
  inputArray = "#aPresidents#"
  returnVariable="foo">

ReturnArray:
<cfdump var="#foo#">
```

This simple web service client starts by building an array—in this case, an array of the first 16 presidents of the United States of America. Next, the `<CFINVOKE>` tag is used with the `WEBSERVICE` attribute, indicating that we are to invoke a web service. The attributes `INPUTARRAY` and `RETURNVARIABLE` are also passed, representing the variable to be sent to the web service as well as the variable that will hold the results. Finally, to show the output from the web service, we run the `<CFDUMP>` tag on the variable specified in the `RETURNVARIABLE` attribute.

Calling this web service in a browser produces the results seen in Figure 20.2.

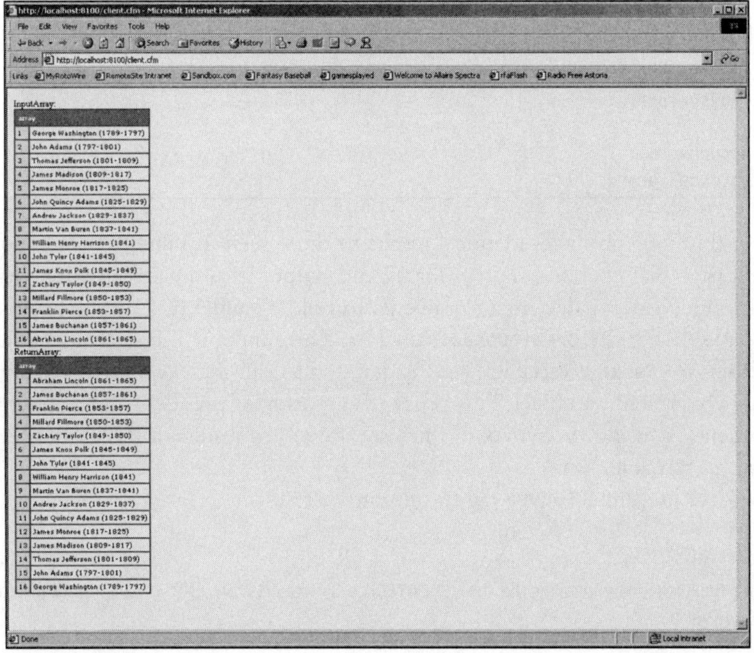

Figure 20.2 Calling `Client.cfm` in a browser shows the array before it is passed to the web service and the results from it.

Web services can also be consumed using the CFSCRIPT syntax. Listing 20.6 shows how.

Listing 20.6 **CFSCRIPT Syntax**

```
 <!--- /cfsClient.cfm
 created 4/25/02 by Jeff Tapper
 Remotesite Technologies
 Jeff.tapper@remotesite.com

Change History:

Usage:
A web service client that uses CFSCRIPT syntax to consume a web service
 --->
 <cfinclude template="aPresidents.cfm">

 InputArray:<br>
 <cfdump var="#aPresidents#">

 <cfscript>
```

continues

Listing 20.6 **Continued**

```
ws = CreateObject("webservice", "http://localhost:8100/
arrayReverse.cfc?wsdl"); foo = ws.reverseArray(aPresidents);
</cfscript>

ReturnArray:
<cfdump var="#foo#">
```

Running this code produces identical results to those seen in Figure 20.2. Again, we include a page that declares an array for us, and output it to the screen with the `<CFDUMP>` tag. Next, we declare a variable `ws` to hold a handle that the `"webservice"` object created with the `CreateObject` function. This function also declares the URL of the web service. Next, a variable `"foo"` is declared to call the `reverseArray()` method of the newly created `ws` object. This is passed our array of presidents (`aPresidents`) as an argument. By using the syntax in this way, the return results of the method are stored in the variable `"foo"`.

Finally, we use the `<CFDUMP>` tag to output the results.

> **Note**
>
> Chapter 5 explains why invoking via the `<CREATEOBJECT>` tag is more efficient than multiple calls with `<CFINVOKE>`.

Registering Web Services Through the ColdFusion Administrator

Another fun feature of ColdFusion MX is the ability to register specific Web Services in the ColdFusion Administrator. This allows you to refer to commonly used Web Services with a simple name (or handle) rather than having to express the entire URL, which is extremely useful for commonly used Web Services because the reference can be set in one place and referred to throughout from there. That way, if the URL should ever change, it's a simple matter of changing it in one place, rather than in every place it's used throughout the codebase.

> **Tip**
>
> Sometimes a developer might not have access to the ColdFusion Administrator. In these cases, consider setting the URL for a web service into a variable that can be referenced throughout the application, rather than coded manually. This way, you can still have the benefit of changing only one reference to the web service, rather than searching through an application for each reference to it.

The first time a web service is called from a ColdFusion page, it is automatically registered in the ColdFusion Administrator. However, it is registered with its complete URL as its handle. Figure 20.3 shows the Administrator with a few Web Services registered with their default handles. (The handles are labeled Web Service Name in the

Administrator.) To make this more useful, you can change the Web Service Name to something shorter and easier to remember. Figure 20.3 shows the Administrator after the Web Service Name for `http://localhost:8100/arrayReverse.cfc?wsdl` has been changed to arrayReverse.

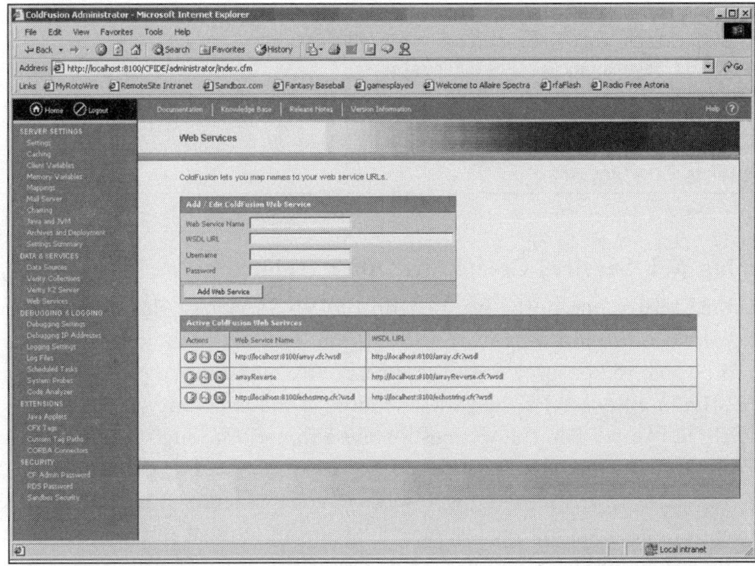

Figure 20.3 The ColdFusion Administrator stores a reference to all Web Services called from the server and offers the ability to create handles, to more easily reference them from the code.

Listing 20.7 shows a page consuming the arrayReverse web service with its handle, rather than the full URL.

Listing 20.7 **Consuming a Web Service by Its Handle**

```
<!--- /cfsClientbyHandle.cfm
created 4/25/02 by Jeff Tapper
Remotesite Technologies
Jeff.tapper@remotesite.com

Change History:

Usage:
A web service client that uses a handle mapped in the ColdFusion Administrator to consume a web service
--->
```

continues

Listing 20.7 **Continued**

```
<cfinclude template="aPresidents.cfm">

InputArray:<br>
<cfdump var="#aPresidents#">

<cfscript>
ws = CreateObject("webservice", "arrayReverse");
foo = ws.reverseArray(aPresidents);
</cfscript>

ReturnArray:
<cfdump var="#foo#">
```

Consuming Web Services Created in Other Technologies

As mentioned earlier, one of the key benefits of Web Services is the complete independence between the platform that produces the service and the platforms that consume it. To be able to consume a web service from ColdFusion, a platform must use the SOAP Binding Style RPC, and use encoding as the encoding style. Viewing a Web Services WSDL can tell you the settings for these things. Although this is a common type of web service, some Web Services do not use this type. For this reason, it becomes important to examine the web service to see whether it is compatible before making use of it. For example, in Listing 20.2, you can see that our web service uses RPC by the following line:

```
<wsdlsoap:binding style="rpc" transport="http://schemas.xmlsoap.org/soap/http"/>
```

And the encoding style can be seen here:

```
<wsdlsoap:body use="encoded"
➥encodingStyle="http://schemas.xmlsoap.org/soap/encoding/"
➥namespace="http://DefaultNamespace"/>
```

After you have verified that these are true, you can consume Web Services to your heart's content.

Listing 20.8 shows the WSDL file for the weather retriever web service from the folks at Learn XML Web Services Development (`http://www.vbws.com/`). This web service takes a zip code as an argument and returns a current weather forecast.

Listing 20.8 **WSDL File for Weather Web Service**

```
  <?xml version="1.0" encoding="utf-8" ?>
- <definitions xmlns:s1="http://tempuri.org/literalTypes"
xmlns:http="http://schemas.xmlsoap.org/wsdl/http/"
xmlns:soap="http://schemas.xmlsoap.org/wsdl/soap/"
xmlns:s="http://www.w3.org/2001/XMLSchema" xmlns:s0="http://tempuri.org/"
xmlns:soapenc="http://schemas.xmlsoap.org/soap/encoding/"
xmlns:tm="http://microsoft.com/wsdl/mime/textMatching/"
```

```
xmlns:mime="http://schemas.xmlsoap.org/wsdl/mime/"
targetNamespace="http://tempuri.org/" xmlns="http://schemas.xmlsoap.org/wsdl/">
- <types>
- <s:schema targetNamespace="http://tempuri.org/">
- <s:complexType name="CurrentWeather">
- <s:sequence>
  <s:element minOccurs="1" maxOccurs="1" name="LastUpdated"
type="s:string"/>
  <s:element minOccurs="1" maxOccurs="1" name="IconUrl" type="s:string" />
  <s:element minOccurs="1" maxOccurs="1" name="Conditions"
type="s:string" />
  <s:element minOccurs="1" maxOccurs="1" name="CurrentTemp"
type="s:float" />
  <s:element minOccurs="1" maxOccurs="1" name="Humidity" type="s:float" />
  <s:element minOccurs="1" maxOccurs="1" name="Barometer" type="s:float" />
  <s:element minOccurs="1" maxOccurs="1" name="BarometerDirection"
type="s:string" />
  </s:sequence>
  </s:complexType>
  </s:schema>
- <s:schema elementFormDefault="qualified"
targetNamespace="http://tempuri.org/literalTypes">
  <s:element name="float" type="s:float" />
  <s:element name="CurrentWeather" type="s1:CurrentWeather" />
- <s:complexType name="CurrentWeather">
- <s:sequence>
  <s:element minOccurs="0" maxOccurs="1" name="LastUpdated"
type="s:string"/>
  <s:element minOccurs="0" maxOccurs="1" name="IconUrl" type="s:string" />
  <s:element minOccurs="0" maxOccurs="1" name="Conditions"
type="s:string" />
  <s:element minOccurs="1" maxOccurs="1" name="CurrentTemp"
type="s:float" />
  <s:element minOccurs="1" maxOccurs="1" name="Humidity" type="s:float" />
  <s:element minOccurs="1" maxOccurs="1" name="Barometer" type="s:float" />
  <s:element minOccurs="0" maxOccurs="1" name="BarometerDirection"
type="s:string" />
  </s:sequence>
  </s:complexType>
  </s:schema>
  </types>
- <message name="GetTemperatureSoapIn">
  <part name="zipCode" type="s:string" />
  </message>
- <message name="GetTemperatureSoapOut">
  <part name="GetTemperatureResult" type="s:float" />
  </message>
- <message name="GetWeatherSoapIn">
  <part name="zipCode" type="s:string" />
  </message>
```

continues

Listing 20.8 **Continued**

```
- <message name="GetWeatherSoapOut">
  <part name="GetWeatherResult" type="s0:CurrentWeather" />
  </message>
- <message name="GetTemperatureHttpGetIn">
  <part name="zipCode" type="s:string" />
  </message>
- <message name="GetTemperatureHttpGetOut">
  <part name="Body" element="s1:float" />
  </message>
- <message name="GetWeatherHttpGetIn">
  <part name="zipCode" type="s:string" />
  </message>
- <message name="GetWeatherHttpGetOut">
  <part name="Body" element="s1:CurrentWeather" />
  </message>
- <message name="GetTemperatureHttpPostIn">
  <part name="zipCode" type="s:string" />
  </message>
- <message name="GetTemperatureHttpPostOut">
  <part name="Body" element="s1:float" />
  </message>
- <message name="GetWeatherHttpPostIn">
  <part name="zipCode" type="s:string" />
  </message>
- <message name="GetWeatherHttpPostOut">
  <part name="Body" element="s1:CurrentWeather" />
  </message>
- <portType name="WeatherRetrieverSoap">
- <operation name="GetTemperature">
  <input message="s0:GetTemperatureSoapIn" />
  <output message="s0:GetTemperatureSoapOut" />
  </operation>
- <operation name="GetWeather">
  <input message="s0:GetWeatherSoapIn" />
  <output message="s0:GetWeatherSoapOut" />
  </operation>
  </portType>
- <portType name="WeatherRetrieverHttpGet">
- <operation name="GetTemperature">
  <input message="s0:GetTemperatureHttpGetIn" />
  <output message="s0:GetTemperatureHttpGetOut" />
  </operation>
- <operation name="GetWeather">
  <input message="s0:GetWeatherHttpGetIn" />
  <output message="s0:GetWeatherHttpGetOut" />
  </operation>
  </portType>
- <portType name="WeatherRetrieverHttpPost">
- <operation name="GetTemperature">
  <input message="s0:GetTemperatureHttpPostIn" />
```

```
<output message="s0:GetTemperatureHttpPostOut" />
</operation>
- <operation name="GetWeather">
<input message="s0:GetWeatherHttpPostIn" />
<output message="s0:GetWeatherHttpPostOut" />
</operation>
</portType>
- <binding name="WeatherRetrieverSoap" type="s0:WeatherRetrieverSoap">
<soap:binding transport="http://schemas.xmlsoap.org/soap/
http" style="rpc" />
- <operation name="GetTemperature">
<soap:operation soapAction="http://tempuri.org/GetTemperature"
style="rpc" />
- <input>
<soap:body use="encoded" namespace="http://tempuri.org/" 105
encodingStyle="http://schemas.xmlsoap.org/soap/encoding/" />
</input>
- <output>
<soap:body use="encoded" namespace="http://tempuri.org/"
encodingStyle="http://schemas.xmlsoap.org/soap/encoding/" />
</output>
</operation>
- <operation name="GetWeather">
<soap:operation soapAction="http://tempuri.org/GetWeather" style="rpc" />
- <input>
<soap:body use="encoded" namespace="http://tempuri.org/"
encodingStyle="http://schemas.xmlsoap.org/soap/encoding/" />
</input>
- <output>
<soap:body use="encoded" namespace="http://tempuri.org/"
encodingStyle="http://schemas.xmlsoap.org/soap/encoding/" />
</output>
</operation>
</binding>
- <binding name="WeatherRetrieverHttpGet" type="s0:WeatherRetrieverHttpGet">
<http:binding verb="GET" />
- <operation name="GetTemperature">
<http:operation location="/GetTemperature" />
- <input>
<http:urlEncoded />
</input>
- <output>
<mime:mimeXml part="Body" />
</output>
</operation>
- <operation name="GetWeather">
<http:operation location="/GetWeather" />
- <input>
<http:urlEncoded />
</input>
```

continues

Listing 20.8 **Continued**

```
- <output>
<mime:mimeXml part="Body" />
</output>
</operation>
</binding>
- <binding name="WeatherRetrieverHttpPost"
type="s0:WeatherRetrieverHttpPost">
<http:binding verb="POST" />
- <operation name="GetTemperature">
<http:operation location="/GetTemperature" />
- <input>
<mime:content type="application/x-www-form-urlencoded" />
</input>
- <output>
<mime:mimeXml part="Body" />
</output>
</operation>
- <operation name="GetWeather">
<http:operation location="/GetWeather" />
- <input>
<mime:content type="application/x-www-form-urlencoded" />
</input>
- <output>
<mime:mimeXml part="Body" />
</output>
</operation>
</binding>
- <service name="WeatherRetriever">
- <port name="WeatherRetrieverSoap" binding="s0:WeatherRetrieverSoap">
<soap:address location="http://www.vbws.com/services/
weatherretriever.asmx"/></port>

- <port name="WeatherRetrieverHttpGet" binding="s0:WeatherRetrieverHttpGet">
<http:address location="http://www.vbws.com/services/
weatherretriever.asmx"/></port>
- <port name="WeatherRetrieverHttpPost"
binding="s0:WeatherRetrieverHttpPost">
<http:address location="http://www.vbws.com/services/
weatherretriever.asmx"/>
</port>
</service>
</definitions>
```

You can see from the following lines that we should have no problem consuming this service from ColdFusion.

```
- <binding name="WeatherRetrieverSoap" type="s0:WeatherRetrieverSoap">
  <soap:binding transport="http://schemas.xmlsoap.org/soap/http"
  ➥style="rpc"/>
  <soap:body use="encoded" namespace="http://tempuri.org/"
  ➥encodingStyle="http://schemas.xmlsoap.org/soap/encoding/" />
```

Listing 20.9 shows a ColdFusion page that acts as a client to this web service. Figure 20.4 shows the result of retrieving current weather conditions.

Listing 20.9 **A ColdFusion MX Client to the VBWS Weather Web Service**

```
<!--- /babelfishclient.cfm
created 4/25/02 by Jeff Tapper
Remotesite Technologies
Jeff.tapper@remotesite.com

Change History:

Usage:
A web service client that leverages the vbws weather service
--->


<cfoutput><form action="http://#cgi.server_name#:#cgi.SERVER_PORT#/
#cgi.script_name#?#cgi.query_string#" method="post"></cfoutput>
<table>
<tr>
<td colspan="2">Enter a zipcode below to retrieve the current weather.
</td></tr>
<tr><td>Zipcode</td><td><input type="text" name="zipcode"></td></tr>
<td colspan="2"><input type="submit" name="submit" value="Get Weather">
</td></tr>
</table>
</form>
<cfif isDefined("form.submit")>
 <cfinvoke webservice="http://www.vbws.com/services/
weatherretriever.asmx?WSDL" method="GetWeather" returnVariable="stWeather"
zipcode="#form.zipcode#"/>

      <cfoutput>
      <h1>Current Weather For #form.zipcode#</h1>
      <table cellspacing="2" cellpadding="2" border="0">
      <tr>
          <td>Last Updated</td>
          <td>#stWeather.LastUpdated#</td>
      </tr>
      <tr>
          <td>Current Temp</td>
          <td>#stWeather.CurrentTemp#</td>
      </tr>
      <tr>
          <td>Current Conditions</td>
          <td>#stWeather.Conditions#</td>
      </tr>
      <tr>
          <td colspan="2"><image src="#stWeather.IconUrl#"></td>
      </tr>
```

continues

Listing 20.9 **Continued**

```
        <tr>
            <td>Barometer</td>
            <td>#stWeather.Barometer#</td>
        </tr>
        <tr>
            <td>Barometer is</td>
            <td>#stWeather.BarometerDirection#</td>
        </tr>
        <tr>
            <td>Humidity</td>
            <td>#stWeather.Humidity#</td>
        </tr>

        </table>
        </cfoutput>
</cfif>
```

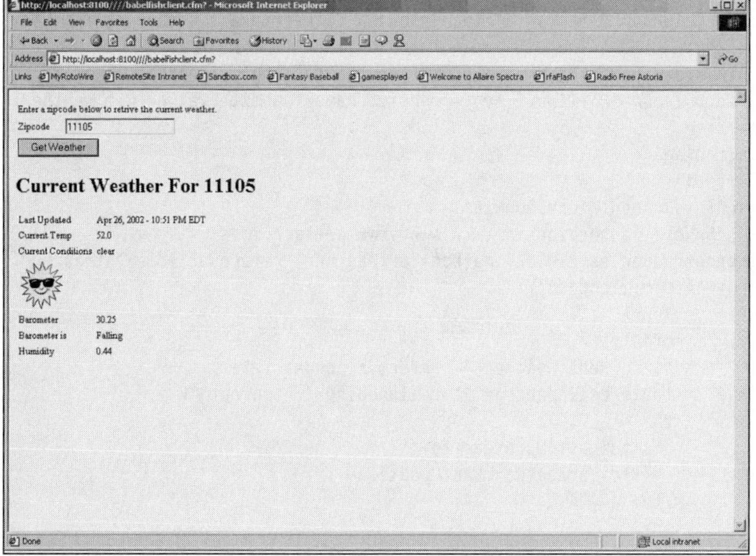

Figure 20.4 The Weather Web Service tells us the skies are clear over Astoria.

Tip

xMethods is a valuable resource for published Web Services that is available to the public and written in a variety of languages. It can be found at `http://www.xmethods.com`.

Conclusion

As you can see, Web Services promise to revolutionize how web applications are architected and constructed. No longer will it be necessary to rebuild core application logic, which can be leveraged from elsewhere, simply because it hasn't been written for ColdFusion.

Incorporating external Web Services into our applications can now be done as seamlessly as adding a custom tag from the Macromedia Developers Exchange.

Additionally, logic we write can be shared with the world, such as the ever-useful ArrayReverse web service we created earlier this chapter. Now everyone can benefit from this much sought-after functionality.

21

Designing a Publishing Engine

by Robin Hilliard and Benjamin Elmore

A KEY THEME IN DYNAMIC PUBLISHING IS the separation of content and presentation information. At the business level, we all know from hard experience that a lot of time can be wasted re-creating content for multiple presentation types. At the code level, we are used to the unmanageable proliferation of HTML documents and the menial task of *content pushing*, which is manually reformatting the same content multiple times to fit a particular situation. With a dynamic publishing solution, we save time and improve control if we can create, approve, and store our content in a presentation-neutral format. Storing it this way in a central repository allows the publishing system to repurpose each piece of content for each presentation type, be it a web page, email message, or Flash PDA application.

Chapter 9, "Centralized Data Persistence," described the application programming interface (API) for our content repository, which allows us to access content homogenously in an arbitrary storage mechanism if we have the appropriate Persistor and PersistentType components. The Persistor component manages the storage type-specific processing, such as how to load or save content in an XML document or search for database records using SQL. The PersistentType component is extended for each class of content to represent an instance of that content (such as a news article, FAQ, or product) after it is retrieved.

We will go on to describe how developers present content in various technologies in Chapter 22, "Assembling a Dynamic Application," but in this chapter, we'll concern ourselves with the needs of these developers when they go to retrieve content for their applications. Accessing content in a presentation-neutral format needs to be a simple task for these reasons:

- Although moving to a dynamic publishing solution greatly reduces the size of your code base, the vast bulk of the remaining code is going to be concerned with retrieving content for presentation. Any improvements in efficiency we can make to the creation of this code will have a relatively significant effect on the project's bottom line.
- The clear separation of presentation logic from the rest of our code is an opportunity to assign our less skilled developers (who might be brilliant designers) to the presentation logic. Their main point of contact with the rest of the system will be when they request content, so it would be best to minimize the learning curve with easy code syntax and strong integrated development environment (IDE) support (such as server behaviors or code snippets in Dreamweaver MX).

It's important to support developers in this task, and that is why an entire layer of our publishing architecture is tasked with facilitating the retrieval of content. The name of this layer is the Publishing Engine (PE). In terms of the success of our architecture, the introduction of the PE is key. Consider that although the separation of content from presentation with the introduction of the Persistence layer is beneficial in terms of content reuse, it is inconvenient for developers who are used to accessing their data directly, who now must access data indirectly through the persistence API. For developers to willingly give up their existing habits, the PE has to provide an attractive API as good or better than the traditional direct content access methods. Refer to Figure 21.1 to see how the PE is responsible for assisting Management and Presentation layer code in retrieving content from the Persistence layer.

In this chapter, we will talk about the requirements of the PE users as they request content. With this in mind, we can discuss the various issues we encounter when we try to build a PE in ColdFusion MX, illustrating with examples from a PE built for the DuvalShock web site.

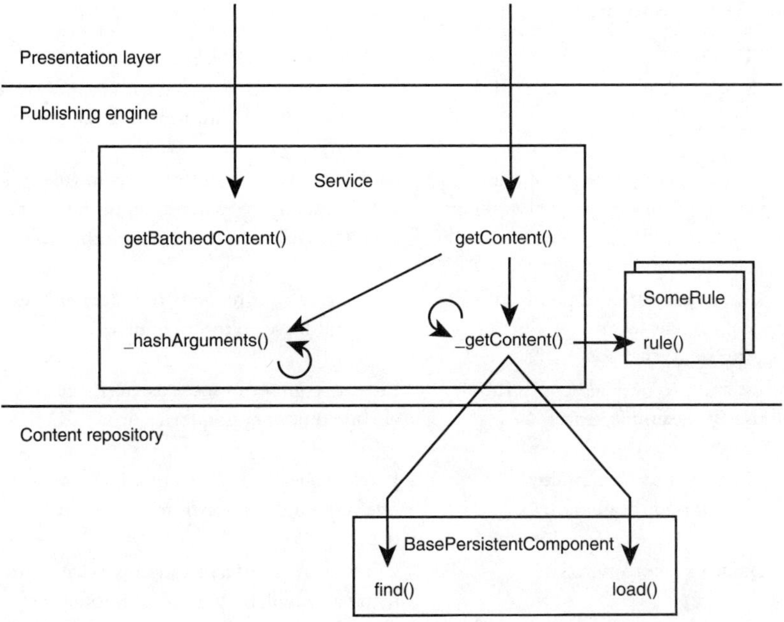

Figure 21.1 A high-level overview of the publishing architecture.

Publishing System Requirements

To start, let's put on our presentation developer hat and make a shopping list of desirable content-retrieval features. To assist us, we can draw a useful analogy with shopping. The content repository API as it stands is equivalent to a warehouse with stacks of product cartons at some remote location. All the content is there, but you have to unpack the boxes yourself, the parking is terrible, and the risk of being hit by a forklift is high. Table 21.1 spells out some of the things the retail industry has done to improve the situation for consumers and vendors.

Table 21.1 **Comparison of Shopping in a Market to Retrieving Content**

Shopping	Retrieving Content
Supermarkets: A one-stop shop for all your shopping needs, whether the products originated on a farm or in a factory. Consistent procedures (that is, checkout). Economies of scale for supermarket owner.	Single service for content retrieval, regardless of original content type and location. Optimal code reuse.

continues

Table 21.1 **Continued**

Shopping	Retrieving Content
Goods organized by category/aisles to make locating them easier.	Search mechanisms (categorization, SQL, full-text index, and so on) to locate the required content.
Standing shopping list: Create a list once and reuse at each shop, tweaking details as required. Can combine or compare with other shopping lists.	Save common content requests in rules that can accept parameters when used in different situations. Allow rules to reuse other rules.
Stock large quantities of goods in close convenient location, reducing shopping time.	Cache results of requests to reduce processing time and increase throughput.
Process and pre-package goods to suit end use (for example, frozen stir-fry vegetables).	Provide content in most useful format to the client: components, queries, arrays, XML, or WDDX.
Shopping carts to hold multiple products on one shopping trip.	Batch requests to return multiple results from one request. Less overhead compared to multiple trips.
Checkout to record purchases.	Content owners want to know what content is being accessed, by whom, and how often.
Security guards, video surveillance, securable premises.	Content owners control who and under what conditions a person has access to the content.

Requesting the Content

Let's explore these in more detail.

A single, consistent way to retrieve content is desirable, from both a training and a code maintainability standpoint. In ColdFusion terms, a clear interface for content requests could be provided as a custom tag or function. When we consider that the code calling the PE API might not be implemented in ColdFusion, the advantage of a component function with remote access via Flash Remoting and web services becomes obvious. The request for content would include the following:

- Information on the general type of content we want to retrieve
- Criteria to narrow the selection, in whatever search grammar is appropriate to the content type
- Options regarding the format of the results

This list is a good starting point. There will be further request arguments related to other requirements, but we can add these as we discuss them.

Specifying Content Search Criteria

The capability to search for the content we want is fundamental. We can search for content in many different ways, each applicable to a particular storage type. If we were searching content in a relational database, we would want full access to the SQL features that database supported. If the database tables had been full-text indexed in Verity, we would want to be able to use Verity search terms, such as *near*, in our search criteria. Because much of the content we access will be categorized, we also want to use the basePersistentComponent `findByMetadata()` function described in Chapter 12, "Categorization of Content." This menagerie of search languages might pose a threat to the simplicity of our search interface except for the useful fact that almost all are expressible as a sequence of commands that we can pass in a string argument. For the remaining search methods, the ability to pass a parameter structure should be sufficient.

Reuse with Publishing Rules

Although some users demand access to the full set of search features that are available, the PE also should provide a way to abstract the details of complex search criteria into a publishing rule. Rules are not used just to hide the details of content searches from our more junior developers; more importantly, rules allow the effort that went into developing the search to be reused. This is not a new idea. Developers who work with relational databases are familiar with the benefits of stored procedures, functions that encapsulate SQL commands into a neat package to be called from database clients. The PE will bring the benefits of stored procedure-like encapsulation not only to relational database content stores (in a vendor-neutral way) but also to any searchable content store type.

PE callers must be able to define rules once and then invoke them repeatedly to return content. Rules are defined either programmatically or by a user using a rule creation UI in the Management layer. When a rule is defined, we might want to specify parts of the search criteria to be substituted with parameters passed at the time the rule is invoked. Imagine a rule that returns all the articles created in a given month. We could create one rule for every month, or we could create a `getArticlesForMonth(month, year)` rule. The second option is more useful.

It also is beneficial if rules can be defined in terms of other rules to increase reuse. Given the preceding rule, we can create a `getArticlesForMonthAndCategory(month, category)` rule to retrieve news articles from a specified month and category, reusing the original rule.

Just as power users want full access to search languages, they also at times want full access to the power of the ColdFusion language. Ideally, the PE can be extended easily by creating rules as ColdFusion functions, which can then be used interchangeably with other rules as necessary. An example of a programmatic rule might be `currentMonth()` or `currentYear()`, either of which would be useful in conjunction with the other rules described so far. For example, we could write `getArticlesForMonthAndCategory(currentMonth(), category)`.

Performance

Performance requirements often are not articulated clearly for Internet projects. A useful way to put performance requirements is as follows:

```
x% of requests handled in < y milliseconds when there are z concurrent user
➥sessions
```

Typical values for a web site might be 99, 2000, and 200; that is, 1 in 100 requests takes longer than 2 seconds when 200 users are refreshing pages on average every 15 seconds. (This is an industry rule-of-thumb for the rate of requests in a normal user session.) The average processing time of your ColdFusion scripts is related directly (by queuing theory) to your ability to meet such a requirement.

Figure 21.2 shows that to deliver the required response to 200 users, the average request-processing time needs to be around 65ms. The shocking point to note is that if this time increases slightly to 110ms, the number of users you can deliver the same response level to will be cut in half—until you spend a lot of money on a second server.

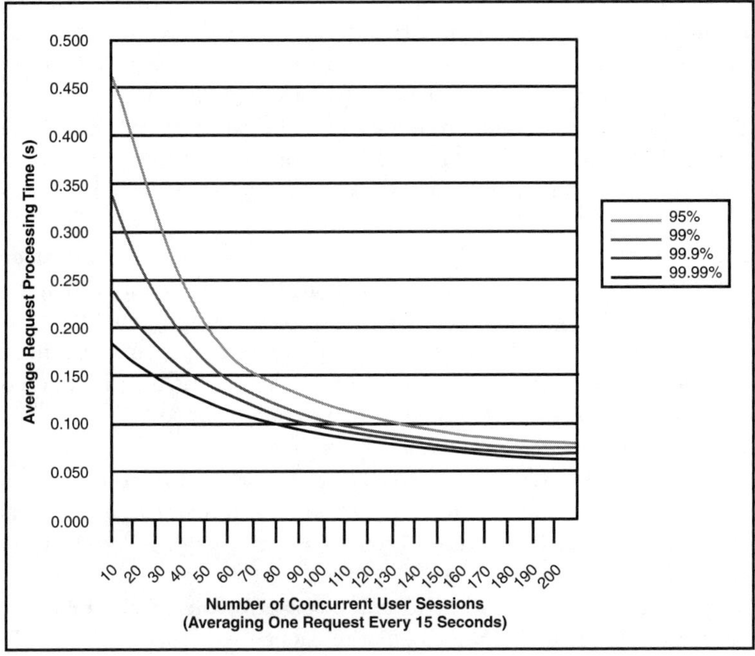

Figure 21.2 Average request processing time required for x percent of requests to be serviced in less than 2 seconds.

This serves to illustrate why performance is so critical to users of the PE, and why they are normally prepared to trade off currency of data for performance gains, which will be the case if the PE caches its results. That said, however, users will want full control of the caching behavior, including the ability to flush the cache and set the cache timeout.

Delivering the Content

Assuming that we have successfully selected the content we require, we must consider the final format that we use to return the results to the client. On a particular client platform, some formats are preferred, whereas others are useless or have no meaning.

To take Flash MX as an example, queries are the preferred result format for the following reasons:

- The Flash MX UI Components support data-aware connections to query resultsets, automating the population of List and ComboBox controls with query result information and greatly speeding development time.
- Flash Remoting supports on-demand loading of query resultsets, so that only the visible rows of a list box or other data-aware components need to be downloaded from the server, and further rows are downloaded as the contents are scrolled.

Sometimes another result format, such as an array of structures or even an XML string, might be more useful to the Flash application than a query. At the opposite end of the usefulness spectrum, an array of ColdFusion Component instances is meaningless to a Flash application.

Table 21.2 summarizes the potential callers of the PE and the content formats they can request.

Table 21.2 **PE Clients and Result Formats**

	Client			
	ColdFusion	**Flash**	**Web Service**	**HTTP Request**
Format				
Array of component instances	P	-	-	-
Array of structures	O	O	P	-
Query	O	P	O	-
XML	O	O	O	O
WDDX	O	O	O	O

P = Preferred, O = Optional

Because all clients can accept more than one format, the client must specify in which format the PE should return the results.

Batch Requests

In some cases, the client needs to make a series of content requests all at once, perhaps because the request came over a message-based transport or because it's the daily update of the content they've subscribed to. It might be a Flash application that normally works offline using local shared objects to store data but then takes advantage of a server connection when it's available to update local information. To assist these clients, the PE should support the batching of requests and responses into a single, multipart request/response transaction.

Content Provider Requirements

We need to consider the needs of the content owners, who are the ones paying for the development and operation of the whole dynamic publishing system.

We often neglect the opportunity to increase the amount of business intelligence gathered with the introduction of a dynamic publishing system. When a bricks and mortar company shows little interest in the number of people in their shop, where and how long customers browse, and what customers are buying, you would probably call it a reckless disregard for the health of their business. Somehow, this perspective has yet to make the transition to the Internet industry as a whole, but those who do take advantage of this information are finding it far richer than that available from a real-world shop, regardless of the number of video cameras, customer survey forms, and radio tracking tags used.

Every time a user requests content, we should log information about the request and result. To decide what information to log, we need to consider the uses that the information will be put to later on. The primarily use of this information will be to populate business intelligence reports. Table 21.3 lists some common report types and identifies the request information that we will need to record to generate them.

Table 21.3 **Request Information Used in Business Intelligence Reports**

	Request Information							
Reporting Use	**Time-stamp**	**Client Identity**	**Content Source**	**Rule/ Parameters**	**Categories**	**Object Ids**	**From Cache?**	**Request Time**
Requests by Object						•		
Requests by Category					•	•		
Requests by Rule				•				
Requests Over Time	•	•	•	•	•	•	•	•
Capacity Planning	•		•	•			•	•

	Request Information							
	Time-stamp	Client Identity	Content Source	Rule/ Parameters	Categories	Object Ids	From Cache?	Request Time
Reporting Use								
Adaptive Caching	•			•			•	•
Client Subscription Charges	•	•		•	•	•		

The Management layer is responsible for creating reports based on the collected information.

Protecting the Content

It's important to protect premium or secure content from unauthorized access, which means that you must have authentication and authorization mechanisms in place when content is requested. Chapter 16, "Securing the Application and User Management," covers these topics in detail, but we will look briefly at the way authorization is applied to a content request.

When a client is authorized to access content, there are three ways to describe the content thus accessed:

- Specify a type of content—for example, news article—that the client can access. All resultsets returned to the client are filtered to eliminate other content types.
- Specify a rule that can be called.
- Tag individual content objects with a list of roles required to view them.

Building a Publishing Engine

In this section, we will build a PE for the DuvalShock web site. The publishing requirements implied by the description of the web site interface in earlier chapters are relatively simple, but that's not to say that as the site grows, the publishing requirements will not increase in scope and complexity. To allow the web site to grow (and for purposes of illustration), we will use all the PE requirements discussed in this chapter to drive our design. DuvalShock will have a PE to be proud of!

Design Approach

With what we know of the PE requirements, it's time to put a few stakes in the ground around a ColdFusion MX solution. To begin, how will the PE be deployed? In the requirements, we have already decided that a component is the ideal solution because it is available to so many types of client. Component functions can be called from ColdFusion, Flash, web service clients, and HTTP clients using `GET`/`POST` methods. Following the lead of the other layers, we'll locate this component under the web root at /components/publishing/service.cfc.

The main function of this component is to facilitate obtaining content for our callers, so let's add a remotely accessible `getContent()` function to our component. The function will take arguments to specify the content to retrieve and return the content in one of the formats listed in Table 21.2.

As we discuss further aspects of the PE implementation, we will build on and modify this design. We will review the completed design again at the end of the chapter.

Specifying Search Criteria

At a minimum, we know that our callers want full access to the search methods that the Persistence layer provides, so we should look to the `basePersistentComponent.find()` function for guidance. This function takes `dataStoreType`, `dataSource`, and `criteria` arguments. We can add these arguments directly to our `getContent()` function, but to reduce the number of separate arguments that our callers have to type when they invoke the function, we will combine the first two into a neater URI-like source argument with the syntax `"dataStoreType:dataSource"`. An example of this (referring to the Persistence layer description) might be `"dbPersistor:myData"`, which is readable and quick to type.

The `criteria` argument contains the search string in a format that the data store type supports, such as SQL or XPath (a standard for specifying nodes in an XML document, supported in ColdFusion MX). The default behavior of `getContent()` will be to pass this argument straight through to the Persistence component.

So far, the PE isn't doing much work for us, but in this case, the best help we can give our caller is to get out of the way.

Maximizing Reuse with Rules

The PE needs to give its callers a way to reuse searches as parameterized rules. The caller normally creates the rules through the publishing API (the caller might be a Management layer UI that end users use to create rules), but we also allow calls to rules created in CFML. The last requirement was to provide a way for rules to call other rules. We need to address three issues here:

- How we define and interpret rules
- Where we keep rules
- How callers invoke rules

A rule takes in some parameters and returns some content, much like a call to our `getContent()` function. In fact, we can think of a rule as a set of arguments passed to `getContent()`—a source and some search criteria. If we can save these arguments under a rule name, then every time we ask for that rule, we can just load and pass the set of arguments to `getContent()`. Many pieces of application code will be able to share a single rule, leveraging the effort that went into creating the rule and isolating the code from underlying changes to the content repository. We can accommodate a change to a content type name or property by updating a single rule rather than chasing up and modifying a wide diaspora of search logic throughout the application.

How about passing parameters to the rule? For the time being, we'll just consider the rules created by the user via the API, not the ones written in CFML. These rules will have a criteria argument saved as a string. Let's allow the criteria argument to be parameterized, so that if the criteria contains the string `"$myParameter$"`, we substitute the value of the parameter `"myParameter"`, passed when the rule is called. The code in Listing 21.1 makes the substitution for us:

Listing 21.1 **A Simple Replace Function Serves as the Backbone for Dynamic Rules**

```
for (param in arguments.stParams) {
      arguments.criteria = ReplaceNoCase(arguments.criteria,
      "$" & param & "$",
      arguments.stParams[param],
      "ALL");
}
```

Now we can write criteria, such as "select * from Products where price < \$maxPrice\$", and pass a different maxPrice with each invocation of the rule.

To allow rules to use the results of other rules, we can take full advantage of the ColdFusion query of queries (QoQ) feature. Instead of passing SQL criteria through to the Persistence layer, we can execute the query in the PE by using the output of other rules as the source queries. To indicate that the caller wants this to happen, he sets the `getContent()` source argument to `"rule"`. To enable the user to indicate where each called rule's output will be used in the new rule, we can extend our parameter syntax so that `"$myRule(arg1=value1, arg2=value2)$"` represents a call to a rule named `"myRule"`, with arguments `arg1` and `arg2`.

If the rule returns a simple value such as a string or number, we insert the returned value into the criteria, replacing the rule invocation. If the rule returns a query, we copy the query to a local variable and insert the variable name into the criteria in a similar fashion. When we pass the criteria to `cfquery` to execute as a QoQ all the query variables the criteria refers to will be in place, and `cfquery` should return a new resultset, formed from a combination of the included rule's results. The code in Listing 21.2 implements this procedure.

Listing 21.2 **Code Block to Process Rules**

```
<cfscript>
   // Incremental suffix to append to created queries
   nextQuerySuffix = 0;
   // Criteria string to process
   criteriaIn = arguments.criteria;
```

continues

Listing 21.2 **Continued**

```
// Processed criteria string
criteriaOut = "";
// Error messages, comma delimited
lErrors = "";
// Keep processing the criteria string until there's none left
while (len(criteriaIn) gt 0) {
    // Break the criteria into chunks at the dollar signs
    chunk = listFirst(criteriaIn, "$");
    criteriaIn = listRest(criteriaIn, "$");
    // Does this chunk look like a rule, i.e. "name(...)"?
    stSubExpr = REFindNoCase("([_a-zA-Z0-9]+)\(([^)]*)\)",
    s, 1,true);
    if ((stSubExpr.len[1] eq len(Chunk)) and
    (arrayLen(stSubExpr.len) eq 3)) {
       // Yes, attempt to parse it. Subexpressions 2 & 3 should
       // contain rule name and parameter list, respectively
       ruleName = "rule:" & mid(chunk, stSubExpr.pos[2],
       stSubExpr.len[2]);
       lParams = mid(chunk, stSubExpr.pos[3], stSubExpr.len[3]);
       // build an arguments structure out of the parameter list
       stArgs = structNew();
       while(len(lParams) gt 0) {
          keyValuePair = listFirst(lParams);
          lParams = listRest(lParams);
          if (listLen(keyValuePair, "=") neq 2)
             lErrors = listAppend(lErrors,
             "'#keyValuePair#' is not a valid parameter name/value");
          else
             stArgs[trim(listFirst(keyValuePair, "="))] =
             trim(listLast(keyValuePair, "="));
       }
       // call the rule
       ruleResult = _getContent(source=ruleName,
       stParams=stArgs,
       returnFormat="query");
       if (isSimpleValue(ruleResult)) {
          // interpolate the result into the criteria string
             criteriaOut = criteriaOut & ruleResult;
       } else if (isQuery(ruleResult)) {
          // store the resultset in a variable, interpolate
          //variable name into criteria string
          queryName = "qRule" &
          incrementValue(nextQuerySuffix);
          setVariable(queryName, ruleResult);
          criteriaOut = criteriaOut & queryName;
       } else {
```

```
            lErrors = listAppend(lErrors,
            "'#ruleName#' did not return a query or simple value");
         }
      } else {
         // no, pass it through to criteriaOut.
         criteriaOut = criteriaOut & chunk;
      }
   }
</cfscript>
<cfif lErrors neq "">
   <!--- Throw errors raised during parsing --->
   <cfthrow message="components.publishing.service.getContent:
   One or more errors encountered while parsing criteria - #lErrors#">
<cfelse>
   <!---
   criteriaOut should contain a valid query of queries expression
   --->
   <cfquery name="result" dbtype="query">#criteriaOut#</cfquery>
</cfif>
```

The processing of rule calls occurs after parameters have been substituted, so parameters can be used in rule argument expressions. Together, parameter substitution and rule invocation give us simple yet powerful semantics for rule reuse. For example, if we had a rule to pick products starting with a particular letter of the alphabet, and another that did currency conversion, users of the PE API could create a third rule that picked products beginning with *k* for less than 10 Australian dollars:

```
SELECT *
FROM $productsStartingWith(letter=k)$
WHERE price < $currencyConvert(from=US,to=AU,amount=10)$
```

Figure 21.3 shows how this criteria expression is parsed by the code in Listing 21.2.

How should the rules be stored? Let's start with the programmatic rules that a programmer creates in CFML to extend the PE for its users. A programmer can do this in quite a few ways, such as using custom tags, but the key point is that the PE can locate and call the rules easily when required. In this implementation, each rule is a component in a Rules subdirectory next to our service.cfc. The component is called *ruleName*.cfc, and it includes one public function called `rule()`.

As stated previously, user-created rules are named backups of a set of arguments submitted to `getContent()`. To save a rule, a user passes a rule name in the saveAsRule argument of `getContent()`. `getContent()` serializes its arguments structure into a `wddx` string, allowing it to be saved in a file under rules/ruleName.wddx. This is easily done using the code in listing 21.3.

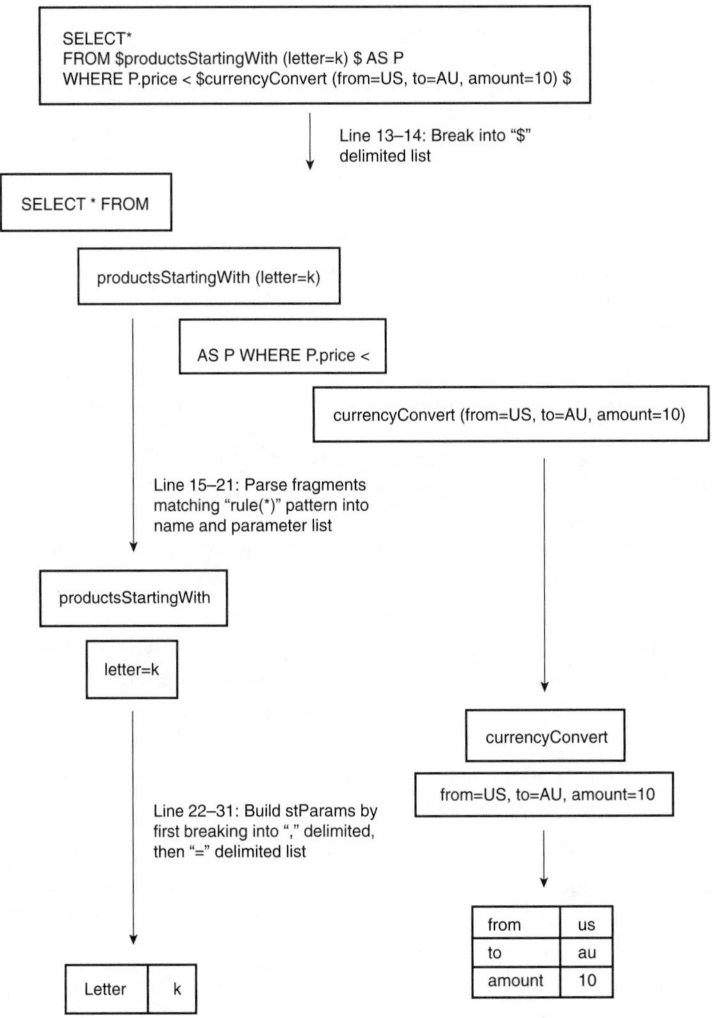

Figure 21.3 Example of parsing rule criteria.

Listing 21.3 Saving Rule Parameters as a WDDX Packet

```
<cfif arguments.saveAsRule neq "">
   <cfwddx action="cfml2wddx"
      input=#arguments#
      output="wArguments">
   <cffile action="write"
      output=#wArguments#
      file=#ExpandPath("/rules/" & arguments.saveAsRule & ".wddx")#
      nameconflict="overwrite">
</cfif>
```

This saveAsRule option is a sort of "query-by-example" feature. Of course, we could create a separate function for creating rules if required. Note also that we could have used the Persistence layer to save the rule in a rule repository, but cfwddx is nice and compact for the purposes of this example. Note that in this approach with all the rules in one place, it becomes a simple matter to list the available rules using a tag such as `<CFDIRECTORY>`. We will leave the implementation of this `listRules()` method to you.

We now need to give users of the PE a way to invoke an existing rule. To do this, the caller passes `"rule:`*`ruleName`*`"` as the source argument to `getContent()`, and passes the rule parameters as a key-value structure in `stParams`. The function checks in the Rules directory to locate a user-defined or programmatic rule that matches the rule name.

If the rule is user defined, we reverse the rule-saving process to get the original `getContent()` arguments back, and we override the saved rule parameters with any parameters that were passed to us. We then can invoke `getContent()` again with our argument structure. If the rule is programmatic, we attempt to call the rule function in the rule component that matches the rule name. Note that you don't need to modify the `getContent()` function to add a new programmatic rule. In this way, the rules are loosely coupled to the publishing service.

Because `getContent()` calls itself to handle rule invocation, we run into an issue with the structure of our component. Several features, such as saveAsRule, security, caching, and auditing only need to be involved in the initial call from the user, and not in subsequent internal rule-processing calls. To fix this, we split `getContent()` into two functions: a public `getContent()` function that handles initial call processing and wraps a second, protected `_getContent()` function, handling the core parameter substitution and rule calling functionality. The `access` attribute of `_getContent()` is set to "protected" so that application code must use the public `getContent()` method, and programmatic rules in the Rules subdirectory can invoke `_getContent()`.

Figure 21.4 provides an example of publishing rules in action. When the user calls `getContent()` to invoke the `"productsStartingWithKUnder10AUD"` rule, `getContent()` handles attribute validation, caching, and logging and passes its arguments through to the private `_getContent()` function. `_getContent()` parses the rule criteria and identifies two rules to be run before it can evaluate its own result. For each of these rules, `_getContent()` extracts the parameters and recursively invokes itself to evaluate the rule's results.

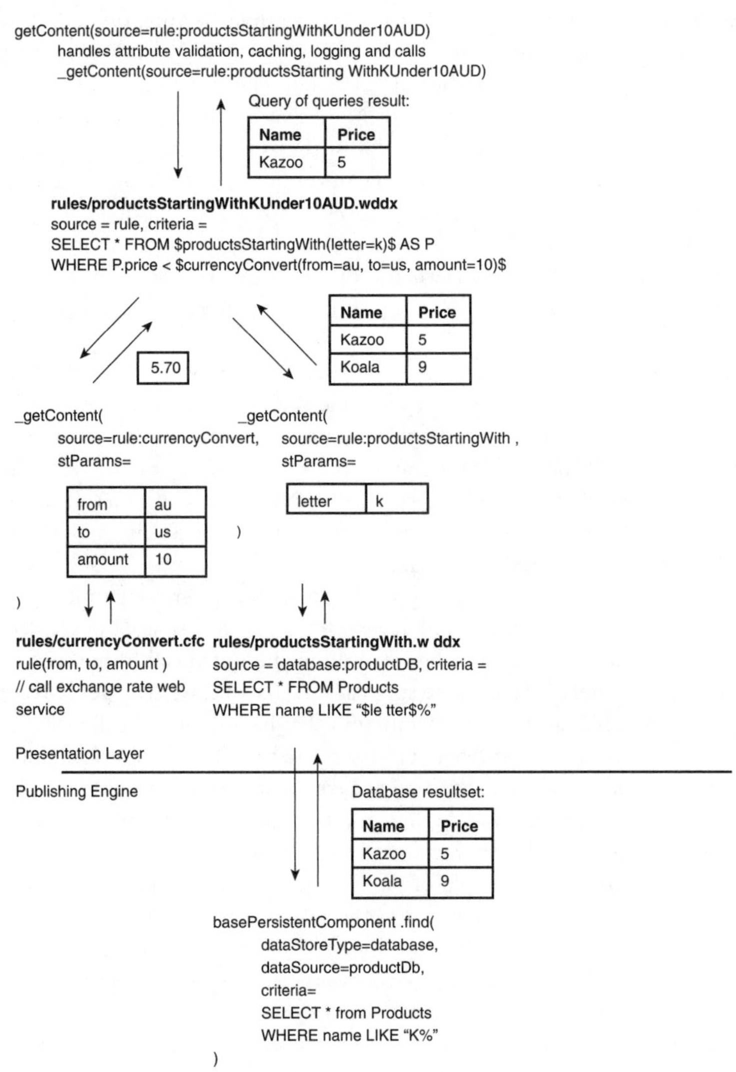

Figure 21.4 Publishing rules in action.

The first rule is programmatic, and `_getContent()` invokes the corresponding component's `rule()` method. The second rule is a database query, and after substituting the `"letter"` parameter, `_getContent()` calls `basePersistentComponent.find()` to return the resultset. The results of these two rules are combined using QoQ to evaluate the original rule's criteria with the results of the two subrules substituted for the rule calls.

Formatting Results

To support the QoQ used to implement nested rules, we have worked with our content in query form. After we have the final resultset in query form, translating it into the format that the caller requires is straightforward. This format is specified in the `returnFormat` argument of `getContent()`.

Conversions to arrays of component instances are carried out with the assistance of the `basePersistentComponent.load()` function. Conversions to arrays of structures and wddx are easy in CFML. A conversion to XML would be just as easy after a DTD was decided upon using standard cfoutput with a `query` attribute. Although formatting adds some overhead to PE processing, it does reduce overhead and complexity in the application code calling the PE. In many cases, the results cannot be sent to the caller without some sort of conversion (see Table 21.2).

Caching for Performance

The PE is a bottleneck in the supply of content to the Client layer, but we can turn this to our advantage when it comes to performance. Because all content requests come to us, the PE is the perfect place to cache results from previous requests for the same content, more than offsetting the overhead incurred by our rules, security, and other processing.

We need to address two issues when caching our `getContent()` results:

- Determine whether a new request is the same as a request we have already cached the results for
- Efficiently retrieve and save the results

To determine if two requests are the same, we need to compare every key and value in the argument structures for equivalence. We could store a copy of the argument structure in each cache and perform a linear search through all the caches looking for a match, but with thousands of cached results, this would be so inefficient that the whole point of caching would be lost. In our PE, we solve this issue by building a hash key of the values in our argument structure with a private component function, `_hashArguments()`. This function concatenates the values of all the structure values into a large string and then uses the ColdFusion `hash()` function to generate a 35-character string with a 1:1 correspondence (as far as we're concerned) to the original string (see Listing 21.4). This string is then used as the key for the cached results in our caching structure. When we're searching for a match, we simply hash the arguments passed to us using `_hashArguments()` and see if a matching key exists in our caching structure. The `hash()` function is handy for indexing tasks such as this.

Listing 21.4 **Function to Generate a Hash Key from a *getContent( )* Arguments Structure**

```
<cffunction name="_hashArguments"
   access="private"
   hint="Generate hash from function arguments structure"
   returntype="string">
   <cfargument name="stArgs"
      type="struct"
      required="true">
   <cfscript>
      concatArgs = "";
      for (key in argument.stArgs) {
         if (isSimpleValue(argument.stArgs[key]))
            concatArgs = concatArgs & argument.stArgs;
         else if (isStruct(argument.stArgs[key]))
            concatArgs = concatArgs &
           _hashArguments(argument.stArgs[key]);
      }
   </cfscript>
   <cfreturn hash(concatArgs)>
</cffunction>
```

If we have a matching key, we can use the existing results, skipping a great deal of processing and reducing request time as a result. Otherwise, we proceed as normal and copy the results to our cache structure for future retrieval. Finally, we allow the caller to force the contents of the cache to be regenerated if the `resetCache` argument is set to `true`. See Listing 21.5.

Listing 21.5 **Caching Results Returned by *getContent( )***

```
<cfset bSave = false>
<cfset cacheKey = _hashArguments(arguments)>
<cflock scope="APPLICATION" type="READONLY" timeout=1>
   <cfset bCacheExists = isdefined("application.PECache." & cacheKey)>
   <cfif bCacheExists>
      <cfset result = application.PECache[cacheKey]>
   </cfif>
</cflock>
<cfif bCacheExists>
   <cfif arguments.resetCache>
      <!--- If resetcache, clear existing cache contents --->
      <cflock scope="APPLICATION" type="EXCLUSIVE" timeout=1>
         <cfset void = structDelete(application.PECache, cacheKey)>
      </cflock>
      <cfset bSave = true>
   </cfif>
   <cfelse>
   <!--- Content not cached, need to save --->
   <cfset bSave = true>
</cfif>
```

```
<cfif bSave>
   <!---
   Need to actually get the content, pass our arguments
   through to private _getContent function
   --->
   <cftry>
      <cfinvoke method="_getContent"
         returnVariable="result"
         argumentcollection=#arguments#/>
      <cfcatch type="any">
         <cfset result = "components.publishing.service:
         ERROR - #cfcatch.message#">
         <cfset bSave = false>
      </cfcatch>
   </cftry>
   <!--- Update cache --->
   <cfif bSave>
      <cflock scope="APPLICATION" type="EXCLUSIVE" timeout=1>
         <cfif not isDefined("application.PECache")>
            <cfset application.PECache = structNew()>
         </cfif>
         <cfset application.PECache[cacheKey] = result>
      </cflock>
   </cfif>
</cfif>
```

In memory, caching of results can result in incredible performance gains. For those who are worried about memory requirements, remember that 52,428 5K caches can be stored in 256Mb. From a server configuration perspective, you need to be aware of the JVM heap size settings in the ColdFusion administrator and adjust them to suit the expected total cache size. As for limits on ColdFusion structures, I have seen (but do not recommend in daily practice) a ColdFusion structure with more than a million keys perform flawlessly.

The caching functionality provided is fairly basic, although it does at least follow locking best practices in dealing with the shared application scope. You could make several additions to this code:

- Add a timeout key to each entry in the caching structure, set by the user, or a fixed time interval after the content was originally cached. If the request occurs after the timeout, set `resetCache` to `true`.
- Add keys to the cache structure to record categorization keywords, objectIDs, and other information that will speed up the collection of reporting data.
- If running out of memory for caching is an issue (usually it isn't—memory is a lot cheaper than a second server), you can look at adaptive caching strategies; for example, only caching the most commonly requested content. One approach is to keep an index of most recent cache access times, and after the upper limit of caches is reached, delete the oldest cache when you add a new one.

- When a result is cached, we can use cfwddx and cffile to back up the cache to disk, using the hash as a filename. When looking for an existing cache, if we can't find the cache in the memory structure, we can check the disk for the cache file.

Some further caching ideas are described in Chapter 22.

Security

With many of us primarily being web developers, it is sometimes easy to forget that just because the PE doesn't have a UI doesn't mean that it's not an external system interface. Our component has to be concerned with securing our content from people who shouldn't get it. There are two parts to security:

- Authentication. (Are you really Robin?)
- Authorization. (Okay, so you're Robin. Here's what you're allowed to do here.)

Authentication happens right up front. There's nothing special about the PE in this regard, so refer to Chapter 16, "Securing the Application and User Management," for the details.

Adding authorization is a bit more involved. In the requirements, we listed three types of authorization that applied to the PE. We need to handle each one at a different point in `getContent`'s processing:

- Rule-based authorization can be checked during validation of the source attribute, before any content is retrieved from rules or the Persistence layer.
- Type and object-based authorization can be checked only after the resultset has been returned because the type and role details are contained in the results. Content for which the caller did not have the required privileges to view would be filtered out of the resultset. We must be careful to make sure that this authorization applied whether or not the results came from the cache.

Auditing/Reporting

As with caching, we can again turn the fact that the PE is a bottleneck in content access to our advantage. After the content has been retrieved from the Persistence layer and rules, and before it is returned to the client, we can log all the salient details for our business intelligence reports. The way the information is logged is driven by the data requirements of the reports to be generated.

Batch Processing

To support the batching of content requests, we added another public function to the PE component, allowing callers to aggregate multiple `getContent()` calls into a single call (see Listing 21.6).

Listing 21.6 **Function to Get Batched Content**

```
<cffunction name="getBatchedContent"
   access="remote"
   hint="Aggregate multiple calls to getContent into a single
   call"
   returntype="array">
   <cfargument name="aParams"
      type="array"
      required="true"
      hint="Array of structures, each one containing a set of
      parameters for getContent">
   <cfloop from=1 to=#arrayLen(arguments.aParams)# index="i">
      <cfinvoke method="getContent"
         returnVariable="arguments.aParams[#i#].result"
         argumentcollection=#arguments.aParams[i]#/>
   </cfloop>
   <cfreturn arguments.aParams>
</cffunction>
```

This function has many uses. You could use it to receive message-based requests (via email) or to generate subscription packages to upload to a remote FTP server.

Architecture Summary

Figure 21.5 shows a completed class diagram of the Service CFC that acts as our PE API. The API exposes two methods to callers: `getBatchedContent()` and `getContent()`. The remaining methods are private. For completeness, a sample programmatic rule `SomeRule` is included in the diagram. It reminds us that the service component depends on `SomeRule`, and other rule components like it to execute rules with a programmatic component.

Figure 21.6 summarizes the interactions of the PE Service CFC methods. Arrows indicate method calls, and curly arrows indicate recursive calls. From the diagram, we can see that API users can call `getBatchedContent()` or `getContent()`. `getContent()` calls `_hashArguments()` (which might call itself to hash nested structures) to get a cache key, and if the content needs to be generated, it calls the protected `_getContent()` method. `_getContent()` can call the following:

- Itself to evaluate nested rules
- Programmatic rules
- `find()` to retrieve content from the repository
- `load()` to convert a resultset into an array of component instances

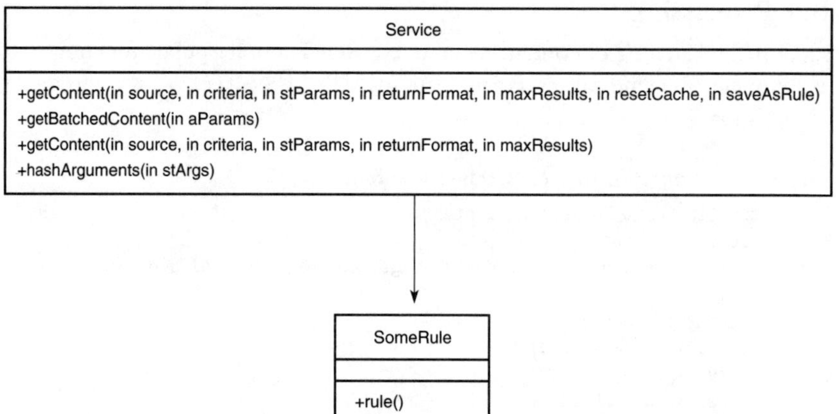

Figure 21.5 Class diagrams for Service and Rule.

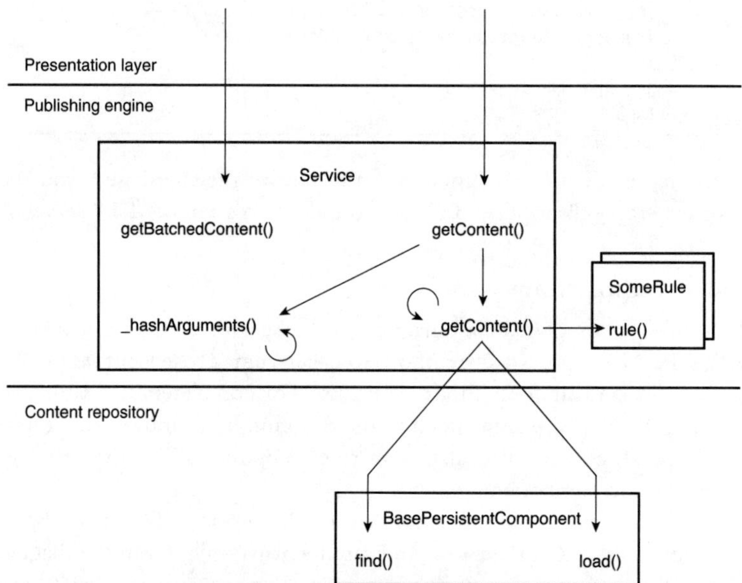

Figure 21.6 Interaction of publishing engine methods.

Conclusion

We started this chapter by discussing the needs of application developers when they retrieve content from the content repository, and why it is important for a dynamic publishing architecture to meet these needs as best as possible. We talked about how users specify and reuse search criteria, and the result formats they might request. We described performance requirements and a way to relate them to request processing times. Finally, we discussed the needs of the content providers—namely, content reporting and content security.

With these requirements in place, we began to build a PE API using ColdFusion components. Initially, `getContent()` passed its arguments to the content repository API largely untouched. With some string and list manipulation, we showed how we could implement a flexible publishing rule capability, bringing the advantages of stored procedure-like reuse and encapsulation to our architecture. We then briefly described how to convert resultsets into various formats, how to implement in-memory caching logic to speed performance, and how to add security and reporting capabilities to our service.

Building a PE is not a trivial task; using one is. If you build one once and use it many times, the net "triviality" of getting content into your application increases, leaving you more time to build non-trivial things, such as applications. This chapter should have provided you with the motivation and the means to implement and use a service like this in your next project.

22

Assembling a Dynamic Application

By Robin Hilliard and Benjamin Elmore

IN A NEW INDUSTRY, EACH COMPANY IMPLEMENTS an independent production process to produce its product. As the industry matures and gains experience, new support businesses offer outsourcing of common production processes at competitive rates, which are possible due to the economies of scale gained through their focus on a particular job. The whole industry benefits from the increases in efficiency and goes on to greater things (or so say the economists).

So far, our discussion of dynamic publishing (DP) has progressed along similar lines. Chapter by chapter, we have identified often-repeated tasks, abstracted the task away into a service, and discussed how such a service could be built. The requirements of each service were to generically simplify or completely hide the details of implementing the task for a developer at a higher architectural layer, closer to the action. Together, the sum effect of the services would be to maximize the efficiency of that developer, and, like our captains of industry, free them up to concentrate on greater things.

This chapter is different because we've now arrived at the scene of the action. Our requirements are no longer driven by the generic needs of friendly application developers building DP systems, but by the ruthlessly specific needs of clients. These needs usually start out along the lines of "everything yesterday for nothing," but rapidly progress into an entirely unique set of needs, constraints, and conundrums that only a skilled analyst can resolve.

That's where the application developer comes in. Software engineering has yet to devise a program that can investigate and understand a real-world problem, work out where a solution fits in, and assemble the solution. In case you have formed another impression while reading the preceding chapters, let us state this clearly. Unlike the developer of a reusable, generic service, the application developer's job is to devise *unique* solutions to unique business requirements, while making the most of the generic services and tools we've created to support them.

In terms of reuse, the application developer is primarily a "reuser." Creating new opportunities for reuse is still desirable, but the closer you get to specific business functionality and client platforms, the more realistic you have to get about the potential benefit of creating reusable code. Where will the code be reused? If the answer isn't immediately obvious, then the extra time invested in designing and developing reusable code is almost certainly wasted effort.

In this chapter, we will begin with a brief review of the new platforms we will be considering for interface development. Aware of the benefits and limitations of these platforms, we will consider some "field tools" that streamline development on these platforms before going on to discuss the process of application development.

Interface Platforms

When it comes to discussing application development, we finally have to leave the safe confines of the ColdFusion environment and consider the multiple platforms we create interfaces on to connect our application with the rest of the world. In this section, we briefly cover the platforms in common use today, along with their advantages and disadvantages.

Web Browser

Most dynamic Internet applications today interact with users via web browsers. Web browsers have the advantage of being more or less ubiquitously deployed across Internet-connected personal computers and devices, and the approachability of HTML has allowed millions of authors to easily publish static documents to a global audience. The web browser is still hard to beat for the display of large bodies of formatted text. However, developers who are using ColdFusion and other technologies to build web applications encounter the limitations of HTML and HTTP every working day. These limitations stem from the document-oriented origins of the web, and include the following:

- **Stateless nature**—Session state must be maintained artificially by an application server using cookies, which can be turned off.

- **Very thin client**—This client is a bit too thin for the demands of interactive web applications. Belated attempts to add client-side interactivity have only half succeeded, with inconsistent support for DHTML and JavaScript on different browsers and browser versions posing a constant headache for designers and developers.
- **Round trip to server**—Because of this "thinness," users have to rely on a round trip to the server for interactivity, incurring significant bandwidth, processing time, and usability penalties.
- **Requests originating with the browser**—There is no bidirectional connection. That is to say, there is no way for the server to request a response from a browser. The only way to simulate this is the awful "Are we there yet?" technique, in which the browser polls the server at short intervals with a page refresh.
- **Reliance on plug-ins for rich media, and little integration with client-side scripting**—Video, audio and other rich media content is displayed using a variety of third-party plug-ins such as the Real Media and Macromedia Flash players. The problem isn't so much that these players aren't available, but more that the integration with DHTML code through the `<OBJECT>` and `<EMBED>` tags is complex, inconsistent across browsers, and limited.

For the time being, end users and developers have come to accept these limitations, but PC desktop applications are a constant reminder to users that the web is really a step backward in terms of usability. For the Internet to truly make a transition from browsing to doing an alternative, technology is needed.

Flash Player

The Flash player is the most widely distributed software in Internet history. At the time of writing, more than 93 percent of Internet-connected devices have a version of the Flash Player installed. Starting as a vector animation tool, Flash quickly established itself on the Internet, helped particularly by the player's small download size. Macromedia has rapidly developed the player and authoring environment to the point at which the Flash 6 Player (supported by the Flash MX authoring environment) has become a viable platform for interactive, rich Internet applications, delivering on the promises of applets and DHTML. The strengths of client application development in Flash MX include these:

- Ubiquitous deployment, available on Windows, Mac, Pocket PCs, mobile phones, game consoles, and other devices. The Flash 6 Player is the only third-party software distributed with Windows XP.

- Low bandwidth. Flash got a bad name for a while as bulky "skip intro" movies took over the web. However, many companies today are finding massive savings in bandwidth and server CPU time by using Flash appropriately. Whereas a web page needs to be regenerated and downloaded each time interactivity is required, Flash downloads the application once and subsequently only requires data to be transmitted to and from the server. Unlike a web page, Flash can start responding to user requests while other parts of the application finish downloading. Responsive, connected Flash applications are completely viable even on a 28K dial-up modem.
- ActionScript, a powerful ECMAscript (European Computer Manufacturer's Association JavaScript standard used worldwide)-based object-oriented scripting language with access to all elements of a Flash application. It's a DHTML coder's dream.
- Flash Components, an object-oriented, open, extensible component technology allowing reuse of Flash code. A library of standard UI Components is included for reduced development time and consistent user interfaces, and new Macromedia and third-party components are becoming available at the time of writing.
- Flash Remoting, an optimized, easy-to-use connection to ColdFusion, JRun, WebSphere, and .NET Components, including full debugging support in the Flash authoring environment. Flash Remoting uses a compressed Action Message Format (AMF) schema to transmit request/response data over the normal HTTP protocol, so you can secure it using HTTPS if required.
- Unprecedented support for simple real-time sharing of data, audio, and video streams using the new Flash Communications Server (FCS) product. FCS facilitates the easy creation of chat, video conferencing, online games, auctions, booking systems, and many new applications that rely on shared, real-time data. Flash applications can subscribe to shared variable scopes and media streams on an FCS server using a new component library and API. On the server, FCS applications are written in ActionScript, accessing a new server API. Applications can call functions running on connected Flash Players or components on other servers using Flash Remoting. They also can control user connections and interact with the same variable scopes and streams seen by connected clients. FCS uses its own protocol that normally runs on port 1935.

Like the web browser, Flash's main application development constraints reflect its origins, this time as an animation tool. Developers who are familiar with event-based UI programming in other technologies can take a while to get used to working with the Flash timeline and frame-based animation concepts. Similarly, Flash's asynchronous style of calling server functionality takes some adjustment for those who are used to function calls that block code execution until results are returned (a concept that is alien to a real-time animation tool needing to get to the next frame on time). On the whole though, Flash offers an exciting alternative or addition to the traditional browser-based Internet application. For more information about developing applications in Flash MX, see `http://www.macromedia.com/desdev/mx/flash/`, or subscribe to the popular Flash coders list hosted by Figleaf Software (`flashcoders-subscribe@chattyfig.figleaf.com`).

Web Services

Web Services are an exciting capability for Internet application developers. For the first time, a wide community of platform vendors has agreed on a standard remote procedure call (RPC) protocol that is relatively easy to use compared to earlier attempts. Until ColdFusion MX however, web services have not been what you might call compellingly easy to create and use.

You can consume web services on a wide variety of platforms, including .NET and Java. They support content and application syndication business models by providing parameter/return value semantics and structured data to external applications over the Simple Object Access Protocol (SOAP)/HTTP protocol.

The limitations of web services are that there are still variations between vendor implementations of SOAP. For instance, .NET doesn't recognize query information that is created on some platforms (including ColdFusion MX), although it has no problems with arrays of structures. SOAP is also a verbose protocol. If high performance is important and you have alternative connection options available (Flash Remoting, direct Java call, COM, CORBA, or custom HTTP format), you might need to use them instead.

Batch and Messaging

An often-overlooked component of an application's external interface, batch- and message-based interfaces have a lot to offer application designers. Consider that in transactions using an online protocol such as SOAP or HTTP, both applications need to be ready to participate in the transaction. If the receiving system is down due to failure or a scheduled outage, the sending system will be unable to continue normal operations. If the sender didn't actually need to immediately know the result of the transaction to continue, the outage of the receiving system would have unnecessarily impacted the sending system. In architecture terms, we would call the caller and sender *tightly coupled*. From an IT operations perspective, this is bad news. Such systems are fragile and constantly run the risk of a single point of failure bringing about a Death-Star-like wider system collapse.

In a batch- or message-based approach, the sender passes the transaction data to a reliable third-party infrastructure that is capable of storing the data until the receiver is available. A perfect example of this is the Internet's most successful and compelling application—email.

Mail servers act as forwarding agents between many types of email client software, which use protocols such as SMTP, POP3, and IMAP to communicate with the server. These are all online protocols, and if the mail server goes down, all our mail clients are in trouble. However, overall reliability and manageability is improved for the following reasons:

- Mail servers are relatively simple, well understood, and tested pieces of software, and they are far less likely to crash than flighty client software.
- You can turn off or reinstall email client software without impacting the rest of the email system.
- You have to deal with relatively few modes of failure, rather than the combinatorial explosion of email client pairs (Outlook × Eudora × Notes × and so on) that we would have to consider for failure if the clients talked to each other directly.

The same principals apply to business applications that use batch or messaging services, increasing reliability and making disaster recovery planning simpler.

Batch interfaces can be as simple as a shared file system, FTP server, or database table. Messaging interfaces can utilize Internet email infrastructure where guaranteed delivery is not necessary. Otherwise, commercial messaging infrastructures, such as Microsoft MQ, IBM MQ-Series, Java Message Service, or Tibco (a commercial Java-based messaging infrastructure), provide various levels of transactional integrity and availability. Both batch- and message-based approaches allow you to create operations-friendly loosely coupled interfaces with external systems.

Field Tools

Now that we've introduced some new platforms for our development efforts, it's time to look at some platform-specific services that have the potential to be factored out and reused across any number of applications on that platform. More specialized than the architectural layers discussed in previous chapters, these services are more accurately characterized as "field tools"—frequently applied point solutions that address common challenges faced by application developers. In the following section, we describe some of the most useful tools and how to build them.

Primordial Tools

Some tools apply to more than one platform. To avoid repetition, we will first describe the features that are common across all the platform-specific descendants of these primordial tools, leaving the remaining details to a later section.

Site Model

The best description of a site model can be found at a site of a different kind: the ancient ruins of the Delphi Oracle in Greece. This site is not only famous for the number of software packages named after it, but also for the inscription *know thyself*, written in the sixth century BC.

Applying this sensible advice to our interface development, a site model is a catalogue of information *about* the interface, for use *by* the interface. By referring to the site model, interface code can carry out many tasks that would otherwise rely on the programmer's knowledge of the interface structure. Each entry in the catalogue describes an interface node, or point of contact with the user/external system. *Node* is a generic term for the building blocks that are familiar to all user interface developers. Examples of nodes include site sections, web pages, GUI forms, Flash movie clips, and areas on pages where content is inserted. The site model structure might be hierarchical, linear, or otherwise—whatever best describes the interface. Site maps, tree navigation panels, and dialog flow diagrams are common manifestations of a site model. The model information is usually stored in a content repository to make the most of Persistence layer and PE services.

Site models are most useful in dynamically generated interfaces, but even static interface code can find it useful to have some amount of information about the interface available at times. We will discuss site models' platform specifics in the following sections.

Localization

International applications often maintain parallel sets of interface captions in multiple languages. As the captions are displayed, the most suitable language for the user needs to be selected according to their locale.

Captions are scattered liberally throughout most interfaces, which means that hitting the Publishing Engine API for a translation of each individual caption is an unwieldy, slow option. A lightweight function or tag to substitute international captions from a cached lookup table greatly speeds development. The team who built the ColdFusion MX administrator application created an excellent example of such a tag. Each caption in the site is written in English and wrapped by the localization tag. The tag has two attributes: a caption identifier and a language. If the language attribute is set to English, the tag does nothing. However, if another language is specified, the tag looks up an alternative caption in a language-specific caption file indexed by caption identifier; then it substitutes the caption for the tag contents.

Tools for the Web

As ColdFusion developers, we are all familiar with the constraints and issues surrounding dynamic web application development—perhaps too familiar. Given the many years elapsed since we started building these sorts of applications, it's surprising that so few tools and frameworks (with the exception of Spectra and Fusebox) have emerged to help us build them more quickly. Reinventing the wheel seems the order of the day. To address this need are three fundamental steel-belted radials of web development: site models, templating, and caching.

Web Site Model

Site models are most prevalent in web applications, primarily due to the popularity (at least among designers and developers) of the tree style site structure and navigation controls inherited from the static web world. The site model is a hierarchical structure of nodes that represents site sections, pages, and areas of content within the page. Efficient implementations are usually a variation on the "Composite" structural pattern, similar to the categorization code in Chapter 12, "Categorization of Content." The properties of each node can include the following:

- A caption for the section, page, or page fragment to be used in automatically generated navigation menus, site maps, and "node management" interfaces
- A logical name for the node, which you can use as a bookmark to refer to that node regardless of its current location in the site model
- A path or URL reference to the node for links
- Arguments to pass to the PE to retrieve the node's content
- References to the templates (see the "Web Templating" section below) that are used to format the content
- Security permissions (authorization roles) that are required to view or edit the node
- Caches of generated HTML content
- Prepared packages of reporting information to log when the node is accessed

Figure 22.1 shows a simplified site map and site model for a part of the DuvalShock web site. Each row in the table describes a site node.

Should a site model be generated based on an existing site, or are sites generated from site models? Both are possibilities, depending on the situation.

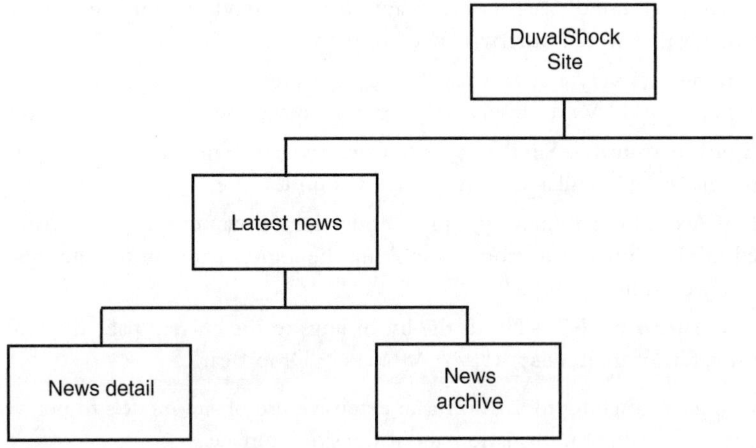

ID	Parent ID	Name	Caption	URL
1		DUVALSITE	DuvalShock	/index.cfm
2	1	LATESTNEWS	Latest news	/news/latest.cfm
3	2	NEWSDETAIL	News detail	/news/detail.cfm
4	2	NEWSARCHIVE	News archive	/news/archive.cfm

Figure 22.1 Site map and site model.

If a site has been created without reference to a site model but one is now required, you can write a script to proactively "crawl" the existing site and build a site model. This could start with something as simple as a recursive directory listing of the web root or a link checker built with the `<CFHTTP>` tag and `REFind` function.

Another more reactive approach is to get pages to register themselves in the site model when they're run. This could be code in application.cfm checking the request URLs, or a tag taking node properties as arguments, called from every page and content area in the site. This method is best if there is already a need for a tag like this on all site pages (for logging or security purposes, for example) that the site model registration code can be added to. Although it adds some overhead to page processing (minimized if the model is cached in memory), if a large team of programmers is constantly adding, updating, and removing pages from the site, this is a good way to keep the site model up to date.

In some sites, the site structure is dynamic and can be modified through a "node management" administration interface. The administration interface reconfigures the site model, which then generates the entire site either at request time or as a scheduled batch update of a collection of static HTML pages.

Interface code can use the site model to automate the rendering of many common web UI elements that would otherwise need to be hand-coded:

- **Site map**— It's very easy to walk through the site model nodes and render the corresponding HTML to display the site map to the user.
- **Navigation menus**—Similar to a site map, navigation menus can be site wide or specific to a particular section or page within the site.
- **Links**—Avoid broken links by using a node's logical name instead of a hard-coded URL. A utility function can look up the logical name in the site model and resolve it into a URL.
- **"Breadcrumb trails"**—This is the list of links to the current page displayed in a header, for example, `Australia` > `Animals` > Drop Bear.

Web templating and caching tools also make extensive use of site models to persist configuration and runtime information about the site interface.

Web Templating

Templating is the most visible manifestation of reuse in a web application. It reflects the fervent desire of web developers everywhere to never have to write the same HTML code twice. It also addresses a universal business requirement to control the content, look, and feel of a web site to comply with corporate branding, legal, and other requirements. These two themes of reuse and control are central to the idea of templating. Many styles of templating are in use today, each one with its own merits and issues.

To begin, let's examine templating options that are used at design time. Most development environments offer a word processor-like template or "snippet" library feature, which allows page development to start with a complete page template or for code fragments to be pasted into the code at the cursor. The developer carries out the integration of the templates manually at design time and has complete control over the result, which becomes a page or possibly a new template to be reused in other pages. This kind of template offers no control and is simply a productivity tool for developers.

Dreamweaver introduced an increased degree of control to design-time templating with the concept of editable regions. These allow the creator of the template to mark up regions where the template consumer is allowed to insert new content; when the template is used, any modification to the original template code is prohibited. This feature is ideal for enforcing consistency across the developers of a dynamic site or the content production team of a static site. Figure 22.2 shows an example of an editable region in Dreamweaver MX. The region is highlighted with an aqua "body" tab and border.

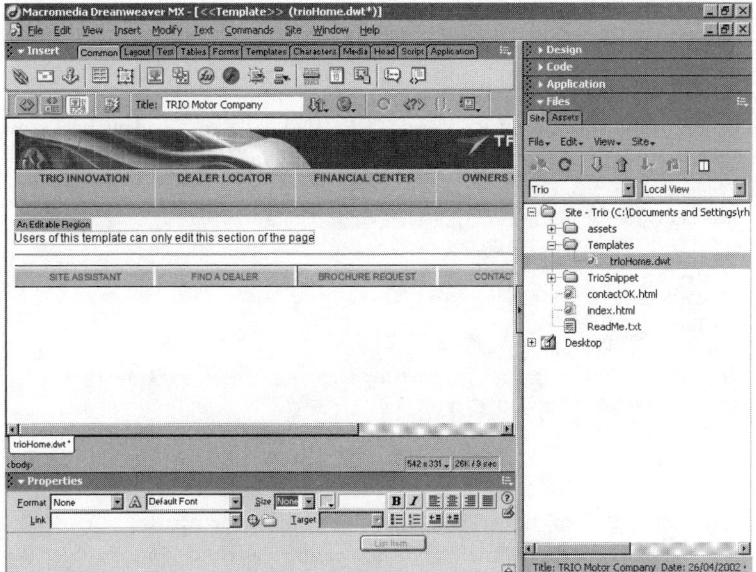

Figure 22.2 Editable region in Dreamweaver MX template.

The same tool has introduced the concept of server behaviors, which are essentially parameterized templates. Adding parameters to templates allows a single template to be applied in a much wider range of situations. Whereas a snippet can contain the skeleton of a `<CFQUERY>/<CFOUTPUT>` tag set, a server behavior can generate a master detail page set or a record entry form for a particular datasource and table. Server behaviors are most useful in hiding the details of an implementation from more junior developers or rolling out coding standards to a development team. A note of caution, however: Point-and-click coding is great, but keeping the developer at arm's length from the code raises the question of who is responsible for the final code—the programmer or the template creator? For more information about these Dreamweaver templating features, see `www.macromedia.com/desdev/mx/dreamweaver/`.

A developer can use the design time template methods we've described so far to compose HTML, CFML, or other files from one or more (possibly parameter-driven) templates. These files are then deployed as components in a web application. Some of the templates might have contained code that accessed and displayed content, but none of the templates would have produced the formatted content itself.

When we talk about runtime templates, however, template composition is driven by the UI code and parameterized by the content/site model rather than the developer. Aside from ColdFusion's familiar `<CFINCLUDE>` and custom tag-based templating options, two main styles of runtime templating are available, which for purposes of discussion, we will name type-oriented templating (TOT) and node-oriented templating (NOT).

Consider the typical ColdFusion script in Listing 22.1, which prints a list of the three most recently created articles, including links to a second page that displays the full article.

Listing 22.1 **Using *<CFQUERY>* and *<CFOUTPUT>* to Display the Latest Three Articles**

```
<cfquery name="qArticle" datasource="duvalDb">
   SELECT TOP 3 id, heading, subheading from Articles
   ORDER BY createdDate DESC
</cfquery>
<h1>Most Recent Articles</h1>
<table>
<cfoutput query="qArticle">
<tr><td><a href="articleFull.cfm?id=#id#">#heading#</a></td></tr>
<tr><td>#subheading#</td></tr>
</cfoutput>
</table>
```

Tens of thousands of ColdFusion developers have made their fortunes with these two tags, which handle the details of connecting to a database and iterating over the results. But it's still not perfect. What if we need to get a list of the top five articles for a Flash application? We could repeat the `select` statement in another part of the site, but that would be ugly; if our table name changed, we would have to search through the site to replace all references to the table. A better option would be to create a "five most recent article headlines" rule in our PE and call it from this page and our Flash application. We could even parameterize the rule to return the most recent *N* articles.

That's the query ready for reuse, which leaves our cfoutput block. Several places in our site interface might need to list articles in this format, so we can either repeat our code or get architectural and put it somewhere central where we can reuse it. That sounds like a job for components, so why not create a function for each template and collect the functions together into a templating component for each type of content in our data model? While we're doing that, it would be good to further streamline the query-output process into a single step. Thinking along these lines, Listing 22.2 presents a base component for all our type template components, components.templating.base.

Listing 22.2 **components.templating.base**

```
<cfcomponent displayname="Base Content Template"
   hint="Base component for content type template components">
   <cffunction name="render" access="public" returntype="string"
   output="true">
      <cfargument name="template"
         type="string"
         default=""
         required="true"
         hint="Name of template to render">
```

```
      <!--- Other formatting option and getContent() arguments --->
      <!--- Pass arguments through to PE to get content --->
      <cfinvoke component="components.publishing.service"
         method="getContent"
         argumentcollection=#arguments#
         returnvariable="qContent"/>
      <table>
      <cfloop query="qContent">
         <cfset stRow=structNew()>
         <cfloop list=#qContent.columnList# index="column">
            <cfset stRow[column] = qContent[column]>
         </cfloop>
         <tr><td>
         <cfinvoke method=#template# argumentcollection=#stRow#/>
         </td></tr>
      </cfloop>
      </table>
      <cfreturn true>
   </cffunction>
</cfcomponent>
```

Listing 22.3 shows an Article templating component that extends the base component.

Listing 22.3 **components.duval.templates.article**

```
<cfcomponent displayname="Article Template"
   extends="components.templating.base"
   hint="Article templates">
   <cffunction name="headSubLink" access="public" output="true">
      <cfoutput>
      <table>
      <tr><td>
      <a href="articleFull.cfm?id=#id#">#heading#</a>
      </td></tr>
      <tr><td>#subheading#</td></tr>
      </table>
      </cfoutput>
   </cffunction>
   <cffunction name="fullArticle" access="public" output="true">
      <cfoutput>
      <table>
      <tr><td><h1>#heading#</h1></td></tr>
      <tr><td><h2>#subheading#</h2></td></tr>
      <tr><td>#body#</td></tr>
      <tr><td>
      <cfset authorParams=structNew()>
      <cfset authorParams.id=authorId>
      <cfinvoke component="duval.templates.author"
```

continues

Listing 22.3 **Continued**

```
            method="render"
            template="shortAuthorBiography"
            source="rule:authorById"
            stParams=#authorParams#/>
        </td></tr>
        </table>
        </cfoutput>
    </cffunction>
</cfcomponent>
```

The base component contains a single function called `render`, which is inherited by all the template components. This function "decorates" the usual call to the PE's `getContent` function, adding a template argument to the list. The function calls the PE to get the results and then loops through each row, calling the function specified in the template argument with the row data passed as the argument collection.

The article component simply implements the various templates without having to worry about iterating over the resultset or laying out the template alongside the rest of the output (although it is a good idea to enclose the template output in its own table). Two templates are available. The first, "headSubLink," renders our original sample cfoutput content, whereas the second, "fullArticle," does what it says. Note that fullArticle calls another template to display a short author biography. There is nothing particularly tricky about doing this. In fact, you can generate whole site maps by using nested template calls.

The code I've described so far is a basic example of a TOT implementation, but you could easily extended it to include the following:

- More layout options in `render()`. For example, specify a separator between content items, lay out templates in multiple columns across and then down, or vice versa.
- A custom tag to provide a shorthand format for cfinvoking a template's render method.
- Built-in caching of HTML results using the caching techniques described in the next section.

Another option might be to have components.templating.base extend components.persistence.basePersistentComponent. With a little tweaking, this would allow the Persistence and Publishing layers to return arrays of component instances with `render` and `template` functions already included.

Now that we've examined TOT, it should be easier to understand NOT, which is a kind of dynamic equivalent to Dreamweaver editable regions. NOT has only one content type, the node, which can be found in the site model. No further data modeling is required using this approach; everything is a node. A node has two properties related to NOT: template and content.

The template property is the name of the template used to format the node, but unlike TOT, it has no corresponding component function to invoke. This is because NOT templates are user definable and stored in a content repository. Recall the user-created and programmatic publishing rules discussed in Chapter 23, "Deployment of a Publishing Application." To draw a parallel, NOT templates are to user-saved rules, what TOT templates are to programmatic rules.

NOT templates need to support a similar markup grammar to user-saved rules. The parsing code in Chapter 23 can be modified to suit. When the template is created, the user needs to mark the point at which to insert the content, as Dreamweaver users do when defining an editable region. The user also can define one or more insertion points for subnodes of the node using the template to display their content. (These are often referred to as content "containers.") For each of these points, the user specifies a name for that subnode and lists the templates that you can use in that position.

In Figure 22.3, a content author created a template called "news" in the management UI and saved it to the template library. The news template includes an area for content and spaces for two templates to the left of the content. The user specified that the templates must be ad(vertisment) templates. As the site grows, another content author (using the node management UI) creates a node called "welcome" which is to display the content "hello" using the news template. She also creates two subnodes, "ad1" and "ad2," to store the content for the two advertisements. When the page is browsed, the templating code does the following:

1. Retrieves the template
2. Substitutes the content in the content area
3. Parses the two subnode insertion points (containers) and asks the subnodes to generate their HTML
4. Substitutes the returned HTML from the subnodes into the page
5. Displays the page

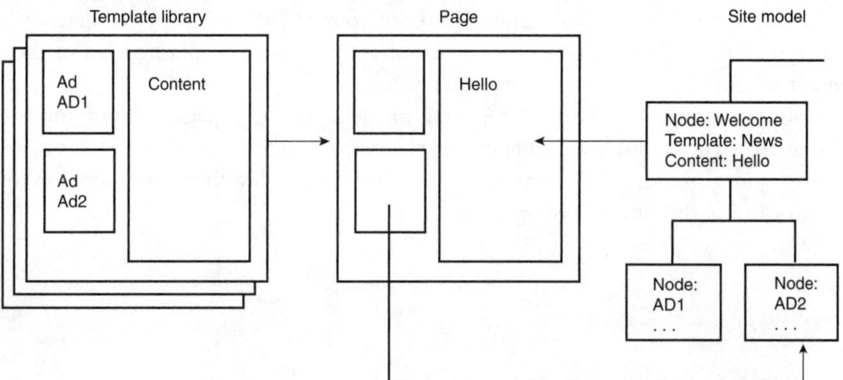

Figure 22.3 Node-oriented templating.

You also can use the NOT template parsing trick by itself to provide inline content insertion in HTML content properties, a useful approach that applies equally well to TOT and NOT templating styles. In large body content properties, it is common for the user to want to insert ad-hoc links and images. The problem is that it is impossible to constrain what images or links are inserted. One solution is to do the following:

- Create image and link content types and template components.
- Ban the use of link and image tags in the content. Filter them out of the content when it is saved.
- Tell the users to use a `<CONTENT>` tag instead that allows the user to specify an image or link, and to use a display template for that image or link (for example, thumbnail, thumbnailWithPopup, originalSize).
- When the property is loaded for display on the site, parse each `<CONTENT>` tag and pass the attributes to the appropriate component's render function. Substitute the render results for the `<CONTENT>` tag in the property.
- When the property is loaded for editing, don't perform the substitution, allowing the user to edit the attributes of the `<CONTENT>` tag.

This technique is not limited to images and links. You could insert any content template output into the property output if your code allows it. Using this approach, TOT can include NOT-like freeform HTML output while maintaining some degree of control over the content.

We have discussed several different approaches to web templating. With this understanding, you will realize that all types of hybrid solutions are possible, and that web templating is an extremely adaptable tool. All but the smallest sites can benefit from using some aspect of web templating.

Caching

With all this CPU-intensive architecture stuff going on, it's always good to remind yourself that caching will save the day, and then some. On the web and especially in ColdFusion, it is easy to cache large chunks of your HTML output into memory or disk, where they can then be retrieved for subsequent requests in a fraction of the time it would take to regenerate from scratch.

ColdFusion provides the `<CFCACHE>` tag to cache an entire page's output, but for reasons that will be discussed later in this chapter, it is often better to cache various parts of your page separately. Several custom tags on the developer exchange do this, or you can use the one in Listing 22.4.

Listing 22.4 **cacheThis.cfm**

```
<cfsetting enablecfoutputonly="Yes">
<!--- CacheThis.cfm --->
<cfif thisTag.executionMode eq "start">
   <cfset thisTag.bSave = false>
   <cflock scope="APPLICATION" type="READONLY" timeout=1>
      <cfset bCacheExists = isdefined("application.cache." &
      attributes.cacheName)>
      <cfif bCacheExists>
         <cfset content = application.cache[attributes.cacheName]>
      </cfif>
   </cflock>
   <cfif bCacheExists>
      <cfif isdefined("url.resetcache")>
         <!--- If url.resetcache defined, clear existing cache
         contents --->
         <cflock scope="APPLICATION" type="EXCLUSIVE" timeout=1>
            <cfset void = structDelete(application.cache,
            attributes.cachename)>
         </cflock>
         <cfset thisTag.bSave = true>
      <cfelse>
         <!--- Otherwise, because it already exists, display contents
         and exit --->
         <cfoutput>#content#</cfoutput>
         <cfexit method="EXITTAG">
      </cfif>
   <cfelse>
      <!--- Cache not created; tell closing tag to save content --->
      <cfset thisTag.bSave = true>
   </cfif>
  <cfelse>
   <cfif thisTag.bSave>
      <cflock scope="APPLICATION" type="EXCLUSIVE" timeout=1>
         <cfif not isDefined("application.cache")>
            <!--- Create cache structure the first time --->
            <cfset application.cache=structNew()>
         </cfif>
         <cfset application.cache[attributes.cacheName] =
         thisTag.generatedContent>
      </cflock>
   </cfif>
</cfif>
```

When the opening tag is processed, it checks to see whether a cache matching the <CACHENAME> tag attribute exists. If it exists, we output the contents and exit; otherwise, we let the body of the tag run and save the generated content in the closing tag. This process is outlined in Figure 22.4.

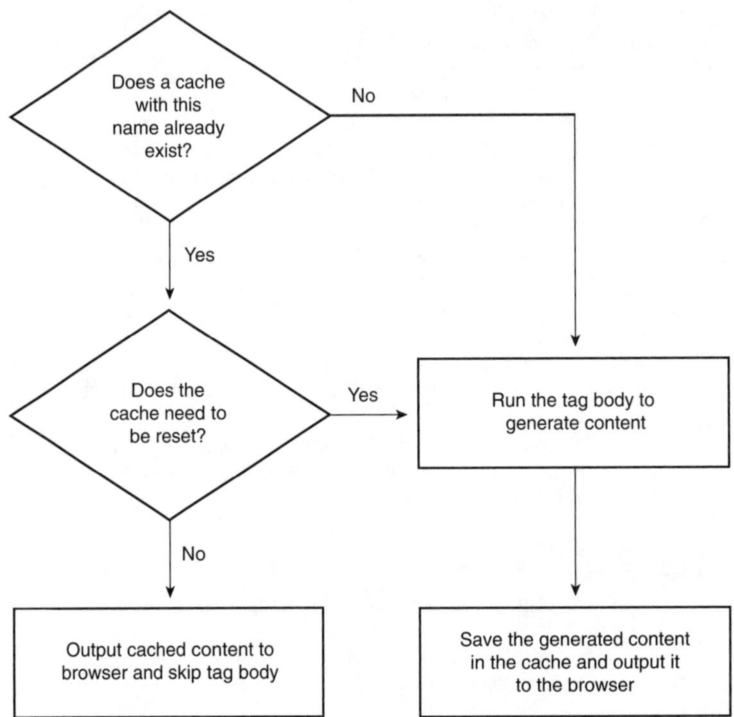

Figure 22.4 Flowchart illustrating caching process.

The main complicating factor in the tag is the locking. That's important, especially given the high frequency of calls to the caching tag. Another feature worth explaining is the resetCache processing in the opening tag. Sometimes clients are wary of caching because they feel they can't trust the site to display the content in the repository. Adding a backdoor mechanism such as a URL parameter to refresh the caches on a page usually eases these concerns.

We could make several improvements to this caching tag. This tag stores its cache in the application scope. When the server is stopped, the cache is lost unless it is backed up. If you are aware of the impending shutdown, it is easy to back up and restore the caching structure with a utility script using `<CFWDDX>` and `<CFFILE>` tags. You also can schedule a cache backup every few minutes if you want something to restore after an unexpected shutdown. Alternatively, you can modify the caching tag to save each cache to disk in a file at the same time you save it to memory, and to check for a disk file if you cannot find a cache in memory.

Another problem to solve when caching content is how to update the cache when content changes. In many cases, the content that is displayed on the site is time-sensitive, such as prices of goods in an online store. Caching solutions is not acceptable to your clients if they delay the updating of this information on the site. If content object *X* changes, we need to find all the caches that contain output based on *X* and delete them so that they will be refreshed the next time they are requested. If all your content is being displayed using template functions, one solution is to modify the render method to insert HTML comments containing the object UUID into the template output. If this doesn't suit, keep a list in the request scope to record the UUIDs. The end tag of the caching tag can add the UUIDs to an index keyed by UUID that records which caches contain each object's output. When an object is updated, look up the object's UUID in the index, delete all the corresponding caches, and remove the cache names from the index.

Using caching is an easy way to quickly improve the scalability of your site. We will discuss some application caching design issues when we talk about assembling web browser interfaces later in this chapter.

Tools for Flash

Although Flash is at an earlier stage of development in terms of dynamic publishing, many developers have successfully transplanted elements of web templating onto the Flash platform. In terms of publishing specific tools, one idea is worth discussing briefly. (This is not a Flash book, after all.)

It would be useful to have a Flash Component version of the TOT render method. This component would first use Flash Remoting to connect to the PE and retrieve content in query form. The component would be configured with the URL of a directory of SWF files, each one corresponding to a content type and containing a shared symbol library of template movies. It would then iterate through the resultset, attach and position the appropriate template movie, and then set local variables corresponding to the row in the resultset.

Tools for Web Services

Web Services need little in the way of tools, which is one of their benefits. The only detail that might prove to be a development time waster is the security implementation. Remember the following two things in this regard:

- ColdFusion MX executes the application.cfm file in a directory of web services before any functions are called.
- The `roles` attribute in cffunction allows you to limit function access to logged on users in a particular role.

For more details about security, see Chapter 16, "Securing the Application and User Management."

Tools for Other Platforms

Given the emphasis usually placed on user interfaces, it's easy to forget about the other types of application interfaces we need to build, and it's even easier for a book on the topic to gloss over the subject. Without the familiar user interface deliverables to refer to, it can be hard to approach the design of these types of interfaces. This section discusses two common services that are useful to consider from a "tool" perspective.

Batch Process Manager

ColdFusion provides basic job scheduling functionality with the `<CFSCHEDULE>` tag and scheduling interface in the ColdFusion administrator, allowing batch processing jobs to be triggered at a particular time. However, what if a particular job can only start when another job, or two jobs, have finished? And how can you monitor the status of jobs as they run? If you recognize these problems but don't have the money to buy expensive enterprise management tools, a homegrown alternative is available.

Create a batch management component with `registerJob`, `start`, `stop`, and `status` functions. The `registerJob` function takes arguments similar to cfschedule, except that instead of specifying a time to start, you specify a list of preconditions. A precondition is just a short string used as a flag to indicate that a particular job has finished with a particular status (success, error, or whatever you require). The function adds the job details to an array of pending jobs, which is saved in a WDDX file (a cheap and cheerful job database) to keep job information across server restarts. An exclusive named lock is used each time the file is accessed to avoid concurrent access, which might corrupt the file.

The `start` function is called by jobs as they start, passing the job ID. The job is moved from the pending to active array and the start time is recorded. The `stop` function is called by jobs as they stop, passing the job ID and a list of conditions. The function moves the job to the finished job array, records the stop time, and adds the preconditions to a list of satisfied conditions. It then rechecks the pending job list to see if any more jobs can be started.

You can call the `status` function at any time, returning a dump of the entire job's file. If you like, you could create a nice graphical console in Flash to display the current status of all jobs.

Mailout Engine

Mass mailouts, used responsibly, are a powerful business tool. However, you need to treat the technology with respect to get it to work satisfactorily. Using `<CFQUERY>`, `<CFLOOP>`, and `<CFMAIL>` to dump thousands of emails at a time into ColdFusion's spool folder is, shall we say, not respectful. The `<CFMAIL>` tag and most SMTP servers are not designed for this rate of traffic.

You can take two approaches. The first option is to spoon-feed `<CFMAIL>` at a reasonable rate. Create a "throttled" `<CFMAIL>` tag or function that validates the parameters (a lot of problems are caused by malformed addresses) and queues the mail parameters and body in its private queue file. A scheduled task is run every minute to check the number of files in the mail/spool directory. If empty, the task takes the next 20 or so messages in the queue and feeds them to `<CFMAIL>`.

Another option is to use one of the many affordable third-party email engines, which are designed for high volume mailouts. All you need is a template method that puts the data into a format accepted by the engine, which you can use to save the data in an input file before starting the program.

Building an Application

No more talk of reusable services and tools—we have an application to build. To reiterate what was said in the introduction, every application is a unique response to a unique set of requirements. Before we start, we need to find out what these requirements are. We then design our application interfaces to these requirements and architect our code to make the most of the reusable services and tools we've created over the course of this book.

Getting Requirements

In the introduction to this chapter, we pointed out that unlike the services in previous chapters, the requirements for the application come directly from the client. A shockingly large number of software projects fail each year due to incorrect or inadequately researched requirements. Good architecture alone cannot save a project that doesn't solve the original problem. You need to build the right software, and build it right.

Although we can't discuss the actual requirements of your next project here as we could for the service chapters, we can briefly talk about the process of eliciting and framing the requirements so that you get useful requirements and some sense of when they are complete. For more information on this topic, read *Practical Software Requirements* by B. Kovitz (published by Manning Press).

To know what code goes in an application, you need to know what interfaces that application presents to the outside world—web pages, web services, batch files, and so on. To know what interfaces need to be built, you need to know what problems the application is to address in the real world. Normally, the problem with software requirements is that the design starts with the interfaces, with no reliable way to check whether they are correct or complete. Even if the real-world problem is described, it usually isn't framed in a way that is easy to test against your interface designs.

To help you frame your dynamic publishing requirements, here is a checklist of information to capture:

- Content types and their properties; categorization; relationships; frequency of changes to content; content source; input/import method (file format, transformation required), and sample content.
- End users/other systems; number; location; connection method/speed; platform (browser and Flash version, OS); accessibility (W3C/Section 508); user type categorization; and usage patterns (peak times, what they're attempting to do via your interface at these times).
- The different ways that users can query the content (list of articles by author, full article, full-text search, subscription sets); common sequences of user actions (use case scenarios, but don't build your entire requirements around these, or you'll have no way to test when you've finished); currency of content (that is, how long can we cache or delay checking the source); exact details of web service/batch interfaces to be provided; content requiring complex transformations before viewing (for example, locate nearest supplier by suburb); personalization; and localization.
- Administrative users (same as end users). How will administrative users manipulate the content—add, edit, delete (security for different categories of user), versioning, promotion, rollback, scheduling of content, editing in place (site edit mode with links to administrative pages inserted in render function)? A common mistake is for designers to describe a dynamic publishing site with a site map alone. This is like describing Microsoft Word with a finished word processing document.
- The controls (workflow) on content going live, auditing, reporting.
- Look and feel can be quantified. A smart creative department lead used to give our clients three words to convey the impression they wanted their web site to give the users. The creative department would mock up 3 to 5 designs (depending on budget) and a panel of users would rate each design against a list of 10 words, including the three the clients wanted. The design with the highest score won.

Most applications do not solve pure dynamic publishing problems. Contact Us, Shop/Checkout, and Chat Rooms are ordinary examples of solutions for other problem types. Don't try to shoehorn requirements for these types of problems into the dynamic publishing frame. Work out what you need to know to build each one and make sure you get that information.

After you have these requirements, you can start a pilot content entry project to test the content schema while you continue with the interface designs. This project will help get content entry off the critical path as well as provide developers with test data early in development.

Interface design is a much written-about topic, so we won't discuss it here except to point out that it is important to test the interfaces against the requirements. If all the interfaces work as described, will the application have the desired affect in the real world? It also is critical to test your interface with real users (on paper or static web site mockup) to ensure that your design is usable. If your project makes it this far, you can move on to designing the system architecture (Chapter 3, "Architecting a Dynamic Publishing Application"), with a good chance of building the right system and making your clients happy.

Build the Content-Related Components

Before you can start building your interfaces, you need to put your content types, categorization hierarchies, publishing rules, and security definitions in place. This is a relatively mechanical mapping of requirements onto the services discussed in previous chapters.

The main thing to consider at this point is how to easily deploy the configuration to another machine. This might be a matter of copying databases or directories, a deployment script, or a combination of both. Manual deployment is error prone, extremely boring, and a waste of resources.

Web Browser Interface

Although we are not starting from a blank slate so to speak, we still need to make a number of design decisions and tradeoffs when we're using DP services and tools to develop a web interface. We can look at each of these in turn.

The style and mix of templating to use on a web site is important to resolve early in the design. In summary, TOT is suitable for highly structured sites with large volumes of typed content to display, such as product catalogs and directories. NOT is more suited to a site of micro-sites, or each site area with its own distinct look but maintaining some branding consistency. Examples of typical NOT sites are magazines, public relations, and one-off promotional campaign sites.

Developers also need to decide when they look at their site map what pages are implemented as a CFML script and what pages are templates being displayed by a CFML script higher in the site hierarchy. Many huge DP sites with thousands of pages indexed on search engines have a disconcertingly small number of browsable CFML scripts running the show. One approach that might help is to put pages that require their own processing (for example, a Contact Us or Search form) in a separate script. The bulk of the site's static content can be displayed through a single CFML template that takes `type`, `template`, and `objectId` URL parameters. One advantage of this is that there are fewer browsable points of entry for malicious users who are attempting to hack URL or form parameters. If you centralize your application URL validation code, your site will be more secure as a result.

Some content types make their way into almost every DP application. An image type with thumbnail and full display methods with "click to view" and caption display options is one. Similarly, a file type with download and inline display templates is another. If you need to secure either of these from unauthorized downloads, you can keep the source outside the web root and create a helper script that checks session credentials before serving the file using cfcontent (the mime type for file downloads is "application/octet-stream"). A link type for external links can render a link to an auditing script that logs the user's departure before redirecting to the target URL. Another link template might bring the target up in a new window.

Caching is easy to use effectively after you are aware of the traps. Developers are often wary of caching because they think that the only option is to cache the entire page, cfcache style. This has obvious disadvantages if there is personalization, browser, or time-specific content on the page; it is a matter of first-come, first-cached. A better option is to cache fragments of the page.

Each cache is named uniquely depending on the parameters that affect the content of the cache. For example, consider a cache that contains the top and left navigation of a page. The only dynamic processing that occurs is that the tab across the top of the page is highlighted to indicate the section of the site the user is browsing, according to a section variable. To make sure this was cached properly, the cache could be called `"top_left_nav_#section#"`. If the number of variables in the name grows large, you might be creating more caches than you need. Try to split the cache into smaller sections with fewer variables.

A typical caching layout on a page might include two or three caches for the header and footer and another cache for the main page content. Don't forget to address cache refreshing and backup as discussed in the "Field Tools" section.

Flash Interface

You can use Flash as a user interface in several ways, from an ad-banner to an offline Flash application running in a stand-alone Flash Player.

Starting small, Flash can be used as a point solution to improve usability and scalability of a particular web site function. The advantage of an independent connection to the server and consequent avoidance of page refreshes is extremely powerful. By way of example, a popular stock-quoting site used to be clogged with millions of requests for stock prices. The web page that the quote form was sitting on was large and took up to 20 seconds to download. The developers replaced the form with a small Flash application that requested stock ticker information from the server, taking no more than two seconds even on a dial-up with no page refresh. You can integrate this sort of Flash application easily into a normal templated web site.

Full screen Flash applications in a browser or the Flash Player are becoming increasingly common, replacing an ungainly collection of web pages used to complete a task with a single, one-screen application. Sites such as these have experienced a massive reduction in customer drop-off rates (statistically 70 percent of attempted web transactions end in failure) by moving to this sort of interface. Coming full circle, some Flash applications that need to display large formatted documents can launch browser windows containing output from ColdFusion servers. ColdFusion developers should be ready to consider Flash in the mixture of interface options available, especially where rich interactivity is required.

Web Services

Web Services are so self contained that outside the service implementation, there is little to consider from an application point of view:

- Is the service going to be registered publicly using a UDDI directory?
- Is there anything we can do for the caller to make using the web service easier? We might want to expose multiple versions of the same component or function, decorated to support a particular class of caller's requirements. Would a facade component that rolled commonly requested sequences of calls into a single function (for example, getBatchedContent) be useful?
- Security. Components that are exposed in the web root as web services can wrap sensitive components in the custom tag path outside the web root, increasing security if the web server is compromised.

Batch and Messaging Interfaces

To create batch interfaces, we perform the following:

- Create the individual processing scripts that carry out our jobs.
- Set up or identify the file systems, FTP servers, database tables, and messaging infrastructures that will be our common ground with our users.
- Configure the ColdFusion scheduling engine with time-based job triggers. This is best done with a script to simplify deployment.
- Create control scripts, which are responsible for automatically registering jobs and preconditions with the batch process manager tools.
- Create monitoring and alerting tools for operational staff to use. Consider integration with ColdFusion MX Enterprise probe feature, or sending SMS messages to site operators. There are several SMS gateways available as web services.

Because batch processing happens away from human supervision, it is important to program defensively and detect errors quickly. A good example of defensive programming is to terminate batch files with a prearranged message and possibly a checksum. That way, if the file is mangled during transit, it is easy to detect before committing to a transaction based on the file.

Writing outward messaging interfaces is similar to writing web pages, except that the target of the content is a messaging API instead of a browser. Consider the level of guarantee you need for message delivery. Is a read receipt required?

Receiving messages depends on the type of messaging infrastructure used. Some require a scheduled task to poll a server (for example, POP3) to determine if new messages have arrived. Other messaging systems might include local agent software that is capable of posting a message to a script in your application.

Conclusion

In this chapter, we discussed how the task of application development differs from the creation of a DP framework covered. We reviewed the platforms used to create application interfaces; then we went into detail about several application tools that are useful in these environments. Finally, we talked about the process of application development, from gathering requirements to the issues you face building particular types of interfaces.

Application development is an extremely broad topic. Therefore, in a single chapter, it is impossible to cover all its aspects in great detail. Some topics were covered at greater length because an understanding of them is so critical to successful dynamic publishing applications. You should be able to practice some of these techniques in your upcoming projects—we wish you luck!

V

The Aftermath

23

Deployment of a Dynamic Publishing Application

by Jeff Tapper

YOU'VE SPENT THE PAST MONTHS PLANNING, developing, testing, and fixing your application. Now you're done, right? Not quite. One crucial step remains: deploying the application. Deployment is the act of moving the completed application from the development/testing servers where it currently resides to the production environment, where the end users will access it.

An often under-planned aspect of application development is deployment. Like other aspects of development, if deployment is not properly planned, it can take considerably longer and numerous difficulties can arise. Like everything else, planning for deployment needs to begin early in the development process.

Many people initially believe that all that is necessary to deploy an application is to copy the code-base to the production servers. Deployment is rarely that simple. In this chapter, we will discuss several aspects of application deployment to help you better understand the intricacies involved.

Deployment Checklist

It's best to create a list containing all the items needed for deployment. The list that follows is one such example, but it is not intended to be a definitive list for all deployments. As you begin to understand the intricacies of application deployment, it is likely that you will modify this list to suit your particular needs or possibly create your own list from scratch.

- Testing
    - Functional
    - Integration
    - User acceptance
    - Load
- Migration
    - Code
    - Objects
    - Server settings
    - Database
- Monitoring
    - Web Server
    - ColdFusion server
    - DB Server
    - Network

Testing

The first items on our deployment checklist pertain to testing. This, you might guess, is to ensure that the application to be deployed works in the manner expected before you move it from one server to the next. By the time you are considering deploying your application, we are assuming that it has been fully unit tested and that integration with any backend components (such as databases, mainframes, COM/Java objects, and so on) has been fully tested. If this level of testing is not yet done, you need to strongly reconsider deploying the application.

Functional

The first and most obvious level of testing to be done prior to deployment is functional testing. The purpose of functional testing is to verify that the application does what it is intended to do. This includes verifying that the proper data is being served on each page, that input is properly written to the database, that emails are sent appropriately, and so on. Far too often, when one begins to investigate why a particular feature isn't working properly in production, the actual reason turns out to be that it didn't work properly in development either. If the application fails to meet the key functional requirements, you should consider revising the application before continuing with deployment.

User Acceptance

Rarely are the people who are building an application the same people who requested the application or who will use it. Nearly every application has a stakeholder who needs to approve that the application built is the application that was requested. User acceptance testing gives a chance for a final review of the application by the stakeholder before it is launched.

Load

Many applications fail because they cannot handle the number of users who might try to access it after it is available on the public Internet. To see if your application can handle the load, you can either open it to the public and hope, or you can load test it. Load testing is done by simulating a number of users accessing the server at once. Most often, this is accomplished through the use of a load testing software package, such as Segue Silk, Rational TeamTest, or Mercury LoadRunner, although a number of cheaper load testing solutions are appearing on the market daily. It also is possible to do some rudimentary load testing with a group of people and a group of machines. This low-tech method uses real users, whereas the software solutions use virtual users.

Bear in mind that running a load test actually tests far more than your code base. It also effectively tests your network, database, and application servers. An application that is not performing as expected is not solely an indicator that the code base is bad. Problems can be caused by the firewall, network, network architecture, server hardware, or configurations within the application server.

By load testing an application, you can know that under prescribed conditions (that is, running this application on a single server with a Dual Pentium Xeon 750MHz processor and 256MB RAM) and a specific number of users, the application performs with certain benchmarks. Watching the benchmarks, you can determine at what point (that is, with how many users) the application's performance is no longer acceptable. After an application's benchmarks are known, you can accurately predict the number of users the application will be able to support in production. If the application is not performing as you expect it, you can either tune the application (by optimizing the code, network, database, and so on) or you can upgrade or add hardware (adding another processor, more RAM, or additional servers to the cluster).

Tip

Brett Cortese's Insights on Load Testing:*

"The biggest thing to think about when planning to handle load is that the entire process of development should be geared toward keeping page times low from the start. Throughout the development process, make sure that debugging is always on and keep all pages' execution times below 300ms. Once you are ready to deploy, it is imperative to have an idea of what your application can handle. This is done by creating virtual load on the machines and monitoring the results. Once you know how your application performs under a specified load on one server, you can accurately predict its performance under the anticipated load in production. For example, if your application needs to service 400 simultaneous users, and you know from load testing that a single server running the application can handle 150 users at once, it will require three servers to handle the expected load. Lastly, remember that load testing is not a one-time event. Each time you make changes to the application, it should be retested to determine the impact the changes have had on the application's performance."

*Cortese is the head of performance tuning and analysis for RemoteSite Technologies.

By knowing how your application performs under anticipated load, you can deploy it with confidence.

Remember: As you load test, you can use some features that are built into the ColdFusion MX application server to identify bottlenecks, such as the Log Slow Pages, and Long Running Queries options available in the administrator. You often can address problems with slow pages by adding indexes to a database (or reworking the database structure, if necessary), eliminating unnecessary blocks of code, and so on.

Migration

As mentioned earlier, migrating an application usually involves more than simply copying the code base. For the dynamic publishing application described throughout this book, migrating the application requires moving the code base, deploying the CFCs (see Chapter 8, "ColdFusion Components with Persistence"), as well as determining whether there is data in development that needs to be migrated. It also includes moving that data as well as migrating any server settings (data sources, mappings, CustomTag paths, and so on).

You can deploy an application manually by moving everything individually, or you can script it using ColdFusion or the Shell Scripting capabilities of the operating system. Manually migrating an application is straightforward and requires little in the way of an explanation. You can achieve each aspect of migration by writing a migration script. Advanced developments might even consider writing an "uber-migration" script, which fires all the other migration scripts in order. In the next several sections, we will see what is in each of the individual migration processes.

Code

Several different means are available to migrate an application's code base, depending on the relationship between the network of the staging server and the production network. If there is a connection between the two networks or if both reside on the same network, then you can perform a simple copy to replicate content from one server to the next.

> **Tip**
>
> Al Everett's Insights on Copying Large Groups of Files:*
>
> If you're performing a file copy across the network, and the server to which you are deploying is already running a production site, be sure to initialize the copy procedure from the staging server, not the production server. Running the copy procedure can be CPU intensive, and it's best not to rob those cycles from a server that is available to the public.
>
> *Everett is the Director of Project Operations for the InnerCrossing Technology Group.

If the staging and production servers are not capable of "seeing" each other across a network, it's necessary to transfer the files using FTP, HTTP, or some other File Transport Protocol. In some extreme cases, it becomes necessary to move files physically from one network to another through the use of Recordable CDs, Zip disks, or another high-capacity removable storage medium.

Always keep in mind that some applications will have geographically redundant production environments to help mitigate outages. This means there are several production networks in different physical locations; that way, if the network in California loses its Internet connection, the New York-based network can still service the requests coming in from around the world. In these cases, it becomes necessary to ensure that the latest code base is transferred to all of the production environments.

Regardless of how the files are to be transported, it is usually a good idea to package them to be transferred into an archive (Zip, Tar, and so on) and move them as a single file, rather than individually. This way, it is easy to have a record of what was transferred; simply look into the archive. Additionally, if you are deploying to multiple servers, you can copy this one archive to each server, rather than having to copy each of the files individually.

ColdFusion MX includes the ability to create archives of files (as well as server settings, as we will see in the next section). These ColdFusion archives (or CARs as they are often referred) are created in the ColdFusion administrator (see Figure 23.1). We will talk about creating and deploying CARs in more detail in the next section, "Server Settings."

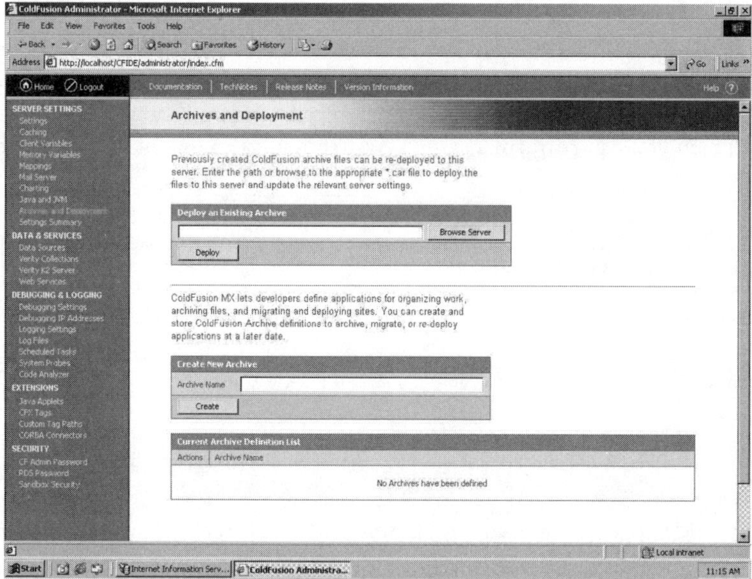

Figure 23.1 The archive page in the ColdFusion administrator.

Server Settings

The options available for migrating a server's settings are much less varied than the options for migrating a code base. With server settings, you can either migrate them manually or with the use of ColdFusion Archives. To migrate them manually, open one browser window containing the ColdFusion administrator of the Staging server, and another window containing the administrator of the Production server, and make each entry in production manually match the setting in staging. If you choose this option, be sure to write down all of the settings so that you can easily re-create them in the future. To create a ColdFusion archive, follow these steps:

1. Open the ColdFusion administrator.
2. Click on the Archives and Deployment link in the left navigation.
3. In the table labeled Create New Archive, enter a name for your archive in the text box labeled Archive Name; then click the Create button.
4. Follow through the wizard, which prompts you for a description of the archive, files and directories, server settings, mappings, data sources, verity collections, scheduled tasks, Java applets, and CFX tags.
5. When you have entered all of your settings, verify them in the Archive Summary page. If they are correct, click on the Close Window button.

6. Back on the Archive and Deployment page, click on the Build Archive button next to the name on your newly created archive. (Note: Build Archive is the middle of the three buttons.)
7. This brings you to a page that is similar to the Archive Summary page from step 5. If this is the archive you want to deploy, click the Next link in the lower-right corner.
8. Next, you are prompted for a location and filename. Enter the location, including the filename, and click Next. (Note: The archive name must end with a .car extension.)
9. Click Generate Archive to finish creating the archive.

After the archive is created, it will contain all of the specified files, as well as the ColdFusion administrator settings specified. This can then be moved to the production server (using a simple file copy, FTP, HTTP, and so on) and deployed.

Deploying an archive is just as simple:

1. Open the ColdFusion administrator.
2. Click on the Archives and Deployment link in the left navigation.
3. In the table labeled Deploy an Existing Archive, enter the path to the archive file you have transferred to the server, or click on the Browse Server button and choose Browse to the File.
4. Click the Deploy button. The Deploy Wizard is launched, showing you an Archive Summary screen.
5. Click the Next link in the lower-right corner.
6. Next, you are prompted for the deploy location. This is the directory to which the files in the archive will be deployed. Enter a location and click the Deploy button.

All the files in the archive are restored in the specified directory and subdirectories to mirror the directory structure from the staging server. When archive deployment is complete, you will see either a `deploy successful` message or a `deploy failed` message.

Objects

By *objects*, we refer to instances of a ColdFusion Component. As we saw in Chapter 9, "Centralized Data Persistence," these instances can be represented as records in a database, XML files, or in several other means. Although these objects often represent application data, such as articles, users, and so on, they occasionally represent application infrastructure. Application data often is not migrated from development to production because it is usually test or dummy data that resides in the development servers. However, application infrastructure might well need to be migrated. One example of application infrastructure that we explored earlier in this book is the Nodes object. (See Chapter 12, "Categorization of Content," for information on the Node CFC.) Nodes are used to store categorizations, and hierarchies of nodes might need to be transferred between development, staging, and production.

An export routine best handles migration of individual objects. This routine is usually a multistep process, first asking the user which types of objects he wants to migrate. When the user has chosen the object types, a next screen displays all objects of the chosen types, allowing the user to select which individual objects will be migrated. Next, these objects have their `export()` methods called, which encapsulates each record into an XML object (WDDX handles this nicely), and write each object to a file. We want a unique name for each file, so we use the ObjectID's as the filename. Finally, these files are archived into a single file (ZIP or TAR) and moved to the destination server.

> **Note**
> The import and export routines mentioned are methods of the BasePersistenceObject covered in Chapter 9.

On the destination server, the files are extracted from the archive into a temporary directory. Using the `<CFDIRECTORY>` tag, a list of all files in the temp directory is generated and looped over. For each file in the loop, we need to determine whether the component representing that type of object has already been deployed on the server. Simply running the `deploy()` method on that component either deploys it if it does not exist, or it does nothing if it does exist. After the component has been deployed, it needs to be imported into the destination server through the use of the `import()` method.

Database

It goes without saying that a dynamic publishing application requires a database. The installation and initial setup of a database is beyond the scope of this chapter, but it is important to have your database tables created in your various environments. A best practice is to have your database generate table creation SQL scripts when you have finalized the database design in development, and to create ColdFusion templates that will run these scripts inside of `<CFQUERY>` tags. When you're deploying to staging or production, you can run these scripts there first, guaranteeing an identical data structure in each environment.

Redeployment

As you can see from the previous few sections, initially deploying an application can be an involved process. Unfortunately, many who remember to plan for the initial deployment often forget to plan for redeployments. Redeployments happen each time a new release of code is added to the existing production site. Only in rare cases will a project deploy initially and then have no changes to the production code base. Most applications have an initial deployment, followed by a seemingly endless number of redeployments afterward, with new features, enhancements, or bug fixes.

The process of redeployment is similar to that of the initial deployment, with the exception that it is not necessary to move all code, objects, databases, and so on. It's only necessary to move the pieces that have changed or are new.

The basic challenge of redeployment involves identifying which pieces of the application have changed and need to be migrated. This often involves finding a means to identify changes in the code base, changes in system objects, changes to settings in the ColdFusion administrator, or changes to the data structure. The "Build Management System" section that follows offers some ideas about identifying changes to the code base; the same object export routine described earlier can be used again for redeployment, allowing for a choice of the objects to be migrated. The Archive Creation Wizard in the ColdFusion administrator allows you to select which server settings need be archived and migrated. You can use tools such as TOAD or ErWin to find changes to database structures and automatically create the proper ALTER TABLE scripts.

Note

You can find more information on ErWin at `http://www3.ca.com/Solutions/Product.asp?ID=260` or on TOAD at `http://www.toadsoft.com/`.

This brings up another good example as to why we want to document all aspects of deployment. Properly documenting this initially can save hours on future redeployments.

Build Management Systems

A number of software packages, usually built into or bundled with version control systems, are capable of associating a group of files together as a build. The idea of associating files together as a build allows for releases of the code base to be moved from one server to another and to be readily associated with each other. With such a concept, it becomes possible to have the most recent version of the code in development, a second version in testing, and another fully stable version in production. In this manner, as a build of the code is certified through testing, it can be safely released to production. As new versions of code are finished in development, they too can be grouped as a build and started in their migratory path to testing on their way to their future home in production.

Although it is not necessary to employ an off-the-shelf build management system to achieve this functionality, attempting to build such a system for yourself can be tedious. If your project employs some form of version control software, you might want to investigate whether a build management system is built into it, or if an additional module serves this function.

Build management is not necessary to redeploy a project, but it certainly serves to ease the pain of redeployment.

Tip

Ben Elmore's Insights on Redeployment:*

A main problem that I have had to deal with [in] the past was...an easy way to push modifications between environments—whether development to testing or testing to development—without having any developer intervention. This allows IT to have much tighter control on their boxes and minimizes the human error in deployments by creating deployable packets.

Here is a trick that I picked up to solve that.

Have a directory that is called /runonce on each of the servers. During the deployment process, move a set [of] deployment files into this directory that contain scripted logic (CFML Code) to deal with items like the following:

- Remote object registration
- Full text searching index creation
- Pre-load data
- Table creation

Each of these deployment files needs to be self contained (not depending upon any outside logic to fire) and use a naming convention that allows for sorting and a priority firing (tableCreation1, tablemodification1, dataModification1, and so forth). This is critical that a naming convention be used because there are dependencies that these files have, such as you can't update a table until it is created.

These deployment files are managed by a run after the handler/component is created. This coordinates the execution of these files by querying the /runonce directory for types of files (tablecreation*.cfm, dataModification*.cfm, and so forth) and then executing them in sequence. After successful completion of the files, this component deletes them from the directory or optionally creates an archive of them somewhere else on the server. You also can log these activities depending on your needs. The decision to make this a component or just a CFM file should be made based on how much auxiliary functionality is needed beyond the execution and deletion of the deployment files.

The actual launch of this run after handler/component needs to be done by the migration process that you are using to move files between environments. Its sequence in the process should obviously be after the movement of the deployment files into the /runonce directory. There have also been times where the kickoff has been manual.

Another similar trick is to allow configurable application preload logic. This thought is to have a directory like /onapplicationload to place a set of preload up files.

These could be things like database checking, loading of server scopes, creating of adapter classes, or checking of database types. These can interact with the application's variables (application or server).

The structure for execution of the files, naming of the files, and other behaviors mirror that of the deployment logic above, but instead of having the trigger of execution be the deployment of files, have it be the nonexistence of a server or application variable on application startup.

*Elmore is the Chief Technology Officer at RemoteSite Technologies.

Monitoring

Another key aspect of deploying an application is enabling the means to monitor the application's health. Although there are a number of devices and services available that can provide monitoring, in this section, we explore a low-cost alternative with a custom-built monitoring solution.

> **Note**
>
> Many decent and affordable site-monitoring solutions are available, including What's Up Gold. (`http://www.ipswitch.com/Products/WhatsUp/index.html`) and SiteScope (`http://www.freshwater.com/SiteScope.htm`).

The first key aspect to remember with monitoring is that you do not want to monitor a server from the same machine. The concept of monitoring involves watching a server, determining if it is okay, and notifying an administrator if it is not. If the server has crashed and we are attempting to monitor from the same machine, we will have no means available to notify the administrator. Instead, we will be monitoring from a separate server, preferably a server on a separate network.

All of the monitoring we do requires two web pages. The first is on the server being monitored, and the other is on the machine doing the monitoring.

Web Server

To monitor whether a web server is responding, we want to create a static HTML page, which has a simple passage of text, such as `Web Server OK`. A page with nothing but this will be created and saved in the web root of the server to be monitored as WSTest.html. The second page we need, on the monitoring server, is a ColdFusion template, which will make a CFHTTP call to the WSTest.html file on the server that is being monitored. Then, with a simple CFIF statement, we can determine whether the text of WSTest.html matches the expected text. If it does, we know the web server is responding properly:

```
All Well
```

If not, we know there is a problem.

CFServer

The next test is to determine whether the ColdFusion server is running properly. To do this, we make a copy of our WSTest.html and save it as CFTest.cfm (see Listing 23.1). One addition is made to the new CFTest.cfm file: adding a `<CFSETTING>` tag to suppress any debug output. The monitoring server makes a call to CFTest.cfm on the server that is being monitored. If the text matches what is expected, then we know the ColdFusion server is running properly. We know this because any request to a .cfm file on a ColdFusion server is handed from the web server to the ColdFusion server for processing, even if the requested page has no ColdFusion tags. If the page is processed with no errors, then the message `All Well` is returned.

Listing 23.1 **CFTest.cfm**

```
<!--- /monitor/cftest.cfm
created 6/20/02 by Jeff Tapper
Remotesite Technologies
Jeff.tapper@remotesite.com

Change History:

Usage:
Displays the phrase All well with no debug output.

---><cfsetting showdebugoutput="0">All Well
```

Database

To test whether ColdFusion is able to talk to a database, we use a simple query, as seen in Listing 23.2. This starts by suppressing any debugging with the `<CFSETTING>` tag. Next, it queries the obj_article table with the intention of running a query to return no results. (Note that you can switch this to any table you know exists in your database. Obj_article was chosen because it was created by code demonstrated earlier in the book.) We accomplish this by using a WHERE clause that reads where `1 = 0`. This serves to effectively run a query that will never return a record. We are not interested in the records in the table, simply in ColdFusion's ability to speak to the database. If the query fails, an error message is thrown, which our monitoring script captures (discussed in the next section). If the query runs successfully (that is, it returns no records, but no error is thrown), then the message `All Well` is returned.

> **Note**
>
> In this example, we are selecting a record from a table created earlier in the book. If you would like a more generic `select` statement to run, you can choose a database-specific query such as this:
>
> ```
> SQL SERVER
> select date() as todaysdateORACLE
> SELECT * From Dual
> ```
>
> Each of these always returns a single record, regardless of what tables exist in the database, and offers a great DB-specific test to verify communication between the ColdFusion and DB servers.

Listing 23.2 **A Simple Database Test Script**

```
<!--- /monitor/dbtest.cfm
created 6/20/02 by Jeff Tapper
Remotesite Technologies
Jeff.tapper@remotesite.com

Change History:
```

```

Usage:
Runs a query designed to return no records. If query runs successfully,
the phrase All Well is returned.

---><cfsetting showdebugoutput="0">

<cfquery name="test" datasource="testdb">
    SELECT * from obj_article where 1 = 0
</cfquery>

<cfif NOT test.recordCount>
All Well
</cfif>
```

Monitoring Script

After the scripts that monitor the web server, ColdFusion server, and database server are in place, a script needs to be on a separate server to call these scripts and run the test. Ideally, the machine that is running the script that tests the production machines should be sitting outside the firewall and should connect to the production machines across the public Internet, as opposed to using a local area network (LAN). This is desirable because it also serves as a de facto test of the production environment's network, firewall, and Internet connection, as if the monitoring script is unable to access the production servers; chances are, the general public can't access the servers either.

Listing 23.3 shows a monitoring script, which, after setting variables indicting the servers to be tested, the administrator's email address who is to be notified, the network address of the SMTP server that will do the notification, and the path of the test files on all the servers, will call each of the test scripts on each of the servers in the list, and email the administrator if any of the tests fails.

Listing 23.3 **A Script to Call the Monitor Pages on the Server Being Monitored**

```
<!--- /monitor/monitoring.cfm
created 6/20/02 by Jeff Tapper
Remotesite Technologies
Jeff.tapper@remotesite.com

Change History:

Usage:
Loops over list of servers, calling the Web Server, ColdFusion and
Database monitoring scripts on each.  If there are any problems
detected, an email is sent to the admin email address provided.

--->
<!---

```

continues

Listing 23.3 **Continued**

```
application-specific variables
Set the email address you would like to use for notifications, the IP
or domain name of your SMTP server, and a comma-delimited list of
machines to be monitored (IP or domain name) here.
--->
<cfset adminemail = "someone@yourdomain.com">
<cfset smtpserver = "127.0.0.1">
<cfset serverlist ="172.168.10.14,172.168.10.15,172.168.10.16">
<!--- declare a new structure to hold results --->
<cfset stResult = structNew()>
<!--- initialize failcount variable, which will determine if there have
been any failures --->
<CFSET failCount = 0>
<!--- list of monitoring files on each of the web servers. Note:
Filename should include path relative to web root --->
<cfset testlist = "monitor/WSTest.html,monitor/cftest.cfm,monitor/dbtest.cfm">
<!--- loop over list of servers --->
<cfloop list="#variables.serverlist#" index="thisServer">
    <!--- declare a new structure for each server --->
    <cfset stResult[thisServer] = structNew()>
    <!--- add a failcount key to each server's structure --->
    <cfset stResult[thisServer].failcount = 0>
    <!--- loop over each file to be used for monitoring --->
    <cfloop list ="#testlist#" index="thisTest">
        <!--- call each file to be monitored --->
        <cfhttp url="http://#thisServer#/#thisTest#"
        method="GET" resolveurl="false">
        <!---
            Each of the monitoring files is set to return the phrase
            "All Well" if it runs properly.
        --->
        <cfif left(trim(cfhttp.fileContent), 8) eq "All Well">
            <cfset stResult[thisServer][thisTest] = "success">
        <cfelse>
            <!---
                 If the first 8 characters (after any extraneous while
                 space has been suppressed) of the results are not
                 "All Well," there has been a problem. The general
                 failcount variable is incremented, as is the failcount
```

```
                  variable for this specific server. The full response
                  is then added to the structure so that it can be emailed
                  to the administrator.
               --->
               <cfset variables.failcount = variables.failcount + 1>
               <cfset stResult[thisServer].failcount =
               stResult[thisServer].failcount + 1>
               <CFSET STRESULT[thisServer][THISTEST] = cfhttp.fileContent>
           </cfif>
       <!--- end loop over files --->
       </cfloop>

   <!--- end loop over servers --->
   </cfloop>

   <!--- initialize an empty string for output --->
   <CFSET OUTPUT = "">

   <!--- check whether there have been any failures --->
   <cfif variables.failcount>
       <!--- loop over all the results --->
       <CFLOOP COLLECTION="#STRESULT#" ITEM="ThisServer">
           <!--- if this server had any failures, process them --->
           <cfif stresult[ThisServer].failcount>
               <!---
               Append the server name and the output from the failed test
               to the output string.
               --->
               <cfset output = output & ThisServer>
               <cfloop
               collection="#stResult[ThisServer]#"
               item="thistest">
                   <CFSET OUTPUT = OUTPUT & "
   " & thistest & "=" & stResult[ThisServer][thisTest] & "

   ">
               </cfloop>
           </cfif>
       </CFLOOP>

       <!---
       after all looping is done, email the administrator the output
       containing the results of all tests on any server that experienced
       any failures.
       --->
       <cfmail to="#variables.adminemail#"
       from="Monitor"
       Subject="Alert, server problemn"
       SERVER="#variables.smtpserver">
   #variables.output#
       </cfmail>
   </cfif>
```

Conclusion

Although the act of deploying an application can be relieving because it often signals the end of a frantic development effort, we need to be careful not to let our guard down until the application is successfully deployed and the monitoring scripts are in place to verify the system's health. Like all aspects of the development process, a successful deployment begins with thorough planning. By understanding each of the tasks involved in the process, the deployment scripts can be written as the application testing is taking place, allowing for a smooth launch of an application. Keep in mind that the initial launch is rarely the end of the deployment. Redeployments are common and should be thoroughly planned as well.

With proper planning, the often-laborious task of releasing an application can be eased, and the headaches, ulcers, and sleeplessness that is common among application developers and project managers can be greatly reduced.

Functional and Technical Documents

by Jeff Tapper

THROUGHOUT THIS BOOK, WE HAVE DESCRIBED the implementation of a dynamic publishing application. When possible, the application described has centered around the requirements defined here.

Requirements

The requirements for the DuvalShock application are divided among business, functional, and visual design requirements.

Business Requirements

DuvalShock's business has been growing, and it needs a means to publish information about its products to its web site with a greater frequency and without requiring the intervention of the technical staff each time. Because DuvalShock continues to add new products and new details about existing products, the current technical staff is over burdened and is unable to complete its new development tasks.

Business users need to be able to create new pages and add new content to existing pages. Additionally, home page content that is older than a specified number of days needs to be moved automatically to an archive page without requiring intervention.

No new content or changes to existing content should be visible on the site until after it has successfully gone through the approval process. (See the section, "Process Model," for more information on the approval process.)

Functional Requirements

The application's functional requirements are broken down into the following categories:

- General site requirements
- Dynamic publishing requirements
- Workflow requirements
- User interface requirements

General Site Requirements

To achieve the goals listed in the "Business Requirements" section, you need the following functionality:

- A dynamic publishing system to allow non-technical employees to create and edit content
- A workflow system
- A rules-based templating system to ensure that the correct visual design is applied to each page

Versions of all content that have been displayed on the web site need to be stored and easily accessible for legal/compliance reasons. A storage mechanism for versions is required, as is an interface to view and revert to previous versions. Versions are created automatically with every creation or change to an object. Therefore, if a previous version is restored for a particular piece of content, a new entry is made for it in the versioning repository.

Dynamic Publishing Requirements

To facilitate the DuvalShock business requirements, a dynamic publishing system is required. This system needs to allow for a customized interface to be created for each type of content on the site. (Although the main type of content is products, there will also be a need for a press release type, a job opportunity type, and so on.) Ideally, this system should allow for a technical employee to create new content types easily. Each type must be capable of having its own customized create/edit interface, as well as one or more display interfaces. Content that is created or edited will go through the workflow process described next. When the content is approved, it will be published to the site using the templating requirements listed.

Workflow Requirements

The DuvalShock workflow begins with a marketing manager (can be expanded to other managers as well) determining that a piece of content needs to be created or edited. When the determination is made, the request is assigned to a qualified author (for products, these are employees of the product manager) who will fulfill the request by creating or editing the content in the new dynamic publishing system. As the author completes the task, the approver (usually the marketing manager who instantiated the workflow) is notified of the new/changed content. The manager then either approves or rejects the content. If the manager rejects the content, he enters some comments about why the content was rejected. Then the author is notified and assigned the task of fixing the content. The iteration between author and approver continues until the content is approved. When the content is approved, the legal department is notified and tasked with reviewing the content for legal/compliance issues. If the legal department rejects the content, the author again is tasked with fixes. If the legal department approves the content, it is launched following the templating rules.

Localization

Because DuvalShock sells its products internationally, we need to be able to have versions of the site's content available in a number of different languages. Depending on the domain name that users use to access the site, different language versions of the site will be accessible to them. To achieve this localization/internationalization, Unicode is used to support the various languages.

Templating Requirements

The system uses a number of specific requirements for each of the templates. Next, you will find details on the key templates home page, body, and archive.

Home Page

A *home page template* has a title description that links to the body template. A publishing rule is created to determine how many product headlines can occur on the home page at one time. Using a first in, first out (FIFO) pattern, as a new piece of content is added, the oldest content in the list is automatically moved to the archive page if the list has more elements than allowed.

The font for the text in the title defaults to Arial at the same size at all times. It was decided in the requirements phase that there would be no flexibility for color, size, or font type in the title area. Titles are automatically hyperlinked to a body page for that content.

Body

The *body template* holds the details of the marketing material. The title description hyperlink points here. The fonts/images/layout of the body pages are at the discretion of the authors and approvers, with the exception of the page title, which appears identically on all body pages and is worded as it is on the home page.

Archive Template

An *archive template* lists bumped home page template title descriptions (15 at a time) in chronological order for the current month. It also has links to previous months' archive templates going back exactly one year.

All titles added for New Products end up on this template with the same font, size, and color as the home page. The titles are in chronological order with the most recent on top. Ten articles are allowed per page, and when the 11th title occurs, a Next Page hyperlink is generated and a new page is dynamically created to handle the overflow as New Product titles are added.

The archive template represents the current month's announcements. At the end of each month, a new template is automatically generated and the previous month's articles are available via a hyperlink shown on the bottom of the page for that particular month. Links to 11 previous months are shown at all times on the archive templates.

At month end, the archive template is restarted to the new month and previous months are separated on a dedicated month template. This is a once-a-month requirement that the development team needs to track manually. Although it's not included in the current scope of this project, it is likely that a future project will include automating this process.

Extensibility

The requirements listed here focus on just the elements of New Products because this was DuvalShock's overarching need. Through the lifecycle of this project, it is expected that we will flesh out similar requirements for other content items, such as press releases, job openings, and so on. If we wanted to describe Company Spotlight, Sales Leaders, and Industry News as additional pieces of metadata, we could easily do this in our workflow application with something as simple as a drop-down box describing the categories. This would be an option before the title and body content are added. You can maximize the reusability if you convince your business to leverage the same publishing rules and properties. You should set the publishing rules company wide, wherever possible, instead of just at the specific content type level. Therefore, if the business logic model is set to account for further changes/additions to the site, minimal changes will be needed for the site itself.

Process Model

As described earlier, a specific process is required to launch new or edited content. This process is diagrammed in Figure A.1.

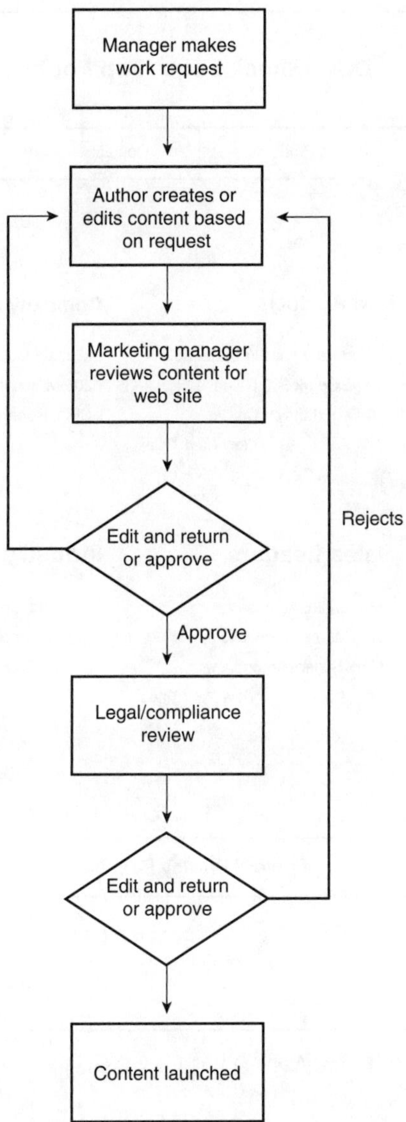

Figure A.1 A visual representation of the workflow process for DuvalShock.

Visual Model

As described earlier, the three templates that follow will comprise our application's visual model (see Figure A.2 to A.4).

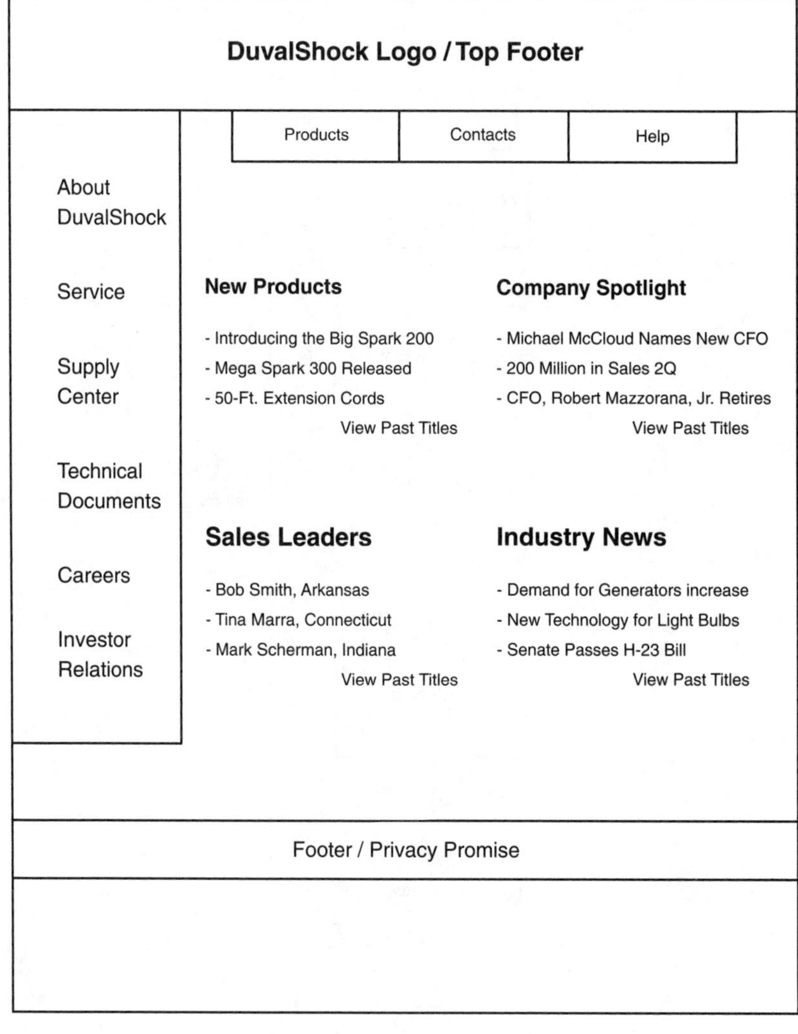

Figure A.2 DuvalShock home page.

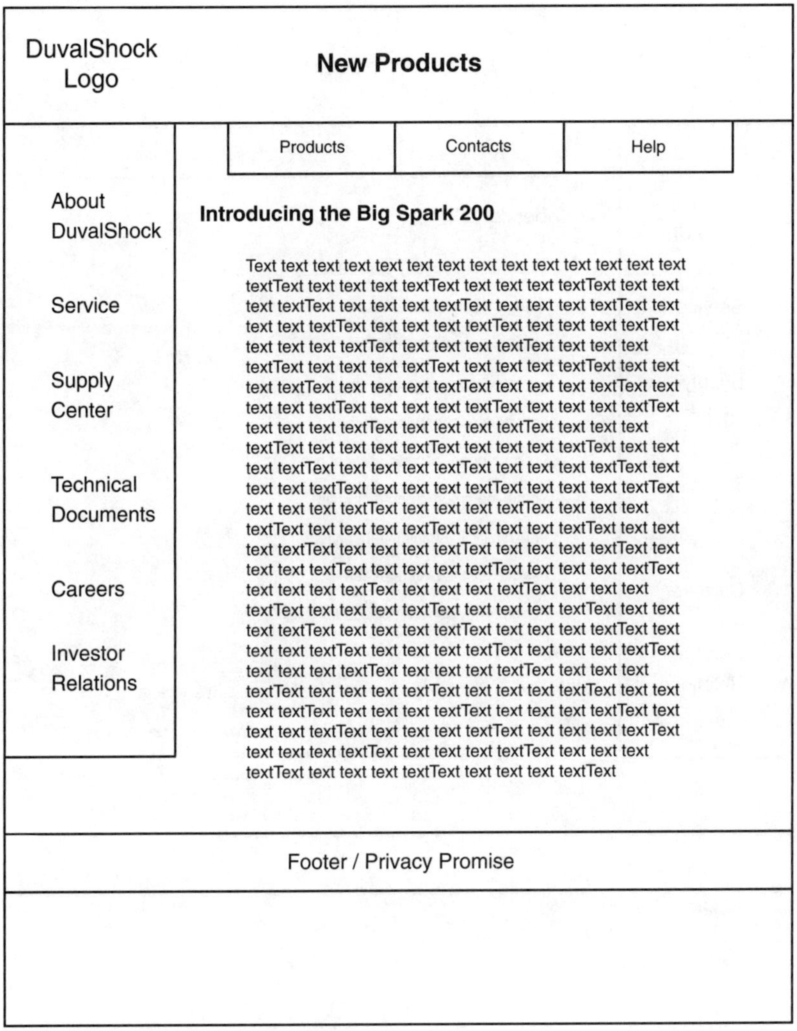

DuvalShock Logo

New Products

Products	Contacts	Help

About DuvalShock

Service

Supply Center

Technical Documents

Careers

Investor Relations

Introducing the Big Spark 200

Text text text text text text text text text text text text text text
textText text text text textText text text text textText text text
text textText text text text textText text text text textText text
text text textText text text text textText text text text textText
text text text textText text text text textText text text text
textText text text text textText text text text textText text text
text textText text text text textText text text text textText text
text text textText text text text textText text text text textText
text text text textText text text text textText text text text
textText text text text textText text text text textText text text
text textText text text text textText text text text textText text
text text textText text text text textText text text text textText
text text text textText text text text textText text text text
textText text text text textText text text text textText text text
text textText text text text textText text text text textText text
text text textText text text text textText text text text textText
text text text textText text text text textText text text text
textText text text text textText text text text textText text text
text textText text text text textText text text text textText text
text text textText text text text textText text text text textText
text text text textText text text text textText text text text
textText text text text textText text text text textText text text
text textText text text text textText text text text textText text
text text textText text text text textText text text text textText
text text text textText text text text textText text text text
textText text text text textText text text text textText

Footer / Privacy Promise

Figure A.3 Product detail page.

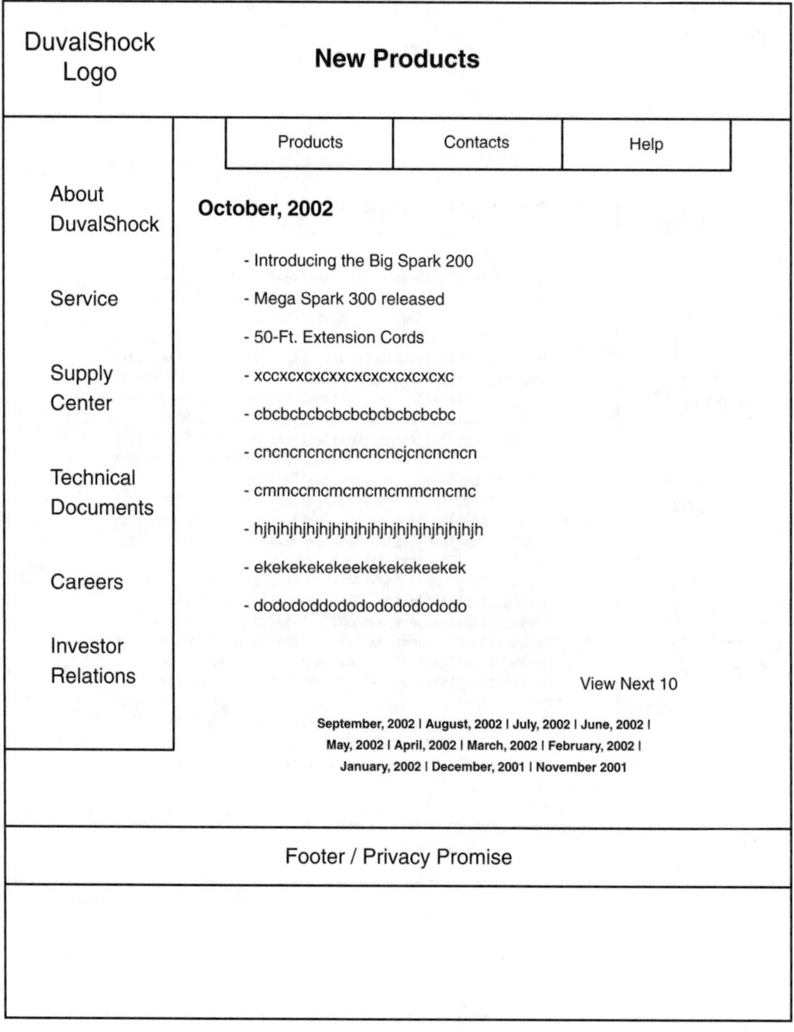

Figure A.4 Archive page.

Class Diagrams

The class diagrams to be used for the DuvalShock application can be seen here in Figure A.5.

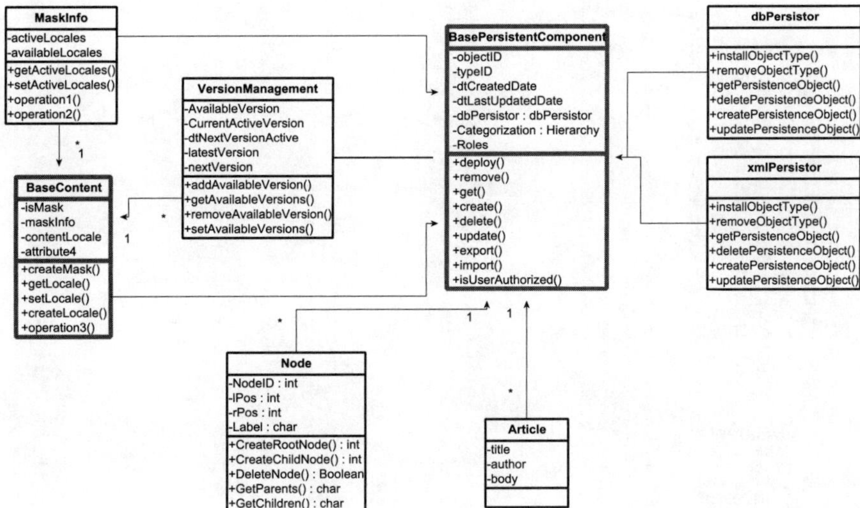

Figure A.5 Class diagram.

Index

A

C

D

E

F

G

H

J

K-L

M

N

O

Q-R

T

V

W

X-Z

HOW TO CONTACT US

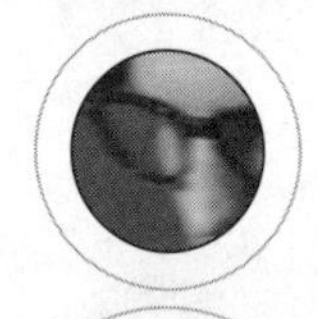
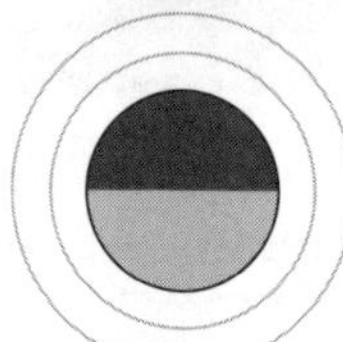

VOICES THAT MATTER

VISIT OUR WEB SITE

WWW.NEWRIDERS.COM

On our web site, you'll find information about our other books, authors, tables of contents, and book errata. You will also find information about book registration and how to purchase our books, both domestically and internationally.

EMAIL US

Contact us at: **nrfeedback@newriders.com**

- If you have comments or questions about this book
- To report errors that you have found in this book
- If you have a book proposal to submit or are interested in writing for New Riders
- If you are an expert in a computer topic or technology and are interested in being a technical editor who reviews manuscripts for technical accuracy

Contact us at: **nreducation@newriders.com**

- If you are an instructor from an educational institution who wants to preview New Riders books for classroom use. Email should include your name, title, school, department, address, phone number, office days/hours, text in use, and enrollment, along with your request for desk/examination copies and/or additional information.

Contact us at: **nrmedia@newriders.com**

- If you are a member of the media who is interested in reviewing copies of New Riders books. Send your name, mailing address, and email address, along with the name of the publication or web site you work for.

BULK PURCHASES/CORPORATE SALES

The publisher offers discounts on this book when ordered in quantity for bulk purchases and special sales. For sales within the U.S., please contact: Corporate and Government Sales (800) 382-3419 or **corpsales@pearsontechgroup.com**. Outside of the U.S., please contact: International Sales (317) 581-3793 or **international@pearsontechgroup.com**.

WRITE TO US

New Riders Publishing
201 W. 103rd St.
Indianapolis, IN 46290-1097

CALL/FAX US

Toll-free (800) 571-5840
If outside U.S. (317) 581-3500
Ask for New Riders
FAX: (317) 581-4663

WWW.NEWRIDERS.COM

Colophon

The cover image, "Tornado During Thunderstorm," was captured by photographer Don Farrall and is available through Photodisc.

This book was written and edited in Microsoft Word, and laid out in QuarkXPress. The fonts used for the body text are Bembo and Mono. It was printed on 50# Husky Offset Smooth paper at R.R. Donnelley & Sons in Crawfordsville, Indiana. Prepress consisted of PostScript computer-to-plate technology (filmless process). The cover was printed at Moore Langen Printing in Terre Haute, Indiana, on 12pt, coated on one side.